NORTH AMERICAN NEW RIGHT

VOLUME 1, 2012

Edited by

GREG JOHNSON

Counter-Currents Publishing Ltd.
San Francisco
2012

Cover image: Lewis Hine, "Power house mechanic working on steam pump," photograph, 1920

Cover design: Kevin I. Slaughter

Published in the United States by
COUNTER-CURRENTS PUBLISHING LTD.
P.O. Box 22638
San Francisco, CA 94122
USA
http://www.counter-currents.com/

ISBN Information:

Limited Hardcover Edition: 978-1-935965-18-3
Paperback: 978-1-935965-19-0
E-book: 978-1-935965-29-9

Library of Congress ISSN Information:

North American new right
ISSN 2165-4409 (hardcover)
ISSN 2165-4409 (paperback)
ISSN 2165-4409 (electronic)

TABLE OF CONTENTS

TOWARD A NORTH AMERICAN NEW RIGHT

GREG JOHNSON[*]

To plant a field or build a house, one must first clear a space. The same is true of an intellectual movement. *North American New Right* was created as a space for dialogue in which a new intellectual movement, a North American New Right, might emerge. This journal began on June 11, 2010, as the "webzine" of Counter-Currents Publishing Limited (http://www.counter-currents.com). But from the very beginning, we also planned a print publication, an annual volume showcasing the best of the online journal as well as new material in a format better suited for appreciating our longer, more scholarly pieces. With this, the first volume of *North American New Right*, that project has now come to fruition.

Our entire project is motivated by consciousness of an existential threat. European peoples, both in our mother continent and scattered around the globe, now live under a cultural, political, and economic system that has set our race on the path to cultural decadence and demographic decline. If these trends are not reversed, whites will disappear as a distinct race. The incomparable light we bring to the world will be extinguished, and the greatness of our achievements will be preserved only in fragments, like the scraps of literature, shards of pottery, and shattered artworks that survived the wreck of pagan antiquity.

We aim to halt and reverse that process here in North America, but we also wish to learn from and contribute to the struggle of our comrades for white homelands around the globe.

The North American New Right is a "metapolitical" move-

---

[*] I wish to thank F. Roger Devlin, Derek Hawthorne, and Matthew Peters for their extensive comments and editorial suggestions, most of which I have followed.

ment modeled on the European New Right, but adapted to our own circumstances. The goal of the North American New Right is to lay the metapolitical foundations for the emergence of a White Republic (or republics) in North America.

"Metapolitics" refers to what comes before the political, i.e., the foundations of politics, including (1) the intellectual case for a new political order, and (2) a concrete community that embodies those ideas in the present and will serve as the seed of a new political order to emerge in the future. As a journal of ideas, *North American New Right* naturally focuses on the intellectual dimension of metapolitics, which centers around three issues: *identity, morality,* and *practicality.*

If we are to defend the idea of a White Republic, we must first answer the question of identity: Who are we? Then we must turn to the moral question: Is it *right* to create a society for our people alone? And if so, we face the question of practicality: How might a White Republic be feasible?

IDENTITY

The question of identity includes such topics as: the inadequacy of "propositional" forms of identity, e.g., the dedication of a society to abstract principles like liberty and equality; existing European regional and national identities; the problem of petty nationalism; the deep roots of our common European identity, including biological race, European history and prehistory, and the cultural diffusions revealed by comparative linguistics and mythology; the concept of collective destiny; occasions for collective pride or self-criticism, i.e., the strengths and weaknesses of our people; the Traditionalism of René Guénon and Julius Evola; the problem of identity in colonial societies like the United States and Canada, where the blending of European stocks is almost universal; and the relationship of the North American New Right to the Western political, philosophical, and cultural tradition.

A corollary of the question of who we are is the question of who we are *not*: the "others." Unavoidably, this includes the Jewish question. In an ideal world, it would be possible to be *for* oneself without being *against* anybody else; but as Carl Schmitt so cogently argues, the political realm is constituted by the friend/enemy distinction, rooted in the potential for existential conflicts between groups.

Yet who and what we are *for* must take priority over the question of who and what we are *against*. Some would prefer to avoid discussion of our own identity as "divisive," but no successful political movement can base itself exclusively on opposition to other groups.

MORALITY

The key moral question is whether it is right to prefer one's own kin over others. Whites, and only whites, have become convinced otherwise. Strict ethnic impartiality would not be destructive of our race if all other races abided by the same principle, but they do not. Moreover, all contemporary Western governments reward non-white appeals to ethnic solidarity. This puts whites at a systematic disadvantage which in time will be sufficient to dispossess us of our homelands.

Indeed, our situation is far worse, for many whites consider it virtuous to *prefer* other groups to their own. They practice what Guillaume Faye calls "ethnomasochism" or "xenophilia." Such attitudes, of course, accelerate white dispossession.

When whites no longer control homelands of our own, our destiny will pass into the hands of other groups, many of which have deep-steated grudges against us. We will, in effect, be a conquered people, and we will share the fates of conquered peoples, most of whom disappear from the pages of history.

Note that the question of ethnic partiality is not the issue of moral "universalism." Partiality to one's own people is a completely universalizable principle. So is ethnic impartiality. So are ethnomasochism and xenophilia. The reason that ethnic impartiality and ethnomasochism/xenophilia are destructive to whites is simply that they are *not* practiced universally and reciprocally.

Another moral issue is the question of utopia. Whites are willing to maintain racially destructive moral attitudes like ethnic impartiality or ethnomasochism/xenophilia because they believe that they are making sacrifices to bring about a better world, a world without ethnic enmity and conflict. We have to destroy this illusion before it destroys us. We need to establish that enmity and conflict are ineradicable.

But we also need to advance our own, more realistic vision of utopia: a peaceful world in which the causes of quarrel are not eliminated, but simply managed. Ethnic diversity in and of itself need not cause conflicts. Ethnic strife is, however, inevitable when diverse groups try to occupy the same living spaces. Therefore, the best way to avoid ethnic hatred and conflict is universal nationalism, i.e., giving every distinct people a country or countries of its own. A durable foundation for world peace is the recognition that all peoples have an interest in preserving the principle of national self-determination. (There is also a common interest in preserving our planetary environment.)

DREAM & REALITY

Before the White Republic can become reality, it must first exist as a dream, a vision of a possible world. Yet to be realizable, even a vision must be realistic. So the North American New Right has the dual task of encouraging both visionaries and realists.

To cultivate our vision, we maintain a strong focus on the arts. Art is an indispensable tool of communicating ideals, for it can reach more people, and stir them more deeply, than mere rational argument. Indeed, imagination is the fundamental source of our ideals themselves.

To encourage contemporary artists, we seek to reconnect them with our tradition. Many of the greatest artists of the last century were men of the Right, and one does not have to go back too far in history before the principles we defend were the common sense of virtually every great creative genius. We also seek to offer contemporary artists constructive criticism, publicity, and opportunities to network and collaborate.

To cultivate realism, we explore the questions of whether a White Republic is feasible and how we might get there from here. These questions can be approached from two complementary angles: theoretical and historical. Philosophy and the human sciences can tell us a good deal about what is possible or impossible, likely or unlikely. History, by contrast, is based on the actual. And if something has actually happened, it is *ipso facto* possible.

The examples of the Irish and the Spanish, for example, show us that European peoples who have been conquered and colonized for centuries can preserve their identities and reconquer their homelands. More recent history also gives us examples of how large, multinational, multiracial empires have collapsed, allowing their constituent nations to free themselves and create ethnically homogeneous states. History thus provides us with a vast store of examples and analogies that can help us shape our ideas and guide them toward realization.

THEORY & PRACTICE[1]

To achieve our political aims, the North American New Right must understand the proper relationship of social theory to social change, metapolitics to politics, theory to practice. We must avoid drifting either into inactive intellectualism or unintelligent and thus possibly counterproductive activism.

Guillaume Faye's *Archeofuturism*[2] offers many important lessons for our project. Chapter 1, "An Assessment of the *Nouvelle Droite*," is Faye's settling of accounts with the French New Right. In the late 1970s and early 1980s, Faye was among their leading thinkers and polemicists before quitting in disillusionment. After twelve years, he returned to the battle of ideas with *Archeofuturism* (1998), which begins with an explanation of his departure and return.

In the 1970s and 1980s, the *Nouvelle Droite*, led by Alain de Benoist, was a highly visible and influential intellectual movement. It published books and periodicals like *Nouvelle École* and *Éléments*; it sponsored lectures, conferences, and debates; it engaged the intellectual and cultural mainstreams. The *Nouvelle Droite* did more than receive mainstream press coverage, it often

---

[1] The rest of this article is adapted from Greg Johnson "Theory and Practice," Counter-Currents/*North American New Right*, September 30, 2010, http://www.counter-currents.com/2010/09/theory-practice/

[2] Guillaume Faye, *Archeofuturism: European Visions of the Post-Catastrophic Age*, trans. Sergio Knipe (London: Arktos, 2010).

set the terms of debates to which the mainstream responded.

The *Nouvelle Droite* was deep; it was highbrow; it was radical; it was relevant; and, above all, it was exciting. It was based on the axiom that ideas shape the world. Bad ideas are destroying it, and only better ideas will save it. It had the right ideas, and it was increasingly influential. Its metapolitical strategy was a "Gramscianism" of the Right, i.e., an attempt to shape the ideas and ultimately the actions of the elites—academics, journalists, businessmen, politicians, etc.—as envisioned in the writings of Italian Marxist Antonio Gramsci.

However, according to Faye, as the 1980s came to a close, the *Nouvelle Droite* became less influential: "Regrettably, it has turned into an ideological ghetto. It no longer sees itself as a powerhouse for the diffusion of energies with the ultimate aim of acquiring *power*, but rather as a publishing enterprise that also organizes conferences but has limited ambitions" (pp. 24–25). The causes of this decline were based partly on objective conditions, partly on the movement's own weaknesses.

Whether fair to the *Nouvelle Droite* or not, two of Faye's criticisms contain universal truths that seem particularly relevant to our project in North America.

(1) The rise of the Front National of Jean-Marie Le Pen caused a decline in the visibility and influence of the *Nouvelle Droite*, whereas one might have expected the Front National's good fortunes to magnify those of the *Nouvelle Droite*. After all, the two movements share much in common, and there can be little doubt that the *Nouvelle Droite* influenced the Front National and brought new people into its orbit.

Faye laments the "airlocks" sealing off different circles of the French Right. In particular, he claims that the *Nouvelle Droite* never engaged the Front National, because its members fundamentally misunderstood Gramsci, whose cultural battle was organically connected with the economic and political struggle of the Italian Communist Party.

The *Nouvelle Droite*, however, treated the battle as entirely cultural and intellectual. Thus they were not really Gramscians. They were actually followers of Augustin Cochin's theory of the role of intellectual salons in paving the way for the French Revolution.[3] Unlike the men of the old regime, however, we do not enjoy the luxury of ignoring party and electoral politics.

The North American New Right aims to change the political landscape. To do that, we must influence people who have power, or who can attain it. That means we must engage organized political parties and movements. No, in the end, white people are not going to vote ourselves out of the present mess. But we are not in the endgame yet, and it may still be possible to influence policy through the existing system. Moreover, parties do not exist merely for the sake of elections. They provide a nucleus for the new order they advocate. Finally, there are other ways to attain power besides elections. Just look at the Bolsheviks.

We know that the present system is unsustainable, and although we cannot predict when and how it will collapse, we know that collapse will come. It is far more likely that whites can turn that collapse to our benefit if we already have functioning political organizations that aim at becoming the nucleus of a new society. Yet we will not have such political organizations unless we engage the presently existing political institutions, corrupt, sclerotic, and boring though they may be.

(2) Even though the *Nouvelle Droite* did not engage with organized politics, it was organized according to "an outdated 'apparatus logic' of the type to be found in political parties, which was not appropriate for a movement and school of thought . . . which led cadres to flee on account of 'problems with the apparatus'" (p. 27). By an "apparatus logic," Faye seems to mean a hierarchical organization in which an intellectual and editorial "party line" is promulgated.

Although Faye does not say so, the inability of the *Nouvelle Droite* to interface with the Front National may in fact be based on the fact that they shared the same structure and thus naturally perceived each other as rivals promulgating slightly different "party lines" and competing for the adherence of the same constituency. If this is true, then the North American New Right can

---

[3] On Cochin, see F. Roger Devlin, "From Salon to Guillotine: Augustin Cochin's *Organizing the Revolution*," *The Occidental Quarterly*, vol. 8, no. 2 (Summer 2008): 63–90.

avoid this problem by configuring itself not as a hierarchical apparatus with a party line but as a lateral network that cultivates dialogue on a common set of questions from various viewpoints.

A PLURALISTIC MOVEMENT

The North American New Right is an intellectual movement with a political agenda, but it is not a hierarchical intellectual sect or a political party. Instead, it is a network of independent authors and activists. We do not have a rigorous and detailed party line, but we do share certain basic premises, questions, and aims. These leave a great deal of latitude for interpretation and application. But that is good.

As an intellectual movement, we embrace a variety of opinions and encourage civil debate. We believe that this is the best way to attract talented and creative people who will advance our agenda. We also believe that debating different perspectives on these issues is the best way to arrive at the truth, or a workable approximation of it.

We collaborate where collaboration is possible. Where differences exist, we seek to build consensus through dialogue and debate. Where differences persist, we agree to disagree and either change the subject or part ways. Because we are a loose network, we can overlap and interface with any number of hierarchical organizations without competing against them.

Just as we reject "apparatus logic," we also reject "representation logic." Because we are a pluralistic movement, there should be no presumption that a given author speaks for me or any other authors who are published here. Every author speaks only for himself.

This is important to understand, because part of every issue of *North American New Right* will be devoted to translations of articles from European New Right thinkers whose positions and aims differ from one another and also from those of the North American New Right. These works are offered for discussion and debate. In their breadth, depth, and originality, they are also exemplars of the kind of work we wish to cultivate in North America.

Even though the North American New Right is a metapolitical movement, and everything we do bears in some way on politics, there will be times when the connections will seem remote and tenuous. Thus we will surely be mocked as pointy-headed, ivory-tower intellectuals or apolitical dandies and poseurs. That is fine. A vibrant and effective intellectual movement has to be exciting to intellectuals, and intellectuals get excited by the oddest things. Besides, bullet-headed pragmatists who see no value in ideas that do not cause an immediate change in poll numbers tend to give up or sell out anyway.

What does that mean for the editorial policy of Counter-Currents Publishing and the journal *North American New Right*? It means, first of all, that those of you who share our concerns but may be holding back because you imagine you diverge from an unstated party line can relax. There is no party line beyond the questions and concerns outlined above. Second, it means that we encourage civil debate and commentary on our articles, interviews, and reviews, including this one. We welcome the challenge.

Counter-Currents/*North American New Right*,
September 30, 2011

DEDICATION

As this volume was going to press, we were saddened to learn of the death of one of our authors, Jonathan Bowden (April 12, 1962–March 29, 2012). We dedicate this volume to his memory.

San Francisco
April 30, 2012

THE DEATH OF
FRANCIS PARKER YOCKEY*

MICHAEL O'MEARA

Fifty years ago today, June 17, 1960, Francis Parker Yockey, fearing he would be lobotomized by the US government, committed suicide while incarcerated in the San Francisco county jail.

Outside of this room, the anniversary of the death of this enigmatic figure—arguably America's most brilliant anti-liberal thinker—is likely to go unobserved in his native land, for his legacy is still unclaimed.

Unlike what Evola called the "false Right," whose alleged anti-liberalism derives from essentially liberal premises (constitutionalism, free markets, bourgeois social forms and sentiments, etc.), Yockey's thought derived from Prussian rather than Anglo-American sources.

As his mentor, Oswald Spengler, argued in *Prussianism and Socialism* (1919), the cultural-political heritage of Prussia's soldier-state grew out of the tradition bequeathed by the medieval knight, Pietism, and ethical socialism, while the market-based Anglo-American world was founded on principles associated with the Vikings, Calvinism, and individualism.

The ramifications of these different traditions were such that America—lacking a proper ruling class and a cultural stratum to sustain its European heritage—came, in time, to scorn its Old World parent, pioneering, in the process, civilizational forms

---

* On June 17, 2010, Counter-Currents Publishing and *North American New Right* hosted a Francis Parker Yockey memorial dinner in San Francisco. Michael O'Meara spoke on Yockey's anti-Americanism and metamorphosis into a supporter of the USSR. This memorial tribute was not included in his speech.

whose materialist occupations and rationalist presumptions have sought to escape the so-called constraints of history, culture, and blood.

During the 19th century, the rising commercial and business classes, communicating vessels of the liberal ethos, allied with the cosmopolitan capitalism of the British Empire and the ascending economic might of America's new low-church empire—an alliance ideologically arrayed under the banner of "Anglo-Saxonism" and implicitly opposed to continental Europeans attached to Listian economics, landed property, authority, and tradition.

In our age, the market forces of American liberalism have managed to denature not just the America's European population, but a good part of the European world.

For though it brought material abundance to some, it also fostered a devastating nihilism that reduces meaning and being to a monetary designation.

If not for America, Yockey believed, the anti-liberal forces of authority, faith, and duty—in the form of National Socialist Germany and Fascist Italy—would have overthrown the liberal *nomos*, anchored in America's "world leadership."

Instead, the very opposite occurred.

First, the colony turned on its mother soil and father culture—then, it subjugated them, ending up, like the snake swallowing its tail, subjugating and denaturing itself—for it (the colony) was European in origin, and origin is inevitably destiny.

Though the "true America," transplant of Europe, shared her destiny, Yockey believed modern liberal America had become an anti-Europe endeavoring not only to subjugate, occupy, and oppress her, but to destroy her unique heritage of blood and spirit.

The only Americans receptive to his anti-liberalism have, relatedly, been those, like him, whose loyalty to Europe's High Culture estranged them from America's culture-distorting—and blood-betraying—liberalism.

* * *

It is a testament, perhaps, to the organic philosophy of history he acquired from Spengler, that Yockey's anti-liberalism grew from his German roots and from his identity with Europe's High Culture, while America's ruling ideas, even on its so-called Right, have stemmed mainly from liberalism's Anglo-Calvinist tradition—and from the Jewish One-World Creed of Mammon it champions.

Counter-Currents/*North American New Right*,
June 21, 2010

SPIRITUAL & STRUCTURAL PRESUPPOSITIONS OF THE EUROPEAN UNION*

JULIUS EVOLA

TRANSLATED BY R. BERKELEY AND BRUNO CARIOU

Circumstances have rendered the need for European unity imperative on our continent. Until now, this need has been fuelled principally by negative factors: the nations of Europe seek a defensive unity, not so much on the basis of anything positive and pre-existing, as because of the lack of any other choice in the face of the threatening pressure of non-European blocs and interests. This circumstance makes it difficult to see the inner form of any possible real European unity very clearly. Thought seems not to go much beyond the project of a coalition or federation, which, as such, will always have an extrinsic, aggregative, rather than organic, character. A unity which would really be organic could be only conceived on the basis of the formative force from inside and from above which is peculiar to a positive idea, a common culture, and a tradition. If we look at the European problem in these terms, it is clear that the situation is painful, and that problematic factors prevent us from indulging in an easy optimism.

Many have drawn attention to these aspects of the European problem. In this respect, a significant work is that of Ulick Varange, entitled *Imperium*.[1] A further examination of the difficul-

---

* Julius Evola, "Sui presupposti spirituali e strutturali dell'unità europea," in *Europa Nazione*, vol. 1, vo. 1 (January 1951). Translation originally published: http://thompkins_cariou.tripod.com/id54.html

[1] Ulick Varange, *Imperium: The Philosophy of History and Politics*, 2 vols. (London: Westropa Press, 1948).

ties which we have mentioned can be based upon this book.

Varange does not propose to defend the project of European unity in purely political terms; rather, he bases himself on the general philosophy of history and civilization which he derives from Oswald Spengler. The Spenglerian conception is well known: according to it, there is no singular and universal development of "culture," but history both builds up and crushes down, in distinct and yet parallel cycles, various "cultures," each of which constitutes an organism and has its own phases of youth, development, senescence, and decline, as do all organisms. More precisely, Spengler distinguishes in every cycle a period of "culture" (*Kultur*) from a period of "civilization" (*Zivilisation*). The first is found at the origins, under the sign of quality, and knows form, differentiation, national articulation, and living tradition; the second is the autumnal and crepuscular phase, in which the destructions of materialism and rationalism take place and the society approaches mechanicalness and formless grandeur, culminating in the reign of pure quantity. According to Spengler, such phenomena occur fatally in the cycle of any "culture." They are biologically conditioned.

Up to this point, Varange follows Spengler, considering the European world, in accordance with Spengler's conception, as one of these organisms of "culture," endowed with its own life, developing an idea which is its own, and following a destiny which is specific to it. Moreover, he follows him in stating that the phase of its cycle through which Europe and the West is currently passing is that of "civilization." However, in opposition to Spengler, who had accordingly launched the new formula of "the decline of the West," he tries to turn the negative into the positive, to make the best of things, and to speak about new forces which would follow an imperative of rebirth, invoking values irreducible to materialism and rationalism. This cyclical development, beyond the ruins of the world of yesterday and the civilization of the 19th century, would push Europe towards a new era: an era of "absolute politics," of supernationality and Authority, and therefore also of the Imperium. To follow this biological imperative in the age of civilization, or to perish, would be Europe's only alternatives.

Accordingly, not only the scientistic and materialistic conception of the universe, but also liberalism and democracy, communism and the UN, pluralistic states and nationalist particularism — all these would be relegated to the past. The historical imperative would be to realize Europe as a nation-culture-race-state unit, based upon a resuscitatory principle of authority and upon new, precise, biological discriminations between friend and enemy, one's own world and an alien, "barbarian" world.

It is necessary to give a good idea of what Varange calls "culture pathology," because this will be useful to our aims. The accomplishment of the inner and natural law of culture-as-organism can be obstructed by processes of distortion (culture-distortion) when alien elements within it direct its energies towards actions and goals which have no connection to its real and vital needs and instead play into the hands of external forces. This finds direct application in the field of wars, since the true alternative is not, according to Varange, between war and peace, but between wars useful and necessary to a culture, and wars which alter and break it up.

The second is the case, not when we go to the battlefield against a real enemy, which threatens biologically the material and spiritual organism of our culture, in which case only a "total war" is conceivable, but when a war of this type bursts within a culture, as has actually happened to the West in the two last cataclysms. In these cataclysms, leaders of European nations themselves have favored the ruin of Europe and the fatal subjection of their homelands to foreign peoples and "barbarians," of the East and of the West, rather than intending to co-operate in the construction of a new Europe which would go beyond the world of the 19th century and reorganize itself under new symbols of authority and of sociality. The fatal, and now quite visible, effect of this has not been the victory of some European nations over others, but that of anti-Europe, of Asia and America, over Europe as a whole.

This accusation is aimed specifically at England, but is extended by Varange to America, since he maintains that the whole system of American political interventionism developed as a result of a "culture distortion," directing itself towards purposes devoid of organic relation to any vital national necessity.

Given this state of affairs, and the increasing tempo of disintegration, the challenge for the West is that of recognizing the biological imperative corresponding to the present phase of its cycle: that of going beyond division into states and of bringing about the unity of the European nation-state, and combining all its forces against anti-Europe.

This task, in its first stage, will be internal and spiritual. Europe must get rid of its traitors, parasites, and "distorters."[2] It is necessary that European culture cleanse itself of the residues of the materialistic, economistic, rationalistic, and egalitarian conceptions of the 19th century. In its second stage, the renewed unity of Europe as civilization or culture will have to find expression in a related political unity, to be pursued even at the cost of civil wars and of struggles against the powers which want to maintain Europe under their own control. Federations, customs unions, and other economic measures cannot constitute solutions; it is from an inner imperative that unity should arise: an imperative which is to be realized even if it appears to be economically disadvantageous, since economic criteria can no longer be considered as determinative in the new era. In the third stage, it will become possible and necessary to attack the problem of the necessary space for the excess population of the

---

[2] Speaking of "traitors, parasites, and 'distorters,'" a point which cannot be stressed enough is that, if we are to believe the contents of certain supposedly top-secret documents from a famous American secret service agency — or even if we don't believe them — the state of affairs in Europe since the end of World War II suggests that the "European Union" is nothing but the continuation, by hidden means, of the "Morgenthau Plan." These documents show, among other things crucial for the true understanding of what has been going on in Europe since the end of World War II, that, in the early 1950s, well-known and highly respectable American mafia-type organizations financed many projects intended, in the terms of their perverse vocabulary, to "rebuild" Europe into the form we know today, and called enthusiastically for the creation of a "European parliament."

European nation, for which Varange sees the best solution as an outlet towards the East, where currently, under the mask of communism, the power of races biologically, immemorially, hostile to Western culture gathers and organizes itself.

This takes us far enough into the ideas of Varange for our current purposes. Let us now evaluate them.

The fundamental symbolism Varange evokes is that of the Imperium, and of a new principle of authority. Nevertheless we do not think that he sees quite clearly what this symbolism involves, if it is to be adopted as it should be; he does not discern the discrepancy between this symbolism and the inherent character of the late phase or "*Zivilisation*" of a culture, in our case of the European one.

In our opinion, Varange is certainly correct when he announces the inadequacy of every federalist or merely economic solution of the European problem. As we have already said, a true unity can only be of the organic type, and for this the plan is quite well-known: it is that already realized, for example, in the European medieval *oecumene*. It embraces both unity and multiplicity and is embodied in a hierarchical participatory system. What this requires us to overcome and to leave behind is nationalism, in the sense of schismatic absolutization of the particular; we must go beyond, or retreat from, this to the natural concept of nationality. Within any national space, a process of integration should then occur — politically — which would coordinate its forces into a hierarchical structure and establish an order based on a central principle of authority and sovereignty. The same thing should then repeat itself in the supranational space, in the European space in general, in which we will have the nations as partial organic unities gravitating into a "*unum quod non est pars*" (to use the Dantesque expression), that is to say into the field of a principle of authority hierarchically superior to each of them. This principle, to be such, should necessarily transcend the political field in the narrow sense, should be based upon itself alone, and should legitimize itself by means of an idea, a tradition, and a spiritual power. Then only would arise the Imperium: the free, organic, and manly European unity, really free from all leveling, liberalistic, democratic, chauvinistic, or collectivistic ideologies, presenting itself, by virtue of this achievement, in a precise separation from both "East" and "West," that is to say from the two blocs which, like the arms of a single pair of pincers, are closing themselves around us.

Therefore, the premise of an eventual development of this type is not the dissolution of the nations into a single nation, in a sort of socially homogeneous single European substance, but the hierarchical integration of every nation. True organic unity, as opposed to mere mixture, is realized not through the bases, but through the summits. Once the nationalistic hubris, which is always accompanied by demagogic, collectivistic, and schismatic forces, is broken, and the individual nations are configured hierarchically, there will exist a virtual unification which will extend itself beyond the nations, while nevertheless leaving them their natural individuality and form.

In this way everything would proceed ideally. The trouble, however, is that the natural context for such an accomplishment is that of a world which is in the phase of "*Kultur*," not of "*Zivilisation*" — to use the Spenglerian terminology. Writers such as Varange mix things belonging to distinct planes, falling into a mistake to which Mussolini also once exposed himself. Mussolini, probably not knowing Spengler's major works, read his *The Hour of Decision*[3] and was struck by the prognosis of a new Caesarism or Bonapartism: this is why he wanted the book to be translated into Italian. However, he did not understand the position in which, according to Spengler, formations of this type fall in the cyclic development of cultures: it is when the world of tradition collapses, when "*Kultur*" no longer exists, but only "*Zivilisation*," when the qualitative values have fallen and the formless element of the "mass" takes the upper hand.

It is only then, in the autumnal or crepuscular phase of a cy-

---

[3] Oswald Spengler, *Jahre der Entscheidung, Erster Teil: Deutschland und die weltgeschichtliche Entwicklung* (Munich: C. H. Beck, 1933); in English: *The Hour of Decision, Part One: Germany and World-Historical Development*, trans. Charles Francis Atkinson (New York: Alfred A. Knopf, 1934).

cle, that the nations disappear and great supranational aggregates are born, under the mark of a pseudo-Caesarism, of a centralized personal power, in itself formless, lacking a superior chrism. All this is only a twisted and inverted image of the Imperium in the traditional and genuine sense; it is not empire, but "imperialism," and, in the Spenglerian view, it represents a last flash, which is followed by the end—the end of a culture, which may be followed by a new and different one without any link of continuity with the precedent.

Now, when Varange speaks of the new period of "absolute politics" and of the blocs which, once the nations of the same culture are absorbed into a single organism, should have as their sole desideratum that of the absolute, existential distinction of enemy and friend (a view taken from Carl Schmitt, who had defined in these terms the essence of the purely political modern units) and of the pure biological imperative, we still remain on the plane of "*Zivilisation*" and of collectivistic, "totalitarian" processes, to be judged more as subnational than as really supranational, whose closest and most consistent realization today can be found in the realm of Stalinism.

Now, it is clear that if the unity of Europe can realize itself only in these terms, i.e., by means of its own brute strength, then the West can perhaps resist the world and reassert itself materially or biologically, as against the extra-European imperialistic powers, but, at the same time, it will have renounced its own interiority, and this will be the end of Europe, of the European tradition; it will become a facsimile of its opponents, a mere product of the plane of the struggle of a brute will to existence and power, under the sway of the general factors of disintegration peculiar to the technicist-mechanicist "*Zivilisation*" which will subsequently overtake all. This is more or less the prognosis made also by Burnham in his consideration of the eventual results of what he calls "the managerial revolution" at work.[4]

What other possibilities are there? It is not easy to say. As

---

[4] James Burnham, *The Managerial Revolution: What is Happening in the World* (New York: John Day, 1941).

far as the nations are concerned, each can maintain its actual individuality and the dignity of an organic "partial whole," while at the same time subordinating itself to a superior order, only under the conditions already indicated: that is, if a really superior authority, one which is not simply political, and which cannot be monopolized by any individual nation in terms of "hegemonism," is directly recognized by it. The alternative which is defined in material terms of usefulness and external necessity is merely extrinsic and quite trivial. The current "authorities" speak willingly of European tradition, of European culture, of Europe as an autonomous organism, and so forth, but unfortunately, when we consider things as they really are, in the light of absolute values, we see that there is little more to this than slogans and sententiousness. Where, then, can we find an avenue of approach to the higher possibility?

On a higher plane, the soul for a European supranational bloc would have to be religious: religious not in an abstract sense but with reference to a precise and positive spiritual authority. Now, even leaving aside the more recent and general processes of secularization and of laicization which have occurred in Europe, nothing like this exists today on our continent. Catholicism is merely the belief of some European nations — and besides we have seen how, in an incomparably more favorable period than the present one, namely the post-Napoleonic one, the Holy Alliance, with which the idea of a traditional and manly solidarity of the European nations dawned, was such only nominally. It lacked a true religious chrism, a universal, transcendent, idea. If in the same way the "new Europe" were to offer only a generic Christianity, it would be too little. It would be something too shapeless and uniform, not exclusively European, which could not be monopolized by European culture. What is more, some doubts cannot but arise regarding the reconcilability of pure Christianity with a "metaphysics of the empire," as is shown by the medieval conflict between the two powers,[5] if this conflict is understood in its true terms.

---

[5] Of emperor and pope — Ed.

Let us leave this plane and pass to the cultural plane. Can we speak today of a differentiated European culture? Or, better, of a spirit which remains unique throughout its various and syntonic expressions in the cultures of the individual European nations? Again, it would be foolhardy to answer in the affirmative, for the reason Christoph Steding has shown in a well-known book entitled *The Reich and the Disease of European Culture*.[6] This reason lies in what this author calls the neutralization of the present culture, a culture no longer appropriate to a common political idea, confined to the private realm, transitory, cosmopolitan, disorientated, anti-architectonic, subjective, neutral, and formless overall because of its scientistic and positivistic aspects. To ascribe all this to a "culture pathology," to an outward and fleeting action of "distortion" by alien elements, as Varange would hold to be the cause of this state of affairs, not only for Europe, but even for America, is rather simplistic.

In general, where can a cultural base differentiated enough to be able to oppose itself seriously to the "alien," the "barbarian," be found today, in this phase of "*Zivilisation*," and where could it be found in the case of previous imperial spaces? We would have to go a long way back, in our work of cleansing and of reintegration, to arrive at such a base, because, although we are certainly right to judge aspects of both the North American and the Russian-Bolshevik civilizations as barbarian and anti-European, we cannot lose sight of the fact that these aspects themselves represent, in both the former and the latter, the extreme development of tendencies and evils which first manifested themselves in Europe.

It is precisely in this that the reason of the weak immunity of the latter against them lies.

Finally, in the situation we are reduced to today, even as far as "tradition" is concerned, there is a misunderstanding. It has already been a long time since the West knew what "tradition" was in the highest sense; the anti-traditional spirit and the

---

[6] Christoph Steding, *Das Reich und die Krankheit der europäischen Kultur* (Hamburg: Hanseatische Verlangsanstalt, 1938).

Western spirit have been one and the same thing since as early as the period of the Renaissance. "Tradition," in the complete sense, is a feature of the periods which Vico would call "heroic ages" — where a sole formative force, with metaphysical roots, manifested itself in customs as well as in religion, in law, in myth, in artistic creations, in short in every particular domain of existence. Where can the survival of tradition in this sense be found today? And, specifically, as European tradition, great, unanimous, and not peasant or folkloric, tradition? It is only in the sense of the leveling "totalitarianism" that tendencies towards political-cultural absolute unity have appeared. In concrete terms, the "European tradition" as culture has nowadays as content only the private and more or less diverging interpretations of intellectuals and scholars in fashion: of this, yesterday, the "Volta Congresses"[7] and, today, various initiatives of the same type have given sufficient and distinctly unedifying proofs.

From these considerations and others of the same kind, we reach a single, fundamental conclusion: a supranational unity with positive and organic features is not conceivable in a period of *"Zivilisation."* In such a period, what is conceivable, at the limit, is the melting of nations into a more or less formless power bloc, in which the political principle is the ultimate determinant and subordinates to itself all moral and spiritual factors, either as the "telluric" world of the "world revolution" (Keyserling), or as the world of "absolute politics" in the service of a biological imperative (Varange), or again as totalitarian complexes in the hands of managers (Burnham), all of which have already become matters of common experience. Unity in function of "tradition" is something very different from this.

Should we then reach a negative conclusion regarding the situation and content ourselves with a more modest, federalist, "social" or socialistic idea? Not necessarily, because, once the

---

[7] The "Volta Congress," convened in 1936 by the Academy of Italy, invited celebrities from various countries to discuss "the question of Europe."

antithesis is noted, all we really need to do is to orientate ourselves accordingly. If it is absurd to pursue our higher ideal in the context of a "*Zivilisation*," because it would become twisted and almost inverted, we can still recognize, in the overcoming of what has precisely the character of "*Zivilisation*," the premise for every really reconstructive initiative. "*Zivilisation*" is more or less equivalent to the "modern world," and, without deluding ourselves, it is necessary to acknowledge that, with its materialism, its economism, its rationalism, and the other involutive and dissolutive factors, the West—let us say Europe—is eminently responsible for the "modern world." In the first place, a revival needs to take place which would have an effect upon the spiritual plane, awakening new forms of sensibility and of interest, and so also a new inner style, a new fundamental homogeneous orientation of the spirit. To this effect, it is necessary to realize that it is not just a matter of, as Varange would have it, going beyond the 19th-century vision of life in its various aspects, because this vision is itself the effect of more remote causes. Then, as regards the biological interpretation of culture by Spengler, precise reservations must be made; above all we must refrain from believing, with the author that we have considered, in an almost inevitable revival which would be heralded by various symptoms. In fact, we must avoid leaning beyond measure on the ideas of the revolutionary and reforming movements of yesterday, since the fact is that different tendencies, sometimes even contradictory tendencies, were present in them, which could only have attained any positive form if circumstances had allowed these movements to develop totalistically, whereas in actuality they were crushed by their military defeat.

Overall, politically speaking, the crisis of the principle of authority seems to us to constitute the most serious difficulty. Let us repeat that we speak of authority in the true sense, which is such as to determine not only obedience, but also natural adherence and direct recognition. Only such authority can lead the elements within a nation to overcome individualism and "socialism," and, in the pan-European area, to reduce the nationalistic hubris, the "sacred prides," and the stiffening of the principle of individual state sovereignty, in a manner better than mere necessity or circumstantial interest can do. If there is something specifically peculiar to the Aryo-Western tradition it is the spontaneous joining together of free men proud of serving a leader who is really such. The only way to a real European unity is via something which repeats on a large scale such a situation, of a "heroic" nature, not that of a mere "parliament" or a facsimile of a joint stock company.

This brings into view the mistake of those who admit a sort of political agnosticism to the European idea, thus reducing it to a kind of formless common denominator: a centre of crystallization is needed, and the form of the whole cannot but reflect itself in that of the parts. On a background which is not that of "civilization," but that of tradition, this form can only be the organic-hierarchical one. The more integration along those lines occurs in each of the partial — that is, national — areas, the more we will approach supranational unity.

The fact that numerous external pressures are now clearly perceptible, so that for Europe to unite is a matter of life or death, must lead to the acknowledgment of the inner problem which must be resolved to give to an eventual European coalition a solid base, which as explained above has a double aspect: on one hand, it is the problem of the gradual and real overcoming of what is characteristic of a period of *"Zivilisation"*; on the other hand, it is the problem of a sort of "metaphysics" by which an idea of pure authority, at once national, supranational, and European, can be justified.

This double problem brings us back to a double imperative. We must see what men are still standing among so many ruins who are able to understand and accept this imperative.

A CONTEMPORARY EVALUATION OF FRANCIS PARKER YOCKEY

KERRY BOLTON

"Thus, the Liberation Front now states to Europe its two great tasks: (1) the complete expulsion of everything alien from the soul and from the soil of Europe, the cleansing of the European soul of the dross of 19th century materialism and rationalism with its money-worship, liberal-democracy, social degeneration, parliamentarism, class-war, feminism, vertical nationalism, finance-capitalism, petty-statism, chauvinism, the Bolshevism of Moscow and Washington, the ethical syphilis of Hollywood, and the spiritual leprosy of New York; (2) the construction of the Imperium of Europe and the actualizing of the divinely-emanated European will to unlimited political Imperialism."

— Francis Parker Yockey[1]

Francis Parker Yockey (a.k.a. Ulick Varange) has enjoyed a renascence over the course of several decades, although his thought was never permitted to die with him in a San Francisco jail in 1960, thanks to the stalwart efforts of individuals such as Willis Carto and H. Keith Thompson, as well as the ongoing efforts of others such as Michael O'Meara. Yockey has been the subject of a major biography[2] and is discussed at length in Martin Lee's book on "neo-Nazism."[3] This writer's Renaissance Press also carries a range of Yockey materials including hither-

[1] Francis Parker Yockey, *The Proclamation of London of the European Liberation Front* (London: Westropa Press, 1949), 29.

[2] Kevin Coogan, *Dreamer of the Day: Francis Parker Yockey and the Post-War Fascist International* (New York: Autonomedia, 1999).

[3] Martin Lee, *The Beast Reawakens:* (Boston: Little, Brown, 1997).

to unpublished manuscripts.[4] Christian Bouchet in France carries material by and about Yockey, and Alfonso De Filippi's Italian translation of *The Proclamation of London* in a nicely bound volume is a sterling effort.[5]

Yockey has been criticized by some "Rightist" luminaries such as David Duke, who has stated that Willis Carto's introduction to Yockey's *magnum opus*, *Imperium*, is of more value than the work itself,[6] while the historical revisionist David McCalden stated that *Imperium* served as a good doorstop. Certainly, Yockey's philosophy does not fit neatly into the racial-nationalist paradigm of genetic reductionism. Like Oswald Spengler's epochal *Decline of the West*,[7] to which Yockey owed a great intellectual debt, Yockey focused on spirit and culture above and beyond genetics.

Just as Spengler was criticized by National Socialist race theorists, primarily by Alfred Rosenberg, who nonetheless conceded that *The Decline of the West* was "great and good" — although by then redundant philosophically;[8] Yockey was not well received by American National Socialist George Lincoln Rockwell, who condemned "Yockeyism" as "dangerous" and "evil." On the other hand, James Madole of the National Re-

---

[4] *Yockey: Four Essays 1939–1960*; *Frontfighter* newsletter; Yockey/Thompson letters to Dean Acheson, 1952; "America's Two Ways of Waging War," 1952; "America's Two Political Factions," 1952; Yockey FBI Report, 1953; Kerry Bolton, *Varange – Life and Thoughts of Yockey* (Paraparaumu, New Zealand: Renaissance Press, 1998), a biography of Yockey drawing from FBI and Intelligence files, newspaper accounts of his capture and death; rare typewritten manuscripts of Yockey; *Imperium*; *The Enemy of Europe*; *The Proclamation of London*. (www.freewebs.com/renaissancepress).

[5] Yockey, *Il Proclama di Londra*, trans. Alfonso De Filippi (Genoa: Effepi, 2005).

[6] David Duke, *My Awakening* (Covington, La.: Free Speech Press, 1999), 474.

[7] Oswald Spengler, *The Decline of the West*, trans. Charles Francis Atkinson, 2 vols. (London: Allen and Unwin, 1971).

[8] Alfred Rosenberg, *The Myth of the Twentieth Century*, trans. Vivian Bird (Torrance, Cal.: The Noontide Press, 1982), 247.

naissance Party was very much influenced by Yockey's ideas.[9]

For those who continue to regard Yockey's paradigm as a seminal method for analyzing events, the lasting contribution of Yockeyan philosophy is that of "cultural morphology," developing Spengler's theory of "culture as an organism," and in particular formulating the diagnostic method of "culture pathology," which includes the concepts of "culture distortion," "culture parasitism," and "culture retardation."[10]

Yockey's diagnostic method allows one to see beyond the surface of problems which are often otherwise reduced to simplistic formulas of white vs. black, Christian vs. Jew, and concepts as banal as "freedom vs. communism," which preoccupied even the "Radical Right" of Rockwell *et al.* — the arguments of which make for a poor showing when confronted by the pseudo-intelligentsia of the Left and its corporate allies.

It was this perspective which, for example, allowed Yockey to see, contra much of the rest of the "Right" during the Cold War era, why the United States is ultimately a much more pervasive, subversive, and degenerate force for the destruction of Europe than a military invasion by the USSR. This is why Yockey referred to the "Bolshevism of Washington," a phrase that much of the "Right" from Yockey's time to our own, would find utterly incomprehensible, if not outright "evil."

During 1948–1949, when his *Imperium* and *Proclamation* were published, Yockey still considered the twin outer enemies of Europe to be the "Bolshevism of Moscow and of Washington." By 1952, Yockey had come to consider the latter the prime enemy. In an unsigned article in *Frontfighter* commenting on Point 5 of the European Liberation Front program, it is stated that the opposition to "the virus of Jewish Bolshevism [is] more readily

---

[9] Coogan, *Dreamer of the Day*, 508–11. Madole published Yockey's "Prague Treason Trial" and other essays and was under the influence of Fred Weiss, a German World War I veteran living in the USA, who was closely associated with both H. Keith Thompson and Yockey. (Thompson to Bolton, personal correspondence; also Coogan, 508–11).

[10] Yockey, *Imperium*, "Cultural Vitalism: (B) Culture Pathology," 367–439. For a very brief summary of these concepts see: Yockey, *The Proclamation of London*, 12–13.

understood, and therefore not as dangerous" as the "ethical syphilis of Hollywood."[11]

As Yockey saw it, the primary problem with Moscow's Bolshevism at the time was its leadership of a world colored revolt against the white world, reminiscent of Spengler's scenario in *The Hour of Decision*.[12] However, Yockey, like many German war veterans such as Major General Otto Remer, whose growing Socialist Reich Party was advocating a neutralist line during the Cold War, saw the primary danger not of a Soviet invasion of Europe but of Europe being subordinated to the US under the guise of protection from "Communism":

> The Liberation Front does not allow Europe to be distracted by the situation of the moment, in which the two crude Bolshevisms of Washington and Moscow are preparing a Third World War. In those preparations, the Culture-retarders, the inner enemies, the liberal-communist-democrats are again at their posts: with one voice the churchills, the spaaks, the lies, the gaulles, croak that Washington is going to save Europe from Moscow, or that Moscow is going to take Europe from Washington. There is nothing to substantiate this propaganda.[13]

Yockey's reorientation towards an openly pro-Soviet position *vis-à-vis* the USA, was determined by the seminal event of the 1952 Prague Treason Trial,[14] which Yockey saw as Mos-

---

[11] "What is the Front Fighting For?," Point 5, *Frontfighter*, no. 23, April 1952.

[12] Oswald Spengler, *The Hour of Decision, Part One: Germany and World-Historical Development*, trans. Charles Francis Atkinson (New York: Alfred A. Knopf, 1934), "The Coloured World Revolution," 204–30. In this chapter many later Yockeyan themes can be found, including even the concept of a "white Imperium" and the repudiation of biological "race purity." Spengler saw "class war" and "race war" as joining together against the West.

[13] Yockey, *The Proclamation of London*, 30.

[14] Yockey, "The Prague Treason Trial, What is Behind the Hanging

cow's definitive break with the "Jewish" faction within Bolshevism which had been vying for control with the Slavic faction, that at heart remained true to the soul of Russia.[15]

In fact, as Yockey now discerned, the break between Moscow and New York came immediately after World War II when Stalin declined to subordinate himself to American internationalist schemes for a new world order via the United Nations Organization and the Baruch Plan for the supposed "internationalization" of atomic energy, which Stalin perceived would in fact mean US control. This laid the basis for the Cold War,[16] despite the insistence of many on the "Right" that there was an ongoing secret alliance between Jews in Washington and Jews in Moscow to rule the world with the Cold War being a cunning plan to bamboozle the *goyim*.

Some saw through this nonsense from the start, either under Yockey's influence or based on their own perceptions of *Realpolitik*. These included the insightful staff writers at the periodical *Common Sense*, Wilmot Robertson of *Instauration*, William Pierce, and the eccentric but sincere and determined James Madole of the National Renaissance Party.[17]

This, then, was Yockey's new orientation in regard to the USSR and the USA during the Cold War:

---

of Eleven Jews in Prague?" (Published in *Yockey: Four Essays* [New Jersey: Nordland Press, 1971]), 1952. According to "D.T.K." (Douglas Thacker Kaye) in the foreword to *Yockey: Four Essays*, Yockey supporters in the USA circulated the manuscript as a mimeographed "press release" dated December 20, 1952.

[15] K. R. Bolton, "Francis Parker Yockey: Stalin's Fascist Advocate," *International Journal of Russian Studies*, no. 2, 2010, http://www.radtr.net/dergi/sayi6/bolton6.htm

[16] K. R. Bolton, "Origins of the Cold War: How Stalin Foiled a New World Order: Relevance for the Present," *Foreign Policy Journal*, May 31, 2010, http://www.foreignpolicyjournal.com/2010/05/31/origins-of-the-cold-war-how-stalin-foild-a-new-world-order/all/1

[17] K. R. Bolton, *Cold War Axis: The Influence of Soviet Anti-Zionism on the American Extreme Right* (Paraparaumu, New Zealand: Renaissance Press, 2009).

The treason trials in Bohemia are neither the beginning nor the end of a historical process, they are merely an unmistakable turning point. Henceforth, all must *perforce* reorient their policy in view of the undeniable reshaping of the world-situation. The ostrich-policy is suicide. The talk of "defense against Bolshevism" belongs now to yesterday, as does the nonsense of talking of "the defense of Europe" at a period when every inch of European soil is dominated by the deadly enemies of Europe, those who seek its political-cultural-historical extinction at all costs.[18]

And further, those who sought the liberation and unity of Europe could play off the USA against the USSR; if they pursued a policy of *Realpolitik* as people such as Remer[19] were themselves advocating:

Henceforth, the European elite can emerge more and more into affairs, and will force the Jewish-American leadership to render back, step by step, the custody of European Destiny to Europe, its best forces, its natural, organic leadership. If the Jewish-American leaders refuse, the new leaders of Europe will threaten them with the Russian bogey. By thus playing off Russia against the Jewish-American leadership, Europe can bring about its Liberation, possibly even before the Third World War.[20]

It was fatuous enough to ask Europe to fight for America, it was silly enough to ask it to "defend itself against Bolshevism" . . . Is there one European—just one—who would respond to this war-aim? But today, openly, without any possible disguise, this is the *raison d'être* of the

---

[18] Yockey, "The Prague Treason Trial," 3.

[19] Lee, *The Beast Reawakens*, 74. The USSR regarded the Socialist Reich Party as a better option than the West German Communist Party, and funds were dispensed accordingly.

[20] Yockey, "The Prague Treason Trial," 7–8.

coalition against Russia, for Russia has named its chief
enemy, its sole enemy, and the sly peasant leadership of
pan-Slavs in the Kremlin is not given to frivolity in its
foreign policy.

[. . .]

We repeat our message to Europe: no European must
ever fight except for sovereign Europe; no European
must ever fight one enemy of Europe on behalf of another enemy.[21]

With the publication of *The Enemy of Europe* in Germany in
1953, primarily as a foreign policy manual for the Socialist
Reich Party, Yockey talked openly of a "new Europe-Russia
Symbiosis," with the occupation of Europe by Russia not resulting in the Russification of Europe, but in the Westernization
of Russia.[22]

Of course the world situation turned out radically different
from what Yockey and others expected, with the implosion of
the USSR and the emergence of a unipolar world under the US.
However, Yockey correctly understood the cultural threat of
the US to Western civilization, and this is why he continues to
be relevant for analyzing the geopolitical situation.

The US ruling stratum is conscious of its anti-Western world
revolutionary mission and deliberately promotes cultural degeneration as part of its agenda. To call the US the "leader of
the West" or any other such term, is not only a misnomer, it is a
travesty; the US is the anti-West *par excellence*, the Great Satan,
as many Muslims refer to it.

That the Soviet bloc, with its spartan values, its martial and
patriotic ethos, its "Socialist Realism" in the arts, was in ruins
several decades after Yockey's death, while the decadent USA
emerged as the unchallenged superpower, attests to the tendency of nations—like individuals—to opt for the soft option,

---

[21] Yockey, "The Prague Treason Trial," 8–9.

[22] Francis Parker Yockey, *The Enemy of Europe* and Revilo P. Oliver,
The Enemy of Our Enemies (Reedy, W.Va: Liberty Bell Publications,
1981), 83.

rather than face hard realities, despite the expectations of Yockey and also the staff of *Common Sense*, who closed up shop in the 1970s, convinced that it wouldn't be long until the Soviets vaporized New York, thus the time for writing articles was past.[23] The method used by the culture distorter is what Aldous Huxley describes as control by "pleasure," an intoxicant that is rotting the soul of the entire world, with militant Islam as a vestige of resistance from a Fellaheen Civilization, and Great Russia the nearest remainder to an unsullied people that might yet break "the dictature of money."

However, if we accept Spengler's theory of the cyclic course of civilizations, one might reasonably expect a renascence of Russian authority and religiosity that will confront US hegemony and force Russia to face new realities and forge new alliances, especially given the scenarios for conflict that can easily arise *vis-à-vis* China and all Asia.[24]

However, for the moment, the US stands victorious, as the harbinger of cultural death throughout the world, spreading the "ethical syphilis of Hollywood," the "spiritual leprosy of New York," and the "Bolshevism of Washington," which outlasted the "Bolshevism of Moscow."

YOCKEY & HUXLEY ON "SOFT" TOTALITARIANISM

Understanding Yockey's views of American "ethical syphilis" and "spiritual leprosy" is aided by a familiarity with Aldous Huxley's 1932 novel *Brave New World*.[25] Huxley was much more prescient than George Orwell and quite precisely described how "world controllers" would impose a global dictatorship not by force of arms, but by the slavery of "pleasure." The ready availability of sex and drugs would be used to create

---

[23] "The End of the Trail," *Common Sense*, May 15, 1972. Much insightful political writing was published in *Common Sense*, and numerous articles have been reprinted as booklets available from this writer.

[24] K. R. Bolton, "Russia and China: An Approaching Conflict?," *The Journal of Social, Political, and Economic Studies*, vol. 34, no. 2, Summer 2009.

[25] Aldous Huxley, *Brave New World* (London: Chatto & Windus, 1969).

a narcotized society where everyone is happy with his servile lot. Appraising *Brave New World* in 1958, Huxley described the regime as:

> . . . The society described in *Brave New World* is a world-state, in which war has been eliminated and where the first aim of the rulers is at all costs to keep their subjects from making trouble. This they achieve by (among other methods) legalizing a degree of sexual freedom (made possible by the abolition of the family) that practically guarantees the Brave New Worlders against any form of destructive (or creative) emotional tension. In *1984* the lust for power is satisfied by inflicting pain; in *Brave New World*, by inflicting a hardly less humiliating pleasure.[26]

A drug called "Soma" maintains social conditioning. Huxley calls this drugged state "not a private vice" but "a political institution":

> It was the very essence of Life, Liberty and the Pursuit of Happiness guaranteed by the Bill of Rights. But this most precious of the subjects' inalienable privileges was at the same time one of the most powerful instruments of rule in the dictator's armory. The systematic drugging of the individuals for the benefit of the State . . . was a main plank in the policy of the World Controllers . . .[27]

In *Brave New World*, population control is enforced and non-reproductive sex, including mass orgies, or "orgy-porgys," in which participants go into a frenzy induced by narcotics and repetitive rhythms.[28] These orgies also serve as religious rites or "solidarity" events.

Yockey had a similar understanding of the workings of soft

---

[26] Aldous Huxley, *Brave New World Revisited* (New York: Harper & Row, 1958), 26–27.

[27] *Brave New World Revisited*, 27

[28] *Brave New World*, ch. 5.

totalitarianism. In *The Proclamation of London,* he writes:

> The degradation of the social life did not merely happen, it was planned, deliberately fostered and spread, and the systematic undermining of the entire life of the West continues today.
>
> The instruments of this assault are the weapons of propaganda: press, radio, cinema, stage, education. These weapons are controlled at this moment in Europe almost entirely by the forces of Culture-disease and social degeneration.

The "chief fount" is Hollywood, which "spews forth an endless series of perverted films to debase and degenerate the youth of Europe" after having successfully destroyed the youth of America.[29]

Concomitantly "a vicious literature" promotes the "destruction of healthy individual instincts, of normal familial and sexual life, of disintegration of the social organism into a heap of wandering, colliding, grains of human sand":

> The message of Hollywood is the total significance of the isolated individual, stateless and rootless, outside of society and family, whose life is the pursuit of money and erotic pleasure. It is not the normal and healthy love of man and wife bound together by many children that Hollywood preaches, but a diseased erotic-for-its-own sake, the sexual love of two grains of human sand, superficial and impermanent. Before this highest of all Hollywood's values everything else must stand aside: marriage, honour, duty, patriotism, sternness, dedication of self to a higher aim. This ghastly distortion of sexual life has created the erotomania that obsesses its millions of victims in America, and which has now been brought to the Mother-soil of Europe by the American invasion.[30]

---

[29] *The Proclamation of London,* 14.
[30] *The Proclamation of London,* 14.

Keep in mind that Yockey was writing this in 1948, not last month, or even a decade ago. We now look back on the era Yockey was describing with such misgivings and consider it a time of innocence and purity in comparison to our own. Who can deny that this process of "social degeneration" has accelerated beyond all ability to calculate?

Yockey also wrote of the rise of "feminism" at a time when we would now barely recognize any such thing as "feminism" in comparison to our own day:

> Hollywood-feminism has created a woman who is no longer a woman but cannot be a man, and a man who is devirilized into an indeterminate thing. The name given to this process is "the setting free" of woman and it is done in the name of "happiness," the magic word of the liberal-communist-democratic doctrine.[31]

Yockey died on the eve of the 1960s with its manufactured "cultural revolution." Yet he surely would have regarded the counter-culture's sexual liberation, feminism, and drug use not as a "revolution" against the US establishment, but merely as a phase of its pursuit of world domination through the destruction of traditional culture and morals.

THE CULTURAL COLD WAR

The origins and implementation of the strategy can now be historically traced with great precision. The seeds of the 1960s were planted as early as 1949, at the start of the Cold War, when Stalin gave the first indications that he was not going to continue the wartime alliance as a subordinate partner in a United Nations-based World State.

The CIA, with funding from the Rockefellers and the like, gathered a gaggle of old Trotskyites, Mensheviks, and other Leftists disaffected with Stalin's uncouth Slavic "Bolshevism." The result was the Congress for Cultural Freedom (CCF) under the direction of "lifelong Menshevik" Professor Sidney Hook

---

[31] *The Proclamation of London*, 14–15.

(who would be awarded the Medal of Freedom by President Reagan, for services to US hegemony), along with his old mentor John Dewey,[32] and luminaries such as Bertrand Russell (who once advocated a pre-emptive nuclear strike on the USSR to insure "world peace"), Stephen Spender, and Arthur Koestler. "Counter-culture rebels" recruited in the 1960s by the US Establishment included Gloria Steinem[33] and Timothy Leary.[34]

The founding conference of the CCF was held at the Waldorf Astoria Hotel in 1949, as a provocation to a Soviet-sponsored peace conference at the Waldorf supported by a number of American literati. The CIA article on this states:

> A handful of liberal and socialist writers, led by philosophy professor Sidney Hook, saw their chance to steal a little of the publicity expected for the [pro-Soviet] Waldorf peace conference. A fierce ex-Communist [should read anti-Stalinist] himself, Hook was then teaching at New York University and editing a socialist magazine called *The New Leader*. Ten years earlier he and his mentor John Dewey had founded a controversial group called

---

[32] Hook and Dewey had in 1937 established a so-called commission of inquiry to investigate the Moscow Trials against Trotskyites, for the purpose of whitewashing Trotsky under the guise of a neutral judicial inquiry. However, one of the commissioners, Carleton Beals, one of the party that went with Dewey *et al.* to Mexico to question Trotsky, resigned in disgust, labeling the inquiry "Trotsky's pink tea party" (Carleton Beals, "The Fewer Outsiders the Better: The Pink Tea Party Trials," *Saturday Evening Post,* June 12, 1937).

[33] On Steinem and the CIA manipulation of the National Students' Association, see Tom Hayden, *Reunion: A Memoir* (London: Hamish Hamilton, 1989), 36–39. Gloria Steinem, the seminal feminist, was an Establishment creation.

[34] Leary was the perfect CIA/Establishment lackey, a mouthpiece for the System-invented psychedelic generation. Journalist Mark Riebling posed the question: "Was the Sixties Rebellion a Government Plot?" in Mark Riebling, "Tinker, Tailor, Stoner, Spy: Was Timothy Leary a CIA Agent? Was JFK the 'Manchurian Candidate'? Was the Sixties Revolution Really a Government Plot?," http://home.dti.net/lawserv/leary.html

the Committee for Cultural Freedom, which attacked both Communism and Nazism. He now organized a similar committee to harass the peace conference in the Waldorf-Astoria.[35]

Through the CCF, the CIA was able to control much of the cultural life of the West during the Cold War era, and subsidized influential magazines such as *Encounter*.[36]

When the CCF was shut down after the implosion of the Soviet bloc, other institutions were established, this time under private auspices, including in particular the Soros network[37] and the National Endowment for Democracy (NED), the latter another collaboration between neo-Trotskyites,[38] the US Government, and neo-conservatives. Both Soros and the NED work in tandem to create revolutions, much like the manipulated "youth revolts" of the 1960s, to install regimes favorably disposed to globalization and privatization, especially in the former Soviet bloc.

The cultural front remains pivotal to the expansion of American global hegemony, the spreading of cultural pathology being far more insidious and intrusive than bombs or even debt, as Yockey was among the first to warn, while much of the rest of the "Right," including Rockwell's American Nazis, aligned themselves with the US Establishment *vis-à-vis* the USSR and

---

[35] Central Intelligence Agency, "Cultural Cold War: Origins of the Congress for Cultural Freedom, 1949–50."

[36] Frances Stonor Saunders, *The Cultural Cold War: The CIA and the World of Arts and Letters* (New York: The New Press, 1999).

[37] The Soros networks support the legalization of narcotics and the promotion of feminism, including liberalized abortion, in states that maintain a vestige of tradition and therefore pose a stumbling block to globalization. The former Soviet bloc is a particular target for Soros subversion. One such Soros front is the Drug Policy Alliance Network, which includes Establishment luminaries such as George Schultz, Paul Volcker, Václav Havel, and Soros himself. Drug Policy Alliance Network, About DPA Network, http://www.drugpolicy.org/about/

[38] The National Endowment for Democracy was the brainchild of Trotskyite Tom Kahn. See below.

American hegemony.

While America sought to export its lethal "culture" in the form of jazz and Abstract Expressionism, to cite two primary examples, Stalin condemned "rootless cosmopolitanism" and was thus fully aware of the consequences of America's cultural exports. Indeed "Abstract Expressionism" became the *de facto* "state art" of the American regime of the "culture distorters," just as Socialist Realism was the *de jure* state art of the USSR.

Abstract Expressionism was the first specifically so-called "American" art movement. Jackson Pollock, the central figure, was sponsored by the Congress for Cultural Freedom. He had worked in the Federal Artist's Project from 1938 to 1942, along with other Leftist artists, painting murals under Roosevelt's New Deal regime, or what Yockey called the second "1933 Revolution."[39] Abstract Expressionism became the primary artistic strategy of the Cold War offensive against the Socialist Realism sponsored by the USSR from the time of Stalin. As in much else, Stalin reversed the original Bolshevik tendencies in the arts, which had been experimental and, as one would expect from Marxism, anti-traditional.[40] On the other hand, Social Realism, which had been the popular American art form until the 1930s, was by the late 1940s being displaced as art critics and wealthy patrons began to promote the Abstract Expressionists.[41]

Many of the theorists, patrons, and practitioners of Abstract Expressionism were Trotskyites or other anti-Stalinist Leftists, who were to become the most ardent Cold Warriors. Modernist art during the Cold War became a factor in the USA's world revolution. In 1947 the US State Department organized a modernist exhibition called "Advancing American Art" which was

[39] Yockey, "The American Revolution of 1933," *Imperium*, 492–501.

[40] See the wailing about this in Trotsky's *The Revolution Betrayed: What is the Soviet Union and Where is it Going?*, trans Max Eastman (New York: Dover, 2004).

[41] K. R. Bolton, "The Art of 'Rootless Cosmopolitanism': America's Offensive Against Civilisation," in *The Radical Tradition: Philosophy, Metapolitics & Revolution in the Twenty-First Century*, ed. Troy Southgate (New Zealand: Primordial Traditions, forthcoming).

intended for Europe and Latin America, reaching as far as Prague.[42]

The two individuals who did most to promote Abstract Expressionism were art critic Clement Greenberg and wealthy
artist and art historian Robert Motherwell[43] who was vigorous
in propagandizing on the subject. Greenberg was a New York
Trotskyite and a long-time art critic for *Partisan Review* and *The
Nation*. He had first come to the attention of the art world with
his article in *Partisan Review*, "Avant-Garde and Kitsch" in
1939,[44] in which he stated that art was a propaganda medium
and condemned the Socialist Realism of Stalinist Russia and the
völkisch art of Hitler's Germany.[45]

Greenberg was a particular enthusiast for Jackson Pollock,
and in a 1955 essay "'American Type' Painting,"[46] he lauded
Abstract Expressionism and its proponents as the next stage of
modernism. Greenberg considered that after World War II the
US had become the guardian of "advanced art," just as others
were to regard America as the only genuine vehicle for a
"world revolution" as a stage for world socialism, as opposed
to the USSR.

Greenberg became a founding member of the American
Committee for Cultural Freedom (ACCF)[47] and was involved

---

[42] *The Cultural Cold War*, 256.

[43] "Motherwell was a member of the American Committee for Cultural Freedom," the US branch of the Congress for Cultural Freedom,
as was Jackson Pollock (*The Cultural Cold War*, 276). Both *Partisan Review* editors Philip Rahv and William Phillips became members of the
American committee of the CCF (*The Cultural Cold War*, 158).

[44] Clement Greenberg, "Avant-Garde and Kitsch," *Partisan Review*, vol. 6, no. 5 (1939): 34–49. The essay can be read at:
http://www. sharecom.ca/greenberg/kitsch.html

[45] Bolton, "The Art of 'Rootless Cosmopolitanism.'"

[46] Clement Greenberg, "'American Type' Painting," *Partisan Review*, vol. 22, Spring 1955.

[47] John O'Brien, "Introduction," *The Collected Essays and Criticism of
Clement Greenberg* (Chicago: University of Chicago Press, 1993), vol. 3,
xxvii.

with "executive policymaking."[48] He continued his support for the CCF even after the 1966 exposé by the *New York Times* and *Ramparts* that the CCF and magazines such as *Encounter* had been sponsored by the CIA. Typical of a good Trotskyite, he continued to work for the US State Department and the US Department of Information.[49]

Another key institution in the service of culture distortion is the Rockefeller dynasty's Museum of Modern Art (MoMA). John J. Whitney, formerly of the US Government's Psychological Strategy Board, was a trustee of the Museum, and he supported Pollock and other modernists.[50]

Note the connection with psychological warfare. William Burden, who joined the museum as chairman of its Advisory Committee in 1940, worked with Nelson Rockefeller's Latin American Department during the war. Burden had been president of the CIA's Farfield Foundation which channeled funds to sundry fronts and lackeys; and in 1947 he was appointed chairman of the Committee on Museum Collections, and in 1956 as MoMA's president.[51] Other corporate trustees of MoMA were William Paley of CBS and Henry Luce of Time-Life Inc., both of whom assisted the CIA.[52] Joseph Reed, Gardner Cowles, Junkie Fleischmann, and Cass Canfield were all simultaneously trustees of MoMA and of the CIA's Farfield Foundation. There were numerous other connections between the CIA and the museum, including that of Tom Braden, who had been executive secretary of the museum through 1947–1949 before joining the CIA.[53]

In 1952 MoMA launched its world revolution of Abstract

---

[48] *The Collected Essays and Criticism of Clement Greenberg*, vol. 3, xxviii.

[49] *The Collected Essays and Criticism of Clement Greenberg*, vol. 3, xxviii.

[50] *The Cultural Cold War*, 263.

[51] *The Cultural Cold War*, 263.

[52] *The Cultural Cold War*, 262. Luce's *Life* magazine featured Jackson Pollock in its August 1949 issue, making Pollock a household name (*The Cultural Cold War*, 267).

[53] *The Cultural Cold War*, 263.

Expressionism via the International Program which had a five year annual grant of $125,000 from the Rockefeller Brothers Fund, under the direction of Porter McCray, who had also worked with Nelson Rockefeller's Latin American Department, and in 1950 as an attaché of the cultural section of the US Foreign Service.[54] Russell Lynes, writing of this period, stated that MoMA now had the entire world to "proselytize" with what he called "the exportable religion" of Abstract Expressionism.[55]

* * *

Communism is gone, but the cultural Cold War continues, now packaged as the "liberation" of states deemed not suitably "democratic." America has its own version of Trotsky's "permanent revolution" which US strategists call "constant conflict." Major Ralph Peters, a prominent military strategist, formerly with the Office of the Deputy Chief of Staff for Intelligence, appears to have coined the term. Peters has written of this in an article by that name. Peters' statements definitively show "culture distortion" to be a contrived strategy for global domination; he reminds us that the regime of the culture distorter now has at its disposal technology far more powerful and pervasive than the cinema and literature of Yockey's time:

> We have entered an age of constant conflict. . . .
> We are entering a new American century, in which we will become still wealthier, culturally more lethal, and increasingly powerful. We will excite hatreds without precedent.
> Information destroys traditional jobs and traditional cultures; it seduces, betrays, yet remains invulnerable. How can you counterattack the information others have turned upon you? There is no effective option other than competitive performance. For those individuals and cul-

[54] *The Cultural Cold War*, 267.
[55] Russell Lynes, *Good Old Modern Art: An Intimate Portrait of the Museum of Modern Art* (New York: Atheneum, 1973), cited by Saunders, *The Cultural Cold War*, 267.

tures that cannot join or compete with our information empire, there is only inevitable failure. . . . The attempt of the Iranian mullahs to secede from modernity has failed, although a turbaned corpse still stumbles about the neighborhood. Information, from the internet to rock videos, will not be contained, and fundamentalism cannot control its children. Our victims volunteer.[56]

Peters is stating that this "global information empire" led by the USA is "historically inevitable." This "historical inevitability" is classic Marx, just as "constant conflict" is classic Trotsky. This is a "cultural revolution," which is buttressed by American firepower. Peters continues:

It is fashionable among world intellectual elites to decry "American culture," with our domestic critics among the loudest in complaint. But traditional intellectual elites are of shrinking relevance, replaced by cognitive-practical elites—figures such as Bill Gates, Steven Spielberg, Madonna, or our most successful politicians—human beings who can recognize or create popular appetites, recreating themselves as necessary. *Contemporary American culture is the most powerful in history, and the most destructive of competitor cultures.* While some other cultures, such as those of East Asia, appear strong enough to survive the onslaught by adaptive behaviors, most are not. The genius, the secret weapon, of American culture is the essence that the elites despise: ours is the first genuine people's culture. It stresses comfort and convenience—ease—and it generates pleasure for the masses. We are Karl Marx's dream, and his nightmare. (Emphasis added.)

Peters' zealous messianic prophecies for the "American Century" are reminiscent of Huxley's *Brave New World* where

[56] Ralph Peters, "Constant Conflict," *Parameters*, Summer 1997, 4–14. http://www.usamhi.army.mil/USAWC/Parameters/97summer/peters.htm

the masses are kept in servitude not by physical force but by mindless narcosis, by addiction to the puerile, everything that is, in a word, "American" since the "Second American Revolution of 1933." Peters continues:

> Secular and religious revolutionaries in our century have made the identical mistake, imagining that the workers of the world or the faithful just can't wait to go home at night to study Marx or the Koran. Well, Joe Sixpack, Ivan Tipichni, and Ali Quat would rather "Baywatch." America has figured it out, and we are brilliant at operationalizing our knowledge, *and our cultural power will hinder even those cultures we do not undermine.* There is no "peer competitor" in the cultural (or military) department. *Our cultural empire has the addicted — men and women everywhere — clamoring for more. And they pay for the privilege of their disillusionment.* (Emphasis added.)

The "constant conflict" is one of world Cultural Revolution, with the armed forces used as backup against any reticent state, as in the cases of Serbia and Iraq. The world is therefore to be kept in a state of flux, with a lack of permanence, which Peters' calls Americas' "strength," as settled traditional modes of life do not accord with the aim of industrial, technical, and economic Darwinian linear historical "progress without end." Peters continues:

> There will be no peace. At any given moment for the rest of our lifetimes, there will be multiple conflicts in mutating forms around the globe. Violent conflict will dominate the headlines, *but cultural and economic struggles will be steadier and ultimately more decisive. The* de facto *role of the US armed forces will be to keep the world safe for our economy and open to our cultural assault. To those ends, we will do a fair amount of killing.* (Emphasis added.)

Peters refers to certain cultures trying to reassert their traditions, and again emphasizes that this universal culture distortion that is being imposed is one of Huxleyan "infectious pleasure." The historical inevitability is re-emphasized, as the "rejectionist" (*sic*) regimes will be consigned to what in Trotsky's term is the "dustbin of history." What Yockey called "culture distortion" is even more forcefully described by Peters as an "infection":

> Yes, foreign cultures are reasserting their threatened identities—usually with marginal, if any, success—and yes, they are attempting to escape our influence. *But American culture is infectious, a plague of pleasure, and you don't have to die of it to be hindered or crippled in your integrity or competitiveness.* The very struggle of other cultures to resist American cultural intrusion fatefully diverts their energies from the pursuit of the future. We should not fear the advent of fundamentalist or rejectionist regimes. They are simply guaranteeing their peoples' failure, while further increasing our relative strength. (Emphasis added.)

Michael Ledeen (formerly a consultant with the US National Security Council, State Department and Defense Department, now with the Foundation for Defense of Democracies, another outfit that works for "regime change") in similar terms to that of Peters, calls on the USA to fulfill its "historic mission" of "exporting the democratic revolution" throughout the world. Like Peters, Ledeen predicates this world revolution as a necessary part of the "war on terrorism," but emphasizes also that "world revolution" is the "historic mission" of the USA and always has been. Writing in the "neo-conservative" *National Review*, Ledeen states:

> . . . [W]e are the one truly revolutionary country in the world, as we have been for more than 200 years. Creative destruction is our middle name. *We do it automatically*, and that is precisely why the tyrants hate us, and are driven to attack us. (Emphasis added.)

Like Peters, Ledeen is affirming a fundamental principle of cultural morphology as the study of the life of a *culture as an organism*, when he refers to the "destructive mission" of America as being something that it does "automatically" (*sic*); that is to say, that it is the innate characteristic of the American cultural organism to behave in such a manner; an inner organic imperative.

> Freedom is our most lethal weapon, and the oppressed peoples of the fanatic regimes are our greatest assets. They need to hear and see that we are with them, and that the Western mission is to set them free, under leaders who will respect them and preserve their freedom.

Ledeen refers to a mission, hence it is seen in such quarters as being of a messianic nature, but of course Ledeen like all other apologists for the global hegemony of culture distortion describes this as a "Western mission"(*sic*), which is a complete misnomer, and one calculated to deceive, just like the USA was heralded as the leader of the "Western world" in opposing "communism" during the Cold War when in fact its strategy was to spread Bolshevism in its most destructive—Trotskyite—sense.[57] Ledeen refers to exporting revolution like a diehard old Trot, yet he claims to speak for American "conservatism," a phenomenon that Yockey would describe as being an element of "Culture retardation," of a bankrupt "leadership" stratum, in a nominal sense, that becomes a hireling of the culture-distorter. American neo-conservatism, it should be noted, is itself a metamorphosis of Trotskyism that had undergone an alchemical change in the distillery of Cold War anti-Stalinism.[58]

Ledeen refers hence in Bolshevik terms to exporting a "democratic revolution" and gives credit to the American re-

[57] K. R. Bolton, "America's 'World Revolution': Neo-Trotskyite Foundations of US Foreign Policy," *Foreign Policy Journal*, May 3, 2010. http://www.foreignpolicyjournal.com/2010/05/03/americas-world-revolution-neo-trotskyist-foundations-of-u-s-foreign-policy/

[58] Bolton, "America's 'World Revolution.'"

gime for having toppled both the Soviet bloc and white rule in South Africa, regimes that in their own way were anachronisms in the "new world order" and therefore had to be removed, as in the case of the Islamic states today, in the interests of what crypto-Mason George H. W. Bush overtly termed the "new world order" in direct reference to the first war against Iraq. Note Ledeen mentions America's "historic mission" and American's "revolutionary burden," again messianic expressions reflecting the same mentality as Marx and Trotsky, and as if to confirm the nature of this mission Ledeen pointedly uses the term *"chutzpah"* to describe the outlook of the American neo-messianists:

> . . . [I]t is time once again to export the democratic revolution. To those who say it cannot be done, we need only point to the 1980s, when we led a global democratic revolution that toppled tyrants from Moscow to Johannesburg. Then, too, the smart folks said it could not be done, and they laughed at Ronald Reagan's *chutzpah* when he said that the Soviet tyrants were done for, and called on the West to think hard about the post-Communist era. We destroyed the Soviet Empire, and then walked away from our great triumph in the Third World War of the Twentieth Century. As I sadly wrote at that time, when America abandons its historic mission, our enemies take heart, grow stronger, and eventually begin to kill us again. And so they have, forcing us to take up our revolutionary burden, and bring down the despotic regimes that have made possible the hateful events of the 11th of September.[59]

American paleoconservative Joseph Sobran remarked in 2001 of this world situation that:

---

[59] Michael Ledeen, "Creative Destruction: How to Wage a Revolutionary War," *National Review* online, September 20, 2001. http://old.nationalreview.com/contributors/ledeen092001.shtml

Anti-Americanism is no longer a mere fad of Marxist university students; it's a profound reaction of traditional societies against *a corrupt and corrupting modernization that is being imposed on them, by both violence and seduction.* Confronted with today's America, then, the Christian Arab finds himself in unexpected sympathy with his Muslim enemy.[60] (Emphasis added.)

The "Bolshevism of Washington" can today just as easily be called "neo-conservatism." While this might seem a paradox, even an absurdity, the nature of this can be readily understood by those who have the higher perspective provided by Yockey-an cultural morphology, which refers to the spirit or inner imperative of doctrines, rather than superficialities. "Bolshevism" in such a context might be used to describe anything of an organically destructive nature involving manipulation of the masses. Hence Yockey saw the "democratic" principles of America as fundamentally communistic, both being forms of materialism arising from the same 19th-century *Zeitgeist*:

The leading values of communism are identical with those of liberal democracy . . . The sole difference between liberal-democracy and communism in practice was that communism was an intensification of those beliefs to the point where they became political.[61]

The American apologists for global hegemony who now call the same principles that were inaugurated by the "1933 Revolution,"[62] "neo-conservatism," often indeed come from a Bolshevik or a Menshevik background, as distinct from — indeed antithetical — to what the American philosopher Paul Gottfried has dubbed "paleoconservatism." The "neo-conservative"

---

[60] Joe Sobran, "Why?," *Sobran's — The Real News of the Month,* vol. 8, no. 11 (November 2001).

[61] *The Proclamation of London,* 13.

[62] Couldn't it be considered that it was with Woodrow Wilson that the "American Revolution" was inaugurated?

movement had major input from Trotskyism, often via the Congress for Cultural Freedom, and has remained basically neo-Trotskyite. I have attempted to trace this back from the Trotsky-Stalin split or what Yockey early perceived as the dichotomy of Slavic Bolshevism vs. Jewish Bolshevism, through to factions within the American Left led by CIA operative Sidney Hook, and in particular by the Trotskyite factionalist Max Shachtman, these tendencies within the American Left becoming so obsessed with opposing Stalinism that they ended up providing the basis for Cold War ideology and operations, which have been transformed into other methods for the post-Soviet era, continuing to spread what is called the "global democratic revolution."[63] Indeed not only did Hook and Shachtman end up supporting Cold War US strategy, so did Trotsky's widow Natalia Sedova, who broke with the Fourth International and commended the USA for its actions in Korea, while positing, like Shachtman, the USSR as being the primary obstacle to world socialism.[64]

From this background emerged the previously mentioned National Endowment for Democracy, taking the place of the redundant Congress for Cultural Freedom in the aftermath of the Cold War, to continue the "Bolshevism of Washington" in new directions. This was founded in 1983 by Shachtmanite Tom Kahn of the AFL-CIO, who had developed a network of contacts with social democrats throughout the Soviet bloc, Africa, and Latin America. Another Shachtmanite, Carl Gershman, became the first president in 1984, and was a founder of

---

[63] As President George W. Bush referred to it in 2003 before a conference of the NED, when stating that just as the Soviet bloc had been "liberated" under Reagan, he would inaugurate the "liberation" of the Muslim world. Fred Barbash, "Bush: Iraq Part of 'Global Democratic Revolution': Liberation of Middle East Portrayed as Continuation of Reagan's Policies," *Washington Post*, November 6, 2003.

[64] Natalia Sedova Trotsky, May 9, 1951, Mexico City, letter to the leadership of the Fourth International and the U.S. Socialist Workers Party, *Labor Action*, June 17, 1951.
http://www.marxists.org/history/etol/newspaper/socialistvoice/natalia38.html

the Social Democrats USA. The NED was introduced to Congress by George Agree, and thus gets Congressional funding for its world revolutionary operations.[65]

When Yockey published *Imperium* in 1948 he viewed Russia as alien to and incompatible with the Western cultural organism and thus as an "outer enemy,"[66] a view that persisted in his final essay, "The World in Flames: An Estimate of the World Situation," written in 1960, the year of his death. Yockey continued to advocate a neutralist position for Europe in the event of a US-Russian conflict, although had long considered Russian occupation of Europe to be less damaging to the cultural organism than the US occupation, and saw the possibility of Westernizing a Russian occupier. He saw the increase in neutralist states as one of the few positive development in the world situation, and in particular the rise of Arab Nationalism, at that time epitomized by "a great and vigorous man," Nasser.[67] He saw a resurgent Islam as providing a bloc that diminished World Zionism without augmenting "Russian-Chinese power." Here Yockey was significantly in error in seeing China-Russia as a bloc. There was no Sino-Soviet bloc during Yockey's time, and there is not one now, despite a temporary pragmatic alliance. The US and China will more likely form a bloc to contain Russia, just as they did during the 1970s. Such a conclusion is within the scope of cultural morphology, although the Russo-Chinese conflict only became apparent shortly after Yockey's death.[68]

However, as with the emergence of Islam, Yockey also saw that a Latin American bloc would likewise pose a nuisance to plutocracy, and he used the example of Cuba at that time. In recent years Hugo Chavez's Venezuela has actively encouraged the formation of a Bolívarian bloc across Latin America, while repudiating both the USA and Zionism, and significantly

---

[65] Bolton, "America's 'World Revolution.'"

[66] *Imperium*, 586.

[67] Yockey, "The World in Flames: An Estimate of the World Situation," VI.

[68] Bolton, "Russia and China: An Approaching Conflict."

has the support of Russia in doing so.[69]

Russia is pregnant with possibilities, and retains the only semblance of a "barbarian horde" with the cleansing power to sweep away the filth of decay that pervades the "West" in its phase of decline. Russia continues to show itself impervious to "democracy" despite the hapless efforts of the "culture retarders" Gorbachev and Yeltsin. The Russian is eternally a "peasant" as Yockey stated, immune from the decadence of the megalopolis. The way the Russian regime deals with oligarchs is a sign of cultural health. While an organic Russo-Western Civilization may or may not be possible, such a conception is not unheard of, De Gaulle proposing a "united Europe from the Atlantic to the Urals"[70] while another French geopolitical thinker, Olivier Vedrine, considers in contrast to Yockey, Russia to be "European," calling for a united front.[71] The world situation as it now stands has changed since Yockey's time, but Yockey's analytical method remains legitimate, even if it leads to conclusions regarding Russia, China, and the US that differ from Yockey's own. But, as his reaction to the 1952 Prague Treason Trial shows, Yockey was above all a realist who was able to radically revise his thinking based on changing circumstances.

Counter-Currents/*North American New Right*,
September 28 & 29, October 1, 2010

---

[69] K. R. Bolton, "An ANZAC-Indo-Russian Alliance? Geopolitical Alternatives for Australia and New Zealand," *India Quarterly*, vol. 6, no. 2 (August 2010), 188.

[70] Yockey regarded De Gaulle as a "cretin" yet saw him as embodying the European desire for neutrality, and stated that "an idiot might save Europe," having "accidentally alighted" upon this "spiritual force" (Yockey, "The World in Flames," VI).

[71] Olivier Vedrine, "Russia is Indeed a European Country," September 2009. Cited by Bolton, "An ANZAC-Indo-Russian Alliance? Geopolitical Alternatives for Australia and New Zealand," 188–89.

THE OVERMAN HIGH CULTURE & THE FUTURE OF THE WEST

TED SALLIS

Can the West and its peoples be saved? And what will this take—particularly if we are concerned with a long-term solution rather than a last ditch "stopgap?" Can a new High Culture of the West arise to secure the existence of the peoples of the West for an extended time frame? What characteristics should such a new culture have?

I will assume the reader is familiar with the civilizational model of Oswald Spengler, a model essentially adopted by Francis Parker Yockey in his various works on the West and its future possibilities. With a Spring, Summer, Autumn, and Winter of a High Culture, "Winter" is the phase of oncoming oblivion. It is clear, at least to me (and it seems that Michael O'Meara agrees with this assessment), that we are in the "Winter" of our current modern Western (i.e., "Faustian") High Culture. And, immersed within this decay, bereft of an overriding organizing principle to provide a spiritual structure for its continued existence, the white race is dying, failing to reproduce, being displaced by aliens, and offering an inadequate level of resistance to the death of the West.

In actual physical weather/climate seasons, spring follows winter. Can the same hold true for particular peoples and their High Cultures? If civilizational (re)birth will lead to long-term racial survival, should we at least consider the possibilities? Of course, one cannot predict with full accuracy if a civilizational (re)birth will take place, much less the precise form such an event would take. Further, one cannot plan and create a High Culture in the manner of a general formulating a strategy and then leading troops into battle. A High Culture must develop along its own lines, according to factors not entirely within (conscious) human control. However, one can, and should, examine the evidence, consider the possibilities, and to the extent it is possible, encourage those trends leading to a civilizational (re)birth. Further, these trends could, and should, be guided, to the extent possible, in directions that would be most fruitful and most consistent with the nature of our people.

A starting point is to consider our present High Culture, the dying remnants of which we see around us. The so-called "Western" or "Faustian" civilization has been described by Spengler and is summarized thus:

> . . . the modern Westerners [are] Faustian. According to its theories, we are now living in the winter time of the Faustian civilization. His description of the Faustian civilization is one where the populace constantly strives for the *unattainable*—making Western Man a proud but tragic figure, for while he strives and creates he secretly knows the actual goal will never be reached.[1]

Here we see two defining characteristics of the "Faustian" civilization of the modern (i.e., post-Classical) West: first, a focus on infinity and the unknown, and second, that the striving toward that focus will always be unsuccessful; the objectives of Western Man are always "unattainable." The second point, and its implications, will be further discussed below. For now, let us accept the Spenglerian model and also accept that we are in the Winter of the Faustian culture. Now, the Spenglerian school, steeped in "stoic acceptance" ("pessimism") will advise us to accept, and make the most of, our circumstances. The era in which we live is what it is, and, like a Roman soldier on guard under erupting Vesuvius, we must stand at our post until the end, until all is enveloped in inescapable decay (civilizational entropy, if you will).

But if race and culture are linked, the dissipation of the culture means the destruction of the race. Or does it? The Faustian is not the first High Culture of Europe; it was preceded by the Classical. Spengler and his follower Yockey break with previous cultural interpretations to stress the sharp discontinuity between

---

[1] http://en.wikipedia.org/wiki/The_Decline_of_the_West, emphasis added.

Classical and Faustian. These are perceived as being two distinct High Cultures, as different from each other as each is to, say, the Egyptian or the Magian.

Therefore, from the same article on Spengler's work, we read (emphasis added):

> Spengler borrows frequently from mathematical philosophy. He holds that the mathematics and art of a civilization reveal its world-view. He notes that in Greek classical mathematics that there are only integers and no real concepts of limits or infinity. Therefore, without a concept of the infinite, all events of the distant past were viewed as equally distant, thus Alexander the Great had no problem declaring himself a descendant of a god. On the other hand, the western world—which has concepts of the zero, the infinite, and the limit—has a historical world-view which places a high amount of importance on exact dates.[2]

Similarly, Revilo Oliver writes (emphasis added):

> Spengler identifies as two entirely separate and discrete civilizations the Classical ("Apollonian"), c. 1100 B.C.–A.D. 300, and the Western ("Faustian"), c. A.D. 900–2200. These are the two for which we have the fullest information, and between them Spengler establishes some of his most brilliant synchronisms (e.g., Alexander the Great corresponds to Napoleon). Even a century ago, this dichotomy would have seemed almost mad, for everyone knew and took for granted that whatever might be true of alien cultures, our own was a continuation, or, at least, revival of the Classical. Spengler's denial of that continuity was the most radical and startling aspect of his historical synthesis, but so great has been his overshadowing influence that it has been accepted by a majority of the many subsequent writers on the philosophy of history, of whom we may mention here only Toynbee, Raven, Bagby, and Brown. The

---

[2] http://en.wikipedia.org/wiki/The_Decline_of_the_West

Classical, we are told, was a civilization like the Egyptian, now dead and gone and with no organic connection with our own. . . . Spengler (whom Brown especially follows in this respect) supports his drastic dichotomy by impressively contrasting Graeco-Roman mathematics and technology with our own; from that contrast he deduces differences in the perception of space and time, exhibited particularly in music, and reaches the conclusion that the Classical *Weltanschauung* was essentially static, desiring and recognizing only a strictly delimited and familiar world, whereas ours is dynamic and exhibits a passionate yearning for the infinite and the unknown. One can advance various objections to the generalizations I have so curtly and inadequately summarized (e.g., is the difference in outlook really greater than that between the "classical" literature of Eighteenth-Century Europe and the Romanticism of the following era?), but the crucial point is whether the differences, which belong to the order that we must call spiritual for want of a better term, are fundamental or epiphenomenal.[3]

I have tended toward the "epiphenomenal" explanation—but in any case, one can agree with Oliver's overarching conclusion in his various works: either the Classical and Faustian are different yet connected phases of the *same* Civilization, or, even if completely distinct, Western Man is capable of producing multiple High Cultures. Either way, one can conclude two things: (1) a successor to the Faustian High Culture is possible and has a precedent, and (2) this successor will be intimately connected in important ways to its predecessor(s) (even if Spengler and Yockey would deny this could be possible).

Therefore, either the Classical and Faustian are indeed linked (by a generalized common gene pool, "racial soul," and Western outlook) or, if they are indeed distinct, they are not *completely* unconnected, as they derive from a common wellspring or foundation (again, the generalized gene pool, "racial soul," and

---

[3] Revilo P. Oliver, *The Enemy of Our Enemies* (Reedy, W.Va.: Liberty Bell Publications, 1981), 16–17.

Western mindset of greater individualism and empiricism compared to other peoples and cultures).

Not only are the Classical and the Faustian in some sense linked but, contrary to Spengler and Yockey—and, indeed, a heresy of the Spenglerian school that rejects a linear history— there is a sense of progression, in that the worldview of the Faustian is broader than that of the Classical; indeed, this greater breadth of vision is a defining characteristic of the Faustian. This breadth being manifested in such phenomena as high level technics, and a mass knowledge base of science, history, philosophy and morality-ethics, the foundation is therefore laid for a new High Culture of a vision even broader than that of the Faustian.

A Spenglerian would argue that any new High Culture of the West, even if possible (and they may deny this possibility), would be completely disconnected to the "Faustian" aspects of the former (i.e., present) Western Faustian High Culture. However, I argue that, having being awakened to the universe at large, it is unlikely that the white man would create a new High Culture that would be insular, rejecting the infinite.

To the (albeit limited) extent we can predict, or even influence, the development of a new High Culture, a potential direction is one that is not purely "Faustian"—in the sense of striving for the *unattainable*. Instead, one can project a future High Culture that is based upon the ultimate and *successful* (eventual) achievement of what was previously considered to be "unattainable."

I would argue that the Christian foundation of the Faustian High Culture is responsible for the fact that the ultimate goals that Western man strives toward end up being "unattainable"— and secretly known by him to be "unattainable." The Christian mindset places inherent limits within the mind of Western man, so he is doomed to ultimately fail even if full success is theoretically possible (eventually). After all, the focus of Christianity is God and not Man, it is "salvation" and not overcoming, and it is a focus on "the next world" and not this, our real world. For man to achieve godhood—or to even have that as a goal—is a form of "blasphemy," it is something that cannot be countenanced. Therefore, ultimate failure *must* occur, for attainment of the "Faustian" goal (attainment itself would then make the event no longer be truly "Faustian") is simply not possible in a High Culture based upon Christianity.

The full development of Western man has been restrained by an alien religion that has placed shackles on his mind and his soul. Nietzsche well recognized the constraints imposed by (Judeo-) Christianity; in his *The Antichrist* we find (emphasis added):

—Has anyone ever clearly understood the celebrated story at the beginning of the Bible—of God's mortal terror of *science?* . . . No one, in fact, has understood it. This priest-book *par excellence* opens, as is fitting, with the great inner difficulty of the priest: *he* faces only one great danger; *ergo,* "God" faces only one great danger.—

The old God, wholly "spirit," wholly the high-priest, wholly perfect, is promenading his garden: he is bored and trying to kill time. Against boredom even gods struggle in vain. What does he do? He creates man—man is entertaining. . . But then he notices that man is also bored. God's pity for the only form of distress that invades all paradises knows no bounds: so he forthwith creates other animals. God's first mistake: to man these other animals were not entertaining—he sought dominion over them; he did not want to be an "animal" himself.—So God created woman. In the act he brought boredom to an end—and also many other things!—Woman was the *second* mistake of God.— "Woman, at bottom, is a serpent, Heva"—every priest knows that; "from woman comes every evil in the world"—every priest knows that, too. *Ergo,* she is also to blame for *science.* . . It was through woman that man learned to taste of the tree of knowledge.—What happened? The old God was seized by mortal terror. Man himself had been his *greatest* blunder; he had created a rival to himself; science makes men *godlike* — it is all up with priests and gods when man becomes scientific!—Moral: science is the forbidden *per se;* it alone is forbidden. Science is the *first* of sins, the germ of all sins, the *original* sin. *This is all there is of morality.* — "Thou shalt *not* know"—the rest

follows from that. — God's mortal terror, however, did not
hinder him from being shrewd. How is one to *protect* one's
self against science? For a long while this was the capital
problem. Answer: Out of paradise with man! Happiness,
leisure, foster thought — and all thoughts are bad
thoughts! — Man *must* not think. — And so the priest invents distress, death, the mortal dangers of childbirth, all
sorts of misery, old age, decrepitude, above all, *sickness* —
nothing but devices for making war on science! The trou-
bles of man don't *allow* him to think. . . Nevertheless — how
terrible! —, the edifice of knowledge begins to tower aloft,
invading heaven, shadowing the gods — what is to be
done? — The old God invents *war*; he separates the peoples;
he makes men destroy one another (— the priests have always had need of war. . . .). War — among other things, a
great disturber of science! — Incredible! Knowledge, *deliver-
ance from the priests*, prospers in spite of war. — So the old
God comes to his final resolution: "Man has become scientific — *there is no help for it: he must be drowned!*". . . . [4]

Indeed. If "the meek shall inherit the Earth" there is no place
for any human striving for the infinite that is *successful*, and
which places Man on the same plane as God. If meekness, humility, the "humble lamb of God" is the foundational archetype
of a culture, then *of course* infinity and the unknown will always
be unattainable. "Thou shalt not know": it is amazing how much
we have achieved despite that, and these remarkable Western
achievements have occurred — not by coincidence — primarily
during the Autumn and Winter periods of the Faustian High
Culture. Only when the constraints imposed by the Christian-
defined culture have to a large extent dissipated has the *a priori*
acceptance of failure been weakened.

The problem is that with a decaying, dying High Culture, this
(partial) emancipation from the cult of humility will go for
naught. Only a new High Culture built upon the fundamental

---

[4] Friedrich Nietzsche, *The Antichrist*, trans. H. L. Mencken (1895)
(Torrance, Cal.: The Noontide Press, 1980), § 48.

concept of human transcendence, and on the attainment of infinity/the unknown, will allow Western Man to fulfill his density. The crumbling ruins of the previous High Culture can serve as building blocks for the future, certainly; they can provide inspiration, certainly; and be a source of pride, certainly. But we need to look toward the Future, and not stand guard over a dying, or dead, Past, analogous to Spengler's Roman soldier.

While I mean no disrespect to anyone's beliefs, be they Christian or Pagan, I do not see a revival of ancient pagan gods as a forward-thinking improvement over the decay of Faustianism. Replacing Jesus with Thor, in my mind, simply replaces one fantasy-crutch with another. White men should no longer require any exogenous gods, whether new or old; we instead should strive toward godhood for our race. It is time for the white man to grow up and put away the fantasies of childhood, fantasies of gods and external intelligent forces controlling a destiny that should be ours, and ours alone, to mold.

The motto of the Classical World was "Know Thyself," while that of the Faustian Age was a combination of "Thou Shalt Not Know" with "Thou Shalt Try to Know and Thou Shalt Fail." I propose that the new High Culture of the West have the motto: "Thou Shalt Know and Thou Shalt Overcome." This will usher in an era in which Western Man unlocks his potential by unlocking the shackles imposed by an assumed inferiority to imaginary gods.

The following quote from Yockey's *The Enemy of Europe* summarizes the palingenetic objective that we could, if we so wished, strive for:

> Our European Mission is to create the Culture-State-Nation-Imperium of the West, and thereby we shall perform such deeds, accomplish such works, and so transform our world that our distant posterity, when they behold the remains of our buildings and ramparts, will tell their grandchildren that on the soil of Europe once dwelt a tribe of gods.[5]

---

[5] Francis Parker Yockey, *The Enemy of Europe*, trans. Thomas Francis

In other words, no imaginary gods. It is Man that will become "God." In the book *The Portable Nietzsche*, editor Walter Kaufmann interprets Nietzsche's "overman" thus: "what is called for is not a super-brute but a human being who has created for himself that unique position in the cosmos that the Bible considered his birthright."[6] That was going well until that last part—about "the Bible." No, Mr. Kaufmann, the Bible does not consider the Overman to be the ultimate birthright of humanity but instead the "last man" as the "prize" instead. It is we who must choose what our "birthright" is, not the wild fantasies of "the Bible."

However, that being so, the rest of the description is sound, if we consider that it is to be applied to the race as a whole and not only to selected individuals within the race. No more "proud, tragic" failure in "striving for the unattainable" in the "Faustian" culture—instead the Overman Culture will be characterized by the proud *successful* attainment of the infinite. That is what a hopeful individual can project as the new High Culture of the West, with links to the Classical and the Faustian, but surpassing both in the aim and objective of the human spirit. That is what Western Destiny can and should be.

What can we do to get things on the right track?

Although the Jewish author Isaac Asimov may not be popular among many white racial nationalists, his *Foundation* series can provide a useful analogy here. "The Foundation" was meant to jumpstart a new civilization after the collapse of the "Galactic Empire," so that the post-collapse "era of barbarism" would be a mere thousand years, instead of 30,000. Facing as we do the collapse of the West through the Winter of the Faustian age, it may be prudent to lay the seeds of a new emergent white, Western civilization for the long term, as we also fight the more short-term and medium-term battles to preserve the white race and save as much of Western Faustian civilization as possible. Without these shorter range objectives, the long term civilizational (re)birth will not be possible. Conversely, without a civilizational (re)birth,

---

(Reedy, W.Va.: Liberty Bell Publications, 1981), 93.

[6] Friedrich Nietzsche, *The Portable Nietzsche*, ed. and trans. Walter Kaufmann (New York: Viking Penguin, 1954), 115–16.

long-term white preservationism would be questionable.

So, there are two things that need to be going on here. First is the ongoing struggle for white racial preservationism and to save as much of the Faustian culture as possible, to serve as a knowledge base and building blocks for the new High Culture of the West. Second, an effort must be initiated to begin the process of laying the groundwork for this new High Culture.

As indicated above, of course a High Culture is an organic phenomenon that cannot be created in a pre-planned form and artificially imposed on a people. However, it *is* possible to plant the seeds and to have some choice as to which seeds are planted. And then, we can nurture the seedling as it grows, and as it develops according to its own inherent character. *This we can do and this we must do.*

This is a serious matter requiring forward-thinking strategy of an extreme visionary character, not something that can be productively "discussed" on "blog threads" or other (typically inane) public forums. It is not something that can occur overnight. This is a long-term, multi-generational project that needs to be undertaken by dedicated individuals who wish to lay the foundation of something great and noble for posterity. This will not be a "quick fix" whose results may be seen in a decade or two; instead, this is a project that has the potential to influence the course of human history, and it must be conducted on that higher level.

Therefore, this essay is simply a call for action and an initial and cursory consideration of the possibilities. If such a project is ever initiated, it should not, and must not, devolve into the mundane "movement" minutiae that many obsess over, nor can it be linked to the more serious, yet short-term, necessary "stopgap" activism required to save our people and culture today. This is another matter, on another level, entirely.

Many are called; few are chosen. The Future Awaits.

Counter-Currents/*North American New Right*,
October 21, 2010

Six Poems for Francis Parker Yockey

Juleigh Howard-Hobson

Birthday Greetings from the Michels

> *"The Michel element of a Culture is not*
> *a pathology and is not a Cultural menace in itself.*
> *Its sole danger is that it is serviceable*
> *to the will-to-annihilate . . ."*

> *"Liberalism is, in one word, weakness.*
> *It wants everyday to be a birthday . . ."*

> — *Francis Parker Yockey*

Here you go, passing it to you now: this
Blighted world. *Happy birthday.* Not that it's
Personal, no, it's bad for all of us —
Especially those of us with all our wits
About us, who can remember the bits
When the world wasn't like this because, no
Matter what they tell you, you need to know:

It wasn't always like this. But you were
Not here when it started to go bad . . . and,
For us, who were already born, we never
Had a chance, no chance at all — we were scammed
Into thinking it was quite alright, planned
Out for the good of us all. What we got
Was this: a world we helped to kill, but not

Because we would have wanted to, no, but
Because we never knew what was at risk
Until it started to stink. Sure, we'd put

Our minds to fixing it back, the thing is,
We can't undo it now, can we? All this
Dun-colored world of the future that they
Sold to us continues. *Happy birthday.*

Einarhjar — Siberia 1947

"With unforgettable dishonor it threw millions of
Western soldiers to the Russian savages, to disappear
forever into the unmarked graves of Siberia."

— Francis Parker Yockey

You have no graveyards, no markers, no names.
We must invoke your memories to do
You honor, since we have no other way.
But, then, it makes no difference: the same
Blood moves inside our veins as moved in you;
The same black sun shone then that shines today.
We need no monuments, no headstones placed
To sanctify your loss. However lost,
Your graves make holy ground from shallow holes,
And you and they can never be disgraced
By lying undisclosed amid the frost
Of that deep frozen foreign land. Your souls
Can never fall away from us — you are
Not truly lost forever, Einarhjar.

MEIN GOLDENER SCHATZ IST VERLOREN
(DIE BERLIN-MUTTER SPRICHT, 1946)

Oh yes. He is gone. And we all know where.
Shot? Not yet, perhaps. Beaten? Starved? Surely . . .
And thin and cold and so very young. He,
With his shy smile, his blue eyes, and his hair —
Once golden, but grown dull from war and cold
Dead hope. The world's gone cold and dead around
Him: all barbed wire, hunger, snowy ground,
A sickly sun and clothes that cannot hold
Back the cut of frost or the bite of wind,
And nothing, nothing ahead but death. That
And nothing else. A quick-step — rat-a-tat!! —
To a hole in the snow. Predetermined
But not recorded. He will lie out there . . .
Smile gone, eyes shut, blood in his golden hair.

SILLY RABBIT

I was never asked to memorize the
Sonnets of Barrett, nor state—even
In general—the years that Crimea
Was a theatre of British war. Seven
Pillars of Wisdom? Nine Noble Virtues?
May as well have never existed for
All that I've been told about them. The truths
That lay unfathomed at my feet are more
Than the truths that were ever revealed by
Way of lessons, books, and socialized cant.

Windswept vistas painted by artists I
Could not suppose to name, (face it Rembrandt
Is more associated with toothpaste
Than with oils), hint at other meanings and
Layers I am not expected—shamefaced,
Realizing an ignorant lack—to stand
Back and try to conceive of. I am not
Enlightened enough to notice, really.

For what is considered a sufficient
Education, the ancient mysteries
Of Pythagoras himself could be dumb
And the universal music of the
Spheres fall silent, for all that has not come
Down of them by the time they've come to me.
For my generation has not been taught
To care for those sort of things. Because my
Generation has had other things, brought
In bright shiny ways that preoccupy
Us while we learn them so that we keep them—
Deep and whole—without knowing that we do.

Four score and twenty years ago, mmmm mmmm
Good, ask any mermaid you happen to
Meet . . .
How do you get to Sesame Street?

SIREN SONG

This form is an Ovillejo ("tangled ball of wool") from
South America

Why do some of you resist?
   We insist
On planning and then manning your defeat.
   It will be sweet,
Once you've all been re-taught
   To be naught,
And you let us dictate culture, form, and thought.

When everything's distorted, retarded, canned,
Just like we've always planned,
We insist it will be sweet to be naught.

BRITTAS BAY

Our time will come to pass again. Slowly,
As cycles turn in natural spirals
That do not consider generations.
Your time must wait, for now. Today, only
Other writers who don't rock cultural
Boats can have their say, for the distortion
Of our way, our world, has made elements
Of alienation that wreck weak souls
Through the insides of their own heads. Secret
Forces forge destiny, though. We are meant
To survive this soullessness, to be whole
Again, although the others will fight it
Because "no age submits quietly to
The spirit of the coming age" (quote you).

Counter-Currents/*North American New Right*,
June 15, 2010

Interview with Alain de Benoist

Bryan Sylvain

Translated by Greg Johnson

Editor's Note

In 2005, Alain de Benoist gave an interview to *The Occidental Quarterly*, which was published as "European Son: An Interview with Alain de Benoist," *The Occidental Quarterly*, vol. 5, no. 3 (Fall 2005): 7–27.

The interview was lengthy, however, and the decision was made to cut it. Thus Benoist's critical discussions of Christianity and the human sciences were removed. Benoist gave me a copy of the French original, and I am translating the "lost" portions here for the first time.

The questions fall naturally under the headings "On Christianity" and "On the Human Sciences," but these designations, as well as the arrangement of the answers, are my own. The questions are reverse-translations from French.

On Christianity

According to the Manifesto of the Nouvelle Droite, the five main characteristics of modernity are individualization, massification, desacralization, rationalization, and universalization. The ND traces the roots of modernity to a secularized form of Christian metaphysics. It is also known for rejecting another product of Christianity: egalitarianism. What then are the "aristocratic values" that the ND intends to promote, and how can they counterbalance each one of these destructive tendencies? And how could everyone adhere to aristocratic values?

To describe egalitarianism as the mere "product" of Christianity is a shortcut that for my part I would no longer take. Things are a little more complex than that. What one can say, on the other hand, is that the advent of modernity can be understood and analyzed only in light of the vast process of secularization that characterizes it. That means that a certain number of themes that were formerly expressed in theological terms have been transferred to the secular sphere.

In the ideology of progress, for example, the promise of salvation in the beyond is transformed into the promise of happiness in the future. The very notion of "progress" is part of the linear vision of history (in opposition to the cyclical or spherical vision of history) privileging the future that was introduced by biblical thought.

The concept of equality (which one should distinguish from egalitarianism) finds its origin in the Christian assertion of an equal relationship of all human souls with God.

The technological enthrallment of the world (*das Gestell*, to use Heidegger's term)—which beginning with Descartes imposes a new perception of the cosmos as entirely available for human control, while consciousness begins to be reduced to an object of natural science—finds its first legitimation in Genesis (so that, as Heidegger saw quite well, technology can be regarded as the completion of metaphysics).

Jean Bodin's theory of the absolute sovereignty of the prince with respect to his subjects is a transposition of the absolute sovereignty of God in relation to creation. This is how Carl Schmitt could say that the principal concepts of modern politics are secularized theological concepts. This process of secularization was also studied in a remarkable way by Karl Löwith.

The New Right, moreover, does not defend "aristocratic" values but the values of any traditional society, i.e., any society not yet conquered by modernity. From the traditional point of view, aristocratic and popular values are about the same. These are all the values inherent in an ethics of honor. In opposition to economic and commercial values, they are also the values of disinterestedness and generosity, as expressed in the system of the gift and the counter-gift.

To the great deontological moral systems, of which Kant is the paradigm, one can still oppose Aristotle's virtue ethics: to pursue personal excellence by practicing the "virtues." In such a system, the good necessarily takes precedence over the just, as Michael Sandel and Charles Taylor very justly argue against John Rawls. Here one returns to Hegel's critique of Kant, i.e., the opposition of *Sittlichkeit* to *Moralität*.

What is your view of the truth of the Christian faith? What is your view of Christian apologetics? A Christian could ask you to offer proof of the falsehood of the Resurrection, since if that were given, Christianity would crumble. How do you answer this challenge?

Strange question. I do not have to "prove" that Jesus was not resurrected any more than I have to "prove" that God did not give the Tables of the Law to Moses on Mount Sinai or that Elvis Presley is not alive and selling pizzas in Brooklyn! The reason is that one cannot prove a negative; one cannot demonstrate non-existence. It is the Christians who have to give proof of their claims, proof that they have not managed yet.

Could you say something about the violent way in which Europe was Christianized? To what extent did the Christianization of Europe rest on fraud?

Christianity was gradually established in Europe by using all available means. Its diffusion was sometimes peaceful, sometimes forcible. The struggle between Christianity and paganism, the history of which has been retold a thousand times, of course included many bloody episodes: forced conversions of whole populations, persecution of pagans, "crusades" internal and external, etc.

However, the Church does not owe its success to force as much as to the skill with which it took over the ancient pagan rites and religious inclinations and twisted them to suit its own purposes. Because it was unable to completely uproot paganism, it got busy "Christianizing" it by giving it new contents.

Churches were built on the sites of old temples, the liturgical calendar was based on the pagan one (Christmas replaced the old festivities of the winter solstice, Midsummer's Day that of the summer solstice, etc.), the legends of the saints took over the powers ascribed to local divinities, many places of pilgrimage were preserved, and the worship of Mary compensated for the absence of a mother goddess, etc. Christianity was thus partially "paganized," becoming at the same time more acceptable to the masses.

But this "paganization" remained superficial, because it touched only the external forms of worship. Nevertheless, it makes it possible to understand the difference that has always existed between popular Christianity and institutional Christianity and its specific theological system.

Is Christianity a foreign religion for Europeans? Does the fact that Christianity was the carrier of a non-European culture, Judaism, which thus became a part of the European heritage, constitute a problem? A whole tradition, according to which the Church is the "New Israel," makes Christians "spiritual Semites." Does it follow from this that the Jewish tradition belongs to the Western tradition?

My critique of Christianity, which is primarily intellectual and philosophical, has nothing to do with the fact that it was born historically outside of Europe. I feel sympathy for certain Eastern religions or spiritualities, like Zen Buddhism or Shintoism, which are not strictly European at all. On the other hand, I am completely hostile to many ideologies that were born in Europe. The provenance of an idea is not a criterion of truth, and the surplus of identity is not reducible to its origin.

Jesus was a Jew of the 1st century of our era who was most likely regarded as a prophet, but who never intend to create a universal "Church," much less a new religion. Convinced of the imminent arrival of the "kingdom of God" (*Olam haba*, "the world that is to come"), it was in the name of the Torah that he opposed the dominant, institutional current of the Judaism of his time. "I was sent only to the lambs of the house of Israel," he says very clearly in a passage of the Gospels (Matthew 15:24) which completely contradicts the words added later found at the end of Mark (16:15) and in Matthew (28:19).

It was only after his death that some who thought he was the Messiah came to see him as the "son of God" come to save all men. Christianity as we know it is above all the work of Paul, and it is in the Mediterranean world, then the Western, that what is essential to its history unfolded.

The concept of a "Judeo-Christian tradition" is, moreover, quite ambiguous. In all rigor, one can speak of Judeo-Christianity only in two precise senses: first historically, to indicate the very first "Nazarene" communities in Palestine which, under the direction of John, vigorously opposed the "Helleno-Christians" led by Paul; then theologically, to indicate the common theological beliefs of Jews and Christians (belief in single god, the distinction between created being and uncreated being, etc).

After the destruction of the Temple in the year 70, the two religions separated completely: the Christians were expelled from the synagogues, and the *Tannaim*, the chief rabbis who then reorganized Judaism based on the Pharisee current, instituted the *birkat-ha-minim*, which curses the partisans of Jesus. For its part, the incipient Christian Church adopted explicit anti-Judaism, which first appears in the Gospel of John, the last of the four canonical Gospels.

Christianity did not become less dependent on its Old Testament roots, but over the centuries it came to adhere to the theology of substitution, which claims that the Church incarnates the true Israel, excluding the Jews while preserving their metaphysical identity (obviously an unbearable claim for the Jews themselves). This rift between its origin and its history is characteristic of Christianity.

But one can grasp the whole of Christianity only by ceasing to regard it as a unitary bloc: early Christianity is different from medieval Christianity, which is not the same thing as Counter-Reformation Christianity, modern Christianity, etc.

How can Celsus, who published polemical writings against the Christians around 178, be used as a guide for the 21st century?

Celsus was a neoplatonic philosopher, the author of an anti-Christian book, the *True Discourse*, the text of which is known to us today only through the attempts to refute it by the Fathers of the Church (this is also the case with the treatises of Julian, Porphyry, etc.). I can't really see how one could make it a "guide for the 21st century." Reading his book—the text of which has been reconstructed by specialists—does, however, help us to better understand the ancient pagan polemics against Christianity.

Does Christianity constitute a viable vehicle for the perpetuation of the European people and their culture, or does it lead to a non-European future because of disappearance of the "Germanic" element that had transformed it in the Middle Ages, as James C. Russell shows so well in his book The Germanization of Early Medieval Christianity: A Sociohistorical Approach to Religious Transformation *(Oxford: Oxford University Press, 2002)? Do you think that there is a reason to preserve Christianity? Can it play a positive role in European culture?*

All told, I do not think that one should be pleased by the appearance of Christianity and its development. The pre-Christian ages of Europe were not spiritually deficient in any way. What is good in Christianity isn't new, and what is new in it isn't good. But as I have just said, Christianity is not a unitary bloc. St. Francis of Assisi and Torquemada gave the same Church quite different faces! There is nothing wrong with preferring the former. I have written a book entitled *On Being a Pagan*, but that has never prevented me from appreciating Catholic authors like Léon Bloy, Charles Péguy, Georges Bernanos, and Gustave Thibon, or from feeling agreement with certain aspects of the social teachings of the Church.

To answer your question more precisely, I do not think that Christianity is a "viable vehicle for safeguarding the European people and their culture." But above all, I believe that it should be well understood that we already no longer live in a Christian society. The dominant public discourse certainly remains impregnated with themes of Christian or biblical origin, but behaviors have changed. There as elsewhere, individualism has taken the lead.

The Churches, just like the parties and the trade unions of

the traditional type, are passing through a deep crisis. In France, less than 8% of the population goes to mass or Sunday worship, the number of ordained priests continues to drop year after year, and nobody obeys the pope any longer regarding sexual morals or manners.

It is different in the United States, where religious belief and practices remain incredibly more widespread than elsewhere. In continental Europe, there is no equivalent of the "creationists" and "born-again Christians," the "Moral Majority," or the ridiculous American "televangelists"! Even in the United States, however, it is no longer possible to speak about a "Christian society." And that is what constitutes the postmodern version of secularization.

Individuals or groups of individuals can of course continue to find reasons in the Christian faith to live and to die, but it has lost the decisive role that it played in the past. It no longer constitutes the total frame of reference and the principal normative criterion of social existence. That means that religious membership today merely has the status of one opinion among many, on the general foundation of indifferentism and practical materialism. It is a radical change in the very definition of religion.

Under these conditions, the question is no longer whether Christianity should or should not be "preserved." The Churches try to survive, clinging nostalgically to a past that no longer corresponds to anything, while seeking on the contrary to adapt to the current world, by reaffirming their universalist vocation, trying to pose as "moral authorities," etc. That is their business. The real issues of the future lie elsewhere.

Why doesn't the New Right refer to Christianity when it preaches a return to the roots of Europe? Paul Piccone and Gary Ulmen, in their introduction to Michael Torigian's "The Philosophical Foundations of the French New Right" (Telos, no. 117, Autumn 1999, pp. 4–5), wonder if two thousand years of Christianity is not sufficient to make this religion an indigenous tradition, even if certain parts of Europe (like Scandinavia and the Baltic States) were Christianized only much later. Are there many political movements eager to return to roots that preach a return to paganism?

The New Right has never preached a "return" to paganism or a "return" to roots, or a return to anything for that matter. Instead, we wish to go beyond current society, but we wish to envision the future through the lens of a clear consciousness of the past. These two approaches are quite different: *recurrence* is not synonymous with *return!* Let us say simply that one can "futurize" the present only by "historicizing" the past.

The problem is that the majority of our contemporaries live in a perpetual present, i.e., a point of view where only the present moment counts and one is no longer capable of awaiting the future or drawing lessons from the past. The past is not limited to the point of origin, which is an always conventional limit anyway, but takes into account all accomplished history. To make any sense of history, we must look at the longest possible term.

Christianity obviously forms part of European history, but Europe was not born with it. When Christianity appeared, Europe already had five or six millennia of culture and civilization behind it. To speak about the "Christian roots" of Europe amounts to denying that the Latin, Greek, Celtic, Germanic, and Slavic cultures of Antiquity ever existed, which is obviously indefensible.

You have sometimes described Christianity as the "Bolshevism of Antiquity." Does the New Right regard Christianity as the ancestor and principal carrier of totalitarianism?

When Christianity was spread in Europe, it necessarily had to destroy the old order. That entailed the struggle against paganism. We have innumerable testimonies on the ways in which the early Christians profaned the old places of worship, destroyed the temples and the statues of the gods, tore down the altars, toppled the colonnades, burned the philosophical and literary works that displeased them, etc. It was indeed a question of "making the past a clean slate." The polemical phrase you quote is alluding to this.

On the other hand, to say that Christianity is the direct origin of totalitarianism is excessive. It nevertheless contributed to it by introducing into the Western realm a type of intolerance—religious intolerance—that was previously unknown.

Paganism quite naturally recognized the legitimacy of the various beliefs professed by the various peoples. With Christianity the concepts of absolute good and evil appear, a single god, orthodoxy, dogma, heresies, inquisitions, wars of religion, etc.

The Christians intended both to convert all humanity and to fight against what they regarded as "idolatry." Their religion being above all a moral religion, they tend to see in their enemies, not just as the adversaries of the moment but as figures of Evil. To eradicate Evil, those who claim to incarnate the Good are quickly led, in all clear conscience, to employ any means.

In modern times, the totalitarian regimes acted no differently: they claimed to carry out "just" wars, declared their adversaries criminals, and were inevitably led to place them outside humanity. One consequence of this way of thinking is the elimination of the *third*: "He who is not with me is against me," said Jesus—a saying recently repeated by President George W. Bush.

ON THE HUMAN SCIENCES

E. O. Wilson describes neuroscience, human genetics, evolutionary biology, and conservation biology as four "frontier disciplines" of the natural sciences that today are bridging the gap between the scientific and humanistic cultures. Does the New Right support Wilson's call for "consilience," i.e., a unified knowledge joining together the life sciences and the human sciences?

Edward O. Wilson is certainly an excellent researcher, but I do not believe that he is a great philosopher. The theme of the "unity of knowledge" ignores the irreducible difference that exists between the exact sciences and social sciences (which Wilhelm Dilthey called the "sciences of the spirit"). Generally, it amounts to an attempt by the former to annex the domain of the latter. The call for "consilience" is in this respect quite similar to the attempt launched in the 1930s by men like Otto Neurath or Philipp Frank to arrive at the "unification of science." The only difference is that Neurath privileged theoretical physics as the supreme discipline, whereas Wilson stresses biology, which today has become the "queen of the sciences."

Wilson writes, "Nature is governed by simple universal

laws of physics, to which all other laws and principles can be reduced" (*Consilience: The Unity of Knowledge* [New York: Knopf, 1998], p. 59). His approach is thus clearly reduction-istic—understanding everything from the point of view of physics, if one takes into account the Copenhagen interpreta-tion of the Uncertainty Principle. To believe that the essence of politics, for example, can be reduced to "simple universal laws of physics" makes one smile. The same applies to all the values that apply to human life insofar as the human realm is a realm of evaluation, in keeping with hermeneutics and phenomenol-ogy: man seeks to give *meaning* to his life, and this meaning necessarily goes beyond the biological order of life. Wilson's "scientific evangelism" reminds one of Auguste Comte's "reli-gion of science." In my view, such projects are doomed to fail.

Specialists in the social sciences are too often ignorant of the findings of the life sciences. Specialists in the life sciences, for their part, tend too often to reject the findings of the social sci-ences as the realm of non-rigorous speculation or "philoso-phy," i.e., non-knowledge. I think they are both wrong.

Both the life sciences and the social sciences should learn how to mutually illuminate one another. The social sciences make it possible to understand and study what is uniquely human, while the life sciences make it possible to better under-stand the foundations of this uniqueness. The social sciences tell us about what in man is changing, while the life sciences tell us about what remains the same. Instead of opposition or unity, the social sciences and the life sciences should seek com-plimentarity.

In 1928, Helmuth Plessner, one of the principal founders of philosophical anthropology, wrote, "No philosophy of man without philosophy of nature." The assertion can be turned around: no philosophy of nature without philosophy of man. One can also quote Aristotle: no kind of thought is valid if it is unaware of its own limits.

Francis Fukuyama (Our Posthuman Future: Consequences of the Biotechnology Revolution *[New York: Picador, 2002]*), *Gregory Stock* (Redesigning Humans: Our Inevitable Genetic Future *[New*

York: Houghton Mifflin, 2002]), and Richard Lynn (Eugenics: A Re-assessment [Westport, Conn.: Praeger, 2001]) are some recent authors who are interested in a possible return of eugenics. What is the New Right's position on eugenics? What are the consequences of today's gap between Western and East Asian nations regarding eugenics?

Historically, in the 19th and 20th centuries, the principal theorists of eugenics were chiefly men of the Left. The United States and the Scandinavian countries, moreover, adopted eugenic policies well before Hitler's Germany. These facts are forgotten today, and eugenics is largely discredited because it is mistakenly seen as specifically "Nazi." But at the same time, all the Western countries practice a minimal eugenics that does not dare speak its name: embryonic sorting, therapeutic abortion, the fight against hereditary diseases, etc. I am not sure that eugenics will ever be rehabilitated as such, but I am certain this trend will continue.

The eugenic practices that the development of the life sciences makes it possible to consider in the earliest stages of embryonic life will not be imposed by the state, but on the contrary they respond to the desire of parents who of course wish to have the best children possible. In my eyes, this desire is perfectly legitimate: a society with fewer sick people is objectively better than a society with more.

The true difficulty begins when one wishes to pass from negative to positive eugenics. Indeed, this raises the crucial question of the criterion of "quality" one selects. The most common answer is general intelligence as measured by IQ (the "g" factor evoked by Spearman in 1927, or the "fluid intelligence" of Raymond B. Cattell, in opposition to "crystallized" intelligence). But this criterion is in many ways debatable. I know quite well the literature about IQ and the polemics to which it is continually subjected. (I published a bibliography about it in 1998.) The work of the London school, from Galton to Robert Plomin, while passing by Eysenck and Jensen, arrived at conclusions that cannot be seriously disputed—even if it is also necessary to take account of Robert J. Sternberg's work on "triarchic" intelligence. The contemporary state of research on intelligence has been quite well-summarized in a recent book: Helmuth Nyborg, *The Scientific Study of General Intelligence: Tribute to Arthur R. Jensen* (London: Pergamon, 2003).

The heritability of intelligence, i.e., the share of inter-individual variations of intelligence that can be attributed to genetic factors—or, if one prefers, the share of the phenotypic variance that can be attributed to genotypic variance—is the subject of increasingly concordant evaluations. This heritability remains, however, relative to a given environment (by definition, if there is no difference in environment, the heritability of the variance is established automatically at 100%).

In addition, the quantification of a quality—and intelligence is primarily a quality—never allows us to completely grasp its nature. This is why I find it much more interesting to know which mental differences can exist between individuals with the same IQ, rather than to know which one has the higher IQ. Lastly, the very concept of a test is a Western concept; this is why, in my opinion, even so-called "culture-free" tests can never be completely successful.

Thus my reservations are not because of the London school's definition of intelligence or the validity of IQ tests, but rather because of the overvaluation of intelligence as the criterion of human value. Indeed, being intelligent does not at all guarantee that one is right: the falsest ideologies are the creations of highly intelligent men, sometimes geniuses. (Marx was not less intelligent than Heidegger, and Richard C. Lewontin is certainly not less intelligent than Arthur R. Jensen.) Besides, if intelligence were always advantageous, it would have always been selected for by natural selection, which was not the case.

This overvaluation of intelligence is quite typical of modern societies. It was foreign to the European mentality throughout most of our history. The Homeric hero, the medieval knight, the French *gentilhomme*, the English gentleman, or the Spanish *caballero*, represent as many ideal types (in Max Weber's sense) which never gave a central place to cognitive capacities, but rather to character traits: courage, a sense of honor, disinterestedness, generosity, fidelity to one's word, will, decisiveness, sensitivity, creativity, etc., all qualities that have nothing to do with intelligence *per se*.

I appreciate intelligence of course: all things being equal, it is more pleasant to deal with intelligent people than with idiots. But I do not make intelligence the sole criterion of human value. I myself joined MENSA around 20 years ago. I left it very quickly, since the extremely intelligent people I met there were also mediocre. We live in a time which, for the first time in history, tends to privilege cognitive capacities alone. This climate facilitates the access of intelligent people who lack character to decision-making jobs. In the long run, it will make us dependent on machines (which already have, in many fields, cognitive powers greater than man's).

Ludwig Klages represented all of European history as a slow rise of the prerogatives of the intellect (*der Geist*) to the detriment of those of sensibility and "heart" (*die Seele*). This critique of the intellect, which is found in continental Europe in a great number of "Right wing" authors, contains at least a share of truth. Georg Simmel, for his part, indeed showed how the diffusion of the money economy supported the prevalence of the strictly intellectual and cognitive functions over the emotive functions and solidarity. Such a description helps to understand the passage from the holist model of *community* ("culture") to the individualistic model of *society* ("civilization"). It also helps us criticize the latter. Since Plato one ought to know that scholars should be especially distrusted in positions of power. Today we need strong spines more than big brains.

The implementation of positive eugenics encounters other obvious difficulties as well. The biological law of regression to the mean (the most intelligent tend statistically to have children less intelligent than they are, and the less intelligent tend to have children more intelligent than their parents) contradicts one of the principal postulates of the eugenic doctrine. Moreover, men in general react more to the beauty of women than to their intelligence.

The inevitable intervention of public authorities is also problematic. Simple incentives can only have a limited effectiveness; more authoritative measures entail social engineering, to which I am completely opposed.

We will see what happens with the Chinese eugenics program. Their ultra-*K* strategy implemented in a coercive way by the authorities frequently results in the selective abortion of girls and will lead in twenty years to a serious imbalance in the ratio between the two sexes. For now, I would prefer to live in Sicily, where people in general have character, rather than in Singapore, a true air-conditioned hell!

In his book Race, Evolution, and Behavior: A Life History Perspective, 3rd ed. *(Port Huron, Mich.: The Charles Darwin Research Institute, 2000), J. Philippe Rushton drew up a list of a whole series of significant statistical differences between blacks, whites, and Asians, which reveals a continuum in which whites regularly occupy an intermediate position between Asians and blacks.*

He cites, in particular, cranial capacity, the number of neurons in the brain, the results obtained by IQ tests, cultural achievements, the proportion of monozygotic twins per 1000 births, hormonal levels, sexual organs, the frequency of sexual relations, permissive attitudes, the rate of sexually transmitted diseases, aggressiveness, impulsiveness, self-image, sociability, the gestation period, motor development, the development of teeth and the skeleton, the median age of the first sexual relations, the median age of the first pregnancy, life expectancy, the stability of marriages, the propensity to obey the law, and mental health.

Are you in agreement with Richard J. Herrnstein and Charles Murray, for whom "Rushton's work is not that of a crackpot or a bigot . . . it is plainly science" (The Bell Curve: Intelligence and Class Structure in American Life *[New York: The Free Press, 1994], p. 643) or do you think, like Cavalli-Sforza and his collaborators, that "the classification of the races appeared a futile exercise for reasons that were already obvious for Darwin"* (The History and Geography of Human Genes *[Princeton: Princeton University Press, 1994])? Could Rushton's work provide a scientific base to the "differentialist antiracism" of the New Right?*

J. Philippe Rushton is certainly not "a crackpot or a bigot," and those who think he is deserve only contempt. The statistical correlations that he highlights are data that must be discussed calmly. The question is what conclusion to draw. The classification of races is one thing, their hierarchization quite another. For my part, I do not believe for an instant that there exists an overarching criterion that makes possible an absolute hierarchy of races. Any attempt to show that A is inferior to B amounts to saying that A is less B than B itself, which is merely a tautology.

Any criterion rests on a subjective choice. Rushton kept a certain number of criteria and set others aside. He says nothing, for example, about the color of the eyes, skin, and hair, which are the phenotypic traits by which the eye immediately distinguishes between the races. And in these three fields, Europeans are by no means "intermediate" compared to the Asians and the blacks. The same goes for many pathological factors or diseases, for which the "continuum" postulated by Rushton does not appear.

Among the criteria retained by Rushton, some are of a doubtful nature: the age of the onset of puberty or the first sexual relations dropped considerably in Europe during the last decades without its population changing "biologically." "Sociability" is an extremely fuzzy concept, which does not have the same meaning in Norway and in Greece. And the great number of early maternities among English teenagers (white ones) is certainly not explained by their ethnic membership. As for the frequency of multiple births among African women, it is certainly an interesting datum—less interesting, however, in my opinion, than the comparison of the myths relating to twinhood among various cultures.

Rushton is also the author of work on the reproductive differences entailed by the *r* strategy [high fertility and low parental investment] and the *K* strategy [low fertility and high parental investment], which he connects with average IQ (the *K* strategy positively correlates with a higher IQ).

This work can also be disputed if one takes account of the speed with which the birth and fertility rates can change inside a "homogeneous" population. The adoption of the *K* strategy by European populations is really only a relatively recent phenomenon: for centuries, in these populations as elsewhere, the large family was the rule. To me it seems imprudent to conclude that Europeans of Antiquity or the Middle Ages had a much lower IQ than we do today.

In Quebec, 200 years ago, the fertility rate was one of highest in the world, whereas today it is one of the lowest. This drop is certainly not explained by the collapse of IQ! In the United States, the white birth rate in 1800 was 55 births per year per 1000 inhabitants, whereas in 1980, it was no more than 14.9 births per annum. Should we think that the first figure expresses a *K* strategy when it is double the current birth rate of black Americans? Or should we think that American whites 200 years ago were twice as "*r*-selected" as black Americans today?

Moreover, if one examines the sexual strategies of males and females—a favorite subject of evolutionary psychology—one notes immediately that women tend to adopt the *K* strategy whereas men, being more naturally polygamous, tend to adopt the *r* strategy. If one accepts the reasoning suggested by Rushton, the average IQ of women should thus definitely be higher than that of men. But this is not the case.

Specialists in evolutionary psychology claim that there are important differences between the sexes, and that these were acquired during the evolution of the species. To what does the New Right appeal to support its "differentialist feminism"?

First to history. From the beginning, in Europe women were never considered mere objects. Male domination, on the other hand, has long been legitimated by Christian theology which, especially in the first centuries, presented women as defective beings and a "place of sin." From the 19th century on, bourgeois society has constantly repressed feminine values. This is what justifies the demands of women.

But there are two forms of feminism: egalitarian feminism and identitarian feminism. The first thinks that the best means of ensuring the promotion of women is to work to gradually blur the distinction between masculine and feminine social roles. Women must be able to do "everything that men do," but in this case it the male social role is implicitly taken as the model. The second, by contrast, holds that one can assert the equality of women only on the basis of their distinctness. The

New Right supports the second tendency, represented in particular by Luce Irigaray, rather than the first, represented in particular by Simone de Beauvoir or Elisabeth Badinter.

For its part, evolutionary psychology shows that the differences between men and women go well beyond their sexual organs. In mankind, the brain itself is sexually dimorphic. Thus sex is not reduced to "gender," to a social construction (as claimed in "gender studies," which are characterized above all by their sterility and their extraordinary monotony). Sex is a biological reality on which multiple social constructions are grafted. Feminism is thus completely legitimate when it demands the recognition of the equal *value* of what is *distinctly* female and what is *distinctly* male. But equal value does not mean indistinctness.

In IQ and the Wealth of Nations *(Westport, Conn.: Praeger, 2002), Richard Lynn and Tatu Vanhanen in a way answered Jared Diamond* (Guns, Germs, and Steel: The Fates of Human Societies *[New York: W. W. Norton & Company, 1999]). To the famous question of Yali: "Why do you whites have so much cargo and have come as far as New Guinea, while we blacks have so little cargo?" Lynn and Vanhanen could have answered, in substance: "Well, Yali, after having reviewed the results of IQ tests and economic indicators from some 81 countries around the world, we concluded that the intelligence of the population constitutes the principal factor determining national differences in economic development. We believe that intelligence is partly determined by environment, but that genetic differences actually explain most of the variation. The environmental factor that most influences the intelligence is the quality of food that fetuses and children receive from their mothers" (cf. Richard Lynn and Tatu Vanhanen, "National IQ and Economic Development: A Study of Eighty-One Nations,"* The Mankind Quarterly, *vol. 41, no. 4, Summer 2000, 415–35). How would you answer Yali?*

The "elites" are by definition always powerful in any political system. In the Soviet Union, they were in the service of the Communist party. In the regime of liberal globalization, they are in the service of capitalism. Thus it is not difficult today to establish a correlation between IQ and development.

This correlation says nothing about the intrinsic desirability of the capitalist system or of the value of "development."

The link between intelligence, social prestige, and the accumulation of riches is not valid, however, for all societies: in many traditional societies, social position is evaluated by the volume of wealth that can be redistributed or destroyed.

Furthermore, the correlations established by Lynn and Vanhanen have the disadvantage of being rather static. Viewed from a historical and dynamic point of view, they become less convincing.

To take only one example, if Argentina today is an economic basket case, whereas in the 1930s it was one of the world's top five economic powers, it is certainly not because the Argentinean IQ abruptly crumbled, but because their country suffered from the liberal policies adopted by their governments under the pressure of the World Bank and the IMF.

Conversely, if China is experiencing extraordinary economic growth today whereas for centuries she was not at all concerned about "development," it is not because Chinese IQ has made a sudden leap.

Today, the 225 richest people in the world together have the equivalent of the annual income of the 2.5 billion poorest. The owners of the largest American firms take on average 475 times the average wages of their employees, against 11 to 24 times for European owners. I doubt that IQ can justify such discrepancies or such positions.

What would I say to Yali? I would initially try to explain to him that the "cargo civilization," which is rich in material things but is spiritually increasingly vacuous, does not make those who live there happy and is not necessarily an example to be followed. After that, I would ask him to teach me what he knows. I would ask him about his language, the origin of his people, their customs and traditions, their beliefs and myths, the way they conceive the world and their names for the stars. I would try to learn from him rather than give him lessons.

Counter-Currents/*North American New Right*,
January 28 & 29, February 9, 11, 14, & 18, 2011

INTERVIEW WITH HAROLD COVINGTON

GREG JOHNSON

Could you give us a brief autobiography and tell us how you became involved in White Nationalism?

I was born in Burlington, North Carolina, in 1953. I had my first dose of racial reality at age 15 when I was thrown into an integrated high school in Chapel Hill, North Carolina, which was bad by the standards of the day (1968) but which of course was a kindergarten compared to the racial situation that exists in our schools today. All we had to worry about back in my time was blacks with knives rather than organized gangs and drug dealers armed with semi-autos, and of course there were the hippy-dippy SDS-type radicals, many of whom I noticed even at the time appeared to be Jews. Homosexuals didn't even come into the equation back in those days, and the drugs at school were just beer and grass and LSD, not ecstasy or coke or crack.

I won't go off into a long digression about the various horrible racial experiences I had in high school, but on the day I finally left there, I looked back and made a silent personal vow that I would devote my life somehow to making sure that no young white person ever again had to go through what I had to go through in that place. Again, I didn't realize how relatively mild my problems had been and how terrible things would become in my lifetime.

For reasons I won't get into, basically having to do with the fact that my father was a psychopath, he ordered me out of the family home, and I went into the United States Army at 17. My experiences in the military provided a further dose of racial reality, although once again I understand they were nothing compared to what young white enlistees go through nowadays when the military has in desperation lowered the recruitment criteria to include drug addicts, criminals, gang-bangers, etc.

I did my basic at Fort Polk, Louisiana, and then was sent for infantry training at Fort Jackson, South Carolina and Ranger School at Fort Benning, Georgia. At Fort Jackson I picked up a paperback book in the day room called *The Order of the Death's Head*, by a German named Heinz Höhne. Rare among studies of the Third Reich, the book was actually reasonably objective, and it had the effect of more or less converting me to National Socialism. I remain a National Socialist in my personal outlook to this day. While I was stationed at Schofield Barracks, Hawaii, I joined the National Socialist White People's Party (NSWPP), which was founded by George Lincoln Rockwell, and was then run by a man named Matt Koehl. I formed a unit of a Party front group called the White Servicemen's League and ended up getting discharged early, albeit under honorable conditions. Nowadays, of course, I'd probably end up in Leavenworth for it.

After I got out of the army I served on permanent NSWPP staff at the headquarters in El Monte, California, under the now-legendary Lieutenant Joseph Tommasi, who was murdered in 1975. I then became editor of the Party newspaper *White Power* in Arlington, Virginia. In 1974 I worked for a construction company in Johannesburg, South Africa, for about six months, and then went to Rhodesia and joined the Rhodesian Army. In 1976 I was deported from Rhodesia for my activities with the proto-NS Rhodesia White People's Party, along with two of my fellow Americans, Eric Thomson and Jeffrey Spencer. That's an interesting example of conservatives being our true worst enemy. I was deported on the personal orders of Ian Smith, and we all know what Mr. Smith's conservatism did to Rhodesia.

From then on it was the usual long Movement history of different groups, different approaches, all of them pretty much dead ends because there basically isn't anything that can be done on an all-America basis in order to reverse the terminal decline of Western civilization on this continent, at least not without the use of a level of armed force which practically speaking, the Movement will never have at its disposal.

In 1982 I more or less went on the run for five years due to a legal situation which I'm still not certain it's completely safe for me to get into, given the paranoid nature of our lords and masters these days and their eagerness to find something, anything, to use as an excuse to plop me down in the cell next to Bill White and Matt Hale. I ended up in Ireland, which at that time had no extradition treaty with the USA, due to the embarrassment and political complications for the Dublin government which would be caused by possibly extraditing IRA men back and forth across the Atlantic.

I learned a lot in Ireland. I didn't just hang out in pubs guzzling Guinness; I read all the newspapers and watched RTE and BBC Northern Ireland; I made trips into the North; I talked to certain people (very carefully), and I sat quietly in certain known IRA pubs nursing a pint or two of Smithwick's, listening and observing. Basically, in Ireland I saw how it's done in the modern world, not in 1930s Germany, and it was an invaluable education.

It's true the IRA didn't win in the main sense of the term, but Communists though they are (and I know that), this small band of dedicated white working class men and women fought a major Western democratic military power to a standstill, and forced the Brits to buy them off instead of crushing them. Like Rocky Balboa, they went a full fifteen rounds with Godzilla and they were still standing at the end of it. The lesson I draw from this and other events in the past 20 years is that it can be done.

In 2000, in the aftermath of what Morris Dees did to Pastor Butler, I finally came out openly for territorial white separatism in the form of the Northwest Imperative.

Can you explain the Northwest Imperative, and tell us how you came to believe in it?

The Northwest Imperative is based on the conviction, an accurate one, that the United States of America in its present form is doomed, and that it is necessary to the physical survival of the white race that we establish a Homeland for all of our people worldwide somewhere on the North American continent. Economics, demographics, and logistics dictate that the best location for such a Homeland is here in the Pacific Northwest. In addition, we have a long history here of commitment and martyrdom here in the Northwest: Bob Mathews and the Order men, Sam and Vicky Weaver, Gordon Kahl, and our latest martyr from the Northwest Front, Jeff Hughes of Vancouver, Canada.

The essence of the Northwest Idea is to reduce the problem to manageable proportions. We are simply too weak, disorganized, and too few to take over the United States, and we need to accept that just ain't gonna happen. Instead of a whole huge continent and 300 million mostly hostile people to worry about, we reduce the problem geographically and demographically to three and a half states with about 12 million people, mostly white. Given the inevitable coming implosion of the United States and the collapse of the central authority in Washington, D.C., when they run out of money to pay their mercenaries, bureaucrats, and enforcers, the Northwest Imperative is do-able in a way that no other plan we've ever come up with is doable.

The Northwest Imperative also reduces the problem to that of a colonial war, and there are numerous models from the last century as to how to wage and win a colonial war. The objective is to make the disputed territory ungovernable and turn it into a massive rathole down which the occupying power bleeds money, manpower, and resources until it can't stand the hemorrhage any longer and cuts its losses. The most important statement in any of my Northwest novels, so important that I have various characters say it over and over again in all four books, is this: "In a colonial war, it's never the generals who surrender. It's the accountants."

Can you tell us what you are doing to promote the idea of a Northwest homeland and to prepare for its concrete realization?

We have formed the "Party" of the Northwest novels, called the Northwest Front, although it isn't really a Party yet and probably won't be for some time. Right now it's just what the name says, a broad front rather than a party. We have participation from people who are involved with other groups and from people who are involved with none. There is no formal membership status, no chain of command, and no hierarchy. We provide what support we can to anyone who lives here or who is willing to come here to the Homeland and work for Northwest independence.

Eventually that will have to change, of course. Eventually there must be a disciplined, fighting revolutionary Party of political soldiers, but that's going to take us a while. White Americans are the sloppiest, laziest, most narcissistic and most undisciplined people in the world, and they simply can't wrap their minds around a European concept such as the political soldier. Not yet. They will have to change, or they will perish from the earth.

Like most of the people in the racialist movement today, my awakening and education were enormously aided by the internet. You yourself have a substantial web presence. Yet you are known as a staunch critic of movement's strong dependence on the internet. Can you explain your views on the virtues and limits of the internet for White Nationalism?

The internet is a reality of 21st century life. I understand and accept that. It can no more be un-invented than gunpowder or nuclear power can be un-invented. The Net has become a necessary evil, but an evil nonetheless, in my opinion.

For one thing, the internet is largely sterile politically. It produces almost nothing except more Net. Somebody sees a great pro-white web site and they are inspired with enthusiasm—to build another web site. There is this immense disconnect between what is essentially a fantasy world in cyber-space and the real world out here where white people are unemployed and foreclosed white families are beginning to live in tent cities called Obamavilles.

The internet gives the white male a feel-good factor which he doesn't have to earn. He sits down at his computer after work with a bowl of nachos and a few cold brewskis, he plays around on VNN or surfs the web looking for racial stuff, maybe he makes a post or two, and then at the end of the evening he gets up and staggers off to bed with the feeling that he has accomplished something, but he hasn't. All he has done is to generate words, and words are no good on earth if they never translate into physical action.

The internet provides the white male with a substitute for action, and with a place where he can hide. Yes, I understand that most of us have jobs and families and homes we have to protect, but the fact remains that at some point in time we are going to have to stand erect once more, like men, and not with our heads hung down and our eyes lowered and our feet shuffling in the presence of our Jewish and liberal lords and masters. The internet does not facilitate the strengthening of the one ancient virtue of our people which we need most of all to rediscover: simple physical courage.

Finally, the internet provides something that our highly dysfunctional people cannot resist: consequences-free misbehavior. This is not just a Movement phenomenon; it's a white thing. The internet is a looney bin, and everyone knows it. The internet is where sick and twisted and often quite deranged people go to vomit. I have never seen anything like some of the filth, the depravity, the idiocy, and the just plain raving madness that I find on the internet every day. I know quite ordinary and apparently stable, functional, and successful people who sit down behind that keyboard, and all of a sudden they get a visit from Mr. Hyde. You've heard of discovering one's Inner Child? It's like the lure of consequences-free misbehavior on the internet unlocks some people's Inner Nut.

All of this having been said, the internet remains the only medium of mass communication we have access to, the only place that provides anything remotely resembling a level playing field, which is probably why the Jews and the government hate it so much. Love the internet or hate it, we seem to be stuck with it.

Many of our people dwell on negative signs, and there are plenty of them. Do you see positive signs? Do you think there are good reasons for hope?

Oh, yes, certainly. So long as one doesn't confuse hope with optimism.

For one thing, it is a historical truism that nothing lasts forever. This Francis Fukuyama rap about liberal democracy being the "end of history" is horse dung. Everything ends, and the present Zionist world order will end as well, quite possibly within the lifetime of those now born. It may not end the way we want it to end, and it may drag the white race and Western civilization down with it, but oh, yes, it will end. Our task in this and coming generations is to make sure that we survive the collapse of this massive evil, along with at least some semblance of Western civilization.

For another thing, for all our weaknesses and flaws we are still the most intelligent and potentially the bravest and most hardy race on earth. It takes more than 100 years of liberal brainwashing, political correctness, and McDonalds' Happy Meals to contaminate and extinguish a whole human genotype. Deep down we are still the men our ancestors were, it's just sometimes it's so deep down we can't read our genetic script.

We can do this thing. We can beat these bastards, any time we so choose. The question is, will we so choose? The *Weltfeind* is counting on his ability to obscure our racial light in a murk of questions, indecision, introspection, corruption, and apathy, to drag the whole world into the shades of grey in which the Jew thrives. If we can achieve moral clarity in our souls we will recover our courage, and when we recover our courage we will rip their hearts out.

One of the things that most struck me about your Northwest Quartet is the attitude of high moral seriousness that these novels communicate, which I think is a valuable corrective to the movement's general ethos of emotional self-indulgence. But you are better at communicating this than I am. Most White Nationalists accept that our race is facing oblivion. What more do they need to get serious?

The stock answer to that is that things have to get so bad that every white man, woman and child is personally affected in their own lives by the current crisis of civilization. They must lose their houses, their jobs, their SUVs, and their plasma TVs and all that nice cold beer in the fridge. This is certainly true as far as it goes, and it is now at long last beginning to happen during this onset of the Obama Depression.

But I believe that more has to happen. There has to be a genuine spiritual awakening that burns away the past several generations of excrement that the Jews have caked around our souls. Our people must once more learn to value something higher than their own private lives and their own creature comforts. I personally found this in National Socialism, others find it in religion, but one of the advantages of turning this into a colonial war is that it allows for the creation of a new (or rather old) idealism in our hearts, a secular nationalism that aspires to the creation of a new country, free of alien oppressors. That will work. Ask the Irish.

Early in your career, you were an avowed National Socialist. How has your thinking changed since then? In your view, what are the enduring truths in National Socialism, and what are its limitations?

I am just as much a National Socialist now as I ever was. The enduring truth of National Socialism lies in one slogan: "Our race is our nation." National Socialism affirms the primacy of race over lesser aspects of human existence such as religion and nationality.

I have, however, come to realize that most Americans are totally spiritually unequipped to accept such a doctrine. They don't speak the language. They simply haven't been engineered that way, and of course 70 years of Jewish hate propaganda, misrepresentation, and distortion hasn't helped. Back in my youth in the old Party, we had the idea that through a process of long and slow education we could wean a sufficient number of our people away from the Jewish narrative and make them see the truth, but we didn't do so hot at that, and now we are out of time. Simply and starkly, it's about racial survival now, and that has to take first place in our strategy.

In order to convince people, you must first put yourself on a credible basis of communication with them, and you can't do that by immediately confronting them with symbols and ideas that they have been conditioned from birth to reject. Every essential principle of National Socialism has a perfectly reasonable and understandable circumlocution that can be used within the American context so as to bypass the socially-engineered rejection mechanisms which have been implanted in white people's brains. Call it National Socialism Lite, if you will. I don't like it, but the urgency of our racial crisis overrides my personal feelings.

What are the books, writers, and historical events that have most shaped your particular version of White Nationalism?

Besides National Socialist works and history? First and foremost there is the life and work of Commander George Lincoln Rockwell. There's the American Civil War, of course. I was born and raised in the last of the Old South, when it was considered entirely normal to have Confederate flags on one's possessions and when it was still possible to see Confederate heroes positively portrayed on TV and in comic books, etc.

Easter 1916 and the Irish War of Independence is another obvious example. I think the situation in Ireland in the 1920s is probably as close a parallel to our situation today as can be drawn. Later on we may draw some insight from the Spanish Civil War, which I always liked — the last war the good guys actually won.

My main Movement mentors were Major William Gaedtke, the last head of the old America First Committee (the Lindbergh one) and Pastor Robert Miles. They taught me the ropes. I learned a lot from Matt Koehl as well. I never thought I'd say this, and I still don't agree with what Koehl did to the NSWPP, but after three decades I now understand why Koehl did a lot of the things he did.

I really enjoy your novels. I have reviewed the Northwest Quartet, and I have also read Slow Coming Dark, Fire and Rain, *and most recently* The Stars In Their Path, *as well as the collection* Other Voices, Darker Rooms. *Who are your main literary influences? Which of your works are your favorites and why?*

My father was a reader of pulp science fiction back in the 1950s and 1960s, and he had these big cardboard cartons of old sci-fi paperbacks in the basement, including a lot of the old Ace doubles that went for 50 cents in those days and would probably go for a couple of hundred bucks apiece today if you could get hold of an intact copy. They were written by all the sci-fi greats of the '50s and '60s: Robert A. Heinlein, Brian Aldiss, Philip K. Dick, Alfred Bester, Edmond Hamilton, Alan E. Nourse, Andre Norton, Ray Bradbury, etc. Those were my first bulk reading, and then, starting about age 14, I somehow (don't remember how) discovered H. P. Lovecraft, and that was love at first sight. I still lug around the three-volume Arkham House set of his complete works with me wherever I go.

My Northwest novels are purely political polemics, wherein I say things that wouldn't be politic to say openly in any other context. They are for the purpose of imparting ideas and disseminating practical information using what Lenin called "Aesopian language," the language of fable. My actual fiction as such, novels like *The Stars In Their Path, The Renegade, Vindictus,* etc. aren't really "influenced" by anyone or anything. They're just stories I get into my febrile brain and which I have to purge by telling them and letting them out.

As to my favorites, excluding the Quartet, which don't count because they're not really novels in the true sense of the word, I'd have to say that *The Madman and Marina* [in *Other Voices, Darker Rooms*] is the best short piece I've ever done. It may possibly even be the best piece, period — I once had an e-mail correspondent in St. Petersburg tell me he didn't believe that my name is Covington, that I had to be a Russian writing under an American pseudonym, because only a Russian could produce such a Dostoyevskyan story. I consider that to be the best review I've ever had.

Personal favorite among the long novels? *The Stars In Their Path,* I'd say. Like all my other books it tells a story, but I use reincarnation as a device to keep on telling the same story over and over and over again, a different way each time and with different characters, rather than draw the same plot out to 100,000 words of padding. I think that was neat, if I do say so myself.

In the Northwest Quartet and Fire and Rain, *I was especially impressed with how you can blend intense drama with light comedy, classical eloquence with pop-culture slang and vulgarity. Joss Whedon and Quentin Tarantino came to mind. Do you pay attention to popular culture? Do you watch movies or television? Name some favorite writers, directors, movies, TV shows.*

I don't watch television any more, and haven't for a long time. It's not just that it's Judaized to the max and politically nauseating, it's just stupid. Moronic. I glance over hulu.com every now and then, and I don't see anything on there that prompts me to get cable again. Why pay $75 a month for drivel?

Movies are another matter. DVDs from the Blockbuster bargain racks are about the only form of recreation I can afford, besides a library card. In that sense yes, I have managed to keep up with enough popular culture, especially among young white people (negrofied though that culture is) so that I can make my young characters believable. I think so, anyway. None of my youthful readers have complained so far.

There are certain movies that just plain creep me out, like *Naked Lunch*, and there are certain flicks I find fascinating because they're incredibly bizarre, like *Dark Star* and the American version of *Kingdom Hospital*, which IMHO is the just plain weirdest thing ever shown on television. My own DVD collection includes *Henry the Fifth* (Kenneth Branagh version), *Zulu*, *The 13th Warrior*, *The Outlaw Josey Wales*, and a few oddballs from the '70s like *Time After Time* and *Absolution*. I gave some friends of mine the first five episodes of *Sharpe's Rifles*. I like a lot of escapist swashbuckling stuff, as you can tell.

Do you plan to write any more novels?

At this point I would say probably not. I'm pretty much NVA'ed out.[1] There is a limit to what can be accomplished through fantasy and the creation of a fictional *mythos*. If I have not yet succeeded in imparting a vision of possibility to our people in the four Northwest novels already extant, I probably never will. I am concentrating henceforth on trying to turn the vision into reality through the Northwest Front, the "Party" of the novels, and it's a five-star bitch. Getting "our" people to peep out from behind their computers and commit a real live physical act out here in the real world is like pulling teeth. Half of my contacts I can't even get to respond to an e-mail.

I still have some bits and pieces of novels and stories lying around in manuscript form and on my computer, plus some ideas I'd like to play with if I ever get the time and the right situation (like the long prison sentence on some ridiculous fabricated charge which I'm sure our lords and masters would like to oblige me with). The main one is a kind of adult version of the Harry Potter series where a secret society of powerful Aryan spirits operating in a kind of netherworld one step above this dimension use their magical powers to try and reverse the destruction of our people wrought by the Sauron-like Jewish overlord of the Dark World, although it would hopefully come across a little more convincing than that. I doubt I'll ever get around to it, though. I need to concentrate what time I have left on building something in the real world.

The Stars In Their Path *surprised me because it is a rather "metaphysical" novel. In my opinion, you are very wise to counsel White Nationalists to be neutral on religious issues. But you are also a private citizen too. So Citizen, can you tell us about your religious and metaphysical beliefs and how you arrived at them?*

I believe in reincarnation because I myself have witnessed and experienced events that indicate to me that it is at least part of the process that happens to the human soul or personality

---

[1] This interview was done in December of 2009. In late 2010, Mr. Covington began writing a fifth Northwest novel, *Freedom's Sons*—Ed.

after death. I won't get into the details of these experiences here, because my present life is all about the 14 Words and such beliefs aren't really germane to my racial work. We are meant to live our lives in this world, not the next. My metaphysical worldview has provided me with one invaluable spiritual asset, in that I do not fear death, although admittedly any Islamic suicide bomber can say the same.

When I went out into the bush in Rhodesia, for example, I was never afraid of being killed. Coming back armless or legless from a landmine, or blind, or in a wheelchair, now that scared the bejesus out of me, but not actual death, and that's a handy spiritual resource to have. I do not, however, insist on these beliefs, nor do I try to impose them on others. I am not missionary about them for the simple reason that I know, and others are going to find out in the fullness of time, and it doesn't really matter what they believe. Whatever floats their boat. For me the question is resolved—again, a good asset for a revolutionary to be packing.

It is depressing to contemplate how much effort goes into things that we would not think twice about if we just came to grips with the fact that we are going to die, and we don't know when. It can happen any day. What do you think gives meaning to human life? Do you think there is a larger meaning and purpose to the universe? Do you think it links up with individual lives?

As opposed to my certainty on reincarnation, I take a rather Zen-ish attitude towards the meaning of each individual life itself. Just because you're going to get more than one go-round is no excuse for slacking. This world is a school where we are sent to learn and to grow as individual spiritual beings. You start out in the equivalent of kindergarten and work your way through grades one through six, junior high, high school, university, maybe some cosmic post-grad work, who knows? You get the idea. Kids who goldbrick and just try to skate through in school don't turn out well as a rule, and neither do human spirits. Karmically speaking it is possible to "fail a grade," many times over, and be forced to keep on repeating the same experiences and facing the same obstacles until one buckles down to it, overcomes those obstacles, and develops properly.

There is nothing at all wrong with spiritual ambition and a drive for excellence, to live one's life for the purpose of leaving behind a better world than one found at birth. Actually that's how we all should be living, although needless to say most don't. Ideally every human life should accomplish something, and this involves overcoming the physical, spiritual, and character-related flaws and obstacles that are part of life. In my view, since the end result as far as the individual's fate is foreordained in any case, how you play the game is indeed the more important aspect of it all, because that's what you will take with you into your next existence.

One thought that comforts me in darker moods is the fact that, long after the Earth is just a burned out cinder in the emptiness of space, radio waves carrying the music of Bach and Mozart and Wagner will still be traveling outwards, perhaps to find ears worthy of them. (Of course all the crap ever broadcast will be out there too.) Does music matter much to you? What are some of your favorite genres, musicians, composers, and why?

Classically speaking I enjoy Wagner, of course, as well as Mozart, Verdi, Gregorian chant and Eastern Orthodox liturgical music, Gesualdo, Hildegard von Bingen, and Aaron Copland, one of the few Jews to whom I would be inclined to award "honorary Aryan" status.

But I don't actually listen to much classical; it demands concentration in order to be appreciated, and most of my mellows I play while I'm working or writing. I did a mix tape I called the Northwest Soundtrack for some of my fans, consisting of key mood pieces I listened to while composing certain sections of the Quartet novels, and it included everything from Celtic symphonic music from the Granuaile, Pilgrim, and Relief of Derry CDs, to rock music from Joe Walsh and Jefferson Airplane, to bagpipes, to movie soundtracks and bluegrass.

My three main music collections I play on my computer while I'm working are entitled "Irish," which includes Enya, the Chieftains, the Corrs, Bothy Band, and Planxty; "Southern," which starts out with Ralph Stanley and moves on to Waylon Jennings, Flatt and Scruggs, Steve Earle, Mike Cross, and Grandpa Jones; and finally "Rock," which has Jefferson Airplane, Phil Collins, the Who, the Rolling Stones, and Runrig, among others.

What are the best things you have done in your life so far, and what things do you most regret doing or leaving undone?

The best thing is my children. They despise me, of course, having been carefully raised to do so by the other members of my family, and that fact has not the slightest iota of effect on my love for them. It's not their fault, and besides, you can never really be angry at someone whose nappies you've changed. The fact is that they exist, and I hope someday they will have children of their own and do better by them than I was able to do.

The thing I regret most is not stepping forward with the Northwest Idea many years ago, when I knew and understood that it was the way to go. Certainly I knew after Ruby Ridge that this was a sacrifice we could not ignore or denigrate by continuing to waste our time on strategies that were proven failures, or even worse, by simply continuing to drift. Why I didn't step forward in 1992 and proclaim what I knew to be the truth involves a lot of complex factors, some of them not very creditable to me. It took the martyrdom of Pastor Butler for me to finally screw my courage to the sticking point. Part of that growing process I mentioned, but it shouldn't have taken me that long, and if the NF is now running short on time, that is in a large degree my fault. I regret that deeply, and hope I can make up for it in the time I have left.

I know a lot of very bright and promising young nationalists. I have recommended your novels to them, even given them copies, and they have definitely been influenced. What is your advice to young nationalists? If you had a son of 19 or 20, embarking on adult life, what would you tell him?

As clichéd as this will sound, my first advice (which I was

never allowed to give to my actual son in real life) would be to learn a trade. Get a marketable skill, something to sell, which will keep food on your table and a roof over your head.

If you are going to be politically effective, you have to start with those basics. You can't participate in a revolution while living under a bridge, and that's where millions of white people are headed. Learn to fix the rich man's toys when they break, learn to do it well and at an economical price, and you will always work. You have to financially bulletproof yourself by acquiring a skill that somebody, somewhere, will always be willing to pay you to exercise. When you've got a roof over your head, a functioning motor vehicle, and your basic needs met, that's your baseline for political activity. You shouldn't attempt it otherwise.

Thank you.

Counter-Currents/*North American New Right*,
July 15, 2010

What is to be Done?

Michael O'Meara
& John Schneider

Introduction

John Schneider and I have opposed the existing regime for nearly forty years, though our original opposition was framed in the ideological and organizational terms of the revolutionary Marxist Left. Neither of us any longer sympathizes with this Left, but we nevertheless accept that it has something still to teach the Right. And though we differ on many things, I think his thoughts on the tasks facing the present anti-system opposition deserve a hearing. — Michael O'Meara

One

Dear Mike,

As always, it was a pleasure chatting with you today. Here is the email I mentioned I would send. Please forgive the first part, in which I unfairly accuse you of a Trotskyite deviation. After our talk I realize that this is not correct, but I would rather send this than attempt to rewrite it. The end is a bit hurried and overwrought but, again, I'd rather send it as it is than worry about revising it.

John

Argument of John Schneider

"Auf tausend Kriege kommen nicht zehn Revolutionen, so schwer ist der aufrechte Gang." — Ernst Bloch

"If you don't hit it, it won't fall." — Chairman Mao

I've been reflecting on your recent email, as well as on your general view regarding what you perceive to be the possible coming collapse of the West. I think that in general I agree with your assessment of the issues facing the system (although you've left out the most salient feature—demography). There remains, however, a disparity in tone and emphasis between us, which I think reflects more than just a difference in mood or style.

While I hate to say it, your focus on the possibility of collapse seems to reflect the fact that *politically* (as opposed to ideologically) your methodology remains a little too Trotskyite.

In your last email, for example, you said:

> But I'm looking for the long shot and judging the possibilities. . . . That said, I still believe that not just the American System, but all of 'Western Civilization' is today in serious trouble.
>
> The difficulties facing the state are unprecedented and potentially system-destroying . . .
>
> A few more catastrophes that add to the growing stresses already afflicting it and the system becomes completely dysfunctional. When this occurs, people will start looking around for alternatives.

All this sounds to me like a white nationalist version of the Trotskyite belief that as the crises of capitalism inevitably worsen, the light bulb will suddenly come on over the collective head of the working class, as it says almost as one: "Oh, the Revolutionary Workers League has had the correct program all along! Let's join them and make a revolution."

In fact, and as a historian you know this, things have never worked out that way. Instead, time after time, the workers have turned to the Social Democrats and the Stalinists because these were the movements which already had deep roots in the class when the crises came. The Trotskyite Cassandras just never got the call, no matter how prescient they may have been.

I also think that while there is no question but that the coming decades will be extremely problematic ones for the system, the notion that it will become "completely dysfunctional" or even collapse has no historical precedent, other than in countries which are quite primitive—think of the Congo—and/or have suffered catastrophic military defeats. As serious as the issues you mention are, I just don't believe that any of them rise to this level on their own or even together.

The problem with relying on the system to collapse under its own weight is not just that it is unlikely to occur.

The bigger issue is that such a view breeds a passive, abstentionist political approach, relying on the production of fierce-sounding tracts and the elaboration of ideologically precise programs to the practical exclusion of any real involvement in the struggles of the day (which are seen as generally irrelevant and futile — or, at best, as simply a means of contacting potential recruits).

The system has survived crisis after crisis, as Bloch recognized, and will likely continue to do so until an agent arises to intervene in these crises to create a different outcome.

RESPONSE OF MICHAEL O'MEARA

John,

You have long chastised me for the implicit passivity inherent in the "politics of catastrophism," just you have repeatedly criticized white nationalists for having no sense of the political.

On both counts, I must concede.

Lenin knew that workers, in struggling against capital, might organize trade unions and other such formations to advance their particular interest within the economic system, but this alone was something very different from a revolutionary class consciousness seeking the system's overthrow.

The breakdowns and crises afflicting every system may therefore provoke "spontaneous" reactions in defense of various social actors, but these reactions "in themselves" are rarely the stuff of revolution.

More generally, I think you're again correct to claim, on Leninist principle, that the advent of a "pre-revolutionary" situation, fostered by crisis and breakdown, almost never culminates in an actual revolution — *if* there does not exist a revolutionary vanguard to concentrate the anti-system forces and lead a concerted assault on the dominant "order" before it manages to recover.

I have one minor and one major difference with you.

The minor difference is perhaps not a difference at all. The age of the revolutionary party—in the classical Bolshevik sense or even in the sense of Mussolini's Blackshirts—seems strangely remote to our postmodern world, where the state is no longer the central actor and where political mobilization is as much about communications and the affirmation of identity as it is about direct action in the public sphere.

What Sam Francis called "Middle American" radicalism—in its half-century long resistance to various elite social-engineering campaigns—took, relatedly, a largely grassroots, localist, and single-issue form.

While we agree that white nationalists and other anti-system actors ought to intervene in these populist movements, the formation of a vanguard party (in the professional, militarist, centralized—i.e., Jesuit—way Lenin advocated) to capture the leadership of these diverse oppositions seems somehow inappropriate to our age.

I suspect the next American revolution will be precipitated more in the way it occurred in pre-1789 France than in early 20th-century Russia or in postwar Italy and Germany. The revolutionary agent, as a result, will probably not be a "party" *per se*, but a new consciousness promoted through the metapolitical activities of salons, societies of thought, blogs, and other traditional and digital media promoting an anti-liberal critique of the dominant system. Once these activities inform the consciousness of a critical mass of like-minded oppositionists, it will perhaps then be possible to organize a party to capture the dominant institutions.

This is not to say that we ought to sit back and await the impending collapse.

Rather, we must, as you stress, do everything to make ourselves worthy of the destiny we claim.

The point I make is Maistre's: Providence has a way of leading men who may think they are leading themselves.

Oppositional "interventions," in any case, will be less centralized and less coordinated (a "leaderless resistance"?) and oppositionists will probably have to go through a period, like that of 1789–92, before they acquire the means and the consensus to create a party that will serve as the vanguard of a new system.

That's the minor point. My major difference is about the nature of the coming crisis, which I believe is not only inevitable but likely to be system-destroying—like those Hollywood disaster films about 13.5 earthquakes.

The single relevant model of rapid *system* collapse is that of the Soviet Union. The American case, I see, is more likely to follow its course than the historically more common forms of gradual civilizational decline and fall.

Why? The Soviet Union was no civilization in any traditional sense—that is, it wasn't something that had organically grown out of Russia's historical distillation of Greek Orthodox High Culture.

Instead, it was an artificial system constructed on certain unworkable ideological tenets. Even before the 1980s, Soviet elites had stopped believing these tenets, realizing the system itself needed a radical overhaul if it were to keep running.

The United States, by contrast, began as an extension of European culture, and however vulgar or superficial its New World civilization may have been, it was something more than an artificially contrived system.

This would change, though, especially after the Gilded Age culminated in the Great Depression of the 1930s—when the country had to be rescued by Roosevelt's "managerial revolution." Since then, the United States has embarked on a permanent project of renewal—of liberal design—that fundamentally and continually transforms the country's nature.

Buttressed by the national mobilization that supported America's intervention in the Second World War, and then more forthrightly with the Cold War and the onset of globalization in the 1990s, America has been progressively turned into a "system"—a counter-civilization—whose political-economic cornerstone is the "military-industrial complex" and whose chief aim is satisfying its Mammon-worshiping corporate sector.

The result: The America of today does not look or sound or

act anything like the America of my childhood.

Given its totalitarian disposition, America's postwar system eliminated all system-impairing legacies—i.e., all those things that might hinder the universalization and rationalization of its world-conquering enterprise.

This meant that the former nation-defining racial hierarchy, the historical basis of American identity, had to be destroyed; that the remnants of its Christian, European culture had to give way to the universal dictates of the empire's multicult; that local and state governments had to bow to the imperatives of Washington's Leviathan; that indigenous and non-indigenous colored people should henceforth achieve "parity" with whites, even if it entailed the massive redistribution of white wealth and opportunity; that the new media-diffused values and behaviors, oriented to hedonist forms of consumption and indifferent to former moral or religious standards, had to replace traditional ones . . .

Everything distinct to America's nativist strain of European culture has, indeed, been hunted down, repressed, extinguished—for the sake of the one-world, market-driven, militarily-aggressive assertion of its elites' global order, arguably as artificial and anti-natural in principle as the Soviet system.

For reasons I can't deal with within the limits of this exchange, the system, especially after 9/11, has assumed a logic of its own, a (logic-free) logic that is increasingly dysfunctional—given the unreal and unnatural, rather than organic principles, steering it.

The best example of this is the military-industrial complex. It was the technological might of America's industrial economy that made the country a world-conquering force. Even though the ensuing desanguination of its population meant that America could no longer produce soldiers capable of fighting on the ground, its vast, high-tech arsenal made it a force no conventional army could possibly defeat.

At this point, though, when American might seemed virtually invincible, the unexpected occurred: Fourth Generation War (4GW). With the advent of this new form of struggle, America's military opponents ceased challenging it on the conventional fields of battle and instead adopted the judo-inspired principle of turning the enemy's strength into a weakness. The folly of Iraq and Afghanistan is the result.

This 4GW dynamic, in which the system is turned against itself, to defeat itself, has not been limited to the field of battle, but is now everywhere infecting the system's "logic."

Thus it is that the more money and power the Pentagon accumulates, the more irrelevant and impotent it becomes in addressing its perceived military threats. In this spirit, Donald Rumsfeld said shortly before 9/11 that the greatest threat to US national security was the Pentagon bureaucracy and its "uncontrollable activism."

Ditto the federal bureaucracy: The more it centralizes power and micro-manages the system, getting into everybody's business, the more unmanageable its ensuing problems.

Even our empire's so-called constitutional system of law, as in the case of Arizona, has become a force for lawlessness (as Obama, in the name of the system's mandated racial egalitarianism, openly aids and abets law-breakers—those illegal immigrants who are bringing not only their unwelcome selves, but Mexico's bloody civil war into our backyards).

Above all, such is the case with the US National Security Complex, which vastly expanded after 9/11. A look at the *Washington Post*'s recent "Top Secret America" series reveals that this expansion, involving seventeen major agencies, scores of new intelligence systems, more than 800,000 employees, and 50,000 top secret annual reports, most of which no one reads, is so Byzantine that terrorists could publish their intentions on the front page of the *New York Times* and this "security" complex would fail to detect it.

In our Maistrian age, not "intelligence," but an institutionalized system of "unintelligence"—increasingly perverse and dysfunctional—reigns.

Putting its radical systemic/systematizing principles above all else, the system has become so unbalanced that its negative tendencies now outweigh its positive ones, sowing, as is more and more evident, the seeds of its own destruction.

The system, as a result, is quite literally out of control. For nobody actually governs it, nobody understands it. And it is totally blind; it can't see the world in front of it—the great metal ship heading, full speed, toward the iceberg. It can't see because the system lives in that bubble of virtual reality, where only its own narrative is told, irrespective of reality.

The coming system crisis will not resemble the one Roosevelt faced in the '30s, but the one Gorbachev confronted in the '80s.

Collapse, I believe, has become an inescapable part of the system—and the system is on auto-pilot, set to self-destruct. It quite simply cannot do anything without screwing up. Conclusion: the "clusterfuck nation" is unreformable. The only question is: *when* it will fall and *what* it will entail.

Given the present converging breakdowns and the consciousness they're creating, I believe we have entered an *interregnum*, whose demands will be as terrifying as they are heroic.

You're certainly right that this is no excuse to sit back or abstain from the many arenas of struggles opened by the impending collapse.

Again: Things may fall apart, but this doesn't mean it will be to our advantage.

Our most important task in this period hovering between two ages is, therefore, to see that things fall in ways favoring our people.

To this end, we'll have to become part of the general movement that is already stirring. No White Nationalist or revolutionary formation will "spontaneously" develop out of the Tea Party or the Militias. We have to intervene as individuals, who bring our distinct racial-secessionist consciousness to this movement, which, however unconscious and cretinized, embodies an implicitly white identity . . . and implies your type of grassroots politicking.

Such a political project, moreover, will take uncharted paths, for the bloodless, liberal system endeavoring to supplant what goes for civilization has today embarked on a course whose culmination can only be the impending destruction of white life in North America.

We must thus, as our overriding aim, encourage the system's collapse and position ourselves to gain from it.

REPLY OF JOHN SCHNEIDER

I completely agree that the time is not right—and may never be right—for the formation of a democratic centralist "vanguard" party, especially as this was understood in the post-1960 era. A look at the history of the New Left is particularly instructive in this regard. During the 1970s, many of the more serious activists radicalized during the antiwar movement became convinced that the creation of an authentically revolutionary Left required the construction of what they perceived to be a Leninist party. In fact, as you and I both experienced during that "party-building" mania, the proliferation of these "vanguard" organizations did nothing to strengthen the Left. Instead, it led to endless infighting and the squandering of massive amounts of energy in ultimately meaningless debates over theoretical and historical questions.

Further, once the construction of the party became *the* key prerequisite for any meaningful politics, the participation of these would-be vanguard parties in the mass movement almost always took on a predatory and divisive character, as the activism of their militants was subordinated to each groupuscule's sectarian maneuvering.

By the 1980s many mass movement activists came to view the members of the various Left parties with deep suspicion. The most successful movements of that period—the Freeze, the Central America anti-intervention/solidarity movement, and the anti-nuclear power movement—were run by non-party activists who, while all committed radicals of one sort or another, functioned through informal leadership networks of like-minded people within their respective movements, while the parties of the Left often remained at the margins.

At present, the anti-system Right is obviously qualitatively weaker than the Left was in the 1970s. Rather than wasting time and energy in grand organizational projects, the need now is simply to coalesce local groupings, to connect them together in informal networks, and to encourage a combined commitment to study, propaganda, and activism. Whatever structures created beyond this can only evolve organically out of the struggles themselves.

Now, regarding your prediction of imminent collapse: I think that the analysis you present here of the system as synonymous with the Military-Industrial Complex is too narrow and owes too much to a paleoconservative perspective.

I would argue instead that our current system can be more properly understood within the context of the global progression of the capitalist economy, which has transcended the limits of nation and human ownership—moving to a stage characterized by transnational corporations run by professional managers without roots in or commitment to any community or nation.

While the transition from national elites to an international one is not complete, it is far advanced, with significant sectors of the elites and the professional-managerial classes having adopted a post-national, and even an anti-national, perspective.

I don't, of course, deny that there is a significantly megalomaniacal element to US foreign policy which has been particularly pronounced since World War II and which often leads to imperial over-reach, with the consequent national humiliation which almost inevitably results—however, I would argue that the imperial element in US politics is *not* essential to the system.

In fact, the US government has shown itself often willing to cut its losses and disengage when the costs become too high. Following the disaster of Indochina, the US essentially abstained from significant ongoing military adventures for the next twenty-five years, and the interventions it did undertake—Grenada, Gulf War One, Serbia, Panama, etc.—were limited in time and/or troop involvement and were often successful. In the first Gulf War, the military and the administration even showed what in hindsight was the remarkable restraint and good sense not to pursue Saddam's troops back into Iraq. In the case of Somalia, where things were clearly going the wrong way early on, Clinton just packed up and went home, subsequently blowing up the aspirin factory to leave them something to remember us by. Similarly Reagan, when the Marine barracks in Lebanon were truck-bombed at the cost of hundreds of American lives, brought the troops home and then had the *USS New Jersey* salve the wound by shelling Syrian and Shiite positions from a safe distance at sea.

I have no doubt that as the world system expands — uprooting traditional ways of life around the globe, depleting resources, and destroying the environment, unleashing a massive population boom in the Third World, reducing the living standards of working people in the First World and creating an increasingly complex and fragile international financial system to sustain itself — it will continue to generate deep crisis and conflict. Overall, however, I think that the elites are far more flexible and much more likely to be able to survive those crises which do arise than your view allows. As I have argued before, only when a movement arises that takes advantage of the opportunities such crises offer will we be able to contemplate the end of the current globalist order.

Two

"The combination of capital has created for [the workers] a common situation, common interests. This mass is thus already a class as against capital, but not yet for itself. In the struggle . . . this mass becomes united, and constitutes itself as a class for itself."
— Karl Marx

Argument of John Schneider

As I mentioned in an earlier email, during the three or so decades from the middle 1950s to the 1980s, the system weathered a storm with many similarities to today's — heightened racial conflict, failed presidencies (Johnson, Nixon, and Carter), military defeat and humiliation abroad, economic stagnation accompanied by unprecedented levels of inflation at home, the oil crisis, seemingly irresolvable conflict in the Middle East, the initiation of terrorist acts against the West, the widespread discrediting of the political class, and an intense culture war.

At home social tensions reached levels not seen since the Great Depression. While the conflict and disruption caused by minorities and the Left are too well-known to repeat here, contrary to current nostalgic accounts, at the time there was real fear that these threatened the very foundations of order.

Although in popular myth the political story of these decades centers on the challenges posed by the counter-culture and the civil rights/black power movement, in fact these years also saw the birth and growth of vital movements of the populist Right across the country. Generally, these movements are now treated as comic-book examples of reprehensible prejudice, serving merely to emphasize the continuing need for the affirmative action regime. At best, they are dismissed as examples of white "backlash."

The story of Dixie's "massive resistance" to desegregation is well-known, but is of less relevance today than are the struggles which took place outside of the deep South. Beginning as early as the 1940s, urban white ethnic communities resisted the remaking of their neighborhoods, which was taking place through a combination of social engineering and black migration. Through the 1950s this resistance often took the form of youth and gang violence in neighborhoods and high schools, as well as in contested public spaces such as amusement parks and public beaches, leading to clashes such as the 1956 Crystal Beach riot near Buffalo, NY. (See Victoria W. Wolcott, "Recreation and Race in the Postwar City: Buffalo's 1956 Crystal Beach Riot," *Journal of American History*, vol. 93, no. 1, June 2006.)

By the 1960s and '70s, in the face of mounting urban criminality, the massive destruction caused by the cycle of Northern race riots which began in 1964, and state efforts to force integration on unwilling white communities via fair housing laws, busing, and the construction of public housing in middle class and blue collar neighborhoods, whites began organizing large and sometimes successful grassroots resistance movements. These included organizations such as Anthony Imperiale's North Ward Citizens' Council, founded in the wake of the 1967 Newark riots, Boston's ROAR (Restore Our Alienated Rights), which waged a mass resistance campaign against forced busing in Boston in the 1970s, and, in the San Francisco Bay Area, the United School Parents, which was able to seize control of the West Contra Costa County Unified School District board from the liberal pro-busing majority in 1969.

At the national level, the support among blue collar and middle class voters in the north and west for George Wallace's presidential campaigns in 1968 and 1972 shocked political observers. In the 1968 election Wallace won almost ten million votes and carried five states, showing that a break with the two-party system was indeed possible.

Meanwhile, a parallel grassroots movements around social and cultural issues began to grow, gathering strength in the '70s, as insurgent groups organized in hundreds of communities around resistance to the introduction of books such as rapist Eldridge Cleaver's *Soul on Ice* into high school libraries and syllabi. Across the country concerned parents battled multiculturalist educrats for control of their children's education. At the same time, resistance to the ERA and abortion mobilized tens of thousands more, causing liberals everywhere to fret over the supposed threat of theocracy.

By the 1980s, however, the system had re-established its equilibrium. As far as the black community was concerned, its elites and middle class were bought off by having political control of many urban areas ceded to them and through the institution of affirmative action policies in business, the government bureaucracy, and educational institutions. Meanwhile, the black masses were pacified by a continued flow of welfare and other government subsidies, as well as trickle-down patronage from black-controlled state and local governments.

Whites on the other hand continued to abandon urban areas with sizable black populations. The defeat of efforts to extend bussing and desegregation into the suburbs in the 1970s allowed the creation of "Whitopias" across the country. In 1990 the US was as residentially segregated as it had been before the civil rights movement began.

The election of a fiscally conservative president in the person of Ronald Reagan helped keep taxes low enough and this—together with the liquidation of most American military adventures around the world, a stabilization in the international oil trade, an end to inflation, and the return of economic prosperity—made whites feel like everything was "just fine." Affirmative action remained an irritant but really didn't affect most people directly and, as for the cities, who really wanted to live in Detroit or Newark anyway? Further, with a good conservative like Reagan in the White House, the culture war seemed well on the way to being won by the good guys.

Indeed, without the demographic transformation now underway, this resolution might arguably have been a reasonable and pragmatic way to neutralize the racial tensions which had been building for decades.

The accommodation of the past twenty-five years, however, is clearly in the process of breaking down. For blacks and the now more numerous Latinos, playing the role of junior partners is becoming increasingly unacceptable. Further, their commitment to the affirmative action/welfare state's entitlements is unwavering, regardless of the system's inability to support an increasingly large population of "clients" on the same terms as when they were a small minority.

For whites, the conjunctural economic recession, coupled with the country's long-term economic decline, threatens the continually increasing standard of living, which allowed them to ignore their common concerns while pursuing individual prosperity. Further, with the shrinking white population, whites, as the most productive sector of the population, will be subject to an increasingly onerous tax burden, as the minority population which in 1970 was only about 15 percent of the population grows to 50 percent and beyond.

Meanwhile, the affirmative action regime will need to become increasingly severe in order to maintain the officially-mandated diversity levels, leading to ever-harsher discrimination against qualified whites. Finally, last century's strategy of white flight to the suburbs and beyond will almost certainly break down in the face of the simple numbers of non-whites, in addition to federal and state governments which may be as hostile to the currently-existing *de facto* segregation as they were to the *de jure* regime of fifty years ago.

Overlaying this process will be the ever more aggressive implementation of the elites' anti-Christian, anti-traditional social agenda. There is every reason to believe that once the Democrats achieve a safe majority — as they have done in California — there will be no limit to the state-sponsored assault on traditional values and their defenders.

Up to now, Middle American whites held enough power by virtue of their numbers to ensure that the federal and most state governments would continue to put limits on the affirmative action regime and at least pay lip service to defending such traditional institutions as marriage and the family. It is clear, however, that, if it has not already vanished, this veto power is rapidly evaporating and in another decade or so will be gone entirely. By mid-century, we will simply be one more competing minority group.

So the question to be faced by all of us — racially conscious conservatives, identitarian anti-system Rightists (like myself), and White Nationalists is: If we can't just sit back and wait for the *deux ex machina* of the catastrophe to bring the system down, then what is to be done?

The task, I think, is twofold. In the first place, grassroots populist resistance movements must be fostered everywhere. As the pressure on them mounts, whites will almost certainly respond as they did between 1955 and 1980, by turning to political activism.

Indeed, the seemingly spontaneous growth of resistance activities around the country is already an encouraging development. The Tea Party movement, in spite of its largely brain-dead leadership, is a particularly exciting phenomenon. While its traditional American libertarian line is a real negative, the NAACP and the commentators of the Left are fundamentally correct about its racial character, since it represents the beginnings of an refusal on the part of whites to pay ever-higher taxes to support the ethnic spoils system and those social engineering projects which threaten to grow out of control once the Democrats really take permanent control of the federal government and the Supreme Court — as they already have done here in California — with predictable results.

Events in Arizona and across the country around immigration control are similarly exciting, especially as the federal government steps in and attempts to reverse the democratic will of the people.

It's time, then, for the conscious anti-system elements to get up from behind their keyboards and learn to think and act *politically*—to descend into the streets, not simply to encourage the growth of these movements, but also to contribute to their political content and work to ensure that they are not once again absorbed and betrayed by the elite politicians of the GOP.

The most valuable victory at this point will simply be the re-creation of American whites as a people *for* itself—as a people that militantly refuses to accept the denigration of themselves and their history, the destruction of their values and culture, the continuation of the anti-white discrimination that goes by the name of affirmative action, and the extortion of taxes to pay for the racial spoils system known as the American welfare state. The most likely way in which this will happen is precisely through the waging of the struggle itself.

The more such a movement gains in strength, the more likely it is that the system's contradictions will be intensified and the more likely it is that some political break will occur. The form of that break and what will emerge from it is impossible to say and pointless to predict—but, regardless, now is the time to take the first steps.

Looking at the existing political resources can be discouraging, but I really believe, as I said to you today, that we're in a position potentially similar to that of the Left in the late 1950s. What remains of the traditional hard Right movements is as generally useless (and even embarrassing) as were the remnants of the CP and SP in those days. Yet, beneath the surface, there was a ferment underway which was able to create a powerful New Left in less than a decade. I think that we, on the Right, have entered a similar age.

RESPONSE OF MICHAEL O'MEARA

John, this is unconcealing (as Heidegger would say) in its overview of the last few decades. Your emphasis on the changing nature of the affirmative-action regime, as it responds to

demographic developments, is particularly good in demon-
strating how the system is beginning to undermine itself.

There are, however, several minor points I would contest, for
they impinge on our larger differences about the present crisis.

First off, I believe this crisis is qualitatively different from
that of the 1970s — that it is, indeed, a terminal crisis. It's true,
as you claim, that in this earlier period there was also a sense of
general decline — "Carter's malaise" — and that racial/cultural
tensions were becoming threatening.

The problems of the '70s may have resurfaced, but because
the general context is so much different from that decade, it
makes these problems qualitatively more serious — and potentially system destroying.

Internationally, the '70s were a decade of humiliating defeat
(Vietnam), lost prestige, and retreat — as the Soviet Union
(which would collapse in the next decade) seemed to be over-
taking the US almost everywhere. The economy was in a slump
and the culture wars of the '60s still simmered. There's no
question that this was experienced as a bleak period for the US.
But no major restructuration of the global order occurred
(though movement was mounting in the Global South to challenge US hegemony). The Cold War *status quo* nevertheless
prevailed, even if the US was forced to retreat here and there.

What has changed since then is the collapse of the Soviet
Union, the advent of unipolarity (which the neocons used to
justify their militarily aggressive empire building in the Middle
East), mass Third World colonization of the First World, and
the devastating economics of globalization. These changes —
whose implications have been world-shattering — are creating a
situation which, I believe, will lead to breaks in the system,
through whose cracks a new global *nomos* will emerge in which
US hegemony becomes a thing of the past.

This will affect the dollar's role as the world's reserve currency and, domestically, add thick new layers of economic
complication to the system's ability to meet its various domestic obligations and pursue its imperial crusades abroad. At
some not-too-distant point these strains are likely to become
unbearable, causing the system (which is already worn out,

dysfunctional, and beset by boondoggles of ever more colossal proportions) to implode.

My view of Ronald Reagan also differs from yours. Yes, he paraded as a fiscal conservative and a defender of traditional values. But, in my mind, this was part of his administration's neoliberal window-dressing. Up to Reagan, Roosevelt's old Social Democratic system, with its labor-management partnership, still prevailed. In cahoots with the insufferable Iron Maiden, Reagan helped dismantle this regime, which had begun to economically stagnate in the '70s, and introduced the neoliberal principles ("supply-side economics") that would deregulate everything and enthrone financial capital: with its globalist ambitions, its maniacal privatizations, its multifront offensive on popular living standards—and the floodgates it opened to Third World immigration.

As Reagan's "conservatism" supplanted notions of the public good with the primacy of the profit motive, it could not but create a social-economic situation, whose market priorities lent themselves to the moral transvaluations and anti-white policies of the Left's Cultural Revolution. Not coincidentally, the social permissiveness of the '60s' anti-materialist hippies gave way to the social permissiveness of the materialist yuppies. It's my impression that even the best conservatives (like Pat Buchanan) still refuse to acknowledge that the other side of Reagan's "market-friendly" policies was a hedonistic consumerism.

I also don't think the Right today is in an analogous situation to the Left of the late '50s—except to the degree that the anti-system forces will need to go through a metamorphosis as significant as that which produced the so-called New Left in the early '60s.

Given America's liberal creedal foundations, the country has always been inherently disposed to "progressive" politics; the Left simply needed to find a way to intersect this disposition, which wasn't too difficult, given that it had already seduced the country's largest cohort group: the TV-educated baby boomers.

By contrast, the present establishment Right, as well as a good deal of the so-called "alternative" and racially-conscious

Right, has, in fact, yet to break with the underlining premises of liberal modernity, especially in its overarching fixation on the economy and its identification with the indefatigable individualism of its Protestant culture and market values.

Ideologically and culturally, virtually all the anti-system forces (including that peculiar cyber tendency which calls itself "White Nationalism") seems congenitally unable to think outside the parameters of the country's liberal Protestant heritage.

A metapolitically-armed Right, I suspect, may possibly (hopefully) emerge from the coming anti-system struggles, but not *vice versa*, as is happening in Europe.

Such an American New Right, if it is to succeed, will, moreover, have to privilege its European heritage or else it will constitute no Right at all. For above all the one thing we seek to conserve amidst the reigning nihilism is the biocultural heritage we inherited from our *patria, Magna Europa.* Indeed, once we recognize that we are an outgrowth of European civilization and that America was no gift of Yahweh (as those Protestant Bolsheviks of the 17th century thought), then perhaps we will finally escape the Americanist ideology that sees the country as somehow free of those historical and cultural restraints which affect other peoples—for it's history and culture, or rather the denial of history and culture, that are, I believe, at the heart of the crisis afflicting not just American, but Western Civilization.

This gets me to my final point. You speak of American whites creating themselves "as a people *for* themselves"—assuming that they already exist as a people "in itself." This Marxist principle—which holds that the objective existence of "a class *in itself*" is historically insignificant until it becomes "a class *for itself*" (i.e., self-consciously ready to assert itself)—was, of course, crucial to the development of the great labor and nationalist movements of the last century and a half. I fully accept the importance you attribute to this process. Nevertheless, in my understanding of US history, it's never been possible to speak of white America as a nation in the European sense.

This is not simply because American identity was historically more racial and ideological than ethnic, but also because the particular evolution of the American "people" was such that the country never experienced the centuries-long ethnogenesis that goes into organically forming a self-conscious nation.

In fact, I would argue that only today, for the first time in US history, the challenge European Americans face presents them with a significant "Other" — the non-white hordes crossing our borders — and thus with the potential to discover, in opposition, who they are.

The truths unconcealed in this struggle, like earlier labor struggle against the bosses, cannot but help European Americans to recognize and affirm the blood-culture that distinguishes them from the non-whites presently representing America's officially designated future.

The battles that lie ahead may therefore possibly make our people more conscious of themselves as a "people" and of the necessity to act "for themselves." This is the way nations arose in the past — as tribal confederations settled conquered lands, growing, under the auspices of their shared myths and struggles, into a single people.

If such a national awakening should occur in the ensuing struggles, perhaps then we'll see the emergence of an American nation — "for itself" — reborn as a nativist offshoot of the European "nation" from which we Americans take our primordial identity.

The type of grassroots and populist struggles, which white people are now beginning to wage, constitute, as you argue, the central arena for all who care to participate in the key political movement of our time.

My quibbling with you here is just a roundabout way of saying that your persuasive argument helps me better understand how the Tea Party will find its way toward the Whiskey Rebellion.

REPLY OF JOHN SCHNEIDER

Your latest response treats so many major questions in such a provocative way that a proper response would take far more space than we have here, so I will limit myself to a few observations.

Regarding the challenges facing our elites at present and in the near future, I think that we both recognize that the system under which we live has survived similar crises in the past. We also agree that the trials it will undergo in the coming period will take place in a context that makes the solutions of the past much less viable. We differ, however, in our evaluation of how likely the powers-that-be will be able to "keep it together" and thereby avoid potentially fatal systemic crises. *Contra* your view, I continue to believe that the elites are probably sufficiently flexible and creative to endure, unless some political agent is able to intervene successfully.

As far as your evaluation of the Reagan era is concerned, I essentially agree with your assessment. I described him above as a "good conservative" in part ironically, but I also would argue, giving him credit for sincerity, that his presidency precisely demonstrates the utter failure of that variant of classical liberalism which poses as conservatism in this country.

In discussing the parallels between the late '50s and today I did not mean to indicate that there is an identity between the two periods. I do believe, however, that like the late '50s/early '60s, when a mass New Left seemed to spring out of nowhere and in the process transcend both the establishment and the alternative institutions of the traditional Left, there is a similar possibility that such a movement of the Right could arise in the coming years.

Like you, I recognize that the current institutions and discourses of both the mainstream and the alternative Right are woefully inadequate—especially in the stubborn insistence across almost the entire spectrum of the Right in clinging to the very ideology, liberal individualism, which lies at the core of the current order. This too, however, is not so different from the position of the Left fifty years ago. The Democratic Party then was completely committed to a Cold War liberalism which would become one of the main targets of the New Left, while the existing organizations of the old Left were in decline and disarray.

I acknowledge, of course, that there are important differences as well. The most important of these, however—and the one which makes clear just how much more difficult our task will be than that of the New Left—lies in the distinction between our movement and theirs as social phenomena. The movements of the 1960s, for all their radical bluster, essentially represented a rebellion by one sector of the elite against another—it was more a matter of the system's growing pains. As you wrote of France's *soixante-huitards* in *New Culture, New Right*:

> Retrospectively, the French student rebellion of May 1968 appears to have been less a revolutionary challenge to the liberal order, which it seemed at the time, than a radical spur to its ongoing subversions. . . . While spouting the revolutionary teachings of Mao Tse-tung or extolling the heroism of Che Guevara, [the student radicals] displayed an occasional idealism. But this was mostly the gloss of an individualism whose anti-authoritarian and hedonistic impetus constituted less a revolt against postwar society, as Herbert Marcuse thought, than a youthful assertion of its underlying tenets. . . . Thus, instead of assailing the socioeconomic structures of bourgeois society, the May Events actually sought the final liberal triumph over whatever "obscurantist" traditionalisms still lingered in European life . . .

Because it did not really challenge the capitalist system—it merely completed the bourgeois revolutions which started hundreds of years ago—the Left's counterculture easily established its hegemony in the decades after the '60s.

Our task, by contrast, will be much more difficult because it will be a truly oppositional one. In insisting on the specific, the organic, and the permanent, we will fundamentally oppose the global, atomized, and soulless "culture of appetite" (E. Michael Jones) which is the natural product of mass consumption capitalism.

Whether we succeed or not (and what "succeeding" actually means) is less important than simply waging the struggle, since the struggle itself is what will make us a people *for ourselves*.

Counter-Currents/*North American New Right*,
August 30 & 31, 2010

PAN-EUROPEAN PRESERVATIONISM

TED SALLIS

As a long-time "pan-Europeanist," I have read a number of critiques of pan-Europeanism focused on that ideology's alleged opposition to the preservation of differences that exist between various European peoples. Further, it is said that pan-Europeanism believes that all whites are identical and interchangeable; therefore, the pan-European worldview has been viewed as fundamentally incompatible with intra-European ethnoracial activism. These critics do not distinguish between a pan-Europeanism that does value, and wishes to preserve, intra-European differences and a more panmictic version of pan-Europeanism that does not.

I would argue that—at least theoretically—a person can be, at the same time, both pan-Europeanist and Nordicist, or pan-Europeanism and pan-Slavist, pan-Germanist, ethnic nationalist, etc., so long as the all the latter "ists" in question are of a "defensive" nature, and that the pan-Europeanism respects and values narrower particularisms. Of course, even if this is true, it is natural to expect that certain levels of ethnic interests[1] would be more important to an activist than others (e.g., a Russian may be a Russian nationalist first, a pan-Slavist second, and a pan-Europeanist third).

More importantly, even if this melding of activist identities does not often occur in the real world, it should, at minimum, be possible for individuals identifying themselves solely as pan-European or Nordicist or pan-Slavic or pan-German or

---

[1] Michael Rienzi, "Pan-European Genetic Interests, Ethno-States, Kinship Preservation, and the End of Politics," *The Occidental Quarterly*, vol. 3, no. 1 (Spring 2003): 31–43.

Basque nationalist-separatist or English/British nationalist to productively and respectfully work together to achieve common objectives, even if there are important points of disagreement remaining between them. Indeed, a British nationalist had the following comments on this subject:

> I think it is perfectly feasible for a British Nationalist to have a hierarchy of levels within which he or she operates and thinks when it comes to the rest of the world around us and its structure and integrity. Ethno British Nationalism need not conflict to any severe degree with racial nationalism as I see it to be, because I don't believe "racial nationalism" seeks to forge the ties mentioned above, just care for and preserve our fellow Nationalists and European peoples by supporting their right to do what we are trying to do.
>
> A calm and rational approach to looking after ourselves first whilst keeping an eye out and an interest in (and a support to) our European counterparts and the order of the world around us is no bad thing in my view, but yes, of course, we have to be careful of what others commonly perceive the definitions to be, and ensure that we split off what to me is "traditional" Nationalism from anything that aims to go further than that.
>
> Does caring about their plight and the wider European nation states and the dwindling European racial presence on planet Earth make me somehow beyond the pale or some wild extremist or supremacist? I do not believe so.[2]

This is reasonable, and stands in contrast to certain British National Party operatives who believe that any concern for the broader race *must* be detrimental to ethnic nationalism. The

---

[2] Independent British Nationalist, "What's in a name? Perhaps some confusion, even on my part," March 7, 2010, http://independent-british-nationalist.blogspot.com/2010/03/whats-in-name-perhaps-some-confusion.html/

opposite is more likely, since a nationalist Britain will more se-cure in a European, white Europe, and infinitely less secure as a lone white island in a continental sea of color.

Although we should never let the opponents of preserva-tionism define us, it is still interesting that "divide and con-quer" is a tactic used against nationalists. One suspects that our opponents would most dread the varied European peoples coming to an agreement on fundamental interests, to work to-gether for Western survival.

Indeed, if we reach the point in which Basque separatists can work with Spanish nationalists, Irish Republican national-ists with Ulster Protestant Unionists, Padanian separatists with Ausonian nationalists, Flemish separatists with Wallonian na-tionalists, Hungarian nationalists with their Romanian coun-terparts, pan-Slavists with pan-Germanists, and American pan-Europeanists with American Nordicists—all in the cause of white, Western survival—this will be a development which will give the enemies of white, Western survival cause for grave concern.

Perhaps pan-Europeanism is best viewed as a flexible meme and not as a rigid set of specific polices; it generally promotes the idea of mutual respect among the varied European peoples, and therefore attempts to search for solutions that will allow for the biological and cultural preservation of all Europeans worldwide.

Pan-Europeanism asserts that all persons of European de-scent should have a "seat at the table" when decisions are made about the fate of the West and its peoples. Pan-Europeanism, properly considered, can be consistent and com-patible with concerns about narrower ingroups: Nordicism, pan-Slavism, pan-Germanism, or whatever ethnic or subracial nationalism one wishes to consider.

What pan-Europeanism introduces to these other ideologies is an additional concern for the broader European family. What if an individual does not care about the broader family of Eu-ropeans, and has an interest solely in his ethnic group or sub-race? There is certainly nothing inherently wrong with that;

everyone has the right to define the limits of his ingroup as he sees fit, and invest in that defined ingroup as is appropriate.

However, the purpose of this essay is not to proselytize, but rather to explain how a specific strain of pan-Europeanism is compatible with the preservation of narrower particularisms, and to place the history of pan-Europeanism within the context of the overarching objectives of "White Nationalism." I will start with the issue of ethnic interchangeability and panmixia, and move on to an examination of other facets of pan-Europeanism, including a very brief historical survey.

INTERCHANGEABILITY & PANMIXIA

One meme asserts that pan-Europeanism means that all whites are "fungible/interchangeable." I do not believe that most responsible pan-Europeanists hold that view. I certainly do not. I believe in a mixture of racial conservationism—making certain that extant ethnoracial stocks are preserved in significant numbers in specific territorial states—and racial palingenesis—which supports eugenics as well as the acceptance of new, stabilized Euro-breeds that may occur in the European Diaspora and that can constitute new ethnies and expand the range of European-specific genetic and phenotypic biological diversity.

When the two ideas are in conflict, racial conservatism trumps racial palingenesis, since the original stocks, once lost, can never be recovered. Hybridization, if it occurs in Diaspora regions, should be carefully monitored so as to create productive new stabilized strains while, at the same time, not resulting in the elimination of parental stocks. This pan-Europeanism, which values and wishes to preserve intra-European differences, can be contrasted to other viewpoints.

One can occasionally encounter a more panmictic vision of pan-Europeanism. For example, in his otherwise useful and interesting preface to Norman Lowell's important book *Imperium Europa*, Constantin von Hoffmeister writes:

The mixing of different European nationalities should

therefore be encouraged. We must support sexual unions between Russian women and German men, Spanish men and Swedish women. Only by radically breaking down the artificial barriers dividing Europe can we create the new breed of man . . .[3]

Von Hoffmeister's overall pan-European vision is positive, I agree with much of it, and he should be commended for his support of Norman Lowell, who is a real fighter for our race and our civilization. However, I do not agree with the specific viewpoint quoted here, which does not represent the totality of pan-Europeanist thought. I believe that we should not be in the business of encouraging mating between Russians, Germans, Swedes, Spaniards, or any other groups within Europe. One could imagine Russian, German, Swedish, and Spanish nationalists — people who may otherwise agree to the basic premises of pan-Europeanism — objecting quite strongly to the idea of a general panmixia involving their respective peoples.

We already have here in America an experiment in intra-European cross-breeding, which may produce productive and useful stabilized blends — all at relatively minimal costs to ethnic genetic interests due to the relative genetic closeness of Europeans. However, responsible stewardship of our ethnoracial-genetic patrimony requires that we at least maintain the original ethnic stocks in their European homelands. If these stocks are completely hybridized out of existence, the loss would be permanent and irreversible. I do not believe that the genetic diversity that currently characterizes the extant European ethnies should be lost; while additional stocks and additional diversity may be created in the Diaspora through cross-ethnic mating and breed stabilization, the original genetic strains of Europe need to be preserved.

Indeed, it is wrong to completely erase *any* legitimate differences between peoples, including groups that are relatively

---

[3] Constantin von Hoffmeister, "Our Motherland: Imperium Europa," in Norman Lowell, *Imperium Europa: The Book that Changed the World* (Imperium Publishing, 2008), 24.

highly related: Norwegians and Swedes are not interchangeable, Englishmen and Danes are not interchangeable, Germans
and the Dutch are not interchangeable, Italians and Greeks are
not interchangeable, Spaniards and Portuguese are not interchangeable, and Russians and Poles are not interchangeable.
And while the differences between the major subraces are certainly greater than that between groups within each subrace,
one cannot draw a line within Europe and say that one group
of differences are *completely* inconsequential, and another
group of differences are *absolutely* essential. At the intra-
continental level, it is a difference of degree. This can be contrasted to the wider gulf that exists between continental
groups, differences that are magnified, in a synergistic fashion,
by the overlay of the great civilizational divides.

In summary, pan-Europeanism is an ideology which respects, strives to preserve, and fights for the interests
of, *all* peoples of European descent worldwide—whether these
peoples are of single ethnic origin or if they are of "combina-
tive" ethnic European ancestry. There is nothing in this definition which asserts that panmixia must take place and certainly
nothing which can be characterized as a lack of interest in preserving various ethnies (keeping in mind, of course, that "ethny" is not always the same as "ethnic group"). To say that pan-
Europeanists *in general* do not see an intrinsic value in individual ethnic groups is simply not true. Thus I argue against the
assertion that pan-Europeanism means that all whites are
"fungible" and "interchangeable" and that this will lead to a
panmixia resulting in a complete loss of biological and cultural
particularisms. Instead, pan-Europeanism is better viewed as a
cooperative effort, aimed toward the objective of Race-Culture
preservation and renewal, an effort that recognizes both the
differences and the commonalities of Western peoples.

History

A brief history of pan-European racial nationalism is summarized below, to contrast to some assertions concerning the
origins of pan-European racial nationalism.

Pre-WWII pan-Europeanism had a varied pedigree, including of course Nietzsche's call to be a "good European," and the thoughts of individuals such as William Penn, Napoleon Bonaparte, Victor Hugo, and Giuseppe Mazzini—all focused on a pan-Europeanism that would preserve the diversity of the European peoples within the large context of unity. What about more recent pan-Europeanism?

In *Dreamer of the Day*,[4] Kevin Coogan describes one strand of pan-European thought that originated from competing visions within National Socialist (NS) Germany. Coogan identifies two SS factions: the so-called *völkisch*, Germanic, Nordicist "Black SS" whose ideology was based on the work of Hans F. K. Günther; and the pan-European, pan-Aryan "Waffen SS" faction led by SS Brigadier General Franz Alfred Six, SS Lieutenant General Werner Best, and SS Colonel Alfred Franke-Gricksch.

For most of the NS regime, the "Black SS" was dominant; however, after Stalingrad, the need for a pan-European crusade against Bolshevism, as well as a growing realization that the war may be lost and the groundwork for a post-war movement needed to be begun, led to a shift in power to the pan-European SS faction.

One consequence of this change in emphasis was the "rehabilitation" within the SS of the Italian theorist Julius Evola, who was recruited into the Germans' pan-European program. The Italian connection to this German-dominated movement also leads us to consider Mussolini's contributions; for example, before he fell into Hitler's orbit, Il Duce promoted such activities as the pan-European "pan-Fascist" Montreux conference of 1934. In addition, in his last years, during the Italian Social Republic, Mussolini promoted the idea of a unified and socialist/fascist (western) Europe.

After the war, a number of individuals and groups continued to promote a pan-European fascist/racial nationalist perspective. Francis Parker Yockey of course comes to mind, as does Oswald Mosley, with his "Europe a Nation" idea. Indeed, the

---

[4] Kevin Coogan, *Dreamer of the Day: Francis Parker Yockey and the Postwar Fascist International* (Brooklyn: Autonomedia, 1999).

following description of Mosley's ideas is of relevance, stressing as it does the fundamental point that a larger scale interest in Europe as a whole does not preclude narrower, national-ethny interests:

In October 1948—the dangerous year of Stalin's blockade of Berlin—Mosley spoke to an enthusiastic meeting of East London workers and called for "the making of Europe a Nation." Yet, as he said in later years, *making Europe into a nation with its own common government did not make him feel any less an Englishman, and an Englishman of Staffordshire where he was born. All other Europeans, Normans and Bretons, Bavarians and Prussians, Neapolitans and Milanese, would through his idea remain Frenchmen, Germans, and Italians, as would Britons remain Britons, yet they would all think and act together as Europeans.*

In those later years he also proposed a three-tier order of governments in Europe, each with a different function. In fact this was taking the best part of the old fascism, the corporate state, and the best of the old democracy, creating something higher and finer than either, through yet another synthesis. The corporate state had envisaged the nation like a human body, having a head, with a brain, with all members of the body working together in political harmony. Thus in Mosley's vision of the future nation of Europe the first tier, the head, would be a common government—freely elected by all Europeans—for Europe's defense and to organize a single continental economy. The second tier would be national governments for all national questions—elected as today—and at the third level many local governments for the regions and small nations like Wales and Scotland. They would have the special task of *preserving the wide diversity of Europe's cultural life*: regional democracy with a new meaning.

Mosley's concept of Europe thus went much further than the present "European Community" and was a direct contrast with it, replacing the national jealousies and economic rivalry of today's "common market" with an essential harmony. "Europe a Nation" included the whole life of the continent from the head organizing a single economy down to the many cultures of Europe. It was perhaps his greatest concept: a new order of governments giving a new meaning to democracy, to be achieved through a synthesis of those two old opponents, pre-war fascism and pre-war democracy.[5]

The journal *Nation Europa*, founded by Arthur Ehrhardt and Herbert Boehme, with support from Swedish far-Rightist Per Engdahl, also strongly promoted a pan-European "Mosleyite" agenda. Coogan discusses other theorists and activists, but it is well established that modern pan-European racial nationalism in Europe has a pedigree going back to the attempts of pre-war, and war-era, (real) fascists and "fascists" to develop an ideology beyond that of narrow single-state nationalism.

In America, before the war, Lothrop Stoddard in *Re-forging America* argued for assimilation of the "white ethnics" and the need for white solidarity against the rising tide of color. Similarly, Charles Lindbergh, in a famous pre-war essay on aviation and race stated:

> We, the heirs of European culture, are on the verge of a disastrous war, a war within our own family of nations, a war which will reduce the strength and destroy the treasures of the White race, a war which may even lead to the end of our civilization. And while we stand poised for battle, Oriental guns are turning westward, Asia presses towards us on the Russian border, all foreign races stir restlessly. It is time to turn from our quarrels and to build our White ramparts again. This alliance with foreign races means nothing but death to us. It is our turn to guard our heritage from Mongol and Persian and Moor, before we become engulfed in a limitless for-

---

[5] Friends of Oswald Mosley, "Oswald Mosley, Briton, Fascist, European," http://www.oswaldmosley.com/briton-fascist-european.htm (emphasis added).

eign sea. Our civilization depends on a united strength among ourselves; on strength too great for foreign armies to challenge; on a Western Wall of race and arms which can hold back either a Genghis Khan or the infiltration of inferior blood; on an English fleet, a German air force, a French army, an American nation, standing together as guardians of our common heritage, sharing strength, dividing influence.[6]

Other factors leading to a pan-European White Nationalism in America include the assimilation of the aforementioned "white ethnics"; the "civil rights movement" which counterposed general white interests with those of Negroes, Levantines, and other "colored" groups; and the mass post-1965 immigration which even more sharply contrasted the differences between white Americans, derived from the Western civilization, and the hordes of others.

A useful simplification suggests that in Europe (where ethnic, single-state nationalism is still a potent force) pan-Europeanism was initially a top-down phenomenon theorized by "far-Right elites," while in America, it has been predominantly characterized by "bottom-up" growth due to "white ethnic" assimilation coupled to a growing and increasingly militant colored populace. Today's global pan-Europeanism, joining like-minded activists in Europe and the European Diaspora, is the result of a convergence of these European and American trends.

The growing race/immigration/Islamic problem in Europe, concerns about Turkey in the EU, along with the understandable reaction to the two World Wars and the consequences of intra-European hostility, has led a growth in "bottom-up" pan-Europeanism in Europe; while the increasing theoretical depth of American White Nationalism, and the recognition that America's race problem is of global scope, has led to increased "top-down" pan-Europeanism in the Diaspora. This conver-

---

[6] Charles Lindbergh, "Aviation, Geography, and Race," *Readers Digest* (1939), http://library.flawlesslogic.com/lindy.htm

gence, over time, may lead to increased integration between European and Euro-American pan-European nationalists.

From a very broad, sweeping historical perspective, Charlemagne, the Holy Roman Empire, Napoleon, Mussolini, and even Hitler, can be viewed as attempts to restore the earlier unity of the Roman Empire; in other words, these were attempts to build a new empire of the West. For centuries in the *modern* historical era, Latin was the common language of educated people throughout the West. Orders like the Knights Hospitallers were drawn from various nations of Western Europe, together fighting for Europe and the West. And the contribution of our eastern European brothers to the defense of the West is also a fact of history (e.g., Poles vs. Turks at Vienna). That the theme of Western Unity has existed as an undercurrent throughout Europe since the birth of the modern "Western" or "Faustian" High Culture cannot be denied.

Also of relevance are Greg Johnson's comments at the Counter-Currents website:

> If you go back far enough in history, you find times, such as the high Middle Ages, when there was a sense of the unity of the European race. Petty state nationalism is a far more modern phenomenon. . . . During the high Middle Ages, *there was a sense of European Unity as "Christendom" that was not explicitly racial but was implicitly so.* The first Crusade in particular was an expression of this sense of unity. Of course even then Christianity was not coextensive with the European race, for there were Nestorian and Arab and African Christians, but the average European did not know that.
>
> If you go back even farther, you find the essential genetic unity of all European peoples. The concept of "whiteness" today can be seen as an attempt to recapture that essential unity. . . . In North America, Australia, New Zealand, and South Africa, the mixing of recently differentiated European stocks is bringing us back to that original unity.

> Whiteness also is natural as a unifying concept in the face of non-whites, particularly in the colonies. . . . In the end, though, the political validity of the concept of whiteness has nothing to do with its temporal pedigree, but with the fact that all whites are perceived by our enemies as essentially the same, thus we are treated as the same. *Our skin is our uniform in the global struggle for domination.*[7]

Which is an effective summary of the fundamental thesis of the current essay.

This historical survey is not meant as an "appeal to authority"; the pan-European idea should today be evaluated on its own merits. However, it is important to contrast the actual historical background with contrary assertions that modern pan-Europeanism is merely the recent invention of ethnically self-interested activists narrowly derived from specific areas of Europe (e.g., Norman Lowell has been unfairly criticized in this regard). Whether or not one agrees with pan-Europeanism, the origins of this worldview have strong roots throughout Europe (at least, Western Europe), and individuals of varied ethnic/subracial European ancestries have championed the idea throughout the centuries — and, in some cases, like the knightly orders, put the idea into practice.

CULTURE, CIVILIZATION, YOCKEY, & SOME BIOLOGY

One thread which is often prominent in modern pan-European thought is the work of its foremost post-war proponent: Francis Parker Yockey. It is therefore important to take a brief look at some of Yockey's relevant statements on this issue.

In *The Proclamation of London* Yockey wrote:

> From the beginning, the Western Culture has been a spiritual unit. This basic, universally formative fact is in

---

[7] Greg Johnson, "Explicit White Nationalism," October 2010, http://www.counter-currents.com/2010/10/explicit-white-nationalism/(emphasis added).

the sharpest contrast to the shallow and ignorant outlook of *those who pretend that the unity of the West is a new idea*, a technical thing which can only be brought about on a limited and conditional basis.

From its very birth-cry in the Crusades, the Western Culture had one State, with the Emperor at its head, one Church and religion, Gothic Christianity, with an authoritarian Pope, one race, one nation, and one people, which felt itself, and *was recognized by all outer forces, to be distinct and unitary.* There was a universal style, Gothic, which inspired and informed all art from the crafts to the cathedrals. There was one ethical code for the Culture-bearing stratum, Western chivalry, founded on a purely Western feeling of honour. There was a universal language, Latin, and a universal law, Roman law. Even in the very adoption of older, non-Western things, the West was unitary. It made such things into an expression of its proper soul, and it universalized them.

More important than anything else, this Culture felt itself to be a power-unit as against all outer forces, whether barbarians like the Slavs, Turks, and Mongols, or civilized like the Moors, Jews, and Saracens. Embryonic national differences existed even then within the West, but these differences were not felt as contrasts, and could not possibly become at that time the focus of a struggle for power. A Western knight was fighting equally for his Fatherland whether in battle against the Slav or the Turk on the Eastern Marshes of Germany, against the Moor in Spain, Italy, or Sicily, or against the Saracen in the Levant. The outer forces recognized as well this inner unity of the West. To Islam, all Westerners whatever were lumped together as Franks, *giaours.*

This higher Cultural unity embraced within its rich possibilities the several Nation-Ideas which were to actualize so much of Western history, for it is obviously a part of the divine plan that a High Culture create as phases of its own unfolding, not only higher aesthetic units, schools of music, painting, and lyric, higher religious and philosophical units, schools of mysticism and theology, higher bodies of nature-knowledge, schools of technics and scientific research, but also higher power-units within itself, Emperor versus papacy, Estates versus Emperor and Pope, *Fronde* versus King, Nation versus Nation. In Gothic times, the intra-Cultural power struggle between Emperor and Pope was always strictly subordinated, by the universal conscience, to the outer tension with the non-member of the Culture, the barbarian and heathen. The Nations existed then, but not as power-units, not as political organisms. The members of the nations felt themselves to be different from one another, but the differences were in no case determining of the whole orientation to life. A Slavic, Turkish, or Moorish attack on Europe was met by forces drawn from all parts of Europe. . . . In this great struggle for the Liberation of Europe, *every European of race, honour, and pride belongs with us, regardless of his provenance.*[8]

And, importantly, considering the issue of preserving intra-European differences:

Local cultures in Europe may be as diversified as they wish, and they will enjoy a perfect autonomy in the European Imperium . . .

Please note that I do not agree with Yockey's oft-cited hostility toward Slavs and other eastern Europeans, for these people need to be fully integrated into the pan-European project. Preferably, the eastern Europeans can join their western brethren in the same racial-civilizational entity, but if this is not possible then at least we need to have closely linked and cooperative dual white entities, perhaps analogous to the western and east-

---

[8] Francis Parker Yockey, *The Proclamation of London*, 1949 http://home.alphalink.com.au/~radnat/fpyockey/proclamation.html (emphasis added).

ern halves of the latter Roman Empire. In any case, we are in this together. Indeed, there are those in Russia who know what is at stake and who are willing to cooperate to save white civilization; for example Dmitry Rogozin.[9]

In *Imperium* Yockey wrote, at different places throughout the book:

> If any Westerner thinks that the barbarian makes nice distinctions between the former nations of the West, he is incapable of understanding the feelings of populations outside a High Culture toward that Culture. . . .
>
> . . . But the greatest opposition of all has not yet been named, the conflict which will take up all the others into itself. This is the battle of the Idea of the Unity of the West against the nationalism of the 19th century. Here stand opposed the ideas of Empire and petty-stateism, large-space thinking and political provincialism. Here find themselves opposed the miserable collection of yesterday-patriots and the custodians of the Future. The yesterday-nationalists are nothing but the puppets of the extra-European forces who conquer Europe by dividing it. To the enemies of Europe, there must be no rapprochement, no understanding, no union of the old units of Europe into a new unit, capable of carrying on 20th century politics. . . .
>
> . . . *Against a united Europe, they could never have made their way in, and only against a divided Europe can they maintain themselves. Split! divide! distinguish! — this is the technique of conquest. Resurrect old ideas, old slogans, now quite dead, in the battle to turn European against European.* . . .
>
> . . . The touching of this racial-frontier case of the Negro, however, shows to Europe a very important fact — *that race-difference between white men, which means Western men, is vanishingly small in view of their common mission of actualizing a High Culture.* In Europe, where hitherto the

---

[9] "Interview with Dmitry Rogozin," Nov. 18, 2008. http://rt.com/Interview/2008-11-18/Interview_with_Dmitry_Rogozin.html

race difference between, say, Frenchman and Italian has been magnified to great dimensions, there has been no sufficient reminder of the race-differences outside the Western Civilization. Adequate instruction along this line would apparently have to take the form of occupation of all Europe, instead of only part of it, by Negroes from America and Africa, by Mongols and Turkestani from the Russian Empire. . . .

. . . Gothic instincts of the Western Culture are still present in the Imperium-Idea. It cannot be otherwise. Also present are the various Ideas which these instincts, within the framework of this Culture, shaped for itself, the religions, the nations, the philosophies, languages, arts and sciences. But they are present no longer as contrasts, but as mere differences.

Gone — forever gone — is any notion that one of these Ideas — national, linguistic, religious, social — has the mission of wiping out another Idea. The adherents of Empire are still distinct from the adherents of Papacy — but this distinction does not rule their minds, for uppermost now is the Idea of Imperium, the return to superpersonal origins, and both of these mighty Ideas have the same spiritual source. The difference between Protestant and Catholic — once excited into a *casus belli* — has gone the same way. Both continue to exist, but it is inconceivable that this difference could again rend the Western Civilization in twain. There have been also the racial and temperamental differences of Teuton and Latin, of North and South. Once these may have contributed to the furnishing of motives to History — this can they no longer do. Again, both are part of the West, even though different, and the Imperium-Idea monopolizes the motivation of History. . . . The former nations, the religions, the races, the classes — these are now the building-blocks of the great Imperial structure which is founding itself. Local cultural, social, linguistic, differences remain — *it is no necessity of the Imperium-Idea that it annihilate its component*

Ideas, the collective products of a thousand years of Western history. On the contrary, it affirms them all, in a higher sense it perpetuates them all, but they are in its service, and no longer in the center of History.[10]

Again, this is no "appeal to authority"; one is free to agree or disagree with Yockey's views as one sees fit. However, Yockey's views can be considered a reasonable summary of pan-Europeanism from a more historical, cultural, civilizational perspective.

So far, this discussion has emphasized culture and civilization, which was Yockey's specialty. I have often brought up biology and genetics elsewhere; here, I will briefly cite the following. In Lao *et al.*, it is reported that European genetic differentiation mirrors geography and that Europe as a whole is *relatively* genetically homogeneous:

> . . . we found only a low level of genetic differentiation between subpopulations, the existing differences were characterized by a strong continent-wide correlation between geographic and genetic distance. . . . This implies that genetic differences between extant European subpopulations can be expected to be small indeed. . . . Overall, our study showed that the autosomal gene pool in Europe is comparatively homogeneous but at the same time revealed that the small genetic differentiation that is present between subpopulations is characterized by a significant correlation between genetic and geographic distance.[11]

This view is supported by Bauchet *et al.*:

---

[10] Francis Parker Yockey ("Ulick Varange"), *Imperium* (Costa Mesa, Cal.: The Noontide Press, 1962).

[11] Lao *et al.*, "Correlation between Genetic and Geographic Structure in Europe," *Current Biology*, vol. 18, no. 16 (2008), 1241–48. PMID: 1869188

In line with previous studies, there is low apparent diversity in Europe, with the entire continent-wide sample only marginally more dispersed than single-population samples from elsewhere in the world.[12]

In other words, the extent of genetic diversity in the entire continent of Europe is in the same range as what is found within single ethnic groups of other continents. Certainly, important racial/genetic differences exist between European peoples, particularly along the north-south and east-west axes. Further, researchers can now distinguish the gene pools of quite closely related European peoples; for example, Norwegians vs. Swedes, or French, German, and Italian-speaking Swiss. All these differences are important; nevertheless, the similarities are important as well.

A pan-Europeanism that respects and preserves genetic and cultural differences, while also respecting genetic and cultural similarities, is wholly consistent with ethnic genetic interests. For example, in *On Genetic Interests*,[13] Frank Salter cites the Civilizations of Huntington[14] as possible core units of ethnic genetic interests for defense against other genetic/civilizational entities. Note that Salter speculated that Huntington's "Orthodox" eastern European bloc may be considered a subsection of the West.

In summary, Europeans are *relatively* genetically similar and share a core civilizational history. This is the fundamental foundational basis for pan-Europeanism.

BALANCING PARTICULARISMS: BROADER & NARROWER

Specifics of how to balance broader and narrower particu-

---

[12] Bauchet *et al.*, "Measuring European Population Stratification with Microarray Genotype Data," *The American Journal of Human Genetics*, vol. 80, no. 5 (2007), 948–56 doi:10.1086/513477

[13] Frank Salter, *On Genetic Interests: Family, Ethny, and Humanity in an Age of Mass Migration* (Frankfurt am Main: Peter Lang, 2003).

[14] Summarized:
http://en.wikipedia.org/wiki/The_Clash_of_Civilizations

larisms are beyond the scope of this essay. However, I point the reader to an examination of pan-European genetic interests[1] as "concentric circles" of genetic interests, which is similar to, and partially based upon an analysis of ethnic relations by Kevin MacDonald[15] as well as, of course, the work of Frank Salter.[13] MacDonald states:

> The problem, then, is how to best create strategies, including control of land areas, which promote ethnic genetic interests in the current environment. There is no precise or entirely natural way to establish the best boundaries for such an endeavor, but it certainly does not follow that such boundaries are arbitrary. It is the sort of problem that is solvable with rational choice mechanisms. For example, in the United States I propose that a grouping of people deriving from Europe, including Eastern and Southern Europe, would be far preferable to a strategy in which there were a large number of separate European groups (e.g., Danish, Scottish, English, Italian, etc.) each acting independently of the others.[16]

Similarly, there is a rational and fitness-preserving pan-East Asian strategy that would follow the same logic as that of pan-Europeanism. Therefore, this Asian strategy would in no way no suggest that the Japanese give up their national identity, or that Koreans or Chinese do the same, or that all Asians intermix and erase all distinctions; nevertheless, they *do* have fundamentally important shared interests in their larger ethnic commonality. Indeed, Asian racial militants in the USA in some cases do adopt such as pan-East Asian policy. Ethnoracial interests can always be considered from a universalist perspective; i.e., to situate particular European interests within a broader framework.

---

[15] Kevin MacDonald, "An Integrative Evolutionary Perspective on Ethnicity," *Politics and the Life Sciences,* vol. 20 no. 1 (2001), 67–79. http://www.csulb.edu/~kmacd/PLS2001-3-067.pdf

[16] Kevin MacDonald, "On the Rationality of Ethnic Conflict," http://www.kevinmacdonald.net/RubinRev.htm

I suppose that in order to build a united Euro-Western front, a pan-European compact, compromise will be necessary. For example, if US immigration policy greatly restricts Asian and African immigration, that benefits all Americans of European descent. However, if it also restricts non-"Celto-Germanic" immigration (e.g., the 1924 act[17]) that will theoretically benefit some American whites more than others (although full assimilation of these others would make the point moot). Alternatively, if it does not discriminate at all between European immigrants (e.g., pre-1924) that could disadvantage the original founding stock American population. Therefore, I believe that the "1924 immigration act" national origins approach is essentially valid, and Stoddard's demand that the earlier Euro-American population maintain control and preeminence while assimilating the later Euro-American "ethnics" is perfectly reasonable.

Of course, the fundamental threat to the interests of all Euro-Americans originates from both elite non-Western groups (e.g., those of Asiatic origin) coupled with a mass of alien lower types (e.g., those of African and Latin American ancestries). In Europe itself, the threat also includes mass migration across racial and civilizational divides from north Africa/Middle East as well as from groups similarly invading the USA (e.g., there is a growing "Latino" population in Spain, and of course sub-Saharan Africans are present as well). Certainly, the narrower particularist viewpoint can be expressed in ethnic genetic interest terms, and that it is valid as far as it goes. But it misses the larger point: the threat is not superficial or temporary but fundamental and encompasses the totality of Western civilization and all of the European peoples. The worldwide racial crisis exists and the fundamental issue remains: European-descended populations are threatened with replacement by Third World peoples.

As a general model for balancing broader and narrower particularisms, one could envision—along the lines of Norman Lowell's Imperium/Dominion split[18]—an overarching pan-European, Western Confederation resting on the framework of

---

[17] http://en.wikipedia.org/wiki/Immigration_Act_of_1924
[18] Lowell, *Imperium Europa*.

internally autonomous states that safeguard their narrower bio-logical and cultural uniqueness. Regardless of these details, the fundamental point remains that all parties to preservationist solutions need to have their voices heard; in particular, all groups that make up the Western family of peoples need to join in this endeavor and participate in the process.

CONCLUSION

An optimal outcome would be if pan-Europeanists, Nordi-cists, pan-Slavists, pan-Germanists, ethnic nationalists, and all the other "ists" and "isms" within the white activist framework can work together in a productive fashion to achieve common objectives, even if fundamental points of important disagree-ment remain. If the majority of such people share a common goal of European, Western survival—albeit with different em-phases, strategies, and tactics—then this could be a starting point to consider the possibilities. Given the immensity of the task before us, it would be helpful to at least be "in the same book," if not "on the same page."

The following quote from Yockey's *The Enemy of Europe* summarizes the palingenetic objective that we could, if we so wished, strive for:

> Our European Mission is to create the Culture-State-Nation-Imperium of the West, and thereby we shall per-form such deeds, accomplish such works, and so trans-form our world that our distant posterity, when they be-hold the remains of our buildings and ramparts, will tell their grandchildren that on the soil of Europe once dwelt a tribe of gods.[19]

That this tribe is not homogeneous, and contains within it-self smaller tribes with unique and valued characteristics, is a given. But I believe, nevertheless, that this greater Western tribe does exist—and that together we can achieve great things,

---

[19] Francis Parker Yockey, *The Enemy of Europe* (York, S.C.: Liberty Bell Publications, 1981), 93.

if we only can take the essential first steps forward. This essay is an open call for a paradigm shift in the relations of the varied types of (Western) ethnoracial nationalism to each other, a shift in the direction of increased cooperation. For approximately the last ten years there has been (sometimes acrimonious and mostly online) debate between proponents of these various "ists" and "isms" with no furthering of those objectives we all hold in common. Careful consideration of the possibilities for cooperation in areas of overlap should occur, and hopefully, these possibilities will become manifest in real-world collegial, productive endeavors.[20] We can and should be able to move forward together to achieve our common objectives. The *status quo* has not been productive.

Counter-Currents/*North American New Right*,
May 31, 2012

---

[20] Some discussion of these issues with respect to white separatism can be found Ted Sallis, "Racial Nationalism and Secession: Ideas, Critiques, Perspective, and Possibilities," *The Occidental Quarterly* vol. 10, no. 4 (Winter 2010–2011): 103–115.

Vanguard, Aesthetics, Revolution

Alex Kurtagić

I have on various occasions criticized the tendency among a subset of racial nationalists to indulge in improbable revolutionary fantasies, where the liberal system collapses, the white masses rise up, and evildoers hang from lampposts in one great Day of the Rope. "Mainstreamers" have, in turn, criticized the tendency among another subset to be bookworm revolutionaries, hermitic, eccentric, and too absorbed in their abstruse intellectual vaporings to be effective harbingers of change in the real world. Both subsets are emblematic of the retreat from reality that results from perceived powerlessness. Both represent vanguardist tendencies. Does that mean that vanguardism is a failed strategy, and that only mainstreamers offer a viable approach?

Far from it.

Vanguardism plays a key role in any movement seeking fundamental change when a system that can no longer be reformed, that has to crumble to make way for a new one, built on different foundations. What is more, it needs not stand in an either-or relationship with mainstreaming: it is possible — indeed it is preferable — to integrate both approaches into a coherent strategy.

Before I begin, I will define the political categories "Right" and "Left" as I intend to use them in this article. By Left I mean those who believe in the ideology of equality and progress; they are associated with liberalism and modernity. By Right I mean those whose outlook is elitist (inegalitarian) and cyclical; they are associated with Traditionalism (in the Evolian sense). By Right I do not mean conservatives, whom I regard as classical liberals, only with socially conservative attitudes.

FROM DYSTOPIA TO UTOPIA

Commentators on the Right are prone to spend most of their energy analyzing and critiquing the modern dystopia. But while this is necessary, it is not sufficient: saying that we have arrived at a wrong destination and that we need to be elsewhere without at the same time indicating where that elsewhere is does not imply motion, only the recognition of the need for motion; therefore it is not a movement. For movement to occur, for an idea to gain adepts who then follow each other in a collective act of motion, the destination must be known, *a priori*, which implies it must be communicable in some way. This destination is the movement's utopia: the perfect accomplishment of its goals.

Utopias exist only in the imagination. Most of the time they are communicated through fantastic art and literature. At best, they are only ever partially and/or imperfectly implemented. At worse, they are highly unrealistic and impractical—most are to some degree. Yet this does not mean they are not useful: they are in fact necessary, and a precondition for movement. Their active ingredient is not their being scientifically accurate, but their capacity to exert an enormous sentimental force on a large enough collective of individuals. And its conception is the charge of the vanguardist, the intellectual outsider, the pioneer, the dreamer, the creator—the individual, or group of individuals, whose task is to break us out of the cognitive cages built by the incumbent system; out of the system-sponsored illusion where anything that is anathema to it seems unthinkable.

Those who adopt mainstreaming approaches often despair at these dreamers because they appear—obviously—impractical, eccentric, and lacking in good sense. The problem is that creative innovators and iconoclasts often are: creative types comprise a peculiar breed, and within that, those who are truly innovative, truly at the vanguard, often shock, worry, and discomfit their less creative peers because they are less fettered by convention. There are undoubtedly good and bad sides to this, but this does not detract from the value of the creative process, even if not all of its byproducts are eventually adopted. The task of the mainstreamer, who abuts the vanguard and the mainstream, is to calculatingly take whatever can be used from the vanguard to stretch the limits of the mainstream, with a view to fundamentally transform the later in the long run.

DREAMER AS PRAGMATIST

Despite having the science, the data, and the logical arguments on its side, the Right has been in retreat for many decades. This alone should be sufficient indication that humans need more than just data, arguments, and truth to be persuaded into a change of allegiance. Yet many who identify with the Right continue operating under the illusion that this is not the case: if people believe in equality it is because they do not know about race differences in IQ; if people believe in multiculturalism it is because they do not know the black-on-white crime statistics; if people believe in liberalism it is because they have not read Gibbon, or Spengler, or Schmitt; and so on.

The irony is that the best example of why this approach is flawed exists all around us: the consumer society. As a child I was irritated by the unrealistic scenarios, the catchy jingles, and the constant sloganizing of television advertising, and I resented the irrational superficiality implied in this method of selling products. I thought that it would be far more logical to have a man in a suit seated at a table, facing the camera, like in a newsroom, and listing the product specifications to the audience in an unemotional monotone, so that viewers may be able to make a rational choice, based on solid data. Any adult with sense knows, even if he cannot explain exactly why, that this would never work in the real world. The reason is simple: the consumer society is not founded on utilitarian logic or reason, but on romanticism, daydreaming, status display, and utopias. And it is founded on these principles because that is what has been found to work — vast sums of money have been spent researching human psychology in the effort to maximize consumer mobilization. Colin Campbell and Geoffrey Miller provide theoretical and evolutionary explanations for the human motivational aspects of consumerism in *The Romantic Ethic and the Spirit of Modern Consumerism* and *Spent* respectively.[1]

---

[1] Colin Campbell, *The Romantic Ethic and the Spirit of Modern Con-*

Therefore it is fair to say that he who daydreams and purposefully induces others to daydream is, in fact, more of a pragmatist than the self-avowed pragmatically-oriented rationalist who seeks to persuade through reason. The former at least understands the irrationality of human nature, and plays (preys?) on it, while the latter fantasizes about abstract humans who act on the basis of rational self-interest.

TRUTH AS A LIFESTYLE CHOICE

Far from an asset, a belief in the power of "the truth" is one of the main obstacles for White Nationalists seeking converts to their cause. If they are frustrated by the failure of individuals to support them despite masses of scientific and statistical data showing heritable race differences in IQ and heritable propensities to violent crime, it is because they have failed to realize that humans choose the truth that suits them best, according to whether it makes them feel good about themselves and about the world, and whether it makes those whose opinion they value feel good about them, at any given point in time and space. Humans are more strongly motivated by the innate need for self-esteem and belonging than by abstract reason. Thus, faced with voluminous, conflicting, and virtually indigestible data and arguments emanating from multiple factions, each claiming a monopoly on the truth, it is easy to choose the most emotionally and socially convenient of available options. For the majority of people this means the truth sponsored by the cultural establishment, because it means easier social integration and higher rewards. Those who choose a truth anathematized by the cultural establishment become reliant on alternative networks and even unconventional methods to survive within a system that seeks to purge them. Ultimately, and perhaps especially in a materialistic society, truth becomes a lifestyle choice.

SUBSTANCE & STYLE

For the above reasons, a strategy purely based on what we

sumerism (Oxford: Basil Blackwell, 1987); Geoffrey Miller, *Spent: Sex, Evolution, and Consumer Behavior* (New York: Viking, 2009).

tend to regard as substance (i.e., empirical data, logical arguments, reasoned conclusions) is doomed to fail. And in the case of White Nationalism, it has long proven a failure. Also for the above reasons, an effective strategy needs to employ a methodology that taps, like consumerism, into the pre-rational drivers of human behavior. The lesson of consumerism does this through the calculating use of style and aesthetics, which in the consumer society are constantly deployed to induce the desired behavior (consumption).

I am familiar with the calculating use of style and aesthetics through my role in the consumer culture, which I played via my record company. Before the advent of MySpace and the free illegal download, whenever I designed an album cover, a logo, an advertisement, a newsletter, or a website; whenever I crafted an album description; even whenever I described an album verbally, I was acutely conscious of the need to appeal and stimulate interest in my target audience. I did not expect them to make rational decisions (especially since to hear the music they had to first buy the CD), but because I successfully triggered an emotional response strong enough to elicit the needed response: an immediate purchase. (Of course, I did not always get it right, and from time to time I got stuck with unsellable stock, something I blamed as much on bad artwork, ill-judged names and titles, and uninspiring logos as I did on the quality of the music.) Advertisement agencies thrive on the exploitation of style and aesthetics for purposes of mobilizing the public into consuming products, supporting a campaign, or voting for a political candidate.

We all know that as far as the white voters are concerned, Obama got elected purely on the basis of aesthetics: he sounded good, was telegenic, and his "blackness" reassured millions of whites eager to prove (mainly to themselves) that they were not racist. Slogans like "Hope" and "Change" contained zero substance; it was all about the Obamicons; and yet they excited the right sentiment among voters who felt hopeless and wanted change. Televised debates about policy emphasized visual presentation and catchy soundbites; they were more about what the candidates looked and sounded like while discussing — but not really—an ostensibly serious topic than about really discussing a serious topic. Annoying? Certainly. But there is no point fighting this. It works.

Having said this, substance is still important. We all know that a strategy based purely on stylistic flash without it being backed by at least some substance eventually implodes. (In the United States, many duped voters have since realized that Obama is an empty suit; in the United Kingdom, many duped voters eventually realized that Blair was a liar.) Emphasize style over substance in too obvious a manner and your strategy will, in fact, turn against you. (This was a major problem for the Blair government during the late 1990s; heavy "spin-doctoring" got Blair elected, but in time everyone was complaining about it.)

It is obvious, therefore, that the winning strategy is one that has both style and substance—substance that backs the style and style that backs the substance—that, in other words, projects the substance as well as the nature of the substance.

This is nothing new, of course, but it is amazing how many fail to realize the importance of style and aesthetics. Is it because we live in an age that is so obviously about style over substance that there is an instinct to rebel against it?

WEAPONIZING AESTHETICS

In a metapolitical context, we can speak then of weaponizing aesthetics: translating ideology into art, high and low, and using it to push culture and society in a predetermined direction, to cause culture and society to undergo fundamental change.

In my experience with various forms of underground music and their associated subcultures, an individual's transformation of consciousness goes through identifiable phases.

First, individuals are exposed to a particular genre of music through their peers; the response, positive or negative, is often immediate, instinctive, the result of a combination of innate biological predisposition, personal history, and sociological factors.

Next, if the individual's response is positive, there begins a process of researching and collecting albums by bands that play in that genre. And if the individual's response is extremely positive, the process is intensive, and becomes gradually more so, causing him eventually to become completely immersed in the associated subculture.

Music-centered youth subcultures are easily identifiable because they are highly stylized and stylistically distinctive. They also have their own ideology, which both emanates and reinforces the values coded in the style of music out of which it has grown. Sometimes the ideology is derivative, an extrapolation, or an exaggeration of certain mainstream values. Sometimes the ideology is fundamentally antagonistic to the cultural mainstream. Also, sometimes the ideology is superficial, sometimes it is not. But in all cases, music fans who have become immersed in the associated subculture come to adopt and internalize its ideology to some extent.

Depending on the nature of this ideology, members of a subculture may undergo a radical change in consciousness—even to the point of becoming proud pariahs—which endures even after they have transcended their membership. They may eventually discard the garb and take up conventional salaried employment, but their allegiance to the music will endure, sometimes as a guilty secret, and traces of their fanatical past will remain in their cognitive structures, lifestyle, home decor, vocabulary, and choice of associations. What is more, even decades after, former members will recognize each other and have a common bond.

And all this is achieved aesthetically, through art. It bears iterating: to the extent that values are absorbed, they are so not because they have been presented logically or scientifically, but because they were presented in an attractive and artful or aesthetically pleasing manner—in a manner that exerts a strong sentimental force on its consumers. And anyone with an awareness of popular culture will know that its power to excite extreme emotion, unite psychologically, and mobilize the masses—to cause them to act irrationally, violently, even against their own rational best interests—cannot be underestimated. When the last volume of the Harry Potter series of novels was published, people queued for hours, in the cold, in the rain, in the wee hours of the morning, to be the first to get their hands on the first hardback edition. And this is a very mild example. We have film evidence from the 1960s showing young women absolutely in hysterics at Beatles concerts, and there is little doubt that their personal lives were partly consumed by thoughts and fantasies involving members of the band. Did their record company present an especially logical argument?

Of course, mass mobilization is possible within popular culture when the product or event in question encodes culturally mainstream values. The less mainstream the values, the less the capacity for mobilization. All the same, in the age of mechanical reproduction we have seen that when a synergistic aesthetic and ideological system is deployed using the methods of popular culture, even radical anti-system propositions are capable, under the right conditions, of mobilizing large enough bodies of people and growing until it establishes itself as a new hegemonic order.

The National Socialists, beginning in Weimar Germany, offer perhaps the most iconic example in the West. Like all political movements, however, National Socialism had metapolitical origins, and arguably occult origins in daydreams of Atlantean and Hyperborean civilizations, which the SS later sought to substantiate. It was more a certain set of ideas and daydreams, a certain sentiment, a certain political romanticism, a certain look, before it was actual politics with an actual label.

The same is true of our modern society: between René Descartes, Adam Smith, John Locke, Karl Marx, and Sigmund Freud on the one hand, and political correctness, immigration, outsourcing, and diversity training on the other, lie a mass of popular novels, films, and albums that consciously or semiconsciously encode, aestheticize, and promote the ideas and narratives of global capitalism and the Freudo-Marxist scholasticism, upon whose metapolitical tradition the modern order is founded.

The weaponization of aesthetics is the creation of an interface that facilitates the translation of the metapolitical into the political, of the vanguard into the mainstream.

CREDIBILITY

Another reason why I put such emphasis on aesthetics in metapolitical discussions is that a well-formulated and perfectly rendered aesthetic system is the fastest way of projecting credibility, and therefore of making a set of values and ideals appear credible to apolitical observers. (To political observers it may inspire pride or fear, depending on their allegiance.) Do we not judge books by their covers? Do we not judge a person by his or her appearance?

I contend that if our values and ideals lack credibility outside our immediate milieu, it is partly because we have yet to find a way to translate our metapolitics into an professionally rendered aesthetic system that is both acceptable and appealing to a wider audience—that reformulates our archaic ideas in a way that is vibrant, relevant, and forward-looking (because people do need hope and change). Needless to say that there are other very significant factors involved (such as the reality of economic sanctions), but this is certainly one of them: without an optimal aesthetic system, actual politics becomes very difficult. One cannot sell an idea without marketing. And one cannot appeal to an elite audience without the right kind of marketing.

This is why we will benefit when talented artists, musicians, designers, and literary stylists who share our sensibilities find congenial outlets and begin making a name for themselves. It is, therefore, necessary that we provide such outlets and offer viable professional and economic opportunities for creative types, lest we continue losing them to the (censoring but remunerated) alternatives offered by the establishment. Only then will we be able to grow a forceful counter-culture.

FINAL THOUGHTS

The age of chaos offers opportunities to those able to "sell" a new dream. Although the present liberal, egalitarian, progressive establishment appears superficially invincible, they do not represent a unified, cohesive, monolithic, totalitarian order: they are, in fact, a rainbow coalition of competing and sometimes contradictory factions that happen to share a set of core beliefs. They are also degenerative and disintegrative, and the logical conclusion of their project is the complete breakdown of society. This has become increasingly apparent since the adoption of multiculturalism as an official government policy, and the adoption of globalism as the modern capitalist paradigm. Worse still, they are contrary to nature, so their continuity results in constant stress and strenuous effort. Division, degeneration, disintegration, stress, and exhaustion grow ever more apparent. And the end of prosperity in the West will make social and cultural upheavals more difficult to contain or diffuse. Thus, in the escalating confusion, even the apolitical, conventionally-thinking citizen will in time become receptive to new, exotic, and even quixotic ideas. Once the confusion becomes severe enough, they will be looking for a radical ideology, a harsh religion, an authoritarian strongman, or a Caesar. They will be looking for meaningful symbolism, for utopian daydreams, for a new romanticism, for something that projects order and strength, is distinctive amid the chaos, and makes them feel powerful and part of something strong.

This might seem grandiose, but the beginning of it is nearer than one thinks: it, in fact, starts with pen and paper, with brush and canvas, with guitar and plectrum; it is founded on the fantasy and the daydreams that animate these utensils.

If revolutions begin with scribbles, scribbles begin with daydreams. And although this may sound fluffy and nebulous to the hard political pragmatist, it bears remembering that such verities always look so after a long period of material prosperity and political stability, while the system appears strong and credible to a majority. But, as it did in the past, following cataclysmic upheavals, when their origins and causes were catalogued by sociologists in their postmortem reports, said verities are likely to look somewhat less nebulous after the tide of culture turns and those once seemingly improbable daydreams start to take form. How long until then? Who knows? But unless we have set the metapolitical bases for our new order, unless we have a virile counter-culture upon which can build it, we might find that by the time the tide turns, others got in well ahead of us while we waited to see if it ever would.

Counter-Currents/*North American New Right*,
May 1, 2012

ABSOLUTE WOMAN:
A CLARIFICATION OF EVOLA'S
THOUGHTS ON WOMEN

AMANDA BRADLEY

One of the central concepts of Julius Evola's philosophy of gender is the distinction between absolute man and absolute woman. But he seldom gives explicit definitions of these terms. Absolute man and woman can be likened to Platonic Forms, thus defining them can be as difficult as defining Justice, Truth, or Love.

The term "absolute woman" inspires more controversy than "absolute man." Since the male principle is associated with light, goodness, and activity, whereas the female principle is associated with darkness, evil, and passivity, feminists can easily claim that Evola's views are inherently misogynist. Another point of controversy is Otto Weininger's influence on Evola. But Evola himself admits that Weininger must be read critically due to "his unconscious misogynous complex."[1]

It is important to address Evola's writings on women so that his views are correctly understood. Since he was opposed to the emerging feminism of his day, it would be easy for those unfamiliar with his ideas to infer that Evola also was anti-woman. By explaining his views and not glossing over any points that do in fact sound misogynistic (as is the case with some Evola devotees) the New Right can set the terms of discourse and accurately elucidate his position.

EVOLA ON THE COMPOSITION OF HUMAN BEINGS

The simplest definition of "absolute woman" is the female principle, the feminine force of the universe. Individual men

---

[1] Julius Evola, *Eros and the Mysteries of Love: The Metaphysics of Sex* (Rochester, Vt.: Inner Traditions, 1991), 157–58.

and woman have varying degrees of the absolute man and woman, although the feminine principle usually is the underlying force in women.

In the modern world (the Kali Yuga) these forces appear in more degenerate forms and also do not always manifest properly. In fact, Evola said that "cases of full sexual development are seldom found. Almost every man bears some traces of femininity and every woman residues of masculinity . . . the traits that we deemed typical for the female psyche can be found in man as well as women, particularly in regressive phases of a civilization."[2] In addition, these "manifest differently depending on the race and type of civilization."[3]

To understand the influence of the "absolute woman," it is first necessary to understand Evola's conception of the human being. He held that humans are comprised of three parts:

- ❖ the outer individual (the personality, or ego);
- ❖ the level of profound being, the site of the *principium individuationis*. This is the true "face" of a person as opposed to the mask of the ego;
- ❖ the level of elementary forces that are "superior and prior to the individuation but acting as the ultimate seat of the individual."[4]

It is at the third level, that of elementary forces, where sexual attraction is aroused.[5] Thus it is here that the elementary forces that comprise the absolute man or woman are located. This matches Evola's description of some modern women, who are able to develop "masculine" skills such as logic or intellectualism. He says they have done so "by way of a layer placed on top of [their] deepest nature."[6] However, they have not succeeded in altering their fundamental nature, only their superficial personalities.

---

[2] *Eros*, 169.
[3] *Eros*, 168.
[4] *Eros*, 36.
[5] *Eros*, 36.
[6] *Eros*, 151–52.

A METAPHYSICAL STARTING-POINT FOR MALE & FEMALE

According to Traditional doctrines, the sexes were meta-physical forces before they manifested in the world. Absolute man and woman exist from the beginning of time, when the Universal One split into a Dyad, which then caused the rest of creation. In most forms of Hinduism, Shiva, the male principle, is identified with pure Being. Shakti, the female principle, is identified with Becoming and Change. In a similar vein, Aristotle associated the male principle with form and the female with matter. According to Evola, form means "the power that determines and arouses the principle of motion, development, becoming" while matter means "the substance or power that, being devoid of form in itself, can take up any form, and which in itself is nothing but can become everything when it has been awakened and fecundated."[7] In the Far Eastern tradition, yang (the male principle) is associated with heaven, while yin (the female principle) is associated with the earth.[8] Thus, form and matter combined to create the manifested universe. From the coitus of Shiva and Shakti "springs the world."[9] (This is in contrast to Oswald Spengler, who believed that becoming was the essential element, rather than steadfast being.)

The male principle is associated with truth, light, the Sun, virility, activeness, and stability. Sometimes it is associated with the Universal One that existed before the Dyad. The female quality is associated with deception, changeability, the moon, the earth, darkness, wetness, passivity, and dependence on another. In Evola's words:

What the Greeks called "heterity," that is, being connected to another or being centered on someone other than oneself, is a characteristic proper to the cosmic female, whereas to have one's own principle in oneself is proper to the pure male . . . female life is almost always devoid

---

[7] *Eros*, 118.

[8] Julius Evola, *Revolt Against the Modern World*, trans. Guido Stucco (Rochester, Vt.: Inner Traditions, 1995), 157.

[9] *Eros*, 122.

of an individual value but is linked to someone else in her need, born of vanity, to be acknowledged, noticed, flattered, admired, and desired (this extroverted tendency is connected to that "looking outside" which on a metaphysical level has been attributed to Shakti).[10]

These forces then manifest in actual men and women. But Evola is clear to maintain that absolute man and woman are not simply aspects of character. Instead, they are "objective elements working in individuals almost as impersonally as the chemical properties inherent in a particular substance."[11] As Evola says:

> before and besides existing in the body, sex exists in the soul and, to a certain extent, in the spirit itself. We are man or woman inwardly before being so externally; the primordial male or female quality penetrates and saturates the whole of our being visibly and invisibly . . . just as a color permeates a liquid.[12]

As such, the absolute woman is not simply an idealized concept of woman. She is defined from the divine down to the human, and is not a human conception of something divine.

THE RELEVANCE OF THE ABSOLUTE WOMAN

The absolute woman is the rod by which all women are to be measured. Evola writes, "the only thing we can do is establish the superiority or inferiority of a given woman on the basis of her being more of less close to the female type, to the pure and absolute woman, and the same thing applies to man as well."[13] In addition, superiority is defined by how closely one realizes the absolute woman or man. "A woman who is perfectly woman is superior to a man who is imperfectly man, just as a farmer

---

[10] *Eros*, 157.
[11] *Eros*, 152.
[12] *Eros*, 32.
[13] *Eros*, 34.

who is faithful to his land and performs his work perfectly is superior to a king who cannot do his own work," says Evola.[14]

Many more characteristics are associated with the female principle than those described below; however, these are the primary ones highlighted by Evola in his writings on the subject.

THE WATERS & CHANGEABILITY

The fundamental feminine characteristic is changeability. Thus, the female is associated with water, which is fluid and adapts to whatever form it is put into, just as matter/Shakti is shaped by form/Shiva. Evola writes that woman "reflects the cosmic female according to its aspect as material receiving a form that is external to her and that she does not produce from within."[15] This fits in with Carl Jung's description of woman's animus, which is not self-created, but instead is a subconscious collection of the thoughts of men.

This changeability is related to woman's tendency to live for someone outside of herself, due to the fluidity and changeability of her nature. For Evola, this means following the path of a mother or lover, fixing herself to a virile force in order to obtain transcendence. In contrast, "modern woman in wanting to be for herself has destroyed herself."[16] By believing that she is merely her personality, she loses her transcendent aspect.

This watery nature is seen in the association of the female with water. According to Evola, water represents "undifferentiated life prior to and not yet fixed in form," that "which runs or flows and is therefore unstable and changeable," and "the principle of all fertility and growth according to the analogy of water's fertilizing action on earth and soil."[17]

Evola also describes the correct relationship between the principle of water and that of fire, associated with the male: "when the feminine principle, whose force is centrifugal, does not turn to fleeting objects but rather to a 'virile' stability in

---

[14] *Eros*, 34.
[15] *Eros*, 153.
[16] *Revolt*, 165.
[17] *Eros*, 119.

which she finds a limit to her 'restlessness.'"[18]

Evola assents that certain modern women may appear very unchangeable, but stresses that this is at an outer level of her being:

> a possible rigidity may follow the reception of ideas due precisely to the passive way she has adopted them, which may appear under the guise of conformity and conservatism. In this way, we can explain the apparent contrast inherent in the fact that female nature is change-able, yet women mainly show conservative tendencies sociologically and a dislike for the new. This can be linked to their role in mythology as female figures of a Demeter or chthonic type who guard and avenge customs and the law — the law of blood and of the earth, but not the uranic law.[19]

Thus, a woman may be quite unchanging in her beliefs about society, etiquette, and morality, but will lack an attachment to a transcendent truth. Many of women's ideas regarding social truths such as honor and virtue are "not true ethics but mere habits," Evola says.[20]

This changeability of women explains the notion that women are at the same time more compassionate and more cruel than men; as woman is associated with the earth, she expresses both the tenderness of the mother and the cruelty of nature. The best example of this duality is the Greek goddess Artemis, who was both the protector of wild animals and the huntress.

WOMAN'S LACK OF BEING OR SOUL

Perhaps the most controversial characteristic of Evola's absolute woman, which he gets from Weininger, is a common conception throughout history: that woman has no soul, or being. Weininger states that woman has no ego, referring to the

---

[18] *Revolt*, 158.
[19] *Eros*, 153.
[20] *Eros*, 155.

Transcendental Ego of Immanuel Kant, which Evola describes as "above the whole world of phenomena (in metaphysical terms one would say 'above all manifestation,' like the Hindu *ātman*)."[21] In some schools of Hinduism, the *ātman* (or "higher self") is identical with the *Brahman*, the infinite soul of the Universe. In other Hindu conceptions, the *ātman* is the life-principle. As manifested existence would be impossible without the *ātman*, this description of woman as lacking a Transcendental Ego should not be taken to mean that women are incapable of developing and solidifying this aspect, though they may be at a disadvantage to men. Also, in the Kali Yuga, all people are the furthest removed from the divine, so modern men and women are likely in the same starting position in terms of development of Being.

Evola expands on the notion, stating that if soul means "psyche" or "principle of life," then "it should signify in fact that woman not only has a soul but is eminently 'soul,'" whereas man is not a soul but a "spirit." He continues: "the point we believe settled is that woman is a part of 'nature' (in a metaphysical sense she is a manifestation of the same principle as nature) and that she affirms nature, whereas man by virtue of birth in the masculine human form goes *tendentially* beyond nature."[22]

DECEPTION & A CONNECTION TO TRUTH

Another attribute of absolute woman is deceitfulness. In fact, Evola states that it is so essential that telling lies has been acknowledged as an essential characteristic in female nature "at all times and in all places by popular wisdom."[23] According to Weininger, this tendency is due to her lack of being. With no fixed essence, most women (and modern men) are attached to no transcendent truth, and therefore there is nothing to lie *against* — Truth only exists when one has substance and values. In Evola's words:

---

[21] *Eros*, 151.
[22] *Eros*, 151.
[23] *Eros*, 155.

Weininger observed that nothing is more baffling for a man than a woman's response when caught in a lie. When asked why she is lying, she is unable to understand the question, acts astonished, bursts out crying, or seeks to pacify him by smiling. She cannot understand the ethical and transcendent side of lying or the fact that a lie represents damage to being and, as was acknowledged in ancient Iran, constitutes a crime even worse than killing. . . . The truth, pure and simple, is that woman is prone to lie and to disguise her true self even when she has no need to do so; this is not a social trait acquired in the struggle for existence, but something linked to her deepest and most genuine nature.[24]

This quality of deceitfulness, while springing from the fundamental makeup of women, should not imply that it must be accepted as a given trait of all women, as Weininger sometimes implies. For, just like man, the ultimate goal of a woman's existence is to connect with and live by the transcendent, which requires a fixation that cannot accept deception.

WOMAN'S INTUITION, MAN'S ETHICS & LOGIC

Another idea Evola gets from Weininger is the notion that absolute woman, since she lacks being, also lacks memory, logic, and ethics.[25] In order to explain this, Evola distinguishes between two kinds of logic: everyday logic, which women can use quite successfully (though sometimes like a "sophist") and "logic as a love of pure truth and inward coherence."[26] This distinction can most commonly be seen when women use logic in arguments as a means to personal ends, rather than to arrive at a truth beyond their desires. Evola writes:

woman, insofar as she is woman, will never know ethics in the categorical sense of pure inner law detached from eve-

---

[24] *Eros*, 155.
[25] *Eros*, 154.
[26] *Eros*, 154.

ry empirical, eudemonistic, sensitive, sentimental, and personal connection. Nothing in woman that may have an ethical character can be separated from instinct, sentiment, sexuality, or "life"; it can have no relationship with pure "being."

Women's primary tool of cognition is not logic but intuition and sensitivity.[27]

In explaining memory, Evola turns to Henri Bergson, who described two types of memory. One is more common in women: the memory connected to the subconscious, which may remember dreams, have premonitions, and unexpectedly recall forgotten experiences. The second type of memory, which women lack due to their fluid nature, is "determined, organized, and dominated by the intellect."[28]

THE FEMALE PRINCIPLE AS POWERFUL, SOVEREIGN, & ACTIVE

Generally the female principle is described as passive, and the male as active. According to Evola, this is only true on the outermost plane. On the subtle plane, he says, "it is the woman who is active and the man who is passive (the woman is 'actively passive' and the man 'passively active')."[29] In Hindu terms the impassible spirit (*purusa*) is masculine, while the active matrix of every conditioned form (*prakriti*) is feminine.[30] To use the creation of a child as an example, man gives his seed, but it is woman who actively creates and gives birth to the child.

Mythology supports the sovereign aspect of woman. Evola gives the examples of the Earth goddess Cybele drawn in a chariot led by two tame tigers, and the Hindu goddess Durga seated on a lion with reins in her hands.[31] Evola states that man knows of this sovereign quality in women, and "often owing to

---

[27] *Eros*, 154.
[28] *Eros*, 154.
[29] *Eros*, 167–68.
[30] *Revolt*, 157.
[31] *Eros*, 167.

a neurotic unconscious overcompensation for his inferiority complex, he flaunts before woman an ostentatious manliness, indifference, or even brutality and disdain. But this secures him no advantage, on the contrary. The fact that woman often becomes a victim on an external, material, sentimental, or social level, giving rise to her instinctive 'fear of loving,' does not alter the fundamental structure of the situation."[32]

ASSOCIATION WITH THE DEMONIC & ASPIRATION

Another "negative" quality of the absolute woman is that of aspiration, in the sense of a sucking quality, which also is associated with the demonic. On a profane level, in a degenerate form, this could be the woman who is constantly demanding more from her husband and others—more time spent together, a better car, a bigger house, or more attention. Since she has no "soul" (as defined above), she must fill the void within herself by sucking the vital force from others in emotional, monetary, or temporal vampirism.

On a metaphysical level, this quality merely refers to the divine female, Shakti, pulling Shiva into the world of manifestation. Thus, it is not good or bad, except to Gnostics and other sects that believe the created world is evil. As Evola states, woman "is oriented toward keeping that order which Gnosticism, in a dualistic background, called the 'world of the Demiurge,' the world of nature as opposed to that of the spirit."[33] This demonic element is expressed in actual life when women draw men to the realm of earth, nature, and children. It is expressed in sex when man's seed is drawn into the woman, creating a child bound by nature. "Although 'woman' can give life," Evola writes, "yet she shuts off or tends to shut off access to that which is beyond life."[34]

In some Eastern thought, the man's seed is thought to be the spiritual manhood—hence the formation of sects that teach men to retain this force to attain liberation rather than wasting

---

[32] *Eros*, 167.
[33] *Eros*, 141.
[34] *Eros*, 142.

it through ejaculation. Women properly trained are said to be able to capture this essence during sex, thus seducing the man into giving up his manhood.

The positive aspect of this trait lies in woman's ability to overcome it, most often by following the path of the mother or lover. In the actions required by these paths (if following them in an attitude of self-sacrifice and not self-aggrandizement), she no longer drains others, but instead learns to build up a vital force within herself through renunciation of desires. By relinquishing the control of the ego/personality by being devoted to others instead, woman is able to fix herself to the transcendent.

Like the other qualities of absolute woman, that of aspiration also can be found in man, especially in the Kali Yuga. Evola refers to sexual practices found in Chinese Taoism, India, and Tibet, where the man sucks the vital female energy from a woman during sex, a technique he describes as bordering on "male 'psychic' vampirism."[35]

THE VALUE OF ABSOLUTE WOMAN IN THE MODERN WORLD

In the Golden Age, we can imagine that the metaphysical elements comprising a person manifested in the proper way. In such a time, the highest classes gave birth to the highest people; race was indicative of a corresponding inner quality; beauty on the outside attested to an inner beauty; and physical gender aligned with the qualities of absolute man or woman.

But in the Kali Yuga, there are pariahs in the highest classes, men who act like women, and men of Aryan stock who do not embody any of the virtues attributed to their race. As Evola says, it is possible for a person to be a different sex in the body than they are in the soul. These cases are similar to those where individuals of one race "have the psychic and spiritual characteristics of another race."[36]

Therefore, men today may not innately possess any virile seed, just as modern women do not necessarily express the absolute female principle. In reading Evola's work, then, we must

---

[35] *Eros*, 249.
[36] *Eros*, 34.

not mistakenly interpret what he says about absolute man or woman as corresponding with individual men and women of today. Modern men and women are almost completely removed from the deepest aspects of themselves, functioning only as personalities. Thus, a person's sex or caste has little importance in determining vocations or social relations. What relevance, then, do Evola's descriptions of absolute man and woman have in the modern world?

An answer is found in the existential *Angst* that defined the 20th century. Martin Heidegger wrote of the inauthentic life, and Jean-Paul Sartre of bad faith; most people today still fit the description of mere personalities, lacking divine connections or the means to find them. In a world that has lost its values and connection to Tradition, discovering these principles in our innermost natures becomes even more important. By examining Evola's work, and that of other Traditionalists, we can find our way back to our true selves, the true relation between the sexes, and a connection to the transcendent.

Counter-Currents/*North American New Right*,
June 17, 2010

D. H. LAWRENCE'S
WOMEN IN LOVE

DEREK HAWTHORNE

D. H. Lawrence's greatest novel is also his most anti-modern. Written between April and October of 1916 in Cornwall, during some of the darkest days of the First World War, *Women in Love* was conceived as a sequel to *The Rainbow*. *Women in Love* continues the story of Ursula Brangwen's life and the fulfillment she finds in a love affair with Rupert Birkin (who does not figure in *The Rainbow* at all). This relationship is, in fact, paired with another: that of Gudrun, Ursula's sister (a very minor character in *The Rainbow*), and Gerald Crich, Birkin's best friend. The novel follows the course of both relationships.

The connection between the two novels seems a tenuous one at best, however, and one can read and appreciate *Women in Love* without any knowledge at all of *The Rainbow*. This has a great deal to do with the dramatic difference in tone between the two. In a letter, Lawrence described the relationship between the two novels as follows: "There is another novel, sequel to *The Rainbow*, called *Women in Love* . . . this actually does contain the results in one's soul of the war; it is purely destructive, not like *The Rainbow*, destructive-consummating."[1]

Women in Love is indeed "purely destructive": it is grimly apocalyptic and misanthropic. There is little sense of the presence of nature this time: the novel moves almost entirely within the conscious and (more importantly) subconscious minds of its four main characters. And the backdrop is the ugly, human-built mechanicalness of the industrialized Midlands. It is easy to attribute the change in tone between the two novels as due

---

[1] Quoted in Keith Sagar, *The Art of D. H. Lawrence* (Cambridge: Cambridge University Press, 1966), 78.

to Lawrence's horror at the war ("The war finished me," he later said).

But one must not lose sight of the fact that the two novels do, in fact, tell one continuous story, and that the switch in tone is appropriate to what the second half of the story depicts: the fragmentary lives of individuals struggling to find fulfillment in the modern world. In his Foreword to the novel Lawrence wrote that it "took its final shape in the midst of the period of war, though it does not concern the war itself. I should wish the time to remain unfixed, so that the bitterness of the war may be taken for granted in the characters." For Lawrence, as for Heidegger, the war was ultimately just an inevitable extension of the industrial age itself.

At the beginning of the story, Birkin is involved in an unhappy love affair with Hermione Roddice, the daughter of an aristocrat and a thinly-disguised portrait of Lady Ottoline Morrell. Birkin is already acquainted with Ursula professionally, as he is the local school inspector and she the school mistress. After they are brought closer together and love begins to grow between them, Birkin abandons Hermione. The memorable episode that precipitates the final break between them involves Hermione trying to bludgeon him to death with a lapis lazuli paperweight.

However, Birkin's relationship with Ursula is, from the first, difficult in its own way. Much of the reason has to do with Birkin's misanthropy and Schopenhauerian pessimism. At some level, Ursula sympathizes with Birkin's views, but she is put off by his extraordinary vehemence, and, more importantly, seems to feel that if he would admit his love for her and fully surrender himself to their relationship he would be freed from his all-consuming hatred of the world. She is carrying on with life, in spite of everything, and eventually she succeeds in drawing him back into life.

The character of Rupert Birkin is universally acknowledged to be a self-portrait of Lawrence, though it would be dangerous to assume that Lawrence has no critical distance from the character (or from himself, for that matter). Nevertheless, Birkin often speaks for Lawrence. Early in the novel Birkin declares that it would be much better if humanity "were just wiped out. Essentially they don't exist, they aren't there." Later, in conversation with Ursula, Birkin declares:

> "Humanity is a huge aggregate lie, and a huge lie is less than a small truth. Humanity is less, far less than the individual, because the individual may sometimes be capable of truth, and humanity is a tree of lies. And they say that love is the greatest thing: they persist in *saying* this, the foul liars, and just look at what they do! . . . It's a lie to say that love is the greatest. . . . What people want is hate—hate and nothing but hate. And in the name of righteousness and love they get it. . . . If we want hate, let us have it—death, murder, torture, violent destruction— let us have it: but not in the name of love. But I abhor humanity, I wish it was swept away. It could go, and there would be no *absolute* loss, if every human being perished tomorrow. . . ."
>
> "So you'd like everybody in the world destroyed?" said Ursula. . . .
>
> "Yes truly. You yourself, don't you find it a beautiful clean thought, a world empty of people, just uninterrupted grass, and a hare sitting up?"
>
> The pleasant sincerity of his voice made Ursula pause to consider her own proposition. And it really *was* attractive: a clean, lovely, humanless world. It was the *really* desirable. Her heart hesitated and exulted. But still, she was dissatisfied with *him*.[2]

If anything, in his own correspondence Lawrence goes further than Birkin. In a letter to his friend S. S. Koteliansky, dated September 4, 1916, while Lawrence was working on *Women in Love*, he declares:

> I must say I hate mankind—talking of hatred, I have

---

[2] D. H. Lawrence, *Women in Love* (New York: Viking Press, 1969; henceforth WIL), 118–19.

got a perfect androphobia. When I see people in the distance, walking along the path through the fields to Zennor, I want to crouch in the bushes and shoot them silently with invisible arrows of death. I think truly the only righteousness is the destruction of mankind, as in Sodom. . . . Oh, if one could but have a great box of insect powder, and shake it over them, in the heavens, and exterminate them. Only to clear and cleanse and purify the beautiful earth, and give room for some truth and pure living.[3]

Where *Women in Love* is most interesting, however, is not in such outpourings of venom, but in Lawrence's attempts to pinpoint why things have gone so disastrously wrong in the modern world. As have many other authors, Lawrence places a great deal of weight on the materialism and mechanism of industrialized modernity. Another, later, exchange between Birkin and Ursula is particularly revealing in this regard. The pair have just bought a chair at a flea market and Birkin states:

"When I see that clear, beautiful chair, and I think of England, even Jane Austen's England — it had living thoughts to unfold even then, and pure happiness in unfolding them. And now, we can only fish among the rubbish-heaps for the remnants of their old expression. There is no production in us now, only sordid and foul mechanicalness."

"It isn't true," cried Ursula, "Why must you always praise the past at the expense of the present? *Really*, I don't think so much of Jane Austen's England. It was materialistic enough, if you like —"

"It could afford to be materialistic," said Birkin, "because it had the power to be something other — which we haven't. We are materialistic because we haven't the power to be anything else — try as we may, we can't bring off anything but materialism: mechanism, the very soul

---

[3] Quoted in Sagar, *The Art of D. H. Lawrence*, 103.

of materialism."[4]

But why did Jane Austen's England have the power to be something else? And what else did it have the power to be? For the answers to these questions we must, in essence, look back to *The Rainbow*. Jane Austen's England still preserved some connection to the land—a sense of belonging to nature. What England then had the "power to be" was nothing grand and idealistic: it had the power simply to be its natural self. The people of Jane Austen's England made and enjoyed beautiful objects—but these objects were an ornament to a life lived in relative closeness to the earth.

In the industrialized world of 1916, however, objects are all that human beings have. The purpose of life itself becomes the production and acquisition of objects. This by itself cannot, of course, provide any sense of "meaning in life," and to fill this void we have introduced idealism and given to our material- ism a moral veneer: we are making Progress, alleviating hun- ger and disease and want, promoting equality, and in general perfecting ourselves and the world through the marriage of science and commerce.

GERALD CRICH & THE MASTERY OF NATURE

In *Women in Love* the coupling of industrial materialism with idealism is personified by Birkin's friend Gerald Crich, son of the local colliery owner. On the train together, the two men speak of the modern world: "So you really think things are very bad?" Gerald asks. "Completely bad," Birkin responds. Throughout the novel, Gerald is drawn to Birkin, fascinated by the man and his notions—yet he is repelled by him at the same time, and frightened. He encourages Birkin to explain what he means, and Birkin obliges him:

"We are such dreary liars. Our idea is to lie to ourselves. We have an ideal of a perfect world, clean and straight and sufficient. So we cover the earth with foulness; life is

---

[4] WIL, 347–48.

a blotch of labour, like insects scurrying in filth, so that your collier can have a pianoforte in his parlour, and you can have a butler and a motor-car in your up-to-date house, and as a nation we can sport the Ritz, or the Empire, Gaby Deslys and the Sunday newspapers. It is very dreary."[5]

But Gerald responds that he thinks the pianoforte represents "a real desire for something higher" in the collier's life.

"Higher!" cried Birkin. "Yes. Amazing heights of upright grandeur. It makes him so much higher in his neighboring collier's eyes. He sees himself reflected in the neighboring opinion, like in a Brocken mist, several feet taller on the strength of the pianoforte, and he is satisfied. He lives for the sake of that Brocken spectre, the reflection of himself in the human opinion."[6]

Material things and the zeal for material things do not lift up the average man. They merely produce what Christopher Lasch aptly called "the culture of narcissism," and what Wendell Berry has called a "consumptive culture." One of the absurdities of modern life is the pretence that human beings who have been reduced to the level of mere consumers are somehow more "advanced" than their ancestors.

But aside from man the consumer, what of man the producer? After all, someone has to produce all those pianofortes. This is where men like Gerald come in. Birkin asks Gerald what he lives for. Gerald answers: "I suppose I live to work, to produce something, in so far as I am a purposive being. Apart from that, I live because I am living." Ursula remarks to Gudrun that Gerald has "got *go*, anyhow" and Gudrun replies, "The unfortunate thing is, where does his *go* go to, what becomes of it?" Ursula suggests, jokingly, that it "goes in applying the latest

---

[5] WIL, 48.
[6] WIL, 48.

appliances!"[7] This remark, however, is truer than she supposes.

The most brilliantly-written chapter of *Women in Love* is "The Industrial Magnate," in which Lawrence depicts Gerald's mastery of the mine. Gerald spends the first few years of his adult life wandering aimlessly, but always in hearty, masculine fashion: living the wild life of a student, becoming a soldier, then an adventurer. Always with Gerald there was an overweening curiosity and a desire truly to master something — a desire which masks a real, inner feeling of helplessness and lostness. He finds his true calling in running the mine, for there he believes he has found the meaning of life:

> Immediately he *saw* the firm, he realized what he could do. He had to fight with Matter, with the earth and the coal it enclosed. This was the sole idea, to turn upon the inanimate matter of the underground, and reduce it to his will. . . . There were two opposites, his will and the resistant Matter of the earth. . . . He had his life-work now, to extend over the earth a great and perfect system in which the will of man ran smooth and unthwarted timeless, a Godhead in process.[8]

By writing "Matter" with a capital M, Lawrence underscores the fact that for Gerald the mine is important not in itself but for what it represents. Gerald sees himself not merely as a colliery owner, but as a titanic being: a participant in the long, historical process of man's divinization through the conquest of nature, now coming to full consummation in the industrial age.

But where has he gotten such ideas? Lawrence tells us that Gerald "refused to go to Oxford, choosing a German university," and that he "took hold of all kinds of sociological ideas, and ideas of reform." It is plain that Gerald has been exposed to a great deal of German philosophy. In depicting Gerald's outlook on life, Lawrence seems to be blending ideas and terminology from three German philosophers: Fichte, Hegel, and Nietzsche.

---

[7] WIL, 41–42.
[8] WIL, 220.

FICHTE & THE MASTERY OF NATURE

Lawrence writes that through Gerald's domination of his will (or his ideals) over Matter "there was perfection attained, the will of mankind was perfectly enacted; for was not mankind mystically contradistinguished against inanimate Matter, was not the history of mankind just the history of the conquest of the one by the other?"[9] The philosophy this is closest to is that of Fichte, though Lawrence is probably thinking of Hegel.

Fichte believed, essentially, that an objective world — an other standing opposed to ego — existed merely as an instrument for the expression of human will. Nature, or what Lawrence here calls "Matter," exists as something that must be overcome and transformed by human beings according to human ideals. In doing so, human beings realize themselves. All of human history for Fichte, indeed all of reality, is the unending imposition of the ideal on the real, or the transformation of material otherness into an image of human will.

Even though Fichte's philosophy, at first glance, appears to be something novel, in a sense it is (and was) nothing new at all: it is the underlying metaphysics of modernity laid bare. In the modern world, again, human beings essentially relate to nature as raw material that must be forced to fit human designs or interests — or at best as a mere background for human action. Further, time is conceived in linear fashion and history as a movement from darkness to light, from primitivism to progressivism.

The humanism of the Renaissance becomes, in the modern period, anthropocentrism. Man is a titanic being without any natural superior, whose vocation is to better the world and other men. It is pointless to ask when, exactly, these modern attitudes took hold. In part, they are an outgrowth of Christian monotheism, which taught the idea that the earth and all its contents has been given to man by God for his exclusive use.

Renaissance humanism, which was in many ways a kind of neo-pagan revolt against Christianity, celebrated the ideal of man as Magus, and as a kind of mini-God here on earth. In

---

[9] WIL, 221.

part, though these Renaissance ideas were bound up with the revival of Hermetic occultism, they paved the way for the scientific revolution represented by men such as Francis Bacon.

By that point in history, belief—real belief—in the God of monotheism was dying, at least among the intelligentsia, who veered more and more toward abstract conceptions of divinity which had little to do with human life. God, in other words, had become irrelevant and human beings found themselves alone in this world that had been given to them for their mastery, with nobody watching from above. It was only a matter of time before man would declare himself God, as Fichte virtually does.

HEGEL'S IDEALISM

Hegel took over Fichte's ideas and, among other things, amplified them with a theological interpretation. God, for Hegel, is pure self-related Idea which becomes real and concrete in the world through human self-awareness—a self-awareness achieved primarily through the analysis and mastery of nature, as well as through art, religion, and philosophy.

Although Hegel insisted that he had not meant to make man God, a great many of his followers and detractors saw that this is precisely what his philosophy had done. The "young Hegelian" Ludwig Feuerbach saw this and in his influential work *The Essence of Christianity* (1841) declared that God was, in fact, nothing but an ideal projection of human consciousness, a stand-in, in fact, for humanity itself.

The Hegelian (or, perhaps, young Hegelian) element in Gerald's metaphysics comes in when Lawrence tells us that Gerald found his "eternal and his infinite" in the endless cycle of machine production. God, as Hegel learned from Aristotle, is an eternal act. The never-ending cycles of modern industrial production—the apex of man's mastery of nature—becomes, for Gerald, God incarnate: "the whole productive will of man was the Godhead."

NIETZSCHE, HEGEL, & THE END OF HISTORY

What seems Nietzschean here is simply the insistence on

Will. In allowing himself to be used as an instrument of the "productive will of man" Gerald believes that he is aggrandizing his own personal power. However, as I noted earlier, in believing so Gerald is deceiving himself, and in the end "the God-motion, this productive repetition *ad infinitum*" simply burns him away in a cold fire. However, there is more to Gerald's Nietzscheanism than this.

The relation of Nietzsche to Hegel is a complex one, but it can be boiled down in the following way. Hegel believed that in the modern period history had, in effect, ended. This assertion seems nonsensical if we make the mistake of confusing history with time. Of course, Hegel did not think time had stopped. He merely believed that the story of mankind had come to an end in the modern age, because it was in the modern, post-Christian age that mankind came to realize its true nature as radically self-determining (and other-determining, as well). With this realization of radical human freedom, and the realization that man actualizes God in the world, Hegel believed that essentially all the important questions and controversies of human history had been answered. The destiny of man was to live in more or less liberal societies, under more or less democratic states, and to practice more or less humanistic versions of Christianity. And in this condition mankind would continue to exist and prosper.

For Nietzsche, on the other hand, the end of history meant the death of everything that ennobles the human race. Without anything to struggle over or to believe in so strongly that one would be willing to fight and die for it, humanity would sink to the level of what Nietzsche called the Last Man, *Homo economicus*: the man whose aspirations do not rise above material comfort, safety, and security. The only hope was the arrival of the Overman, who would create new values, new systems of belief, and initiate new conflicts among human beings. In short, the Overman would re-start history. Nietzsche's writings, in their trenchant critique of all Western beliefs and values, can be seen as an attempt to actually hasten the collapse of the modern world and usher in the Overman.

NIETZSCHE'S WILL TO POWER

Essentially, Gerald Crich represents the Nietzschean Over-man—or at least someone who believes himself to be a Nietzschean Overman. Gerald, himself a "great blonde beast," is riding the tiger by riding his employees, expressing his "will to power" through mastering the mines. What Gerald doesn't realize is that, in Nietzschean terms, he is merely the *instrument* of will to power, expressing itself in the modern age as industrialism and mechanization. As Colin Milton has discussed at some length, this may actually indicate a confusion, or at least an inconsistency, in Lawrence's understanding of Nietzsche.[10]

Nietzsche is explicitly invoked in the novel when Ursula identifies Gerald with *"Wille zur Macht."* The episode which prompts this comment from her is one of the most famous in the novel. In the chapter "Coal Dust," Ursula and Gudrun go for a walk, but when they come to the railway crossing, they must wait for the colliery train to pass. As they stand there, Gerald Crich trots up riding a "red Arab mare." The mare is frightened by the locomotive and moves away from it, but Gerald forces her back again and again, cutting into her flesh with his spurs. Ursula is horrified and cries "No—! No—! Let her go! Let her go, you fool, you *fool*—!" Gudrun, on the other hand, is fascinated by Gerald's show of brute force over the mare and cries out only as he rides away, "I should think you're proud." As we shall see, Gudrun is Gerald's counterpart, a portrait of the other, purely destructive side of modern will.

The episode with the mare is a good example of Lawrence's sometimes obvious, but very effective symbolism. The mare represents nature—any and all natural beings—forced into submission before the designs and mechanisms of modernity. There is no other way to bring nature into accord with modern unnaturalism, other than by force and sheer bullying. And so later on Ursula refers to "Gerald Crich with his horse—a lust for bullying—a real *Wille zur Macht*—so base, so petty."

---

[10] See Colin Milton, *Lawrence and Nietzsche: A Study in Influence* (Aberdeen: Aberdeen University Press, 1987).

In his essay "Blessed are the Powerful" Lawrence remarks, "A will-to-power seems to work out as bullying. And bullying is something despicable and detestable."[11] In short, in *Women in Love* Lawrence seems to understand *Wille zur Macht* as a kind a kind of egoistic self-aggrandizement. In fact, however, what Nietzsche teaches is the *surrender* to *Wille zur Macht*, as an impersonal force that expresses itself through us.

Interestingly, perhaps the clearest parallels to Gerald Crich's philosophy of life, and Lawrence's treatment of it, are two thinkers Lawrence knew nothing about when he wrote *Women in Love*: Oswald Spengler and Ernst Jünger, both of whom were strongly influenced by Nietzsche.

SPENGLER: FAUSTIAN MAN & TECHNOLOGY

The first volume of Spengler's major work *Der Untergang des Abendlandes* (*The Decline of the West*) was published in 1918, two years after Lawrence first began working on *Women in Love*. According to Spengler, "Faustian man" creates a human world of artifacts and schemes not out of any economic motivation but rather out of a sheer desire for mastery.

However, Spengler believed that in the modern world, at the very height of his technological prowess, Faustian man has begun to decline. In *Der Mensch und die Technik* (*Man and Technics*, 1932), Spengler argued that technology had, in effect, taken on a life of its own. In building a technological world, humanity has been caught in the logic and the inevitable course of technology itself.

Technology rapidly becomes indispensable and human beings find themselves unable to do without it. Technological problems inevitably require technological solutions, and the sheer amount of gadgetry that the average human has to be conversant with grows exponentially. Technology comes to dominate the economy, so that most people find themselves not just being served by technology but working most of their

---

[11] *Phoenix II: Uncollected, Unpublished, and Other Prose Works by D. H. Lawrence*, Warren Roberts and Harry T. More, eds. (New York: Viking Press, 1970), 437.

lives for its advancement. In short, Faustian man, who had originally created the machines, now comes to be ruled by them.

Gerald certainly presents us with a vivid portrait of Spengler's Faustian man. Lawrence does not explicitly make anything like Spengler's argument concerning technology, but something like it lies beneath the surface of *Women in Love* and some of his other writings. Certainly Lawrence conveys the idea that Gerald foolishly believes himself to be master of the machines. Lawrence writes, "It was this inhuman principle in the mechanism he wanted to construct that inspired Gerald with an almost religious exaltation. He, the man, could interpose a perfect, changeless, godlike medium between himself and the Matter he had to subjugate."[12]

The medium Lawrence refers to is technology. "And Gerald was the God of the machine, *Deus ex Machina*."[13] In *Man and Technics*, Spengler writes: "To construct a world for himself, himself to be God—that was the Faustian inventor's dream, from which henceforth arose all projects of the machines, which approached as closely as possible to the unachievable goal of perpetual motion."[14] Of course, what Gerald doesn't realize is that he is Spengler's Faustian man caught in the trap: servant of that which he had created.

ERNST JÜNGER & THE *GESTALT* OF THE WORKER

Ernst Jünger's Promethean, Nietzschean philosophy of technology comes uncannily close to Gerald's own ideas. Jünger's views were forged on the battlefields of World War I, at the very same time Lawrence was writing *Women in Love*. The war affected both men profoundly, but in profoundly different ways. As I have already mentioned, much of the misanthropy and apocalyptic quality of *Women in Love* is to be at-

---

[12] WIL, 220.

[13] WIL, 220.

[14] Quoted in Michael E. Zimmerman, *Heidegger's Confrontation with Modernity: Technology, Politics, and Art* (Bloomington, Ind.: Indiana University Press, 1990), 27–28.

tributed to Lawrence's horror of the war and what it had reduced men to. Jünger himself regarded the war as horrifying,
and his memoir of his days as a soldier, *In Stahlgewittern* (*The
Storm of Steel*, 1920), is as frightening and chastening an account
of war as has ever been written. For Jünger, as for Lawrence
(and, later, Heidegger) the war was essentially a technological
phenomenon.

However, Jünger came to believe that technology—
including the technology of war—was, in effect, a natural phenomenon: the product of some kind of primal, expressive force
not unlike Schopenhauer's Will or Nietzsche's Will to Power.
The very title *In Stahlgewittern* suggests this understanding of
things. Michael E. Zimmerman writes in *Heidegger's Confrontation with Modernity*:

> On the field of battle, [Jünger] experienced himself at
> times as a cog in a gigantic technological movement. Yet,
> unexpectedly, by surrendering himself to this enormous
> process, he experienced an unparalleled personal eleva-
> tion and intensity which he regarded as authentic indi-
> viduation. Generalizing from this experience, he con-
> cluded that the best way for humanity to cope with the
> onslaught of technology was to embrace it wholehearted-
> ly.[15]

In *Der Arbeiter* (*The Worker*, 1932) Jünger heralded the coming of what Zimmerman calls his "technological Overman."
The productive power underlying all of reality shall body itself
forth in the "*Gestalt* of the worker," who is essentially a steely-
jawed soldier on perpetual march to the technological transformation and mastery of nature. Zimmerman writes:

> Jünger asserted that in the nihilistic technological era, the
> ordinary worker either would learn to participate willingly
> as a mere cog in the technological order—or would perish.
> Only the higher types, the heroic worker-soldiers, would be

15 Ibid., 49.

capable of appreciating fully the world-creating, world-destroying technological-industrial firestorm.[16]

This passage rather uncannily brings to mind Lawrence's description of the effect that Gerald's managerial style has on his workers. This is a crucially important passage and I shall quote it at length:

> But they submitted to it all. The joy went out of their lives, the hope seemed to perish as they became more and more mechanized. And yet they accepted the new conditions. They even got a further satisfaction out of them. At first they hated Gerald Crich, they swore to do something to him, to murder him. But as time went on, they accepted everything with some fatal satisfaction. Gerald was their high priest, he represented the religion they really felt. His father was forgotten already. There was a new world, a new order, strict, terrible, inhuman, but satisfying in its very destructiveness. The men were satisfied to belong to the great and wonderful machine, even whilst it destroyed them. It was what they wanted. It was the highest that man had produced, the most wonderful and superhuman. They were exalted by belonging to this great and superhuman system which was beyond feeling or reason, something really godlike. Their hearts died within them, but their souls were satisfied.[17]

One can see here that Lawrence seems to accept the Spengler-Jünger thesis that there is an inexorable logic to the modern, technological society and that a fundamental change has come over humanity which makes it possible for men to become servants of the machine. The passage above continues, "It was what they wanted, otherwise Gerald could never have done what he did." Lawrence clearly believes that there is something inevitable about what human beings are becoming — but unlike

---

[16] Ibid., 54–55.
[17] WIL, 223.

Jünger he cannot embrace it. The Nietzschean-Jüngerian answer to modernity — to ride the tiger — is perhaps the best that
one can do to harmonize oneself with the technological world
and its apparent dehumanization. But Lawrence absolutely rejects it, and paints Gerald as a tragic, deluded figure. Why? In
answering this question, we confront Lawrence's central objec-
tion to modernity.

HISTORY: PROGRESSIVE OR CYCLICAL?

In the deleted Prologue to *Women In Love* (which is interesting for a good many other reasons), Lawrence describes Birkin
in the early days of his affair with Hermione as "a youth of
twenty-one, holding forth against Nietzsche." Yet when Lawrence introduces us to Birkin's own views they seem strikingly
Nietzschean. First, however, Lawrence describes how Birkin
had studied education (and become a school inspector) under
the influence of what seems unmistakably like a warmed-over
Hegelianism:

> He had made a passionate study of education, only to
> come, gradually, to the knowledge that education is
> nothing but the process of building up, gradually, a
> complete unit of consciousness. And each unit of con-
> sciousness is the living unit of that great social, religious,
> philosophic idea towards which mankind, like an organ-
> ism seeking its final form, is laboriously growing.[18]

But Birkin quickly becomes disillusioned with this vision, and
responds to it in true Nietzschean fashion:

> But if there *be* no great philosophic idea, if, for the time
> being, mankind, instead of going through a period of

---

[18] D. H. Lawrence, *Women in Love* (Cambridge: Cambridge University Press, 1987), 505. It may help here to read "philosophic idea" as
"philosophic Idea." That he describes the idea as "social, religious,
philosophic" seems an allusion to Hegel's treatment of Spirit in its
Objective and Absolute forms.

growth, is going through a corresponding process of decay and decomposition from some old, fulfilled, obsolete idea, then what is the good of educating? Decay and decomposition will take their own way. It is impossible to educate for this end, impossible to teach the world how to die away from its achieved, nullified form. The autumn must take place in every individual soul, as well as in all the people, all must die, individually and socially. But education is a process of striving to a new, unanimous being, a whole organic form. But when winter has set in, when the frosts are strangling the leaves off the trees and the birds are silent knots of darkness, how can there be a unanimous movement towards a whole summer of fluorescence? There can be none of this, only submission to the death of this nature, in the winter that has come upon mankind, and a cherishing of the unknown that is unknown for many a day yet, buds that may not open till a far off season comes, when the season of death has passed away.[19]

What is Nietzschean here is Birkin's conviction that he is living at the end of history—but, contra Hegel, it is a time of disintegration and decay. However, unlike Nietzsche and his followers (including Gerald), Lawrence and Birkin do not see any way to transmute this situation into something that becomes life-advancing. What Gerald cannot see, but Birkin and Lawrence clearly can, is that the submission of the miners to "the *Gestalt* of the worker" represents the first stage in the complete breakdown of the Western world. The same passage quoted earlier from "The Industrial Magnate" chapter continues:

[Gerald] was just ahead of [his workers] in giving them what they wanted, this participation in a great and perfect system that subjected life to pure mathematical principles. This was a sort of freedom, the sort they really wanted. It was the first great step in undoing, the first

---

[19] Ibid., 505–506.

great phase of chaos, the substitution of the mechanical principle for the organic, the destruction of the organic purpose, the organic unity, and the subordination of every organic unit to the great mechanical purpose. It was pure organic disintegration and pure mechanical organisation. This is the first and finest state of chaos.[20]

Submission to or mastery of the modern, technological world—whether that world represents an advance or a degeneration—is not the answer for Lawrence because he believes that true human fulfillment lies in submission to something higher, or perhaps deeper: the true unconscious. Gerald offers his miners a kind of "freedom," but it is the illusory freedom of the mind and ego from the call of the natural self.

Essentially, for Lawrence, the modern world is characterized by the subordination of the organic to the mechanical; of the natural to the planned, automated, and "rational." But in severing the tie to the organic and placing themselves in the service of the machine and the idea, men lose their fundamental being, and their sense of having a place in the cosmos.

The real problem with Nietzsche is that although he talks a great deal about the body and about "instincts," everything for him is still, to borrow Lawrence's language, "in the head." In his *Genealogy of Morals*, Nietzsche presents us with an attractive discussion of the healthy, "natural" morality of the master type, which values such things as health, strength, and beauty. But Nietzsche's own approach to morals amounts to a conscious and willful desire to relativize all values—to declare that there is *no* natural source, and no natural values. The Overman, in fact, gets to simply posit new values. This appears to be a purely intellectual, and largely arbitrary affair. The idea of "creating" values is psychologically implausible: how can anyone believe in, let alone fight for, values and ideals that they have consciously dreamed up?

---

[20] WIL, 223.

THE IMPOTENT *ÜBERMENSCH*

In his characterization of Gerald Crich, Lawrence gives us a realistic portrait of what would become of an "Overman" in real life. Keep in mind that it is Lawrence's belief that when we abstract ourselves from the natural world, and from the promptings of the nature within us, we suffer and even, in a way, go mad. This is, in effect, what becomes of Gerald. In the concluding passages of the "Industrial Magnate" chapter Lawrence describes the psychological toll that mastery of Matter has taken on Gerald:

> And once or twice lately, when he was alone in the evening and had nothing to do, he had suddenly stood up in terror, not knowing what he was. And he went to the mirror and looked long and closely at his own face, at his own eyes, seeking for something. He was afraid, in mortal dry fear, but he knew not what of. He looked at his own face. . . . He dared not touch it, for fear it should prove to be only a composition mask.[21]

Inevitably, Gerald's sense of dissociation displays itself in a sexual manner:

> He had found his most satisfactory relief in women. . . . The devil of it was, it was so hard to keep up his interest in women nowadays. He didn't care about them anymore. . . . No, women, in that sense, were useless to him anymore. He felt that his mind needed acute stimulation, before he could be physically roused.[22]

The clear suggestion is that Gerald is practically impotent. Like Clifford in *Lady Chatterley's Lover*, whose impotence has a purely physical cause, Gerald is physically numb; he lives from the mind alone. Disconnected from his natural being, he no longer feels spontaneous, animal arousal for the opposite sex.

---

[21] WIL, 224.
[22] WIL, 225.

188 North American New Right, vol. 1, 2012

He has become "re-wired," so to speak, so that the route to the sexual center, in his case, is by way of the intellect; he can only become sexually aroused through his mind.

The irony here is that Gerald is portrayed throughout the novel as handsome, strong, and virile in both a physical and spiritual sense: he is a master of matter, and of women. In fact, however, both his physical and spiritual virility is mere appearance. He is master neither of himself nor of his world. Nor is he even master of his erection. On the other hand, Birkin, who is portrayed as physically weaker, is at least truly virile in a spiritual sense. This is the reason he manages to avoid becoming "absorbed" by Ursula.

Lawrence is famous for characterizing relations between the sexes as a battle, or, more accurately, a struggle unto death. In *Women in Love*, the two couples battle each other continuously, but most of the fighting is done by the women against the men. (The famous nude wrestling match between Gerald and Birkin is a purely honest, physical contest, whose only psychological undertones are homoerotic.)

Birkin compromises with Ursula in settling for love rather than something "higher." But despite this he maintains his integrity and individuality. It is a difficult feat, and even at the novel's end we see Ursula working to try and undermine his desire for another kind of love in his life: "Aren't I enough for you?" she asks him.

Gerald, however, cannot pull it off. He lacks Birkin's spiritual virility: his ability to maintain himself, inviolate, even in giving himself to a woman. Gudrun's onslaughts are much more destructive and insidious than Ursula's, and in the end the "manly" Gerald is broken by them.

GUDRUN BRANGWEN, THE MODERN WOMAN

Gerald Crich is only one half of Lawrence's portrait of the "modern individual." The other half is Gudrun Brangwen. Of course, Birkin and Ursula are modern individuals, though in a different sense. The latter couple are both seeking some fulfilling way to live in, or in spite of, the modern world. They (especially Birkin) have achieved some critical distance from it.

Gerald and Gudrun, however, are both creatures of modernity. Gerald has consciously embraced the modern rootless Prometheanism; Gudrun unconsciously. Further, Gudrun is not simply a female version of Gerald. Her "modernity" consists in certain traits which complement those of Gerald. What complicates matters is that Ursula and Gudrun also represent, for Lawrence, the two halves of femininity, and not just modern femininity.

In the first chapter of the novel, Gudrun reacts with revulsion to one of the locals as she and Ursula walk through Beldover: "A sudden fierce anger swept over the girl, violent and murderous. She would have liked them all annihilated, cleared away, so that the world was left clear for her." It is interesting to compare this with Birkin's (and Lawrence's) fantasies of annihilation. Birkin, the complete misanthrope, wants to wipe the earth clean of humanity, *including himself,* so that there is only "uninterrupted grass, and a hare sitting up." In Gudrun's fantasy, she is left sitting up and *everyone else* is wiped away.

This small detail gives us an important clue to Gudrun's character, which is fundamentally egoistic. A thoroughgoing egoism is always nihilistic, for it wills that all limitation or opposition to the ego be cancelled. But even the mere existence of other human beings (or anything else, for that matter) constitutes a limitation on the ego.

Just as Lawrence does with Gerald, this "self-assertion" on Gudrun's part is connected, by allusion, with Nietzsche. This time, however, the allusion is put into the mouth of the character herself in what seems on the surface like a purely innocent remark. Enjoying the snowy Tyrol, Gudrun exclaims, "Isn't the snow wonderful! Do you notice how it exalts everything? It is simply marvellous. One really does feel *übermenschlich* — more than human."[23]

Like Gerald, Gudrun lives in a state of abstraction from the body and from nature. In sex she remains perfectly detached. Writing of the aftermath of Gudrun's first sexual encounter with Gerald, Lawrence emphasizes again and again her full

---

[23] WIL, 385.

consciousness, while Gerald lays on top of her, asleep and sati-
ated. He tells us "she lay fully conscious." And: "Gudrun lay
wide awake, destroyed into perfect consciousness." And: "She
was suspended in perfect consciousness — and of what was she
conscious?"[24] (He does not truly answer the question.)

Gudrun is revolted by the rhythms of nature and by natural
objects — even though, ironically, it is small animals that she
depicts in her sculpture (perhaps this is the only way she can
encounter them, as things she molds and creates herself). Holding Winifred Crich's pet rabbit Bismarck, who puts up quite a
struggle, "Gudrun stood for a moment astounded by the thun-
derstorm that had sprung into being in her grip. Then her col-
our came up, a heavy rage came over her like a cloud. . . . Her
heart was arrested with fury at the mindlessness and bestial
stupidity of this struggle, her wrists were badly scored by the
claws of the beast, a heavy cruelty welled up in her."[25]

The mechanical succession of day after day revolts her. Very
early in the novel she confesses to Ursula, "I get no feeling
whatever from the thought of bearing children." She looks at
Ursula, who is clearly flustered by this, with a "mask-like ex-
pressionless face." When Ursula, intimidated by her sister,
stammers out a reply, "A hardness came over Gudrun's face.
She did not want to be too definite."[26] This desire to remain
indefinite is essential to Gudrun's character.

In fact, the essence of Gudrun is nothingness. In the first
chapter, Lawrence tells us "there was a terrible void, a lack, a
deficiency of being within her."[27] In conversation with Gerald,
Birkin describes her as a "restless bird," and says that "She
drops her art if anything else catches her. Her contrariness pre-
vents her from taking it seriously — she must never be too serious, she feels she might give herself away. And she won't give
herself away — she's always on the defensive. That's what I

[24] WIL, 338.
[25] WIL, 232.
[26] WIL, 3.
[27] WIL, 11.

can't stand about her type."[28]

Gudrun's "type" is the modern individual who cannot stand to be tied to anything, who is in constant flux, wary of anything that would compel her to make a commitment, whether to a relationship or a career, or whatever. Plato in the *Republic* essentially winds up describing this modern type when he attempts to characterize the sort of character produced by a democracy:

> "Then," [said Socrates], "he also lives along day by day, gratifying the desire that occurs to him, at one time drinking and listening to the flute, at another downing water and reducing; now practicing gymnastic, and again idling and neglecting everything; and sometimes spending his time as though he were occupied with philosophy. Often he engages in politics and, jumping up, says and does whatever chances to come to him; and if he ever admires any soldiers, he turns in that direction; and if it's money-makers, in that one. And there is neither order nor necessity in his life, but calling this life sweet, free, and blessed, he follows it throughout."
>
> "You have," [said Adeimantus], "described exactly the life of a man attached to the law of equality."[29]

Near the end of the novel, Lawrence tells us of Gudrun:

> Her tomorrow was perfectly vague before her. This was what gave her pleasure. . . . Anything might come to pass on the morrow. And to-day was the white, snowy iridescent threshold of all possibility. All possibility—that was the charm to her, the lovely, iridescent, indefinite charm—pure illusion. All possibility—because death was inevitable, and *nothing* was possible but death. She did not want things to materialize, to take any definite shape.

---

[28] WIL, 87.

[29] *The Republic of Plato*, trans. Allan Bloom (New York: Basic Books, 1991), 239–240, 561c–e.

> She wanted, suddenly, at one moment of the journey to-
> morrow, to be wafted into an utterly new course, by
> some utterly unforeseen event, or motion.[30]

When Gudrun is asked the question *wohin?* (where to?) Lawrence tells us that "She never wanted it answered."[31]

The quintessential modern individual does not, in fact, want
to be anything at all, for to be something definite would close
off other possibilities. And so the modern individual is always
oriented toward the future, which contains all possibilities, rather than toward the present. In this respect, Gudrun's character perfectly complements Gerald's. Gerald has completely abstracted himself from the present by regarding everything else
as "Matter" to be transformed according to his will.

This is what Heidegger tells us is the modern perspective on
nature.[32] Because everything is merely raw material to be made
over into something else, nothing is ever regarded as pos-
sessing a fixed identity. The essence of everything, really, is to
become something else, something better. The being of things
is thus something projected into the future; something that will
be revealed at a later date, through human ingenuity. The result of this treatment of things as raw material is that it produces individuals who live for the future: for what will be, and
for what they will be. This is how "abstraction" from the present occurs. A key ingredient in this, of course, is a kind of radical subjectivism and anthropocentrism: the being of things is
something that will be created by human beings.

The modern world is therefore a world of individuals who
are, mentally, quite literally elsewhere. On the one hand they
are disconnected from the natural world (which to them is essentially "stuff") and from their own nature, which they erro-
neously believe is something they can decide on or even re-

---

[30] WIL, 459–60.

[31] WIL, 461.

[32] See Heidegger's essay "The Question Concerning Technology,"
in *The Question Concerning Technology and Other Essays*, trans. William
Lovitt (New York: Harper Torchbooks, 1982).

make. They are disconnected, in fact, from presentness in general.

At one point Lawrence reveals to us that Gudrun suffers from the nagging feeling that she is merely an "onlooker" in life whereas her sister is a "partaker."[33] Indeed she is an onlooker and this is the key to her weird "consciousness" in the sex act. Gerald is an onlooker too, hence the sense of *unreality* he experiences when looking at himself in the mirror. They are both creatures of the mind, of idealism, and of futurity.

And this is truly the heart of Lawrence's critique of modernity: that we have lost touch with the sense of being a part of nature, and of being in our bodies, in present time. The ultimate result of such abstraction from nature, the body, and the present is the destruction of nature, of any possibility of inner peace and fulfillment, and of community.

Both Gerald and Gudrun are fundamentally destructive, nihilating individuals, but of the two Gudrun represents destruction in its purest form. Gerald destroys in order to transform and, as we saw earlier, he believes himself to be an agent of history and of social reform. (Or, at least, this is the moral veneer he paints over his activities.) With Gudrun, there is no such self-justification. Of course, ultimately Gerald's transformation of Matter is perfectly destructive, and so one can plausibly claim that in a sense Gudrun is the more honest of the two, though she is not self-aware in her destructiveness.

Gudrun represents the inner truth of Gerald's Prometheanism laid bare. This point is conveyed through the structure of Lawrence's novel itself. Gudrun is a presence throughout the entire book, but by the last few chapters the story becomes focused very much on her. And it is here that the pure nihilism of her character is brought to the fore. At the same time, Gerald, who had earlier been a relatively strong figure, is reduced to inefficacy and becomes almost a shadowy presence. His physical death comes, in a way, as merely an outward expression of an internal death that had already taken place in his soul.

---

[33] WIL, 157.

GUDRUN & LOERKE

What seems to immediately precipitate Gerald's suicide is that Gudrun gives every indication of leaving him for an artist named Loerke who she has met in the Tyrol. Loerke, better than Gerald, personifies Jünger's Promethean modernism. Loerke is a sculptor who shares with Gudrun and Ursula his plans for a granite frieze for a huge factory in Cologne. Churches, he tells the two sisters are "museum stuff," and since the world is now dominated by industry, not religion, art should come together with industry to make the modern factory into a new Parthenon:

> "And do you think then," said Gudrun, "that art should serve industry?"
> "Art should *interpret* industry as art once interpreted religion," he said. . . .
> "But is there nothing but work—mechanical work?" said Gudrun.
> "Nothing but work!" he repeated, leaning forward, his eyes two darknesses, with needle-points of light. "No, it is nothing but this, serving a machine, or enjoying the motion of a machine—motion, that is all. . . ."[34]

Loerke exhibits the same destructive, modern will we find in Gerald and Gudrun, but come to *full* consciousness of itself. This is what attracts Gudrun to Loerke. She has realized that Gerald is weak—he possesses the destructive will, but cannot own up to it; he must hide it under his idealism. Loerke has embraced the Will to Power without illusion:

> To Gudrun, there was in Loerke the rock bottom of all life. Everybody else had their illusion, must have their illusion, their before and after. But he, with a perfect stoicism, did without any before and after, dispensed with all illusion. He did not deceive himself in the last issue. In the last issue he cared about nothing, he was troubled

---

[34] WIL, 415.

about nothing, he made not the slightest attempt to be at one with anything. He existed a pure, unconnected will, stoical and momentaneous. There was only his work.[35]

Birkin describes him a bit later as "a gnawing little negation, gnawing at the roots of life."[36] Loerke is completely detached from nature and from the body. His sexuality is indeterminate. Though he has a male lover, he is drawn to Ursula. But he tells her that it wouldn't matter to him if she were one hundred years old: all that matters is her mind. (Loerke and Ayn Rand would have made a great pair.)

The Gudrun-Gerald relationship plays itself out, and reaches its tragic end, in the Alps. The choice of locations is significant. Lawrence often depicts his protagonists as either "watery" or "fiery." Gudrun and Gerald are the "watery" couple in *Women in Love*, whereas Birkin and Ursula are "fiery." The novel's climax involves Gerald trudging off into the Alps and, in an apparent act of suicide, freezing to death. It is as if his inner essence as water (in the form of ice) finally wins out and destroys him. Though Gudrun and Ursula are bound together by blood, the deeper bond is between Gudrun and Gerald, and it is metaphysical. They are the two aspects of the modern soul: one productive without a purpose; the other destructive, nihilating.

URSULA'S PRIMACY

In a sense it is strange to argue as I did earlier that *Women in Love* represents the continuation of Ursula's story. For one thing, the novel seems to focus more directly on the Birkin-Gerald relationship. Further, Gudrun is actually a more vivid character than Ursula. Nevertheless, I would still argue that Ursula is the central character. She is the most "natural" of any major character in the novel, the least in conflict with herself.

We are made to feel closer to Birkin, as he is transparently Lawrence's self-portrait. But Birkin is "abstracted" from life in

---

[35] WIL, 417.
[36] WIL, 419.

his own way. He berates Hermione for having everything in her head and lacking real sensuousness. Yet so much of Birkin is theory and *talk*. He wants some kind of total, transformative experience that would give him a real sense of being alive—yet he wants to hold onto his ego boundaries. He wants love, but then again he doesn't. He wants to give himself to Ursula, but not *totally*. Admirers of Lawrence the man often miss the rather obvious flaws in Birkin's character, and are thus oblivious to how Lawrence may have achieved a critical distance from Birkin (and from himself).

In the end, Birkin's "problems" are in large measure solved by the oldest means in the world: the force of natural love, and the institution of marriage. Up to a point (but only up to a point) Birkin simply surrenders his abstract ideas about relationships—about finding something "more" than love—and surrenders to Ursula. Ursula knows from deep within herself, the falsity of Birkin's ideals. Through her he comes to know what Lawrence would call "the sweetness of accomplished marriage." There is only one part of him that remains unfulfilled. But that is a subject for another essay . . .

Counter-Currents/*North American New Right*,
January 10–13, 2011

"THE FLASH IN THE PAN"
FASCISM & FASCIST INSIGNIA IN THE SPY SPOOFS OF THE 1960S

JEF COSTELLO

One of my guiltier pleasures is the "Matt Helm" films of the 1960s. There were four of these, all produced by Irving Allen and starring Dean Martin as secret agent Matt Helm. The first (*The Silencers*) appeared in 1966. The story behind these films is an interesting one. In the 1950s Irving Allen was partnered with Albert R. ("Cubby") Broccoli. Things came to an end, however, when Broccoli announced that he was interested in purchasing the film rights to the James Bond novels by Ian Fleming. Allen thought this a terrible idea, and according to legend told Fleming over lunch that he didn't think his novels were good enough even for television(!). Broccoli and Allen went their separate ways, the former partnering with Harry Saltzman. Their first film together was 1962's *Dr. No*, starring Sean Connery.

The result left Mr. Allen with a considerable amount of egg on his face. Not to be deterred—and apparently burdened by neither a sense of irony nor of shame—he purchased the rights to Donald Hamilton's series of Matt Helm spy novels. These books were actually the antithesis of Fleming's: Helm was a cold-blooded, no-nonsense American assassin, a character as devoid of charm as Hamilton's realistic plots were devoid of Bondian fantasy. Irving launched a phoney, "world-wide" search for an actor with the balls enough to play Helm—but in reality Dean Martin apparently had the part all along.

With a vocal style uncomfortably close to that of Bing Crosby, Martin had carefully cultivated the image of a boozy, lovable playboy. (In reality, he was by all accounts a serious, introverted man whose on-stage glasses of "whisky" were actually iced tea.) He was an odd choice for an American James Bond. But the Matt Helm films were consciously aimed at an unsophisticated, lower-middle-class American audience. The people who thought Bond was just a wee bit too toffee-nosed and foreign. The cinematic Matt Helm was Bond if Bond had been from Long Island. Helm was a boozing, womanizing wastrel. Incorrigibly lazy, he is depicted in three of the four films as unable to get out of bed to answer a call from the head of I.C.E. (Intelligence Counter-Espionage). But somehow he is always the only man who can save the world.

The Helm films borrow shamelessly from Bond but exaggerate all the Bondian elements. Instead of Maurice Binder's tasteful nude silhouettes, the credits sequence of the first Helm film features a strip show (the title "The Silencers" appears over the boobs of one of the girls, when she flings off her top). Unlike the spiritually virile Bond, who attracts women by actually seeming to be rather indifferent to them, Helm is a leering, eye-popping adolescent sex maniac. Instead of an Aston Martin complete with lethal accessories, Helm drives a 1965 Mercury Parklane station wagon complete with a bar and a bed (convenient for roadside quickies).The Helm films also frequently push the limit in sexual innuendo and double entendres. (The poster for the first film features Martin astride the barrel of a huge gun, under the words "Matt Helm Shoots the Works!") Perhaps the most amusing of these is the name of the evil organization Helm confronts in three of the four films: B.I.G.O.

Pronounced "Big Oh," the letters stand for Bureau of International Government and Order. Evil organizations with acronyms for names were a staple of the Bond-inspired films and television shows of the 1960s. The granddaddy of all of these was Fleming's S.P.E.C.T.R.E.: The Special Executive for Counter-Intelligence, Terrorism, Revenge, and Extortion. S.P.E.C.T.R.E. had been introduced in Fleming's 1961 novel *Thunderball*, which he had actually based (without attribution) on a screenplay written with Kevin McClory and Jack Whittingham.

S.P.E.C.T.R.E. was conceived by Messrs. Fleming, McClory, and Whittingham as a relatively small organization made up of the greatest criminal brains of the world. Headed by the sinister, asexual German-Greek Ernst Stavro Blofeld (Fleming's villains were often foreign mongrels) the organization was apolitical, and aimed simply at making a profit—it is never depicted as motivated by any sort of political ideology. (For example, in *Thunderball* S.P.E.C.T.R.E. steals two nuclear bombs with the intention of extorting £100 million from the United States and Great Britain.)

In the Bond films, which eventually completely eclipsed the novels in the popular imagination, S.P.E.C.T.R.E. became a vast organization equipped with its own secret island (*From Russia with Love*), steel-lined Paris headquarters (*Thunderball*), and steel-framed rocket base concealed inside an inactive volcano (*You Only Live Twice*). Blofeld really loved steel. In *For Your Eyes Only* (1981), Bond disposes of a Blofeld-like character who begs for his life, promising to build Bond "a delicatessen in stainless steel" (I am not kidding—watch it and see for yourself). And in the films S.P.E.C.T.R.E. has its own insignia: a stylized amalgam of a ghost and an octopus.

B.I.G.O. uniform patch from THE SILENCERS (1966)
(The circle is blue; the flash is red; the background is white.)

When S.P.E.C.T.R.E. became B.I.G.O. in the Matt Helm films, however, a curious thing happened. B.I.G.O. was not merely a vast criminal organization—it was a vast Right-wing conspiracy. The aim of the Bureau of International Government and Order was world domination: the creation of one world, fascist-style government. And, of course, it had to have its own insignia, just like S.P.E.C.T.R.E., and this is where things get really interesting: B.I.G.O.'s emblem was a lightning bolt through a circle (an "O"), uncannily similar to the official symbol of Sir Oswald Mosley's British Union of Fascists (even the red, white, and blue color scheme is the same).

Derisively referred to by critics of the B.U.F. as "the flash in the pan" (I have to admit that this is witty), the "Flash and Circle" was adopted by the organization in the summer of 1935, replacing the fasces. It was supposed to represent "the flash of action within a circle of unity" and was designed by Eric Hamilton Percy, Commander of the Fascist Defence Force.[1] A similar insignia was adopted by the Canadian Union of Fascists (a lightning bolt over a maple leaf), and in 1948 Mosley revived the flash and circle as the emblem of his new party, the Union Movement.

The "Flash and Circle" of the British Union of Fascists
(The disk is blue; the flash and circle are white; the background is red.)

The B.I.G.O. "flash and circle" was introduced in *The Silencers,* but it features even more prominently near the beginning of the second Helm film *Murderers' Row* (also 1966). In this film, the head of the organization is played to hammy perfection by Karl Malden, who is seen wearing a flash and circle ring (like the S.P.E.C.T.R.E. octopus rings prominently featured in *Thun-*

---

[1] See John Millican, *Mosley's Men in Black: Uniforms, Flags and Insignia of the British Union of Fascists 1932–1940 and Union Movement* (London: Brockingday Publications, 2004), 16.

derball) and seated in a kind of throne festooned with flashes and circles.

As a fascist superpower, B.I.G.O. was by no means unique among the '60s spy spoofs. Indeed, one of the interesting features of that cinematic phenomenon—the vast scope of which (from about 1965 to 1969) is largely forgotten today—is that the villains in the American films and television shows were almost always in the B.I.G.O. mold: quasi-fascist secret organizations out to "take over the world." On the other hand, the British and Continental spy films of the period usually feature villains moved by pure profit, not ideology—or by some strangely personal motivation. (For example, the 1966 Dino de Laurentiis-produced *Se Tutte le Donne del Mondo*—released in the U.S. as *Kiss the Girls and Make Them Die*—features a villain who plans to kill off the human race and repopulate the planet by inseminating a bevy of beautiful women kept in a state of suspended animation.)

The reason for this difference between the American and European spy extravaganzas is not hard to discern. Americans had been sold on entering the Second World War with the claim that the fascists were out to "take over the world." (While we allied ourselves with Stalin, who really did aim at world domination.)

This ridiculous fabrication is still believed almost universally by Americans. Thus villains assimilated to this "fascist" model were very easy for Americans to understand, and so Blofeld was transmuted into a plethora of little Hitlers and Mussolinis and Mosleys, armed this time with all the "secret weapons" we were frightened that the fascists might be developing in hollowed-out mountain lairs: death rays and flying saucers and doomsday devices of all kinds.

I started watching the '60s spy spoofs as a child, when local TV stations would run them in the afternoons. Bond was always a big TV event back then. He was only shown around my bedtime, and always with parental warnings (which seem absurd today). As a consequence, I was exposed to the Bond spoofs prior to ever being exposed to Bond. I thrilled to the adventures of Matt Helm, Derek Flint, *The Man From U.N.C.L.E.*,

Mission: Impossible, and *The Avengers*. The odd thing was that I usually found the villains more attractive than the heroes. The villains, for one thing, had those terrific, steel-lined underground lairs. They had snazzy uniforms (with thrilling lightning-bolt insignia). They were ruthless and efficient. They were serious and disciplined. They seemed bent on doing something important. The heroes, on the other hand, were usually wise-cracking hedonists—the most extreme example, of course, being Matt Helm.

Was this childhood attraction to B.I.G.O. and Thrush and Galaxy (we'll come to the latter two organizations in a moment) a sign of my incipient fascism? Probably. But much more interesting is what these American spy spoofs reveal about the modern American soul. Let's focus just on Matt Helm for the moment, as paradigmatic of the genre. It's discipline, order, duty, and iron will (the villains) . . . against hedonism, debauchery, and selfish abandon (the hero). (I didn't mention this earlier but Matt Helm always has to be talked into taking a break from chasing tail so that he can save the world.)

The conflict between America and fascism in World War II was presented as the conflict between freedom and slavery. In Matt Helm, however, the truth is laid bare and the conflict revealed for what it really was. The freedom of Matt Helm is mere license. He's out to make the world safe not for democracy and individual rights, but for boozing and boinking and sleeping till noon. That's the American Dream, and he is living it. And so when those handsome, uniformed, lock-step, lightning-bolted troops in their spotless lairs are blown to kingdom come we can all cheer. Who did they think they were, anyway?

Flint is another interesting case, almost forgotten today. He was played by James Coburn in two films: *Our Man Flint* (1966) and *In Like Flint* (1967). These are actually among the most significant '60s spy films, simply because they had some of the highest budgets (still not as high as the Bond films—but getting there). Derek Flint is a kind of absurdly exaggerated amalgamation of James Bond and Doc Savage. He is a scientist, a surgeon, an expert in several martial arts, an accomplished ballet dancer (and teacher!), a war hero, a marine biologist, and a linguist. He is able to stop his heart to feign death. Most memorable of all is his specially-designed cigarette lighter with its 82 functions ("83 if you wish to light a cigar").

Flint is what my mother would call "higher class" than Matt Helm (whom my mother would dismiss as "ethnic"). Nevertheless there are significant parallels—and very interesting ones, given the above analysis of the Americanization of the Bond genre. Just like Helm, Flint is a hedonist. He lives in a swanky, high tech apartment (like Helm's, only in better taste), located on Central Park West (unlike Helm, who parks his station wagon in the burbs—I kid you not). Flint is part Hugh Hefner, living with four beautiful girls ("there were five at one time, but that got to be a little much," he explains).

Just like Helm, Flint has to be convinced to set aside his personal projects to save the world. (Although Helm technically works for I.C.E., Flint is a completely free agent.) In both films, in fact, Flint ultimately agrees to go on his mission only after something happens which affects him personally. In the first film, he only really gets serious when the villains kidnap his girlfriends. Apparently saving the world from their infernal weather machine was not enough of a motivating factor for him.

In *Our Man Flint*, the villains—the ones with the weather machine—work for "Galaxy" (apparently not an acronym). Of course, they have their own insignia. Not a lightning bolt this time (that would be too perfect) but a G on a circle with Saturn-like rings encircling it (the exact same insignia, it is interesting to note, was used on the TV series *Land of the Giants*, also produced by Twentieth-Century Fox). Again, however, they are ideologically-motivated and vaguely fascist.

Galaxy is a bit different from B.I.G.O., however. They are headed by three white-coated, idealistic scientists who aim to pacify the world and create a conflict-free utopia. Ideologically, this actually puts them further to the Left, but there are strongly authoritarian overtones to Galaxy (nifty uniforms, a *"Führer-Prinzip"* of absolute loyalty to the three leaders, etc.). At the climax of the film, as Flint is poised to destroy the weather machine, one of the mad scientists pleads with him to desist: "Ours would be a perfect world!" he cries. "Not my kind of

world," Flint responds, as he proceeds to demolish their hand-
iwork.

Again, everything here is on personal terms. Our hero goes
on his mission because *his* life is adversely affected; he foils the
villains' scheme because their vision is not *his*. No conception
of duty is at work in Flint, and no high-minded ideals. He is
just looking out for number one. (It is noteworthy that on its
release, *Our Man Flint* received a positive review in Ayn Rand's
journal *The Objectivist*.[2])

Galaxy uniform patch from OUR MAN FLINT (1966)

Flint is consciously and deliberately presented in the films
as an American hero — and an American answer to Bond (in the
first film, he beats up a Connery lookalike dubbed "Triple-O-
Eight"). Flint infiltrates Galaxy's secret island but is captured
when an eagle swoops down and attacks him. One of the
guards explains that the eagle is trained to spot and attack
Americans. Flint smiles ruefully and says, "The anti-American
eagle. Diabolical!" Here we Americans are supposed to recognize that although the villains of this film are not the Soviets,
it's still about Us vs. Them. Us vs. them foreign interllectuals
with their books and their high-minded ideals. (The villains in
the Helm films are always foreign and often—interestingly—
aristocratic. What a delight it is to see the noble and the digni-

---

[2] Barbara Branden, Review of *Our Man Flint*, *The Objectivist*, 5, no.
2 (February 1966), in *The Objectivist*, Volumes 5–10 (1966–1971) (Palo
Alto, Cal.: Palo Alto Book Service, 1982), 30–31.

fied toppled by the hometown boy!)

At least Bond still works for Queen and Country. For all his high living, it is clear that he still has a strong sense of duty. The American versions of Bond jettison all that is noble about the character and turn him into a grinning lothario, a self-involved hedonist, a perpetual adolescent, a vulgar operator always on the make. And please keep squarely in mind that this was done so that American audiences would have a character they could more easily identify with and root for. The American soul is rotten to the core.

Perhaps the most interesting of all the quasi-fascist spy villains is the one that figures in virtually all 105 episodes of *The Man From U.N.C.L.E.*: Thrush. U.N.C.L.E. creator Sam Rolfe invented Thrush actually as a fall-back villain. Recognizing that it would be difficult to invent new villains every week, with new motivations, Rolfe thought Thrush would be a convenient, regular foil for the do-gooding U.N.C.L.E. organization (that's the United Network Command for Law and Enforcement). Thrush was initially supposed to be mysterious. We were not even supposed to know what the name "Thrush" meant: it could be the name of the organization, or the code-name of the organization's leader (in one 1964 episode, "The Double Affair," Thrush is actually referred to as "him").

As the series progressed, however, the writers came up with more definite ideas about Thrush. First, the name became fixed as the name of the organization (though why it was called that was never explained in the series). Rolfe decided that Thrush was a "supra-nation" spread all over the earth. (In the pilot episode, one of the villains says "Thrush is my country.") Its center was "The City of Thrush," though this was always referred to in the series as "Thrush Central": a mobile headquarters always shifting from place to place. Thrush's agents had cover roles within their communities.

Borrowing a term from the ancient Persians, Rolfe referred to the individual, local outposts of Thrush as "satraps," each of which would be disguised in some ordinary way: as a shop, an office block, a school, a mortuary, a garage, a winery, etc. This concept, of course, was equivalent to that of the "communist cell." And Thrush, in fact, is a unique amalgam of elements of the Left and Right—but, as always with these spy baddies—the accent is on the Right.

Thrush's stated purpose is taking over the world and imposing a fascist-style state. "Thrush believes in the two-party system: the masters and the slaves," our hero Napoleon Solo intones in an early episode. "Very nicely put," concurs his Thrush captor. Like B.I.G.O. and Galaxy and all the other fascistic spy villains, Thrush is depicted as highly disciplined and regimented (the "Thrush Uniform Code of Procedure" is mentioned in two episodes written by Peter Allan Fields, the man principally responsible for much of the detail about Thrush introduced in the series; many of Rolfe's original ideas were never used). Thrush agents, again, wear snazzy uniforms (complete with black berets). They carry specially-designed guns equipped with bizarre-looking night scopes. And Thrush is always coming up with some doomsday device: an earthquake machine, a "volcanic activator," a deadly hiccup-inducing gas, a death ray, another death ray, and still another death ray.

David McDaniel, author of several of the U.N.C.L.E. paperback novels (published by Ace Books), eventually decided that Thrush was an acronym standing for Technological Hierarchy for the Removal of Undesirables and the Subjugation of Humanity. Though this is often mentioned in retrospectives on U.N.C.L.E., in fact it was never used in the series and is not considered "canonical." Still, McDaniel did a nice job here in highlighting the "fascistic" nature of Thrush (at least insofar as fascism is popularly conceived).

The heroes of U.N.C.L.E.—Napoleon Solo and Illya Kuryakin—are a cut above Helm and Flint. Rolfe conceived U.N.C.L.E. as an FBI-like organization, utilizing only educated men of high moral character. And though Solo is a bit of a womanizer, both he and Kuryakin are depicted chiefly as stalwart, straight-arrow types. Still, the motives and raison d'être of U.N.C.L.E. are more than a bit vague. In the narration that opens the first several episodes of the series we are told that U.N.C.L.E. is involved in "maintaining political and legal order anywhere in the world." But what does this mean?

In a 1965 essay partly dealing with U.N.C.L.E., Ayn Rand rightly asked:

> If "U.N.C.L.E." is dedicated to international law enforcement, does this mean that it protects indiscriminately any sort of government? . . . If so, then would "U.N.C.L.E." have protected the Nazi government against the Jewish refugees? Would it protect Castro's government against the Cuban refugees? Would it protect the Soviet government against the refugees from one-third of the globe? The presence of Illya Kuryakin [a Russian agent] among the knights of "U.N.C.L.E." would seem to indicate the affirmative, which is pretty sickening.[3]

The truth seems to be that U.N.C.L.E. is out to maintain the *status quo* in our post-historical world of Last Men. U.N.C.L.E.'s only ideological commitment is opposition to Thrush, who are the quasi-fascistic Nietzschean Overmen bent on re-starting history. In other words, the good guys.

Thrush insignia from THE MAN FROM U.N.C.L.E.

---

[3] Ayn Rand, "Bootleg Romanticism," *The Objectivist Newsletter*, January 1965, p. 3. The version of "Bootleg Romanticism" published in Rand's *The Romantic Manifesto: A Philosophy of Literature*, 2nd ed. (New York: New American Library, 1975) is a shortened one, with all the material on U.N.C.L.E. excised.

Thrush's symbol was an angry, stylized bird inside a kind of shield. However, when U.N.C.L.E. was revived in the shockingly lame 1983 TV movie *The Return of The Man From U.N.C.L.E.: The Fifteen Years Later Affair,* the producers (who were not involved with the original series) forgot about this insignia. And when their designer was asked to come up with a symbol for Thrush, guess what he produced. That's right: a lightning bolt!

The American producers of the Bond-inspired spy spoofs made their villains fascists for the simple reason that Americans have been so well trained to see fascists as the bad guys. There was no need to provide any elaborate explanation for why these villains were bad—we all know these sorts of guys are bad, don't we? And yet they possess an enduring fascination and allure, with their sleek black uniforms, their arresting insignia, their discipline, their ruthlessness, their unity, and, yes, their great underground steel lairs.

Another part of the appeal is that they have rejected all of the equality and democracy bullshit—the bullshit all Americans pay lip service to (terrified of each other, as Tocqueville pointed out), but only the most craven actually believe in. The dirty little secret is that B.I.G.O. and Galaxy and Thrush are a kind of fantasy wish fulfillment for us. Fear not: at the end of the film, our oversexed playboy hero (with whom we guiltily identify) will vanquish the morally superior bad guys and we can all give three cheers for the American way. But we all know whose way is *really* superior—and that that lightning bolt in fact strikes at the worst within us, the worst which, in our modern world, reigns ascendant.

Give me the lightning bolt and pass me the black coveralls, I want to join Thrush!

Counter-Currents/ *North American New Right,*
May 11, 2011

THE LESSON OF
CARL SCHMITT*

GUILLAUME FAYE & ROBERT STEUCKERS

TRANSLATED BY GREG JOHNSON

We met Carl Schmitt in the Westphalian village of Pletten-berg, the place of his birth and retirement. For four remarkable hours we conversed with the man who remains unquestiona-bly the greatest political and legal thinker of our time. "We have been put out to pasture," said Schmitt. "We are like do-mestic animals who enjoy the benefits of the closed field we are allotted. Space is conquered. The borders are fixed. There is nothing more to discover. It is the reign of the *status quo . . .*"

Schmitt always warned against this frozen order, which ex-tends over the Earth and ruins political sovereignties. Already in 1928, in *The Concept of the Political*,[1] he detects in the univer-salist ideologies, those "of Rights, or Humanity, or Order, or Peace," the project of transforming the planet into a kind of de-politicized economic aggregate which he compares to a "bus with its passengers" or a "building with its tenants." And in this premonition of a world of the death of nations and cul-tures, the culprit is not Marxism but the liberal and commercial democracies. Thus Schmitt offers one of the most acute and perspicacious criticisms of liberalism, far more profound and original than the "anti-democrats" of the old reactionary Right.

He also continues the "realist" manner of analyzing of poli-tics and the state, in the tradition of Bodin, Hobbes, and Machi-avelli. Equally removed from liberalism and modern totalitari-

---

* http://guillaumefayearchive.wordpress.com/2009/09/06/la-lecon-de-carl-schmitt/

[1] Carl Schmitt, *The Concept of the Political*, trans. George Schwab (Chicago: University of Chicago Press, 1996) — trans.

an theories (Bolshevism and fascisms), the depth and the modernity of his views make him the most important contemporary political and constitutional legal theorist. This is why we can follow him, while of course trying to go beyond some of his analyses, as his French disciple Julien Freund, at the height of his powers, has already done.[2]

The intellectual journey of the Rhenish political theorist began with reflections on law and practical politics to which he devoted two works, in 1912 and 1914,[3] at the end of his academic studies in Strasbourg. After the war, having become a law professor at the universities of Berlin and Bonn, his thoughts were focused on political science. Schmitt, against the liberal philosophies of Law, refused to separate it from politics.

His first work of political theory, *Political Romanticism* (1919),[4] is devoted to a critique of political romanticism which he opposes to realism. To Schmitt, the millennialist ideals of the revolutionary Communists and the *völkisch* reveries of the reactionaries seemed equally unsuitable to the government of the people. His second great theoretical work, *Die Diktatur* [*The Dictator*] (1921),[5] constitutes, as Julien Freund writes, "one of the most complete and most relevant studies of this concept, whose history is analyzed from the Roman epoch up to Machiavelli and Marx."[6]

---

[2] Cf. Julien Freund, *L'Essence du politique* (Paris: Sirey, 1965), and *La Fin de la Renaissance* (Paris: PUF, 1980).

[3] Carl Schmitt, *Gesetz und Urteil. Eine Untersuchung zum Problem der Rechtspraxis* [*Law and Judgment: An Investigation into the Problem of Legal Practice*] [1912] (Munich: C. H. Beck, 1968) and *Der Wert des Staates und die Bedeutung des Einzelnen* [*The Value of the State and the Meaning of the Individual*] (Tübingen: J. C. B. Mohr [Paul Siebeck], 1914) — trans.

[4] Carl Schmitt, *Political Romanticism*, trans. Guy Oakes (Cambridge, Mass.: The MIT Press, 1985). — trans.

[5] Carl Schmitt, *Die Diktatur: Von den Anfängen des modernen Souveränitätsgedankens bis zum proletarischen Klassenkampf* [*The Dictator: From the Origins of Modern Theories of Sovereignty to Proletarian Class Struggle*] (Berlin: Duncker & Humblot, 1921) — trans.

[6] In his Preface to the French edition of *The Concept of the Political*: Carl Schmitt, *La notion de politique* (Paris: Calmann-Lévy, 1972).

Schmitt distinguishes "dictatorship" from oppressive "tyranny." Dictatorship appears as a method of government intended to face emergencies. In the Roman tradition, the dictator's function was to confront exceptional conditions. But Machiavelli introduces a different practice; he helps to envision "the modern state," founded on rationalism, technology, and the powerful role of a complex executive: this executive no longer relies upon the sole sovereign.

Schmitt shows that with the French jurist Jean Bodin, dictatorship takes the form of a "practice of the commissars" which arose in the 16th and 17th centuries. The "commissars" are omnipotent delegates of the central power. Royal absolutism, established on its subordinates, like the Rousseauist model of the social contract which delegates absolute power to the holders of the "general will" set up by the French Revolution, constitutes the foundation of contemporary forms of dictatorship.

From this point of view, modern dictatorship is not connected with any particular political ideology. Contrary to the analyses of today's constitutionalists, especially Maurice Duverger, "democracy" is no more free of dictatorship than is any other form of state power. Democrats are simply deceiving themselves to think that they are immune to recourse to dictatorship and that they reconcile real executive power with pragmatism and the transactions of the parliamentary systems.

In a fundamental study on parliamentarism, *The Crisis of Parliamentary Democracy* (1923),[7] Schmitt ponders the identification of democracy and parliamentarism. To him, democracy seems to be an ideological and abstract principle that masks specific modalities of power, a position close to those of Vilfredo Pareto and Gaetano Mosca. The exercise of power in "democracy" is subject to a rationalist conception of the state which justified, for example, the idea of the separation of pow-

---

[7] Carl Schmitt, *The Crisis of Parliamentary Democracy*, trans. Ellen Kennedy (Cambridge, Mass.: The MIT Press, 1986). See also Carl Schmitt, *Political Theology: Four Chapters on the Theory of Sovereignty* [1922], trans. George Schwab (Cambridge, Mass.: The MIT Press, 1986) — trans.

ers, the supposedly harmonious dialogue between parties, and ideological pluralism. It is also the rationality of history that founds the dictatorship of the proletariat. Against the democratic and parliamentarian currents, Schmitt places the "irrationalist" currents, particularly Georges Sorel and his theory of violence, as well as all non-Marxist critiques of bourgeois society, for example Max Weber.

This liberal bourgeois ideology deceives everyone by viewing all political activity according to the categories of ethics and economics. This illusion, moreover, is shared by liberal or Marxist socialist ideologies: the function of public power is no longer anything but economic and social. Spiritual, historical, and military values are no longer legitimate. Only the economy is moral, which makes it possible to validate commercial individualism and at the same time invoke humanitarian ideals: the Bible and business. This moralization of politics not only destroys all true morals but transforms political unity into neutralized "society" where the sovereign function is no longer able to defend the people for whom it is responsible.

By contrast, Schmitt's approach consists in analyzing the political phenomenon independently of all moral presuppositions. Like Machiavelli and Hobbes, with whom he is often compared, Schmitt renounces appeals to the finer feelings and the soteriology of final ends. His philosophy is as opposed to the ideology of the Enlightenment (Locke, Hume, Montesquieu, Rousseau, etc.) and the various Marxian socialisms as it is to Christian political humanism. For him, these ideologies are utopian in their wariness of power and tend to empty out the political by identifying it with evil, even if it is allowed temporarily — as in the case of Marxism.

But the essence of Schmitt's critique relates to liberalism and humanism, which he accuses of deception and hypocrisy. These theories view the activity of public power as purely routine administration dedicated to realizing individual happiness and social harmony. They are premised on the ultimate disappearance of politics as such and the end of history. They wish to make collective life purely prosaic but manage only to create social jungles dominated by economic exploitation and incapable of mastering unforeseen circumstances. Governments subject to this type of liberalism are always frustrated in their dreams of transforming politics into peaceful administration: other states, motivated by hostile intentions, or internal sources of political subversion, always emerge at unforeseen moments. When a state, through idealism or misunderstood moralism, no longer places its sovereign political will above all else, preferring instead economic rationality or the defense of abstract ideals, it also gives up its independence and its survival.

Schmitt does not believe in the disappearance of the political category. It can be invested in any type of activity. It is a concept which concerns collective anthropology. For this reason, political activity can be described as substantial, essential, enduring through time. The state, on the other hand, enjoys only conditional authority, i.e., a contingent form of sovereignty. Thus the state can disappear or be depoliticized without the political, but the political—as substantial—does not disappear. The state cannot survive unless it maintains a political monopoly, i.e., the sole power to define the values and ideals for which the citizens will agree to give their lives or to legally kill their neighbors—the power to declare war. Otherwise partisans will take over political activity and try to constitute a new legitimacy. This risk particularly threatens the bureaucratic states of modern liberal social democracies, in which civil war is prevented only by the enervating influence of consumer society.

These ideas are expressed in *The Concept of the Political*, Schmitt's most fundamental work, first published in 1928, revised in 1932, and clarified in 1963 by its corollary *Theory of the Partisan*.[8] Political activity is defined there as the product of a polarization around a relation of hostility. One of the fundamental criteria of a political act is its ability to mobilize a population by designating its enemy, which can apply to a party as well as a state. To omit such a designation, particularly through idealism, is to renounce the political. Thus the task of a serious

---

[8] Carl Schmitt, *Theory of the Partisan: Intermediate Commentary on the Concept of the Political*, trans. G. L. Ulmen (New York: Telos Press, 2007)—trans.

state is to prevent partisans from seizing the power to designate enemies within the community, and even the state itself. Under no circumstances can politics be based on the administration of things or renounce its polemical dimension. Any sovereignty, like any authority, is forced to designate an enemy in order to succeed in its projects; here Schmitt's ideas meet the research of ethologists on innate human behavior, particularly Konrad Lorenz.

Because of his "classical" and Machiavellian conception of the political, Schmitt endured persecution and threats under the Nazis, for whom the political was on the contrary the designation of the "comrade" (*Volksgenosse*).

The Schmittian definition of the political enables us to understand that the contemporary political debate is depoliticized and connected with electoral sideshows. What is really political is the value for which one is ready to sacrifice one's life; it can quite well be one's language or culture. Schmitt writes in this connection that "a system of social organization directed only towards the progress of civilization" does not have "a program, ideal, standard, or finality that can confer the right to dispose of the physical life of others." Liberal society, founded on mass consumption, cannot require that one die or kill for it. It rests on an apolitical form of domination: "It is precisely when it remains apolitical," Schmitt writes, "that a domination of men resting on an economic basis, by avoiding any political appearance and responsibility, proves to be a terrible imposture."

Liberal economism and "pluralism" mask the negligence of the state, the domination of the commercial castes, and the destruction of peoples anchored in a culture and a history. Along with Sorel, Schmitt pleads for a form of power that does not renounce its full exercise, that displays its political authority by the normal means that belong to it: power, constraint, and, in exceptional cases, violence. By ignoring these principles the Weimar Republic allowed the rise of Hitler; the techno-economic totalitarianism of modern capitalism also rests on the ideological rejection of the idea of state power; this totalitarianism is impossible to avoid because it is proclaimed humanitarian and is also based on the double idea of social pluralism and individualism, which put the nations at the mercy of techno-cratic domination.

The Schmittian critique of internal pluralism as conceived by Montesquieu, Locke, Laski, Cole, and the whole Anglo-Saxon liberal school, aims at defending the political unity of nations, which is the sole guarantor of civic protection and lib-erties. Internal pluralism leads to latent or open civil war, the fierce competition of economic interest groups and factions, and ultimately the reintroduction within society of the friend-enemy distinction which European states since Bodin and Hobbes had displaced outwards.

Such a system naturally appeals to the idea of "Humanity" to get rid of political unities. "Humanity is not a political con-cept," writes Schmitt, who adds:

The idea of Humanity in doctrines based on liberal and individualistic doctrines of natural Right is an ideal social construction of universal nature, encompassing all men on earth. . . . which will not be realized until any genuine possibility of combat is eliminated, making any grouping in terms of friends and enemies impossible. This univer-sal society will no longer know nations. . . . The concept of Humanity is an ideological instrument particularly useful for imperialistic expansion, and in its ethical and humane form, it is specifically a vehicle of economic im-perialism. . . . Such a sublime name entails certain conse-quences for one who carries it. Indeed, to speak in the name of Humanity, to invoke it, to monopolize it, dis-plays a shocking pretense: to deny the humanity of the enemy, to declare him outside the law and outside of Humanity, and thus ultimately to push war to the ex-tremes of inhumanity.[9]

To define politics in terms of the category of the enemy, to refuse humanitarian egalitarianism, does not necessarily lead to contempt for man or racism. Quite the contrary. To recog-

---

[9] Cf. *The Concept of the Political*, 53–54—trans.

nize the polemical dimension of human relations and man as "a dynamic and dangerous being," guarantees respect for any adversary conceived as the Other whose cause is no less legitimate than one's own.

This idea often recurs in Schmitt's thought: modern ideologies that claim universal truth and consequently consider the enemy as absolute, as an "absolute non-value," lead to genocides. They are, moreover, inspired by monotheism, Schmitt being a Christian pacifist and convert. Schmitt claims with good reason that the conventional European conception that validated the existence of the enemy and admitted the legitimacy of war—not for the defense of a "just" cause but as eternally necessitated by human relations—caused fewer wars and induced respect for the enemy considered as adversary (as *hostis* and not *inimicus*).

Schmitt's followers, extending and refining his thought, have with Rüdiger Altmann coined the concept of the *Ernstfall* (emergency case), which constitutes another fundamental criterion of the political. Political sovereignty and the credibility of a new political authority is based on the capacity to face and solve emergency cases. The dominant political ideologies, thoroughly steeped in hedonism and the desire for security, want to ignore the emergency, the blow of fate, the unforeseen. Politics worthy of the name—and this idea pulverizes the abstract ideological categories of "Right" and "Left"—is that which, secretly, answers the challenge of the emergency case, saves the community from unforeseen trials and tempests, and thereby authorizes the total mobilization of the people and an intensification of its values.

Liberal conceptions of politics see the *Ernstfall* merely as the exception and "legal normality" as the rule. This vision of things, inspired by Hegel's teleological philosophy of history, corresponds to the domination of the bourgeoisie, who prefer safety to historical dynamism and the destiny of the people. On the contrary, according to Schmitt, the function of the sovereign is his capacity to decide the state of the exception, which by no means constitutes an anomaly but a permanent possibility. This aspect of Schmitt's thought reflects his primarily French and

Spanish inspirations (Bonald, Donoso Cortès, Bodin, Maistre, etc.) and makes it possible to locate him, along with Machiavelli, in the grand Latin tradition of political science.

In *Legality and Legitimacy* (1932),[10] Schmitt, as a disciple of Hobbes, suggests that legitimacy precedes the abstract concept of legality. A power is legitimate if it can protect the community in its care by force. Schmitt accuses the idealistic and "juridical" conception of legality for sanctioning Hitler's rise to power. Legalism leads to the renunciation of power, which Schmitt calls the "politics of non-politics" (*Politik des Unpolitischen*), politics that does not live up to its responsibilities, that does not formulate a choice concerning the collective destiny. "He who does not have the power to protect anyone," Schmitt writes in *The Concept of the Political*, "also does not have the right to require obedience. And conversely, he who seeks and accepts power does not have the right to refuse obedience."

This dialectic of power and obedience is denied by social dualism, which arbitrarily opposes society and the sovereign function and imagines, contrary to all experience, that exploitation and domination are the political effects of "power" whereas they much more often arise from economic dependency.

Thus Schmitt elaborates a critique of the dualistic state of the 19th century based on the conceptions of John Locke and Montesquieu aiming at a separation between the sphere of the state and the private sphere. In fact, modern technocracies, historically resulting from the institutions of parliamentary representation, experience interpenetrations and oppositions between the private and public, as shown by Jürgen Habermas. Such a situation destabilizes the individual and weakens the state. According to Schmitt, it is this weakness of the democracies that allowed the establishment of one-party regimes, as he explains in *Staat, Bewegung, Volk* [*State, Movement, People*].[11]

---

[10] Carl Schmitt, *Legality and Legitimacy*, trans. Jeffrey Seitzer (Durham, N.C.: Duke University Press, 2004) — trans.

[11] *Staat, Bewegung, Volk: Die Dreigleiderung der politischen Einheit* [*State, Movement, People: The Three Organs of Political Unity*] (Hamburg: Hanseatische Verlagsanstalt, 1934) — trans. It concerns a series of

North American New Right, vol. 1, 2012

This type of regime constitutes the institutional revolution of the 20th century; in fact, it is today the most widespread regime in the world. Only Western Europe and North America preserved the pluralist structure of traditional democracy, but merely as a fiction, since the true power is economic and technical. The one-party state tries to reconstitute the political unity of the nation, according to a threefold structure: the state proper includes civil servants and the army; the people are not a statistical population but an entity that is politicized and strongly organized in intermediate institutions; the party puts this ensemble in motion (*Bewegung*) and constitutes a portal of communication between the state and the people.

Schmitt, who returns again and again to Nazism, Stalinism, theocracies, and humanitarian totalitarianisms, obviously does not endorse the one-party state. He does not advocate any specific "regime." In the old Latin realist tradition inherited from Rome, Schmitt wants an executive who is both powerful and legitimate, who does not "ideologize" the enemy and can, in actual cases, make use of force, who can make the state the "self-organization of society."

War thus becomes a subject of political theory. Thus Schmitt is interested in geopolitics as a natural extension of politics. For him, true politics, great politics, is foreign policy, which culminates in diplomacy. In *The* Nomos *of the Earth* (1951),[12] he shows that the state follows the European conception of politics since the 16th century. But Europe has become decadent: the bureaucratic state has been depoliticized and no longer allows the preservation of the history of the European peoples; the *jus publicum europaeum* which decided inter-state relations is declining in favor of globalist and pacifist ideologies that are incapable of founding an effective international law. The ideology of human rights and the vaunted humanitarianism of international institutions are paradoxically preparing a world where

---

studies on one-party states, primarily Marxist, that appeared in 1932.

[12] Carl Schmitt, *The* Nomos *of the Earth in the International Law of* Jus Publicum Europaeum, trans. G. L. Ulmen (New York: Telos Press, 2006) — trans.

force comes before law. Conversely, a realistic conception of the relations between states, which allows and normalizes conflict, which recognizes the legitimacy of will to power, tends to civilize the relationship between nations.

Schmitt is, along with Mao Tse-Tung, the greatest modern theorist of revolutionary war and of the enigmatic figure of the partisan who, in this era of the depoliticization of states, assumes the responsibility of the political, "illegally" designates his enemies, and indeed blurs the distinction between war and peace.[13]

Such a "false pacifism" is part of a world where political authorities and independent sovereignties are erased by a world civilization more alienating than any tyranny. Schmitt, who influenced the constitution of the Fifth French Republic—the French constitution that is most intelligent, most political, and the least inspired by the Enlightenment idealism that France has known—gives us this message: liberty, humanity, peace are only chimeras leading to invisible oppressions. The only liberties that count—whether of nations or individuals—are those guaranteed by the legitimate force of a political authority that creates law and order.

Carl Schmitt does not define the values that mobilize the political and legitimate the designation of the enemy. These values must not be defined by ideologies—always abstract and gateways to totalitarianism—but by mythologies. In this sense, the functioning of government, the purely political, is not enough. It is necessary to add the "religious" dimension of the first function, as it is defined in Indo-European tripartition. It seems to us that this is the way one must complete Schmitt's political theory. Because if Schmitt builds a bridge between anthropology and politics, one still needs to build another between politics and history.

Counter-Currents/ *North American New Right*,
July 11, 2011

---

[13] Cf. "The Era of Neutralizations and Depoliticizations" (1929), trans. Matthias Konzett and John P. McCormick, *Telos* no. 96 (Summer 1993)—trans.

HOMER:
THE EUROPEAN BIBLE[*]

DOMINIQUE VENNER

TRANSLATED BY GREG JOHNSON

François Jullien, one of the sharpest minds of our time, recalled:

> When I was in school, people called me and a friend "the Homerists" . . . And I was more and more convinced that, if one seeks the decisive categories of European thought (categories of "action" as well as categories of "knowledge"), one should go to Homer or Hesiod far more than Plato. . . . Unite [the *Iliad* and the *Odyssey*] and you obtain the fundamental outlines of Greek philosophy.[1]

The founding poems also conceal the first expression of historical thought. At the beginning of *The Peloponnesian War*, Thucydides refers to the *Iliad* to paint in broad strokes the ancient history of the Greeks, thus recognizing that Homer laid the foundations. But this merit was seldom recognized by oth-

---

[*] http://www.dominiquevenner.fr/#/la-bible-des-europeens/3228811

[1] François Jullien, interview with Thierry Marchaisse, *Penser d'un dehors (la Chine). Entretiens d'Extrême-Occident* (Paris: Le Seuil, 2000), 47. Philosopher and sinologist François Jullien is professor at the University of Paris-7. He is member of the Academic Institute of France and director of the Institute of Contemporary Thought. In order to discover the authentic nature of European thought, he compared it with something completely different, that of China, which had developed in an autonomous way, without any connection with the Indo-European languages.

ers. Inspired by the gods and poetry, which are all the same, Homer bequeathed to us the hidden source of our tradition, the Greek expression of all the whole Indo-European heritage, Celtic, Slavic, or Scandinavian, with a clarity and formal perfection without equivalent. This is why Georges Dumézil read the whole *Iliad* every year.

Who was Homer? Let us set aside scholarly debates. All that matters is what the Ancients thought. For them, there was no doubt about the reality of the divine poet. Likewise, they never doubted his double paternity of the *Iliad* and the *Odyssey*.[2]

THE RELEVANCE & TRANSMISSION OF HOMER

The relevance of Homer was highlighted in 2007 by an exposition organized by the Bibliothèque nationale de France (BNF).[3] It presented for the first time the rich collections of its Cabinet des médailles. As Patrick Morantin, the organizer of the exhibition, wrote:

> . . . first we must be appreciate the fact that a work of this magnitude has survived 3,000 years. What veneration must have attended the work of the Poet, whatever the times, that this body of work survived the wars, vandalism, accidents, censors, ignorance! How many works of late Antiquity were lost while today we can read the *Iliad* and the *Odyssey* in their entirety!

And Morantin added: "The *Iliad* is perhaps, with the New Testament, the work which we know from the greatest number of sources."

Plato said that Homer was "the educator of Greece." Thus he was also ours. His works, first passed down orally, go back to the 8th century before our era. Two centuries later, three Athenian statesmen, in particular Pisistratus, established the

---

[2] Jacqueline de Romilly, *Homère* (Paris: PUF, 1985).

[3] The BNF exposition "Homère. Sur les traces d'Ulysse" [Homer: On the Trail of Ulysses] was accompanied by an excellent catalog published by Seuil, realized by its three organizers, Olivier Estiez, Mathilde Jamain, and Patrick Morantin.

first written edition which thus dates back to the 6th century
BCE. Later, the exhibition organizers add, between the 2nd and
3rd centuries before our era:

> At the Library of Alexandria, Homer was the most-
> studied author; he was also the first to have a true critical
> edition. This critical edition began with Zenodotus of
> Ephesus in the first half of the 3rd century BCE and cul-
> minated with Aristarchus of Samothrace in the first half
> of the following century. . . . Beginning in the 2nd centu-
> ry BCE, the text becomes uniform. The work of the Alex-
> andrian scholars had set a standard to which everyone
> referred from then on.

The common source was the edition established in Athens in
the 6th century BCE at the request of Pisistratus.

FROM THE MIDDLE AGES TO THE RENAISSANCE

The memory of the poems had dimmed after the end of the
Western Roman Empire, without however disappearing:

> Although in the medieval West the bonds with the origi-
> nal texts of Homer were broken, the name of the Poet
> never ceased being venerated, and his heroes and their
> adventures were not forgotten. Homer indirectly contin-
> ued to nourish the imagination of the Middle Ages
> through the traditional Latin poets like Virgil, Ovid, Sta-
> tius, the Latin summaries of the *Iliad*, the apocryphal
> books of Dares the Phrygian and Dictys of Crete, the me-
> dieval romances like the *Romance of Troy* [of Benoît de
> Sainte-Maure] and their prose adaptations . . . so that the
> heroes and subject of the epics were known to the edu-
> cated public until the Renaissance, when the *Iliad* and the
> *Odyssey* were rediscovered in the original Greek.

Paradoxically, in spite of its Christianization, the Byzantine
Empire:

> . . . saw to the transmission of the old authors. The classi-

cal tradition was thus maintained in Byzantium where, from 425 to 1453, the schools of Constantinople remained its pillars. This is why it is unsuitable to speak about the "Renaissance" in the Eastern Roman Empire. In the West, on the other hand, the rediscovery of Homer was a striking fact for the first Italian humanists.

At the request of Petrarch, who did not read Greek, the first Latin translation of the *Iliad* was made in 1365–66.

The decisive event was the fall of Constantinople in 1453. Shortly before, many learned Byzantines had taken refuge in Italy. Thus in Florence in 1488 the first edition in Greek of the *Iliad* and the *Odyssey* appeared. The first French translation of the *Iliad* was done in 1577 by Breyer.

In an interview at the beginning of the BNF catalog, Jacqueline de Romilly stressed that the *Iliad* and the *Odyssey* reveal a high degree of civilization in the sense of refinement of manners. The historian added: "My teacher Louis Bodin, a great specialist in Thucydides, told me just before his death: 'Now, for me, there is nothing any more but Homer.' And it is much the same for me now; one goes back to the essential, to the completely pure."

ALWAYS BE THE BEST

In these poems circulates the sap of eternal youth. They are the source of our literature and an important part of our imagination. At first, their prodigiously inventive style can seem a little disconcerting, with the repetitive descriptions that were used as reference marks by the ancient listeners.[4] But once you

---

[4] No French translation is really satisfactory. To soak up the *Iliad*, one should refer to the translation of Paul Mazon (Gallimard, Folio Traditional), to which the Preface of P. Vidal-Naquet adds nothing. For the *Odyssey*, one should especially refer to the poetic translation of Philippe Jaccottet (La Découverte, 1982; Poche, 2004). The Bouquin collection, *Homère. L'Iliade et l'Odyssée* [*Homer: the Iliad and the Odyssey*], translated by Louis Bardollet, includes a useful critical apparatus. One can also profit from the essay by Jacqueline de Romilly, *Hector* (Éditions de Fallois, Livre de Poche, 1997). One should also consult Marcel Conche, *Essais sur Homère* (PUF, 1999). Finally, see

get into the text, you become enchanted by it.

By composing the *Iliad*, Homer became the creator of the very first tragic epic, and with the *Odyssey* that of the very first novel. Both poems place the individuality of the characters in the center of the story, something one does not find in the tradition of any other civilization. As André Bonnard emphasized, the *Iliad* is a world populated by innumerable distinct characters. To bring them to life, Homer does not describe them. It is enough for him to lend them a gesture or a word. Hundreds of warriors die in the *Iliad*, but with a specific trait, the Poet gives them a singular life at the instant of death: "And Diores fell into dust, on his back, his arms reaching out towards his comrades" (Book IV, 565). Just one gesture, and today we are touched by this unknown Diores and his love of life.

Death comes to the Trojan Harpalion, a brave man who cannot control a movement of horror: "Turning back, he rejoined the group of his comrades, looking around, so that bronze might not strike his flesh." He fell back in the arms of his companions and, on the ground, his body expressed its outrage while twisting "like a worm" (Book XIII, 654).

Almost all the characters of the *Iliad*, except women, children, and old men, are warriors. The majority are brave, but not in the same way. The bravery of Ajax, son of Telamon, first of the Greeks after Achilles in his impressive stature, strength, and cool, flinty, awe-inspiring bravery:

> He went forth like great Ares [the god of war], when he goes into battle. . . . So the great Ajax, rampart of the Achaeans, charged forth, a smile on his savage face. And his feet took great strides, as he held high a spear whose shadow grew. At this sight, the Argives [Achaeans] were in great joy. A terrible shudder shook every Trojan's limbs, and even Hector's heart pounded in his chest. . . . Ajax approached like a tower . . . (Book VII, 208–19)

A single combat, a duel, followed, full of fire, between Ajax

---

Dominique Venner, *Histoire et traditions des Européens* [*History and Traditions of Europe*] (Le Rocher, 2004), chs. 4–6.

and Hector who, after many assaults, was wounded in the neck. "The spear made black blood ooze." As the night fell, the heralds intervened to separate the two combatants. Homer shows us the point where combat answers to chivalrous rules. The two adversaries agree to suspend the fight until the following day, each returning to his camp, even exchanging their weapons (Book VII, 303–5). However stubborn, Ajax agrees, feeling that he has triumphed in this duel.

Different is the bravery of the young Diomedes. He has the ardor and dash of youth. He is the youngest of the heroes of the *Iliad* after Achilles. He is never tired. After a hard day of combat, he still volunteered for a perilous night expedition to the Trojan camp, in the company of Ulysses, a warrior as brave as he is crafty and circumspect.

Diomedes is also one of the chivalrous characters in the Poem. One day, ferociously fighting a Trojan, at the moment of striking with his lance, he suddenly learns he is Glaucos, son of a patron and friend of his father:

> Then brave Diomedes was seized with joy, and, planting his lance in the nourishing earth, he addressed his noble adversary these words full of friendship: "In truth, you are a patron of my father's house, and our bonds are very old. . . . By your father and mine, let us be from now on be friends." Thus spoke Diomedes . . . .
>
> Upon this, the two warriors jumped from their chariots, clasped hands, and agreed to be friends (Book VI, 229).

Homer honors rooted individuality, not "individualism," which is its perversion. With the respect of the adversary, in spite of implacable combat, they are bases of our tradition. One finds traces of this in the modern *Iliad*, Ernst Jünger's *In Storms of Steel*. These living roots dominate the whole European psyche: tragedy and philosophy. They are engraved into art beginning with Greek sculpture; they sustain law and political institutions.

Homer does not conceptualize, as philosophers later did. He

makes visible; he shows living examples, teaching the qualities that make a man a *"kalos k'agathos,"* noble and accomplished. "Always be the best," Peleus told his son Achilles, "better than the rest" (*Iliad*, Book VI, 208). To be noble and brave for a man, to be gentle, loving, and faithful for a woman. The Poet bequeathed a digest of what Greece offered thereafter to posterity: nature as model, the striving towards beauty, the creative force that strives always to surpass, excellence as the ideal of life.

THE *ILIAD*, POEM OF DESTINY

The *Iliad* is not just a poem about the Trojan War, it is a poem about destiny as perceived by our Borean ancestors, whether they are Greek, Celtic, German, Slavic, or Latin.[5] The Poet tells of nobility in the face of the plague of war. He tells of the courage of heroes who kill and die. He tells of the sacrifice of defenders of their fatherland, the sorrow of the women, the farewell of a father to his son going forth, the despondency of the old men. He tells of many more things still: the ambition of the leaders, their vanity, their quarrels. He tells also of their bravery and cowardice, their friendship, their love and tenderness. He tells of the thirst for glory that raises men to the level of gods. This poem where death reigns tells of the love of life and of honor placed higher than life, to which they were devoted even more than the gods.

In 16,000 verses in 24 books, the Poet reports a brief episode at the end of the ten year siege of Troy, probably in the 13th century BCE. Troy, also called Illion (hence *Iliad*) was a powerful fortified city built at the entrance to the Dardanelles on the Asiatic side of the Hellespont, the enduring frontier between West and East. Like modern historians, the ancients Herodotus and Thucydides, did not doubt the reality of the events that provided the framework of the *Iliad*. The Trojans were Boreans (Europeans), the same race as their Greek adversaries, the Achaeans "with the blonde hair," also called Argives (originat-

---

[5] The neologism "Borean" has a broader sense than "Indo-European," which is a linguistic category. It refers to the Greek myth of Hyperborean origins.

ing in the Argolide) or Danaens (descendants of the mythical Danaos). Despite this small difference, the Trojans are associated with Asia, and not only for geographical reasons. Their army contained contingents of barbarians (foreigners to the Greek world), which was confirmed by archaeological discoveries in the 20th century of their relations with the very diverse Hittite empire.

According to tradition, the conflict had a mythic origin: the intervention of the gods who divided themselves between the two camps. Out of vengeance, Aphrodite (Venus for the Latins) gave Paris, the young prince of Troy, son of the aged King Priam, the power to carry off Helen, the most beautiful of women, already married to "blonde haired" Menelaus, an Achaean, the king of Sparta. The abduction of a royal spouse by a foreigner was a crime that shocked all the Achaeans. At their wedding, all the lords of Greece had sworn to respect the union of Menelaus and the terribly tempting Helen. Thus an army assembled in Aulis with its fast vessels, like the Viking ships to come, and departed towards the Asian shores of the Troad. They went to punish Troy and bring back Helen. Thus the war began: "The whole earth, far and wide, flashed with the gleam of bronze . . ."

THE ANGER & REMORSE OF ACHILLES

After ten years of a very long siege, along with raids in the area, a quarrel opposed Agamemnon, chief of the Achaean coalition, and Achilles, the most famous hero of his camp. Abusing his power, Agamemnon seizes Briseis "with the lovely cheeks," the young captive loved by Achilles. Such is the pretext and the beginning of the poem: "Sing, goddess, of Achilles' disastrous anger . . ." This goddess who sings the epic is the Muse, whose interpreter is the Poet, which underlines his bonds with the divine world.

In the grip of righteous indignation, after having copiously insulted Agamemnon, Achilles decided to abandon the battle and "retire to his tent" (a much imitated phrase) as did his followers (the Myrmidons).

This anger of Achilles, principal hero of the *Iliad* along with the Trojan Hector, is the pivot of the poem. His withdrawal with his men had the gravest consequences for the Achaeans. Victory is abandoned. In the plain, under the walls of Troy, they will suffer three increasingly disastrous defeats. The attackers are put on the defensive. They must even build a fortified camp around their ships. This retrenchment was then attacked by the Trojans, led by Hector, the most famous son of Priam. The enemy managed to set fire to the Greeks' vessels and push them to the sea.

Throughout these hard battles, which fill the poem with carnage and exploits, the absence of Achilles is nothing but a sign declaring his force and power. The bravest of the Achaean chiefs — the massive Ajax, the impetuous Diomedes, the skillful Ulysses — vainly try to replace him.

One night of black tragedy, between two disasters, while Achilles, in his tent, putrefies in the inactivity to which he has condemned himself, he sees the approach of an embassy led by the two great leaders of the army, Ajax and Ulysses. With them is the aged Phoenix, who tries to make him hear the voice of his father. In the face of the danger, Agamemnon repented. He returned Briseis and offered sumptuous gifts in reparation. The embassy fails. Achilles, wallowing in resentment, put himself at fault in his turn (Book IX).

The following day, the Trojans forced the defenses of the Greeks. Hector set fire to a ship. At the other end of the camp, Achilles saw the rising flames. In spite of his obstinacy, he could not remain deaf to the pleas of his friend Patroclus, his other self. He sent his troops into battle, dressing Patroclus in his own armor. This counterattack drives back the Trojans. But Patroclus is killed by Hector. Achilles' grief is terrifying. But it brings him back to life, unleashing a fury and rage of vengeance against Hector, the killer of Patroclus.

Thus there is a complete reversal of the dramatic action that had been frozen by the withdrawal of Achilles. Maddened by pain, the Achaean hero returned to combat: "Like a vast fire, raging through the deep valleys of dry mountains, burning the forest, driven in all directions by the whirling wind, Achilles leaped in all directions. He went forth, like the night . . ." (Book XVIII). After a fierce duel, he killed Hector, then stripped his body and dragged it though the dust behind his chariot.

ACHILLES & HELEN AGAINST DESTINY

For Achilles, to the pain of the death of his friend was added the certainty of his own fate. An old prophecy warned that he would be killed as soon as he took Hector's life. Achilles always knew it. Unlike the other heroes killed in battle, he knew his destiny in advance and chose it. He does not submit to fate in Oriental fashion, he faces it. As a young man, he was offered the choice of a long and peaceful life far from strife, or an intense life cut short in the flash of battle. He chose the latter, bequeathing to the men of the future a model of tragic grandeur. Free of illusions, he knew that he will not have another life: "A man's life," he says in Book IX, "does not come again; one can never grasp or seize it again once it has escaped one's clenched teeth . . ." It is a thought that speaks to us today.

Compared to the sacred texts of other peoples and cultures, the freedom and sovereignty of the heroes of Homer are unique. Admittedly, the gods intervene in the *Iliad*, at fortunate and unfortunate times, but without really canceling the autonomy of men. Their many interventions do nothing but precipitate what would have happened anyway. And it really seems that Homer does not take them completely seriously (except perhaps Athena), which scandalized Plato's stilted and moralistic sensibility. In reality, the gods of Homer are allegories of the forces of nature and life.

The last book of the *Iliad* is a drama of reversal: when the aged Priam comes to beseech the return of the body of Hector, his son, one sees Achilles allowing himself to become more and more susceptible to compassion. Transformed by his own suffering, the hero appears more complex than his wild violence suggested.

There are more than heroes and warriors in the *Iliad*. There are also women (Helen, Hecuba, and Andromache), children (Astyanax), old men (Priam). There are more than just brave men. There is Paris, whose strange love of Helen is the origin of the Trojan War. Carrying out the will of Aphrodite, he was the seducer and the kidnapper of Helen. Unintentional author of the war, he also brings it to a close by killing Achilles with a treacherous arrow, an episode that the Poem does not report, which is suggested only by the prophecy formulated by Hector at the moment he dies (Book XXII, 359–60).

Paris, the often cowardly and conceited fop, is the opposite of his brother Hector, who scorns him. Hector is the pure hero, the guardian of Troy, whereas Paris is the "plague of his fatherland." Helen, the woman he seduced and abducted, scorns him and does not fear to rebuke him: "You have returned from battle! You should have died out there, under the blows of the strong warrior who was my first husband!" (Book III, 450–55). She detests him, but, by the will of Aphrodite, she is controlled by his sexual magnetism. Once again, Homer does not explain, he tells, and what he says is full of complex truth.

Helen is the opposite of Paris. She is moral, her lover amoral. She revolts against the physical submission to him imposed by Aphrodite. Her nature was made for order. She always regrets leaving her old life: "I left my bridal room, my close relations, my cherished daughter. . . . I languished in tears." Nothing predisposed her to take the role of adulteress, instrument of the ruin of two peoples. Nothing, except the intervention of the gods, in other words, fate.

With a great and moving truth, the *Iliad* thus shows several antagonistic natures, Helen and Paris, Achilles and Hector.

THE STOICISM & PATRIOTISM OF HECTOR

Achilles is the incarnation of youth (he is not yet 30). He is also the incarnation of Force. It is the radiant and untamed Force before which everything submits. A Force subjected to passion. Achilles does not dominate anything. He suffers everything: Briseis, Agamemnon, Patroclus, Hector. Circumstances unleash in him one storm after another. Everything in him defies death. He never thinks of it, although he knows it is near. He loves life enough to prefer its intensity to its duration. Strange destiny! His love of glory, his impatience, and his anger keep him far from battle during the first 18 books of the Poem, to the point of endangering his own. To save the army, he need only rise, which Ulysses says to him: "Rise and save the army . . ."

Awakened by the death of Patroclus, the Force rises: "Achilles rose . . . A great brightness radiated from his head to the sky, and he strode to the edge of the ditch. There, upright, he let out a cry, and this voice caused an inexpressible tumult among the Trojans" (Book XVIII).

Homer implicitly sympathizes with Hector. This Poem of the Achaeans thus treats their principal enemy as an exemplar. Is there any equivalent to this nobility in our national epics or the holy books of the Near or Far East? Though he is as brave as Achilles, Hector's courage is not blind. He is the very incarnation of stoic courage. He is not immune to fear. But he conquers it. Even though he knows that all is lost, he fights to the limit of his endurance.

Hector is also the incarnation of patriotism. For him, honor merges with duty. He is ready to die, not for his own glory, but for his country, his wife, and his child. He will defend them against all hope, because he knows Troy is lost.

Nothing is more carnal than Hector's love for his fatherland, of whom his woman and son are the concrete images. He does not hide his fears for Andromache before leaving her for battle:

> I know that the day will come when holy Troy will perish, and Priam, and the people of Priam. But neither the future misfortunes of the Trojans, nor that of my mother, or King Priam and my courageous brothers, afflict me as much as a bronze armored Achaean taking your freedom and leading you away in tears. . . . May the heavy earth claim me in death before I hear you cry, before I see you snatched away from here . . . (Book VI, 447–65)

With these words, he stretches his arms towards his son. But the child bursts into tears, terrified by the gleaming helmet of his father. Laughing, Hector takes off his helmet and gives the child to Andromache, who takes him in her arms "with laughter in tears." Here Homer's poetic genius shines forth. Hector tactfully corrects his dark predictions: "Don't cry," he says to Andromache, "Nobody can send me beneath the earth before the appointed hour."

The moment before, Andromache begged Hector not to go. She does so no longer. She understands that he defends their freedom and mutual affection. In this last conversation of two spouses, there is something unique in all ancient literature: a perfect equality in love. One never ceases discovering the incomparable richness of the *Iliad*, which concludes with the preparation of Hector's funeral. The death of Achilles and the "Trojan horse" are briefly evoked only in the *Odyssey* (Books XI and VIII).

THE *ODYSSEY*: THE PLACE OF MAN IN THE COSMOS

The second of the great Poems recounts, in 12,000 verses and 24 books, the difficult return of Ulysses to his fatherland. A return opposed by a thousand terrifying obstacles. The *Odyssey* is thus a poem of homecoming and of justified vengeance.

But the *Odyssey* is more than that. Under narrative pretexts different from *Iliad*, the second poem suggests the "worldview" suitable for Hellenes. It shows the place of man in nature and in relation to the mysterious forces that order it.

Putting mortals in harmony with the cosmic order is at the heart of the Homeric poems. But Homer's Heaven is placed beyond the primitive times of the foundation of cosmos evoked by the old myths, whose contents were formalized in Hesiod's *Theogony*: the confrontation of Ouranos and Cronos, the combat of the Olympian gods and their victory over the Titans. From all that, the Poet retains only the Olympian light, without worrying about building a coherent system. In Homer, the coherence is not in the discourse. It is in himself.

The departure from and return to the cosmic order form the framework of the *Odyssey*. Ulysses unintentionally provokes Poseidon's anger by blinding his son, the Cyclops Polyphemus. This is the way of man's destiny. Unintentionally, we provoke the anger and the punishment of the gods (representations of the forces of nature). Thus we must fight and endure their torments to return to the harmony we have lost.

This is the fate of Ulysses. Facing the terrifying tests imposed by Poseidon, who plunged him into a world of chaos, monsters (Scylla and Charybdis), and of possessive or perverse nymphs

(Calypso, Circe, the Sirens)—not to mention a visit to the realm of the dead—the navigator tirelessly fights to escape the traps and to find his place in the order of the world. Thrown into mortal peril, Ulysses will spend ten years returning home.

This is not merely the pretext for Homer to charm his audience with fantastic stories. The long voyage of Ulysses is drawn by the invincible desire of men, the "eaters of bread," to escape chaos and find an orderly cosmos. No doubt the love for Penelope and longing for Ithaca are at the heart of his desire to return. But they merely exemplify the hope to again fit in to the order of the world. Having found and reconquered his fatherland, Ulysses will be able to re-establish in the chain of generations, a fragment of eternity.

In the last sequence, every step of the reconquest of Ithaca is imprinted in the memory up to the massacre of the "suitors" (usurpers of Ithaca). How the hero is recognized by his son Telemachus and how they weave a meticulous plan of revenge. How Ulysses arrives at his manor, disguised as a beggar, who is recognized only by his old dog Argos, who dies of joy. How he is recognized by his nurse, Eurykleia, who sees an old scar, a souvenir of a memorable boar hunt. And then there is Penelope, anxious, worried, inquisitive. Then comes the moment of just vengeance in an orgy of bloodshed. And reunion with Penelope is finally possible. Then Athena intervenes, which delays the arrival of "rosy-fingered" Dawn, so that the night of the return lasts longer . . .

In the *Odyssey*, Homer does not only laud the memory of the heroes. He glorifies Eurykleia, Ulysses' nurse, and Eumaios, his swineherd, two subordinate characters who are nevertheless exemplars of intelligence and fidelity. Their role in the reconquest of Ithaca is capital. Thanks to Homer, they live on today.

THE POEM OF WOMANHOOD RESPECTED

Because of the marked presence of Penelope, the *Odyssey* is also the poem of independent and respected womanhood. When Penelope appears in the great hall of the palace of Ithaca, grand and beautiful, her brilliant veils drawn back on her cheeks, like golden Aphrodite, the knees of the "suitors" go weak and desire invades their hearts (*Odyssey*, Book XVIII, 249).

Lover, wife, and mother, Penelope takes charge of the small kingdom of Ithaca in the absence of Ulysses, a sign of the consideration given to womanhood. Many other women are present in Homer. In the *Iliad*, Helen, Andromache, Hecuba, and Briseis. In the *Odyssey*, Helen again, Calypso, and the charming Nausicaa. But Penelope eclipses all, except perhaps Helen, who is in a class by herself.

Compelled, like women of our time, to develop the knack of remaining feminine in a social world dominated by male values, she suffered often but never gave up. She remains beautiful and desirable in spite of time. She also knows the importance of modesty to live in the company of men. When tormented too much, she takes refuge in sleep, under Athena's watch. Against the avid pack of suitors, she does not use masculine violence. She charms, smiles, and invents the stratagem of the perpetually rewoven shroud, turning to her advantage the cupidity of which she is the object, and which perhaps does not displease her.

However, with the return of Ulysses, the craftiest of men, she deceives him somewhat as well, pretending not to recognize him even after he massacred the "suitors" with the assistance of their son Telemachus. He will first have to prove his identity by the test of the secret of the conjugal bed, before she agrees to give herself to him. In which sacred story of other cultures can one find the equivalent of Penelope and her radiant femininity?

THE POLITICAL ORDER OF THE SHIELD OF ACHILLES

Behind the story, there is also a vision of the world and life that awakens the memory of a lost wisdom. In Homer, the forests, the rocks, the wild beasts have souls. The whole of nature merges with the sacred, and men are not isolated from it.

If the cosmos is the model for Homer's world, the model of society is found in the allegory of Achilles' shield forged by Hephaestus (*Iliad*, Book XVIII). Depicted there are two cities, one in peace, the other in war, the two faces of life. One sees that the Greek city to come, with its citizens, institutions, and reciprocal duties, is already present in the Homeric world. Hector says explicitly that he dies for the freedom of his fatherland (*Iliad*, Book VI, 455–528).

The foundation of social organization and civil peace is the ethnic unity of the city and respect for the laws guaranteed by the ancients. Men are happy in a happy society, one that always remains the same, where one marries as one's ancestors married, where one plows and harvests as one always plowed and harvested. Individuals pass, but the city remains.

As Marcel Conche stresses, a society that can read its future in its past is a society at rest, without concern. This permanence grounds a sense of security. But innovations, "progress," will bring disorder. When one dreams of the ideal city and better days to come, everyone's peace of mind is destroyed. Then dissatisfaction with oneself and the world predominates. What, on the contrary, is illustrated on the shield of Achilles, is a happy society, filled with love of life, as it has always been. The weddings are joyous, equity reigns, civic friendship is shared by all. When war comes, the city closes ranks and mounts the ramparts. The enemy has not a single ally in the place. What peace of mind!

DESTINY COMMANDS BOTH GODS & MEN

Homer's heroes are not, however, models of perfection. They are prone to error and excess in proportion to their vitality. They pay the price, but they are never subject to a transcendent justice punishing sins defined by a code foreign to life. Neither the pleasures of the senses or of force, nor the joys of sexuality are likened to evil.

In Book III of the *Iliad* (161–75), the too beautiful Helen is invited by old King Priam onto the walls of Troy, in order to show her the two armies, for a truce had just been concluded. Quite conscious of being the involuntary cause of the war, Helen groans, saying that she would rather be dead. Priam then responds with an infinite gentleness that surprises us to this day: "No, my daughter, you are not guilty of anything. It is the gods who are responsible for it all!" What delicacy and high-mindedness from the old king, whose sons will all be killed.

But what generous wisdom also, which releases human beings from the guilt that so often overpowers other beliefs.

In placing these words in the mouth of Priam, Homer does not say that men are never responsible for the misfortunes that strike them. He shows elsewhere how much vanity, desire, anger, folly, and other failings can cause calamities. But in the specific case of this war, as in many wars, he stresses that everything escapes the will of men. It is the gods, fate, or destiny that decides.

History teaches us how judicious this interpretation is. How can one not be struck by its wisdom, when so many religions claim that human beings and their supposed sins are the cause of all the disasters of which they are victims, including earthquakes?[6]

But the words of Priam have a broader meaning still. They suggest that in the life of man, many of one's imagined faults are actually caused by fate. This distance regarding the mysteries of existences, this respect for others, are constants in the Homeric poems. This goes to show the very high level of civility and wisdom of the world Homer describes, by comparison to which ours often seems barbaric.

Homer thus bequeathed us, in their unaltered purity, our models and principles of life: nature as foundation, excellence as goal, beauty as horizon, the mutual respect of man and woman. The Poet reminds us that we were not born yesterday. He restores the foundations of our identity, the paramount expression of an ethical and aesthetic inheritance that is "ours," that he held in trust. And the principles that he brought to life in his models never cease to reappear to us, proof that the hidden thread of our tradition could not be broken.

Counter-Currents/ *North American New Right*,
September 8, 9, & 11, 2010

---

[6] One thinks of the famous interpretations of the tidal waves that destroyed Lisbon in 1755, inspired by what the Bible says of Sodom and Gomorrah, destroyed, it is said, because of the immorality of their inhabitants . . .

MARS & HEPHAESTUS:
THE RETURN OF HISTORY[*]

GUILLAUME FAYE

TRANSLATED BY GREG JOHNSON

Allow me an "archeofuturist" parable based on the eternal symbol of the tree, which I will compare to that the rocket. But before that, let us contemplate the grim face of the coming century.

The 21st century will be a century of iron and storms. It will not resemble those harmonious futures predicted up to the 1970s. It will not be the global village prophesied by Marshall McLuhan in 1966, or Bill Gates' planetary network, or Francis Fukuyama's end of history: a liberal global civilization directed by a universal state. It will be a century of competing peoples and ethnic identities. And paradoxically, the victorious peoples will be those that remain faithful to, or return to, ancestral values and realities — which are biological, cultural, ethical, social, and spiritual — and that at the same time will master techno-science. The 21st century will be the one in which European civilization, Promethean and tragic but eminently fragile, will undergo a metamorphosis or enter its irremediable twilight. It will be a decisive century.

In the West, the 19th and 20th centuries were a time of belief in emancipation from the laws of life, belief that it was possible to continue on indefinitely after having gone to the moon. The 21st century will probably set the record straight and we will "return to reality," probably through suffering.

The 19th and 20th centuries saw the apogee of the bourgeois

---

[*] http://guillaumefayearchive.wordpress.com/2007/07/12/mars -et-hephaistos-le-retour-de-lhistorie/

spirit, that mental smallpox, that monstrous and deformed simulacrum of the idea of an elite. The 21st century, a time of storms, will see the joint renewal of the concepts of a people and an aristocracy. The bourgeois dream will crumble from the putrefaction of its fundamental principles and petty promises: happiness does not come from materialism and consumerism, triumphant transnational capitalism, and individualism. Nor from safety, peace, or social justice.

Let us cultivate the pessimistic optimism of Nietzsche. As Drieu La Rochelle wrote: "There is no more order to conserve; it is necessary to create a new one." Will the beginning of the 21st century be difficult? Are all the indicators in the red? So much the better. They predicted the end of history after the collapse of the USSR? We wish to speed its return: thunderous, bellicose, and archaic. Islam resumes its wars of conquest. American imperialism is unleashed. China and India wish to become superpowers. And so forth. The 21st century will be placed under the double sign of Mars, the god of war, and of Hephaestus, the god who forges swords, the master of technology and the chthonic fires.

TOWARDS THE FOURTH AGE OF EUROPEAN CIVILIZATION

European civilization—one should not hesitate to call it higher civilization, despite the mealy-mouthed ethnomasochist xenophiles—will survive the 21st century only through an agonizing reappraisal of some of its principles. It will be able if it remains anchored in its eternal metamorphic personality: to change while remaining itself, to cultivate rootedness and transcendence, fidelity to its identity and grand historical ambitions.

The First Age of European civilization includes antiquity and the medieval period: a time of gestation and growth. The Second Age goes from the Age of Discovery to the First World War: it is the Assumption. European civilization conquers the world. But like Rome or Alexander's Empire, it was devoured by its own prodigal children, the West and America, and by the very peoples it (superficially) colonized. The Third Age of European civilization commences, in a tragic acceleration of the historical process, with the Treaty of Versailles and end of the civil war of 1914–18: the catastrophic 20th century. Four generations were enough to undo the labor of more than forty. History resembles the trigonometrical asymptotes of "catastrophe theory": it is at the peak of its splendor that the rose withers; it is after a time of sunshine and calm that the cyclone bursts. The Tarpeian Rock is next to the Capitol!

Europe fell victim to its own tragic Prometheanism, its own opening to the world. Victim of the excess of any imperial expansion: universalism, oblivious of all ethnic solidarity, thus also the victim of petty nationalism.

The Fourth Age of European civilization begins today. It will be the Age of rebirth or perdition. The 21st century will be for this civilization, the heir of the fraternal Indo-European peoples, the fateful century, the century of life or death. But destiny is not simply fate. Contrary to the religions of the desert, the European people know at the bottom of their hearts that destiny and divinities are not all-powerful in relation to the human will. Like Achilles, like Ulysses, the original European man does not prostrate himself or kneel before the gods, but stands upright. There is no inevitability in history.

THE PARABLE OF THE TREE

A Tree has roots, a trunk, and leaves. That is to say, the principle, the body, and the soul.

(1) The roots represent the "principle," the biological footing of a people and its territory, its motherland. They do not belong to us; one passes them on. They belong to the people, to the ancestral soul, and come from the people, what the Greeks called *ethnos* and the Germans *Volk*. They come from the ancestors; they are intended for new generations. (This is why any interbreeding is an undue appropriation of a good that is to be passed on and thus a betrayal.) If the principle disappears, nothing is possible any longer. If one cuts the tree trunk, it might well grow back. Even wounded, the Tree can continue to grow, provided that it recovers fidelity with its own roots, with its own ancestral foundation, the soil that nourishes its sap. But if the roots are torn up or the soil polluted, the tree is finished.

This is why territorial colonization and racial amalgamation are infinitely more serious and deadly than cultural or political enslavement, from which a people can recover.

The roots, the Dionysian principle, grow and penetrate the soil in new ramifications: demographic vitality and territorial protection of the Tree against weeds. The roots, the "principle," are never fixed. They deepen their essence, as Heidegger saw. The roots are at the same time "tradition" (what is handed down) and *"arche"* (life source, eternal renewal). The roots are thus the manifestation of the deepest memory of the ancestral and of eternal Dionysian youthfulness. The latter refers back to the fundamental concept of deepening.

(2) The trunk is its *"soma,"* the body, the cultural and psychic expression of the people, always innovating but nourished by sap from the roots. It is not solidified, not gelled. It grows in concentric layers, and it rises towards the sky. Today, those who want to neutralize and abolish European culture try to "preserve" it in the form of monuments of the past, as in formaldehyde, for "neutral" scholars, or to just abolish the historical memory of the young generations. They do the work of lumberjacks. The trunk, on the earth that bears it, is, age after age, growth and metamorphosis. The Tree of old European culture is both uprooted and removed. A ten year old oak does not resemble a thousand year old oak. But it is the same oak. The trunk, which stands up to the lightning, obeys the Jupiterian principle.

(3) The foliage is most fragile and the most beautiful. It dies, withers, and reappears like the sun. It grows in all directions. The foliage represents *psyche*, i.e., civilization, the production and the profusion of new forms of creation. It is the *raison d'être* of the Tree, its assumption. In addition, which law does the growth of leaves obey? Photosynthesis. That is to say, "the utilization of the force of light." The sun nourishes the leaves which, in exchange, produce vital oxygen. The efflorescent foliage thus follows the Apollonian principle. But watch out: if it grows inordinately and anarchically (like European civilization, which wanted to become the global Occident and extend to the whole planet), it will be caught by the storm, like a badly

rigged sail, and it will pull down and uproot the Tree that carries it. The foliage must be pruned, disciplined. If European civilization wishes to survive, it should not extend itself to the whole Earth, nor practice the strategy of open arms . . . as foliage that is too intrepid overextends itself, or allows itself to be smothered by vines. It will have to concentrate on its vital space, i.e., Eurosiberia. Hence the importance of the imperative of ethnocentrism, a term that is politically incorrect, but that is to be preferred to the "ethnopluralist" and in fact multiethnic model that dupes or schemers put forth to confuse the spirit of resistance of the rebellious elite of the youth.

One can compare the tripartite metaphor of the Tree with that of that extraordinary European invention the Rocket. The burning engines correspond to the roots, with chthonic fire. The cylindrical body is like the tree's trunk. And the capsule, from which satellites or vessels powered by solar panels are deployed, brings to mind foliage.

Is it really an accident that the five great space rocket series built by Europeans—including expatriates in the USA—were respectively called Apollo, Atlas, Mercury, Thor, and Ariadne? The Tree is the people. Like the rocket, it rises towards the sky, but it starts from a land, a fertile soil where no other parasitic root can be allowed. On a spatial basis, one ensures a perfect protection, a total clearing of the launching site. In the same way, the good gardener knows that if the tree is to grow tall and strong, he must clear its base of the weeds that drain its roots, free its trunk of the grip of parasitic plants, and also prune the sagging and prolix branches.

FROM DUSK TO DAWN

This century will be that of the metamorphic rebirth of Europe, like the Phoenix, or of its disappearance as a historical civilization and its transformation into a cosmopolitan and sterile Luna Park, while the other peoples will preserve their identities and develop their power. Europe is threatened by two related viruses: that of forgetting oneself, of interior desiccation, and of excessive "opening to the other." In the 21st century, Europe, to survive, will have to both regroup, i.e., return to its memory, and pursue its Faustian and Promethean aspirations. Such is the requirement of the *coincidentia oppositorum*, the convergence of opposites, or the double need for memory and will to power, contemplation and innovative creation, rootedness and transcendence. Heidegger and Nietzsche . . .

The beginning of 21st century will be the despairing midnight of the world of which Hölderlin spoke. But it is always darkest before the dawn. One knows that the sun will return, *sol invictus*. After the twilight of the gods: the dawn of the gods. Our enemies always believed in the Great Evening, and their flags bear the stars of the night. Our flags, on the contrary, are emblazoned with the star of the Great Morning, with branching rays; with the wheel, the flower of the sun at Midday.

Great civilizations can pass from the darkness of decline to rebirth: Islam and China prove it. The United States is not a civilization, but a society, the global materialization of bourgeois society, a comet, with a power as insolent as it is transitory. It does not have roots. It is not our true competitor on the stage of history, merely a parasite.

The time of conquest is over. Now is the time of reconquest, inner and outer: the reappropriation of our memory and our space: and what a space! Fourteen time zones on which the sun never sets. From Brest to the Bering Strait, it is truly the Empire of the Sun, the very space of the birth and expansion of the Indo-European people. To the south-east are our Indian cousins. To the east is the great Chinese civilization, which could decide to be our enemy or our ally. To the west, on the other side of the ocean: America whose desire will always be to prevent continental union. But will it always be able to stop it?

And then, to the south: the main threat, resurging from the depths of the ages, the one with which we cannot compromise.

Loggers try to cut down the Tree, among them many traitors and collaborators. Let us defend our land, preserve our people. The countdown has begun. We have time, but only a little.

And then, even if they cut the trunk or the storm knocks it down, the roots will remain, always fertile. Only one ember is enough to reignite a fire.

Obviously, they may cut down the Tree and dismember its

corpse, in a twilight song, and anaesthetized Europeans may not feel the pain. But the earth is fertile, and only one seed is enough to begin the growth again. In the 21st century, let us prepare our children for war. Let us educate our youth, be it only a minority, as a new aristocracy.

Today we need more than morality. We need hypermorality, i.e., the Nietzschean ethics of difficult times. When one defends one's people, i.e., one's own children, one defends the essential. Then one follows the rule of Agamemnon and Leonidas but also of Charles Martel: what prevails is the law of the sword, whose bronze or steel reflects the glare of the sun. The tree, the rocket, the sword: three vertical symbols thrust from the ground towards the light, from the Earth to the Sun, animated by sap, fire, and blood.

Counter-Currents/*North American New Right*,
June 29, 2010

POST-MODERN CHALLENGES:
BETWEEN FAUST & NARCISSUS[*]

ROBERT STEUCKERS

TRANSLATED BY GREG JOHNSON

In Oswald Spengler's terms, our European culture is the product of a "pseudomorphosis," i.e., of the grafting of an alien mentality upon our indigenous, original, and innate mentality. Spengler calls this innate mentality "Faustian."

THE CONFRONTATION OF THE INNATE & THE ACQUIRED

The alien mentality is the theocentric, "Magian" outlook born in the Near East. For the Magian mind, the ego bows respectfully before the divine substance like a slave before his master. Within the framework of this religiosity, the individual lets himself be guided by the divine force that he absorbs through baptism or initiation.

There is nothing comparable for the old-European Faustian spirit, says Spengler. *Homo europeanus*, in spite of the Magian/Christian varnish covering our thinking, has a voluntarist and anthropocentric religiosity. For us, the good is not to allow oneself to be guided passively by God, but rather to affirm and carry out our own will. "To be able to choose," this is the ultimate basis of the indigenous European religiosity. In medieval Christianity, this voluntarist religiosity shows through, piercing the crust of the imported "Magianism" of the Middle East.

Around the year 1000, this dynamic voluntarism appears gradually in art and literary epics, coupled with a sense of infinite space within which the Faustian self would, and can, ex-

---

[*] http://euro-a-synergies.hautetfort.com/archive/2008/07/21/defis-postmodernes-entre-faust-et-narcisse.html

pand. Thus to the concept of a closed space, in which the self finds itself locked, is opposed the concept of an infinite space, into which an adventurous self sallies forth.

FROM THE "CLOSED" WORLD TO THE INFINITE UNIVERSE

According to the American philosopher Benjamin Nelson,[1] the old Hellenic sense of *physis* (nature), with all the dynamism this implies, triumphed at the end of the 13th century, thanks to Averroism, which transmitted the empirical wisdom of the Greeks (and of Aristotle in particular) to the West. Gradually, Europe passed from the "closed world" to the infinite universe. Empiricism and nominalism supplanted a Scholasticism that had been entirely discursive, self-referential, and self-enclosed. The Renaissance, following Copernicus and Bruno (the tragic martyr of Campo dei Fiori), renounced geocentrism, making it safe to proclaim that the universe is infinite, an essentially Faustian intuition according to Spengler's criteria.

In the second volume of his *History of Western Thought*, Jean-François Revel, who formerly officiated at *Point* and unfortunately illustrated the Americanocentric occidentalist ideology, writes quite pertinently: "It is easy to understand that the eternity and infinity of the universe announced by Bruno could have had, on the cultivated men of the time, the traumatizing effect of passing from life in the womb into the vast and cruel draft of an icy and unbounded vortex."[2]

The "Magian" fear, the anguish caused by the collapse of the comforting certitude of geocentrism, caused the cruel death of Bruno, that would become, all told, a terrifying apotheosis . . . Nothing could ever refute heliocentrism, or the theory of the infinitude of sidereal spaces. Pascal would say, in resignation,

---

[1] Benjamin Nelson, *On the Roads to Modernity: Conscience, Science, and Civilizations* (Totowa, N.J.: Rowman & Littlefield, 1981).

[2] Jean-François Revel, *Histoire de la pensée occidentale* [*History of Western Thought*], vol. 2, *La philosophie pendant la science (XVe, XVIe et XVIIe siècles)* [*Philosophy and Science (15th-, 16th-, and 17th-Centuries)*] (Paris: Stock, 1970). Cf. also the masterwork of Alexandre Koyré, *From the Closed World to the Infinite Universe* (Baltimore: Johns Hopkins University Press, 1957).

with the accent of regret: "The eternal silence of these infinite spaces frightens me."

FROM THEOCRATIC LOGOS TO FIXED REASON

To replace Magian thought's "theocratic logos," the growing and triumphant bourgeois thought would elaborate a thought centered on reason, an abstract reason before which it is necessary to bow, like the Near Easterner bows before his god. The "bourgeois" student of this "petty little reason," virtuous and calculating, anxious to suppress the impulses of his soul or his spirit, thus finds a comfortable finitude, a closed-off and secured space. The rationalism of this virtuous human type is not the adventurous, audacious, ascetic, and creative rationalism described by Max Weber[3] which educates the inner man precisely to face the infinitude affirmed by Giordano Bruno.[4]

FROM THE END OF THE RENAISSANCE, TWO MODERNITIES ARE JUXTAPOSED

The petty rationalism denounced by Sombart[5] dominates the cities by rigidifying political thought, by restricting constructive activist impulses. The genuinely Faustian and conquering rationalism described by Max Weber would propel European humanity outside its initial territorial limits, giving the main impulse to all sciences of the concrete.

From the end of the Renaissance, we thus discover, on the one hand, a rigid and moralistic modernity, without vitality, and, on the other hand, an adventurous, conquering, creative modernity, just as we are today on the threshold of a soft post-modernity *or* of a vibrant post-modernity, self-assured and potentially innovative. By recognizing the ambiguity of the terms "rationalism," "rationality," "modernity," and "post-

---

[3] Cf. Julien Freund, *Max Weber* (Paris: PUF, 1969).

[4] Paul-Henri Michel, *La cosmologie de Giordano Bruno* [*The Cosmology of Giordano Bruno*] (Paris: Hermann, 1962).

[5] Cf. essentially: Werner Sombart, *Le Bourgeois. Contribution à l'histoire morale et intellectuelle de l'homme économique moderne* [*The Bourgeois: Contribution to the Moral and Intellectual History of Modern Economic Man*] (Paris: Payot, 1966).

modernity," we enter one level of the domain of political ideologies, even militant *Weltanschauungen*.

The rationalization glutted with moral arrogance described by Sombart in his famous portrait of the "bourgeois" generates the soft and sentimental messianisms, the great tranquillizing narratives of contemporary ideologies. The conquering rationalization described by Max Weber causes the great scientific discoveries and the methodical spirit, the ingenious refinement of the conduct of life and increasing mastery of the external world.

This conquering rationalization also has its dark side: It disenchants the world, drains it, excessively schematizes it. While specializing in one or another domain of technology, science, or the spirit, while being totally invested there, the "Faustians" of Europe and North America often lead to a leveling of values, a relativism that tends to mediocrity because it makes us lose the feeling of the sublime—of the telluric mystique—and increasingly isolates individuals. In our century, the rationality lauded by Weber, if positive at the beginning, collapsed into quantitativist and mechanized Americanism that instinctively led by way of compensation, to the spiritual supplement of religious charlatanism combining the most delirious proselytism and sniveling religiosity.

Such is the fate of "Faustianism" when severed from its mythic foundations, of its memory of the most ancient, of its deepest and most fertile soil. This caesura is unquestionably the result of pseudomorphosis, the "Magian" graft on the Faustian/European trunk, a graft that failed. "Magianism" could not immobilize the perpetual Faustian drive; it has—and this is more dangerous—cut it off from its myths and memory, condemned it to sterility and dessication, as noted by Valéry, Rilke, Duhamel, Céline, Drieu La Rochelle, Morand, Maurois, Heidegger, and Abellio.

CONQUERING RATIONALITY, MORALIZING RATIONALITY, THE DIALECTIC OF ENLIGHTENMENT, THE "GRAND NARRATIVES" OF LYOTARD

Conquering rationality, if it is torn away from its founding myths, from its ethno-identitarian ground, its Indo-European matrix, falls—even after assaults that are impetuous, inert, emptied of substance—into the snares of calculating petty rationalism and into the callow ideology of the "Grand Narratives" of rationalism and the end of ideology. For Jean-François Lyotard, "modernity" in Europe is essentially the "Grand Narrative" of the Enlightenment, in which the heroes of knowledge work peacefully and morally towards an ethico-political happy ending: universal peace, where no antagonism will remain.[6] The "modernity" of Lyotard corresponds to the famous "Dialectic of the Enlightenment" of Horkheimer and Adorno, leaders of the famous Frankfurt School.[7] In their optic, the work of the man of science or the action of the politician must be submitted to a rational reason, an ethical corpus, a fixed and immutable moral authority, to a catechism that slows down their drive, that limits their Faustian ardor. For Lyotard, the end of modernity, thus the advent of "post-modernity," is incredulity—progressive, cunning, fatalistic, ironic, mocking—with regard to this metanarrative.

Incredulity also means a possible return of the Dionysian, the irrational, the carnal, the turbid, and disconcerting areas of the human soul revealed by Bataille or Caillois, as envisaged and hoped by Professor Maffesoli,[8] of the University of Stras-

---

[6] Jean-François Lyotard, *The Postmodern Condition: A Report on Knowledge*, trans. Geoff Bennington and Brian Massumi (Minneapolis: University of Minnesota Press, 1984).

[7] Max Horkheimer and Theodor Adorno, *The Dialectic of Enlightenment*, trans. Edmund Jephcott (Stanford: Stanford University Press, 2002). Cf. also Pierre Zima, *L'École de Francfort. Dialectique de la particularité* [*The Frankfurt School: Dialectic of Particularity*] (Paris: Éditions Universitaires, 1974). Michel Crozon, "Interroger Horkheimer" ["Interrogating Horkheimer"] and Arno Victor Nielsen, "Adorno, le travail artistique de la raison" ["Adorno: The Artistic Work of Reason"], *Esprit*, May 1978.

[8] Cf. chiefly Michel Maffesoli, *L'ombre de Dionysos: Contribution à une sociologie de l'orgie* [*The Shadow of Dionysus: Contribution to a Sociology of the Orgy*] (Méridiens, 1982). Pierre Brader, "Michel Maffesoli: saluons le grand retour de Dionysos" [Michel Maffesoli: Let us Greet

bourg, and the German Bergfleth,[9] a young nonconformist philosopher; that is to say, it is equally possible that we will see a return of the Faustian spirit, a spirit comparable with that which bequeathed us the blazing Gothic, of a conquering rationality which has reconnected with its old European dynamic mythology, as Guillaume Faye explains in *Europe and Modernity*.[10]

THE ENCYSTED METANARRATIVE . . .

Once the Enlightenment metanarrative was established—"encysted"—in the Western mind, the great secular ideologies progressively appeared: liberalism, with its idolatry of the "invisible hand,"[11] and Marxism, with its strong determinism and

---

the Great return of Dionysos], *Magazine-Hebdo*, no. 54 (September 21, 1984).

[9] Cf. Gerd Bergfleth et al., *Zur Kritik der Palavernden Aufklärung* [*Towards a Critique of Palavering Enlightenment*] (Munich: Matthes & Seitz, 1984). In this remarkable little anthology, Bergfleth published four texts deadly to the "moderno-Frankfurtist" routine: (1) "Zehn Thesen zur Vernunftkritik" ["Ten Theses on the Critique of Reason"]; (2) "Der geschundene Marsyas" ["The Abuse of Marsyas"]; (3) "Über linke Ironie" ["On Leftist Irony"]; (4) "Die zynische Aufklärung" ["The Cynical Enlightenment"]. Cf. also R. Steuckers, "G. Bergfleth: enfant terrible de la scène philosophique allemande" ["G. Bergfleth: enfant terrible of the German philosophical scene"], *Vouloir*, no. 27 (March 1986). In the same issue, see also M. Kamp, "Bergfleth: critique de la raison palabrante" ["Bergfleth: Critique of Palavering Reason"] and "Une apologie de la révolte contre les programmes insipides de la révolution conformiste" ["An Apology for the Revolt against the Insipid Programs of the Conformist Revolution"]. See also M. Froissard, "Révolte, irrationnel, cosmicité et . . . pseudo-antisémitisme," ["Revolt, irrationality, cosmicity and . . . pseudo-antisemitism"], *Vouloir* nos. 40–42 (July–August 1987).

[10] Guillaume Faye, *Europe et Modernité* [*Europe and Modernity*] (Méry/Liège: Eurograf, 1985).

[11] On the theological foundation of the doctrine of the "invisible hand" see Hans Albert, "Modell-Platonismus. Der neoklassische Stil des ökonomischen Denkens in kritischer Beleuchtung" ["Model Platonism: The Neoclassical Style of Economic Thought in Critical Eluci-

metaphysics of history, contested at the dawn of the 20th century by Georges Sorel, the most sublime figure of European militant socialism.[12] Following Giorgio Locchi[13]—who occasionally calls the metanarrative "ideology" or "science"—we think that this complex "metanarrative/ideology/science" no longer rules by consensus but by constraint, inasmuch as there is muted resistance (especially in art and music[14]) or a general disuse of the metanarrative as one of the tools of legitimation.

The liberal-Enlightenment metanarrative persists by dint of force and propaganda. But in the sphere of thought, poetry, music, art, or letters, this metanarrative says and inspires nothing. It has not moved a great mind for 100 or 150 years. Already at the end of the 19th century, literary modernism expressed a diversity of languages, a heterogeneity of elements, a kind of disordered chaos that the "physiologist" Nietzsche analyzed[15] and that Hugo von Hoffmannstahl called *die Welt der Bezuge* (the world of relations).

---

dation"], in Ernst Topitsch, ed., *Logik der Sozialwissenschaften* [*Logic of Social Science*] (Cologne/Berlin: Kiepenheuer & Witsch, 1971).

[12] There is abundant French literature on Georges Sorel. Nevertheless, it is deplorable that a biography and analysis as valuable as Michael Freund's has not been translated: Michael Freund, *Georges Sorel, Der revolutionäre Konservatismus* [*Georges Sorel: Revolutionary Conservatism*] (Frankfurt am Main.: Vittorio Klostermann, 1972).

[13] Cf. G. Locchi, "Histoire et société: critique de Lévi-Strauss" ["History and Society: Critique of Lévi-Strauss"], *Nouvelle École*, no. 17 (March 1972), and "L'histoire" ["History"], *Nouvelle École*, nos. 27–28 (January 1976).

[14] Cf. G. Locchi, "L'idée de la musique' et le temps de l'histoire" ["The 'Idea of Music' and the Times of History"], *Nouvelle École*, no. 30 (November 1978), and Vincent Samson, "Musique, métaphysique et destin" ["Music, Metaphysics, and Destiny"], *Orientations*, no. 9 (September 1987).

[15] Cf. Helmut Pfotenhauer, *Die Kunst als Physiologie: Nietzsches ästhetische Theorie und literarische Produktion* [*Art as Physiology: Nietzsche's Aesthetic Theory and Literary Production*] (Stuttgart: J. B. Metzler, 1985). Cf. on Pfotenhauer's book: Robert Steuckers, "Regards nouveaux sur Nietzsche" ["New Views of Nietzsche"], *Orientations*, no. 9.

These omnipresent interrelations and overdeterminations show us that the world is not explained by a simple, neat and tidy story, nor does it submit itself to the rule of a disincarnated moral authority. Better: they show us that our cities, our people, cannot express all their vital potentialities within the framework of an ideology given and instituted once and for all for everyone, nor can we indefinitely preserve the resulting institutions (the doctrinal body derived from the "metanarrative of the Enlightenment").

The anachronistic presence of the metanarrative constitutes a brake on the development of our continent in all fields: science (data-processing and biotechnology[16]), economics (the support of liberal dogmas within the EEC), military (the fetishism of a bipolar world and servility towards the United States, paradoxically an economic enemy), cultural (media bludgeoning in favor of a cosmopolitanism that eliminates Faustian

---

[16] Biotechnology and the most recent biocybernetic innovations, when applied to the operation of human society, fundamentally call into question the mechanistic theoretical foundations of the "Grand Narrative" of the Enlightenment. Less rigid, more flexible laws, because adapted to the deep drives of human psychology and physiology, would restore a dynamism to our societies and put them in tune with technological innovations. The Grand Narrative — which is always around, in spite of its anachronism — blocks the evolution of our societies; Habermas' thought, which categorically refuses to fall in step with the epistemological discoveries of Konrad Lorenz, for example, illustrates perfectly the genuinely reactionary rigidity of the neo-Enlightenment in its Frankfurtist and current neo-liberal derivations. To understand the shift that is taking place regardless of the liberal-Frankfurtist reaction, see the work of the German biocybernetician Frederic Vester: (1) *Unsere Welt — ein vernetztes System* [*Our World — A Networked System*], dtv, no. 10118, 2nd ed. (Munich, 1983) and (2) *Neuland des Denkens. Vom technokratischen zum kybernetischen Zeitalter* [*New World of Thinking: From the Technocratic to the Cybernetic Age*] (Stuttgart: DVA, 1980). The restoration of holist (*ganzheitlich*) social thought by modern biology is discussed, most notably, in Gilbert Probst, *Selbst-Organisation, Ordnungsprozesse in sozialen Systemen aus ganzheitlicher Sicht* [*Self-Organization: Order Processes in Social Systems in Holistic Perspective*] (Berlin: Paul Parey, 1987).

specificity and aims at the advent of a large convivial global village, run on the principles of the "cold society" in the manner of the Bororos dear to Lévi-Strauss[17]).

THE REJECTION OF NEO-RURALISM, NEO-PASTORALISM ...

The confused disorder of literary modernism at the end of the 19th century had a positive aspect: its role was to be the magma that, gradually, becomes the creator of a new Faustian assault.[18] It is Weimar — specifically, the Weimar-arena of the creative and fertile confrontation of expressionism,[19] neo-Marxism, and the "conservative revolution"[20] — that bequeathed us, with Ernst Jünger, an idea of "post-metanarrative" modernity (or post-modernity, if one calls "modernity" the Dialectic of the Enlightenment, subsequently theorized by the Frankfurt School). Modernism, with the confusion it inaugurates, due to the progressive abandonment of the pseudo-science of the Enlightenment, corresponds somewhat to the nihilism observed by Nietzsche. Nihilism must be surmounted, exceeded, but not by a sentimental return, however denied, to a completed past. Nihilism is not surpassed by theatrical Wagnerism, Nietzsche fulminated, just as today the foundering of the Marxist "Grand Narrative" is not surpassed by a pseudo-rustic neoprimitivism.[21]

---

[17] G. Locchi, "L'idée de la musique et le temps de l'histoire" ["The Idea of Music and Historical Time"].

[18] To tackle the question of the literary modernism in the 19th century, see: Malcolm Bradbury, James McFarlane, eds., *Modernism 1890–1930* (Harmondsworth: Penguin, 1976).

[19] Cf. Paul Raabe, ed., *Expressionismus. Der Kampf um eine literarische Bewegung* [*Expressionism: The Struggle of a Literary Movement*] (Zurich: Arche, 1987) — a useful anthology of the principal expressionist manifestos.

[20] Armin Mohler, *La Révolution Conservatrice en Allemagne, 1918–1932* [*The Conservative Revolution in Germany, 1918–1932*] (Puiseaux: Pardès, 1993). See mainly text A3 entitled "*Leitbilder*" ("Guiding Ideas").

[21] Cf. Gérard Raulet, "Mantism and the Post-Modern Conditions" and Claude Karnoouh, "The Lost Paradise of Regionalism: The Crisis

In Jünger—the Jünger of *In Storms of Steel, The Worker,* and *Eumeswil*—one finds no reference to the mysticism of the soil: only a sober admiration for the perennialness of the peasant, indifferent to historical upheavals. Jünger tells us of the need for balance: if there is a total refusal of the rural, of the soil, of the stabilizing dimension of *Heimat,* constructivist Faustian futurism will no longer have a base, a point of departure, a fallback option. On the other hand, if the accent is placed too much on the initial base, the launching point, on the ecological niche that gives rise to the Faustian people, then they are wrapped in a cocoon and deprived of universal influence, rendered blind to the call of the world, prevented from springing towards reality in all its plenitude, the "exotic" included. The timid return to the homeland robs Faustianism of its force of diffusion and relegates its "human vessels" to the level of the "eternal ahistoric peasants" described by Spengler and Eliade.[22] Balance consists in *drawing in* (from the depths of the original soil) and *diffusing out* (towards the outside world).

In spite of all nostalgia for the "organic," rural, or pastoral— in spite of the serene, idyllic, aesthetic beauty that recommend Horace or Virgil—Technology and Work are from now on the essences of our post-nihilist world. Nothing escapes any longer from technology, technicality, mechanics, or the machine: nei-

---

of Post-Modernity in France," *Telos,* no. 67 (March 1986).

[22] Cf. Oswald Spengler, *The Decline of the West,* 2 vols., trans. Charles Francis Atkinson (New York: Knopf, 1926) for the definition of the "ahistorical peasant" see vol. 2. Cf. Mircea Eliade, *The Sacred and the Profane: The Nature of Religion,* trans. Willard R. Trask (San Diego: Harcourt, 1959). For the place of this vision of the "peasant" in the contemporary controversy regarding neo-paganism, see: Richard Faber, "Einleitung: 'Pagan' und Neo-Paganismus. Versuch einer Begriffsklärung" ["Introduction: 'Pagan' and Neo-Paganism: Essay in Disambiguation"], in Richard Faber and Renate Schlesier, *Die Restauration der Götter: Antike Religion und Neo-Paganismus* [*The Restoration of the Gods: Ancient Religion and Neo-Paganism*] (Würzburg: Königshausen & Neumann, 1986), 10–25. This text was reviewed in French by Robert Steuckers, "Le paganisme vu de Berlin" ["Paganism as Seen in Berlin"], *Vouloir,* nos. 28–29, April 1986, 5–7.

ther the peasant who plows with his tractor nor the priest who plugs in a microphone to give more impact to his homily.

THE ERA OF "TECHNOLOGY"

Technology mobilizes totally (*Total Mobilmachung*) and thrusts the individual into an unsettling infinitude where we are nothing more than interchangeable cogs. The machine gun, notes the warrior Jünger, mows down the brave and the cowardly with perfect equality, as in the total material war inaugurated in 1917 in the tank battles of the French front. The Faustian "Ego" loses its intraversion and drowns in a ceaseless vortex of activity. This Ego, having fashioned the stone lacework and spires of the flamboyant Gothic, has fallen into American quantitativism or, confused and hesitant, has embraced the 20th century's flood of information, its avalanche of concrete facts. It was our nihilism, our frozen indecision due to an exacerbated subjectivism, that mired us in the messy mud of facts.

By crossing the "line," as Heidegger and Jünger say,[23] the Faustian monad (about which Leibniz[24] spoke) cancels its sub-

---

[23] On the question of the "line" in Jünger and Heidegger, cf. W. Kaempfer, *Ernst Jünger*, Sammlung Metzler, Band 201 (Stuttgart, Metzler, 1981), 119–29. Cf also J. Evola, "Devant le 'mur du temps'" ["Before the 'Wall of Time'"] in *Explorations: Hommes et problems* [*Explorations: Men and Problems*], trans. Philippe Baillet (Puiseaux: Pardès, 1989), 183–94. Let us take this opportunity to recall that, contrary to the generally accepted idea, Heidegger does not reject technology in a reactionary manner, nor does he regard it as dangerous in itself. The danger is due to the failure to think of the mystery of its essence, preventing man from returning to a more originary unconcealment and from hearing the call of a more primordial truth. If the age of technology seems to be the final form of the Oblivion of Being, where the anxiety suitable to thought appears as an absence of anxiety in the securing and the objectification of being, it is also from this extreme danger that the possibility of another beginning is thinkable once the metaphysics of subjectivity is completed.

[24] To assess the importance of Leibniz in the development of German organic thought, cf. F. M. Barnard, *Herder's Social and Political Thought: From Enlightenment to Nationalism* (Oxford: Clarendon Press, 1965), 10–12.

jectivism and finds pure power, pure dynamism, in the universe of Technology. With the Jüngerian approach, the circle is closed again: as the closed universe of "Magianism" was replaced by the inauthentic little world of the bourgeois — sedentary, timid, embalmed in his utilitarian sphere — so the dynamic "Faustian" universe is replaced with a Technological arena, stripped this time of all subjectivism.

Jüngerian Technology sweeps away the false modernity of the Enlightenment metanarrative, the hesitation of late 19th century literary modernism, and the *trompe-l'oeil* of Wagnerism and neo-pastoralism. But this Jüngerian modernity, perpetually misunderstood since the publication of *Der Arbeiter* [*The Worker*] in 1932, remains a dead letter.

THE BABBITT WITH THE SARTREAN PARADOX

In 1945, the tone of ideological debate was set by the victorious ideologies. We could choose American liberalism (the ideology of Mr. Babbitt) or Marxism, an allegedly de-bourgeoisified version of the metanarrative. The Grand Narrative took charge, hunted down any "irrationalist" philosophy or movement,[25] set up a thought police, and finally, by brandishing the bogeyman of rampant barbarism, inaugurated an utterly vacuous era.

Sartre and his fashionable Parisian existentialism must be analyzed in the light of this restoration. Sartre, faithful to his "atheism," his refusal to privilege *one* value, did not believe in the foundations of liberalism or Marxism. Ultimately, he did not set up the metanarrative (in its most recent version, the

---

[25] The classic among classics in the condemnation of "irrationalism" is the *summa* of György Lukács, *The Destruction of Reason*, 2 vols. (1954). This book aims to be a kind of *Discourse on Method* for the dialectic of Enlightenment vs. Counter-Enlightenment, rationalism vs. irrationalism. Through a technique of amalgamation that bears a passing resemblance to a Stalinist pamphlet, broad sectors of German and European culture, from Schelling to neo-Thomism, are blamed for having prepared and supported the Nazi phenomenon. It is a paranoiac vision of culture.

North American New Right, vol. 1, 2012

vulgar Marxism of the Communist parties[26]) as a truth but as an "inescapable"*categorical imperative* for which one must militate if one does not want to be a "bastard," i.e., one of these contemptible beings who venerate "petrified orders."[27] It is the whole paradox of Sartreanism: on the one hand, it exhorts us not to adore "petrified orders," which is properly Faustian, and, on another side, it orders us to "magically" adore a "petrified order" of vulgar Marxism, already unhorsed by Sombart or De Man. Thus in the '50s, the golden age of Sartreanism, the consensus is indeed a moral constraint, an obligation dictated by increasingly mediatized thought. But a consensus achieved by constraint, by an obligation to believe without discussion, is not an eternal consensus. Hence the contemporary oblivion of Sartreanism, with its excesses and its exaggerations.

THE REVOLUTIONARY ANTI-HUMANISM OF MAY 1968

With May '68, the phenomenon of a generation, "humanism," the current label of the metanarrative, was battered and broken by French interpretations of Nietzsche, Marx, and Heidegger.[28] In the wake of the student revolt, academics and

---

[26] To understand the fundamental irrationality of Sartre's Communism, one should read Thomas Molnar, *Sartre, philosophie de la contestation* (Paris: La Table Ronde, 1969). In English: *Sartre: Ideologue of Our Time* (New York: Funk & Wagnalls, 1968).

[27] Cf. R.-M. Alberes, *Jean-Paul Sartre* (Paris: Éditions Universitaires, 1964), 54–71.

[28] In France, the polemic aiming at a final rejection of the anti-humanism of '68 and its Nietzschean, Marxist, and Heideggerian philosophical foundations is found in Luc Ferry and Alain Renaut, *French Philosophy of the Sixties: An Essay on Anti-Humanism*, trans. Mary H. S. Cattani (Amherst: University of Massachusetts Press, 1990) and its appendix, *'68–'86. Itinéraires de l'individu* [*'68–'86: Routes of the Individual*] (Paris: Gallimard, 1987). Contrary to the theses defended in first of these two works, Guy Hocquenghem in *Lettre ouverte à ceux qui sont passés du col Mao au Rotary Club* [*Open Letter to Those Went from Mao Jackets to the Rotary Club*] (Paris: Albin Michel, 1986) deplored the assimilation of the hyper-politicism of the generation of 1968 into the contemporary neo-liberal wave. From a definitely polemical point of view and with the aim of restoring debate, such

popularizers alike proclaimed humanism a "petite-bourgeois" illusion. Against the West, the geopolitical vessel of the Enlightenment metanarrative, the rebels of '68 played at mounting the barricades, taking sides, sometimes with a naïve romanticism, in all the fights of the 1970s: Spartan Vietnam against American imperialism, Latin American guerillas ("Che"), the Basque separatists, the patriotic Irish, or the Palestinians.

Their Faustian feistiness, unable to be expressed though autochthonous models, was transposed towards the exotic: Asia, Arabia, Africa, or India. May '68, in itself, by its resolute anchorage in Grand Politics, by its guerilla ethos, by its choice to fight, in spite of everything took on a far more important dimension than the strained blockage of Sartreanism or the great regression of contemporary neo-liberalism. On the Rght, Jean Cau, in writing his beautiful book on Che Guevara[29] understood this issue perfectly, whereas the Right, which is as fixated on its dogmas and memories as the Left, had not wanted to see.

With the generation of '68 — combative and politicized, conscious of the planet's great economic and geopolitical issues — the last historical fires burned in the French public spirit before the great rise of post-history and post-politics represented by the narcissism of contemporary neoliberalism.

---

as it is, in the field of philosophical abstraction, one should read Eddy Borms, *Humanisme — kritiek in het hedendaagse Franse denken* [*Humanism: Critique in Contemporary French Thought*] (Nijmegen: SUN, 1986).

[29] Jean Cau, the former secretary of Jean-Paul Sartre, now classified as a polemist of the "Right," who delights in challenging the manias and obsessions of intellectual conformists, did not hesitate to pay homage to Che Guevara and to devote a book to him. The "radicals" of the bourgeois accused him of "body snatching"! Cau's rigid Right-wing admirers did not appreciate his message either. For them, the Nicaraguan Sandinistas, who nevertheless admired Abel Bonnard and the American "fascist" Lawrence Dennis, are emanations of the Evil One.

THE TRANSLATION OF THE WRITINGS OF THE FRANKFURT SCHOOL ANNOUNCES THE ADVENT OF NEO-LIBERAL NARCISSISM

The first phase of the neo-liberal attack against the political anti-humanism of May '68 was the rediscovery of the writings of the Frankfurt School: born in Germany before the advent of National Socialism, matured during the California exile of Adorno, Horkheimer, and Marcuse, and set up as an object of veneration in post-war West Germany. In *Dialektik der Aufklärung*, a small and concise book that is fundamental to understanding the dynamics of our time, Horkheimer and Adorno claim that there are two "reasons" in Western thought that, in the wake of Spengler and Sombart, we are tempted to name "Faustian reason" and "Magian reason." The former, for the two old exiles in California, is the negative pole of the "reason complex" in Western civilization: this reason is purely "instrumental"; it is used to increase the personal power of those who use it. It is scientific reason, the reason that tames the forces of the universe and puts them in the service of a leader or a people, a party or state. Thus, according to Herbert Marcuse, it is Promethean, not Narcissistic/Orphic.[30] For Horkheimer, Adorno, and Marcuse, this is the kind of rationality that Max Weber theorized.

On the other hand, "Magian reason," according to our Spenglerian genealogical terminology, is, broadly speaking, the reason of Lyotard's metanarrative. It is a moral authority that dictates ethical conduct, allergic to any expression of power, and thus to any manifestation of the essence of politics.[31] In France, the rediscovery of the Horkheimer-Adorno theory of reason near the end of the 1970s inaugurated the era of depoliticization, which, by substituting generalized disconnection for concrete and tangible history, led to the "era of the vacuum"

---

[30] Cf. A. Vergez, *Marcuse* (Paris: PUF, 1970).

[31] Julien Freund, *Qu'est-ce que la politique?* [*What is Politics?*] (Paris: Seuil, 1967). Cf. Guillaume Faye, "La problématique moderne de la raison ou la querelle de la rationalité" ["The Modern Problem of Reason or the Quarrel of Rationality"], *Nouvelle École*, no. 41, November 1984.

described so well by Grenoble Professor Gilles Lipovetsky.[32] Following the militant effervescence of May '68 came a generation whose mental attitudes are characterized quite justly by Lipovetsky as apathy, indifference (also to the metanarrative in its crude form), desertion (of the political parties, especially of the Communist Party), desyndicalisation, narcissism, etc. For Lipovetsky, this generalized resignation and abdication constitutes a golden opportunity. It is the guarantee, he says, that violence will recede, and thus no "totalitarianism," red, black, or brown, will be able to seize power. This psychological easygoingness, together with a narcissistic indifference to others, constitutes the true "post-modern" age.

THERE ARE VARIOUS POSSIBLE DEFINITIONS OF "POST-MODERNITY"

On the other hand, if we perceive — contrary to Lipovetsky's usage — "modernity" or "modernism" as expressions of the metanarrative, thus as brakes on Faustian energy, post-modernity will necessarily be a return to the political, a rejection of para-Magian creationism and anti-political suspicion that emerged after May '68, in the wake of speculations on "instrumental reason" and "objective reason" described by Horkheimer and Adorno.

The complexity of the "post-modern" situation makes it impossible to give one and only one definition of "post-modernity." There is not *one* post-modernity that can lay claim to exclusivity. On the threshold of the 21st century, *various*

---

[32] G. Lipovetsky, *L'ère du vide: Essais sur l'individualisme contemporain* [*The Era of the Vacuum: Essays on contemporary individualism*] (Paris: Gallimard, 1983). Shortly after this essay was written, Gilles Lipovetsky published a second book that reinforced its viewpoint: *L'Empire de l'éphémère: La mode et son destin dans les sociétés modernes* (Paris: Gallimard, 1987); in English: *The Empire of Fashion: Dressing Modern Democracy*, trans. Catherine Porter (Princeton, N.J.: Princeton Univeristy Press, 1994). Almost simultaneously François-Bernard Huyghe and Pierre Barbès protested against this "narcissistic" option in *La soft-idéologie* [*The Soft Ideology*] (Paris: Laffont, 1987). Needless to say, my views are close to those of the last two writers.

post-modernities lie fallow, side by side, diverse potential post-modern social models, each based on fundamentally antagonistic values, primed to clash. These post-modernities differ — in their language or their "look" — from the ideologies that preceded them; they are nevertheless united with the eternal, immemorial, values that lie beneath them. As politics enters the historical sphere through binary confrontations, clashes of opposing clans and the exclusion of minorities, dare to evoke the possible dichotomy of the future: a neo-liberal, Western, American and American-like post-modernity versus a shining Faustian and Nietzschean post-modernity.

THE "MORAL GENERATION" & THE "ERA OF THE VACUUM"

This neo-liberal post-modernity was proclaimed triumphantly, with Messianic delirium, by Laurent Joffrin in his assessment of the student revolt of December 1986 (*Un coup de jeune* [*A Coup of Youth*], Arlea, 1987). For Joffrin, who predicted[33] the death of the *hard* Left, of militant proletarianism, December '86 is the harbinger of a "moral generation," combining in one mentality soft Leftism, lazy-minded collectivism, and neo-liberal, narcissistic, and post-political selfishness: the social model of this hedonistic society centered on commercial praxis, that Lipovetsky described as the *era of the vacuum*. A political vacuum, an intellectual vacuum, and a post-historical desert: these are the characteristics of the blocked space, the closed horizon characteristic of contemporary neo-liberalism. This post-modernity constitutes a troubling impediment to the greater Europe that must emerge so that we have a viable future and arrest the slow decay announced by massive unemployment and declining demographics spreading devastation under the wan light of consumerist illusions, the big lies of advertisers, and the neon signs praising the merits of a Japanese photocopier or an American airline.

On the other hand, the post-modernity that rejects the old

---

[33] Cf. Laurent Joffrin, *La gauche en voie de disparition: Comment changer sans trahir?* [*The Left in the Process of Disappearance: How to Change without Betrayal?*] (Paris: Seuil, 1984).

anti-political metanarrative of the Enlightenment, with its metamorphoses and metastases; that affirms the insolence of a Nietzsche or the metallic ideal of a Jünger; that crosses the "line," as Heidegger exhorts, leaving behind the sterile dandyism of nihilistic times; the post-modernity that rallies the adventurous to a daring political program concretely implying the rejection of the existing power blocs, the construction of an autarkic Eurocentric economy, while fighting savagely and without concessions against all old-fashioned religions and ideologies, by developing the main axis of a diplomacy independent of Washington; the post-modernity that will carry out this voluntary program and negate the negations of post-history — this post-modernity will have our full adherence.

In this brief essay, I wanted to prove that there is a continuity in the confrontation of the "Faustian" and "Magian" mentalities, and that this antagonistic continuity is reflected in the current debate on post-modernities. The American-centered West is the realm of "Magianisms," with its cosmopolitanism and authoritarian sects.[34] Europe, the heiress of a Faustianism much abused by "Magian" thought, will reassert herself with a post-modernity that will recapitulate the inexpressible themes, recurring but always new, of the Faustianness intrinsic to the European soul.

Counter-Currents/*North American New Right*,
December 13, 15, & 29, 2010

---

[34] Cf. Furio Colombo, *Il dio d'America: Religione, ribellione e nuova destra* [*The God of America: Religion, Rebellion, and the New Right*] (Milan: Arnoldo Mondadori, 1983).

JEAN THIRIART:
THE MACHIAVELLI OF UNITED EUROPE[*]

EDOUARD RIX

TRANSLATED BY GREG JOHNSON

A diligent reader of Hobbes, Machiavelli, and Pareto, the Belgian Jean Thiriart (1922–1992), founder of the mythic pan-European transnational Jeune Europe (Young Europe), is the unsurpassable theorist of a Greater Europe united from Galway to Vladivostok.

Born in 1922 to a liberal family in Liège, Belgium, Jean Thiriart was a young militant in the ranks of the Marxist extreme Left as part of the Unified Socialist Young Guard and the Socialist Antifascist Union. He greeted the Molotov-Ribbentrop pact of 1939 with enthusiasm: "The most beautiful, the most exciting part of my life," he would admit, "was the German-Soviet pact."[1] Because, for him, "National Socialism was not an enemy of Communism, but a competitor."[2]

FROM ONE WAR TO ANOTHER

In 1940, at the age of 18, he joined the Amis du Grand Reich allemand (AGRA–Friends of the Greater German Reich), the association in occupied French-speaking Belgium of secular and socialist supporters of collaboration, not Rexists. He also belonged to the Fichte Bund, a movement based in Hamburg that emerged from the National Bolshevik current. Condemned to three years of prison after the liberation, he gave up all political activity.

He became re-engaged only in 1960, at the age of 38, during

---

[*] *Réfléchir & Agir*, no. 21, Fall 2005, 44–47.
[1] C. Bourseiller, *Extrême-droite. L'enquête* (F. Bourrin, 1991), 114.
[2] Ibid.

the decolonization of the Belgian Congo, taking part in the foundation of the Comité d'action et de défense des Belges d'Afrique (CADBA—Committee of Action and Defense of the Belgians of Africa). Quickly, the defense of the Belgians of the Congo transformed into a fight for the European presence in Africa, including the French in Algeria, and CADBA turned into the Mouvement d'action civique (MAC—Movement of Civic Action). Thiriart, assisted by Dr. Paul Teichmann, transformed this Poujadist-inflected group into a revolutionary structure that effectively organized Belgian support networks for the OAS.[3]

On March 4, 1962, at a meeting in Venice under the aegis of Sir Oswald Mosley, the leaders of MAC, the Movimento Sociale Italiano (MSI—Italian Social Movement), the Union Movement, and the *Reichspartei* moved to found a "National European party centered on the idea of European unity." But nothing concrete came of it.

Vowing to create a true European revolutionary party, in January 1963 Jean Thiriart transformed MAC into Young Europe, a transnational European movement under the sign of the Celtic cross. Although established in six countries, it never had more than 5,000 members in all of Europe, and this, even Thiriart admitted, "only by scraping the bottom of the barrel." Of the total, two-thirds were concentrated in Italy. In France, because of its support of the OAS, Young Europe was banned, which forced the movement to remain semi-clandestine and explains its weak influence, its manpower not exceeding 200 members.

NATIONAL EUROPEAN COMMUNITARIANISM

In 1961, in *Le Manifeste à la Nation Européenne* (*Proclamation of the European Nation*), Jean Thiriart declared himself for "a united powerful, communitarian Europe . . . opposed to the Soviet and US blocs."[4] He presented his ideas at greater length in a

---

[3] L'Organisation armée secrète, the Secret Army Organization—the French resistance to the decolonization of Algeria—Ed.

[4] *Nation-Belgique*, no. 59, September 1, 1961.

book published in 1964, *Un Empire de 400 millions d'hommes: L'Europe (An Empire of 400 Million Men: Europe)*. Quickly translated into the seven principal European languages, this work — which was supplemented in 1965 by a booklet of 80 pages, *La Grande Nation: L'Europe unitaire de Brest à Bucarest (The Great Nation: United Europe from Brest to Bucharest)*, deeply influenced the cadres of the European extreme Right, particularly in Italy.

The originality of Young Europe lies in its ideology, National European Communitarianism, that Thiriart presents as a "European and elitist socialism," de-bureaucratized and given a spine by European nationalism. Challenging the romantic concept of the nation inherited from the 19th century, which falls under a determinism that is ethnic, linguistic, or religious, he prefers the concept of a dynamic nation: moving, becoming, corresponding to the nation/community of destiny described by José Ortega y Gasset. Without rejecting the common past completely, he thinks that "this past is nothing compared to the gigantic common future . . . What makes the Nation real and viable is its unity of historical destiny."[5]

Describing himself as a "Greater European Jacobin," he wanted to build a united nation and advocated the "fusion state," centralized and transnational, the political, legal, and spiritual heir of the Roman Empire, which will give all its inhabitants European omni-citizenship. In 1989, he summarized: "The main axis of my politico-historical thought is the unitary state, the centralized political state, and not the racial state, the nostalgic state, the historical state, the religious state." Nothing is more foreign for him than the "Europe of a hundred flags" of Yann Fouéré or the "Europe of the carnal fatherlands" dear to Saint-Loup.

Thiriart's nationalism is based solely on geopolitical considerations. According to him, the only nations that have a future are those of continental scale like the United States, the USSR, or China. Petty traditional nationalisms are obstacles, even anachronisms, manipulated by the great powers. Thus to re-

---

[5] J. Thiriart, *La Grande Nation. L'Europe unitaire de Dublin à Bucarest* (1965), 9.

turn to grandeur and power, Europe should be unified.

Unification would take place under the aegis of a European Revolutionary Party, organized on the Leninist model of democratic centralism, which would organize the masses and select the elites. A historical party—following the example of Third World experiments like the FLN in Algeria or the NLF in Vietnam—would be an embryonic state developing into the united European state. It would have to carry out the national liberation struggle against the American occupation, its dedicated collaborators, thousands of "Quislings" from the System parties, and the colonial troops of NATO. Thus Europe would be liberated and unified from Brest to Bucharest, 400 million strong, and would then be able to conclude a tactical alliance with China and the Arab states to break the American-Soviet condominium.

In spite of their geopolitical lucidity, Thiriart's theses, rationalist and materialist to the extreme, are perplexing in their eminently modern character. As the Traditionalist Claudio Mutti, a former militant of Giovane Europa, stressed:

> . . . the limit of Thiriart consisted precisely in his secular nationalism, supported by a Machiavellian worldview and deprived of any justification of a transcendent nature. For him, historical confrontations were resolved by brute power relations, while the state is nothing more than incarnated Nietzschean Will to Power in service of a project of European hegemony marked by an exclusivist, blind, and conceited pride.[6]

On the economic plane, Thiriart offered, as an alternative to "the profit economy" (capitalism) and the "utopian economy" (Communism) an "economy of power," whose only viable dimension is European. Taking as a starting point the economists Fichte and List, he recommended "the autarky of great spaces."

---

[6] Notes by C. Mutti on G. Freda, "La désintégration du système" ["The Disintegration of the System"], supplement to *Totalité*, no. 9 (1980).

Europe would have to leave the IMF, adopt a single currency, protect itself by tariff barriers, and work to preserve its self-sufficiency.

FROM YOUNG EUROPE TO THE EUROPEAN COMMUNITY PARTY

After 1963, dissensions in connection with South Tyrol caused a radical schism, which led to the birth of the Europa Front in Germanic countries like Germany, Austria, and Flanders.

However, the year 1964 marks the militant apogee of the movement, which played a leading role, thanks to Dr. Teichmann, in the strike of Belgian doctors opposed to the nationalization of their profession, and took part in communal elections in Quiévrain. Its working class members organized themselves as the Syndicats communautaires européens (SCE—European Community Trade Unions). In August 1964, the journalist Emile Lecerf and Dr. Nancy resigned because of ideological differences with Thiriart. Lecerf went on to head the Révolution européenne group, more or less aligned with the positions of Europe-Action in France, a "nostalgic" and "literary" movement according to Thiriart. The departure of this historic leader, followed in December 1964 by that of Paul Teichmann, caused the militant decline of the organization.

In 1965, Young Europe became the Parti communautaire européen (PCE—European Community Party). Doctrinal concerns then distracted it from militant activism. The theoretical review *L'Europe communautaire* came out monthly while the *Jeune Europe* weekly became semi-monthly. After October 1965 the party's Cadre Schools took place across Europe, Thiriart having worked out a "physics of politics" based on the writings of Machiavelli, Gustave Le Bon, Serge Tchakhotine, Carl Schmitt, Julien Freund, and Raymond Aron.

Moreover, the party published, between 1965 and 1969, a monthly magazine in French, *La nation européenne*, and Italian, *La Nazione Europea*, which offered a counter-current to the traditional extreme Right by placing the continental unit above the nation, opposing NATO and promoting the autonomous deterrent force wanted by De Gaulle, denouncing America as the new Carthage, viewing the regimes of Eastern Europe as a kind of national Communism, and taking an interest in the liberation struggles of the Third World to the point of describing Cuba, the Arab countries, and North Vietnam as allies of Europe! The magazine, distributed by the Nouvelles Messageries de la Presse Parisienne in France, had 2,000 subscribers and printed 10,000 copies of each issue.

In June 1966, Jean Thiriart met in Bucharest with the Chinese Prime Minister Zhou Enlai on the initiative of Ceausescu. Beijing then spoke about a "tri-continental" struggle. Thiriart advocated a "quadri-continental" struggle, proposing to foment a Vietnam within Europe. For that, he envisaged creating "European brigades" on the Garibaldian model, which, after having fought in the Middle East or in Latin America, would return to fight a war of liberation in Europe.

It should be noted that following this discussion, the Italian militants of Giovane Europa carried out united actions with local Maoists, unified by a minimal common program of hostility to the two superpowers, rejection of the Yankee occupation of Europe, anti-Zionism, and support for Third World liberation struggles.

This collaboration was not without consequences. Various National European cadres ultimately joined the Maoist ranks. Thus in 1971 Claudio Orsoni, nephew of the fascist leader Italo Balbo and a founding member of Giovane Europa, would create the Center for the Study and Application of Maoist Thought. In 1975, Pino Bolzano, the last director of *La Nazione Europea*, went on to lead the daily paper of the extreme Left group Lotta Continua (The Struggle Continues). Renato Curcio would join the Marxist-Leninist Italian Communist Party before founding . . . the Red Brigades!

Young Europe had supporters in certain countries in Eastern Europe and the Middle East. Thus, on August 1, 1966, Thiriart published an article in Serbo-Croatian, entitled "Europe from Dublin to Bucharest," in the official diplomatic review of the Yugoslav government, *Medunarodna Politika*. Ferociously anti-Zionist, the Belgian leader was in contact with Ahmed Shukeiri, predecessor of Arafat as the head of the PLO, and the first European to fall with weapons in hand at the side of the Palestinians was a French engineer and member of Young Europe, Roger Coudroy.

Thiriart also had ties to Arab secular-socialist regimes. In the autumn of 1968, he made a long voyage to the Middle East at the invitation of the governments of Iraq and Egypt. He had discussions with several ministers, gave interviews to the press, and took part in the congress of the Arab Socialist Union, the party of Nasser, whom he met on this occasion. Disappointed by the lack of concrete support from these countries, in 1969 he renounced militant combat, causing the breakup of Young Europe.

THE EURO-SOVIET EMPIRE

He would continue, however, his rich theoretical reflections. When Washington approached Beijing in the 1970s, he suggested a Euro-Soviet alliance against the Sino-American axis, in order to build a "very large Europe from Reykjavik to Vladivostok," which he thought was the only way to resist the new American Carthage and billion-strong China. This is what led him to declare in 1984: "If Moscow wants to make Europe European, I preach total collaboration with the Soviet enterprise. I will then be the first to put a red star on my cap. Soviet Europe, yes, without reservations."[7]

Thiriart's dream of a Euro-Soviet Empire, which he described as a "hyper-nation state equipped with a de-Marxified hyper-communism,"[8] merges with Eurosiberia: "Between Iceland and Vladivostok, we can join together 800 million men . . . and find in the soil of Siberia all our strategic and energy needs. I say that Siberia is the economically most vital power for the European Empire."[9] He then worked on two books: *The Euro-Soviet Empire from Vladivostok to Dublin: After-Yalta* and, in collaboration with José Cuadrado Costa, *The Transformation of*

---

[7] *Conscience Européenne*, no. 8, July 1984.

[8] Ibid.

[9] J. Thiriart, "L'Europe jusqu'à Vladivostok," in *Nationalisme & République*, no. 9, September 1992.

Communism: Essay on Enlightened Totalitarianism, which remained on the drawing board because of the sudden collapse
of the USSR. He left his political exile only in 1991 to support
the creation of the Front européen de libération (FEL—
European Liberation Front). In 1992, he went to Moscow with a
delegation of the FEL and died of a heart attack shortly after
his return to Belgium, leaving a controversial but original body
of theoretical work, which inspires to this day Guillaume Faye,
the preacher of Eurosiberia, and Alexander Dugin, the prophet
of Eurasia.

Counter-Currents/*North American New Right,*
September 20, 2010

TOWARD THE WHITE REPUBLIC

MICHAEL WALKER

Michael O'Meara
Toward the White Republic
Edited by Greg Johnson
San Francisco: Counter-Currents Publishing, 2010

Toward the White Republic is a collection of essays and talks by Michael O'Meara, who has been active in recent years translating works by European New Right authors and writing for *The Occidental Quarterly*. The succinct Foreword to this collection of essays lays out the author's purpose very clearly. In his words:

> Since falling victim to that brood of vipers, the Judeo-capitalist elites, the country [the USA] has been redesigned as a "universal nation." . . . The essays here address the trifold character of this assault: (1) describing the nightmare world the elites are creating, (2) suggesting a politically feasible alternative to it, and (3) alerting whites to various false flags raised by conservatives, philistines, and others. Common to all these essays is the author's intent to make whites more conscious of their destiny as a people—and to remind them, thus, of what needs to ensure the continuation of their kind, unique gift of Europe's blood and spirit.

My first and immediate quibble, or more than a quibble if I am honest, is with the comparative term "more conscious." For whom is this book intended? Those who are already conscious, the readers for example, of *The Occidental Quarterly*? Or for whites who are somewhat conscious, but not enough? Judging by the contents of the book, I should say that the writer is addressing the already converted, in which case there is no need to make such readers "more conscious" of their destiny as a people. They are very conscious already. The question for them is not consciousness but guidelines as to what they should do about it, not awareness but solutions.

Awareness is an issue for the millions of whites who are not conscious of their destiny, but for such people far too much is taken as read in this book, starting with the assumption that the reader will not blink at the expression "brood of vipers, the Judeo-capitalist elites."

In fact—and I suspect Dr. O'Meara would concur with me on this—a racial group only becomes aware of its ethnicity when dramatically and materially placed in juxtaposition with the ethnicity of others. Neither nationalism nor racial con-sciousness are created by intellectual or scientific idealism or discoveries of any kind; they are the creations of experience.

To an extent the writer shows he is aware of this, yet like the majority (or all?) writers on the subject, he has no time to dis-cuss how consciousness through experience can be raised or channeled constructively. The hypothesis, the primacy of the white race and its impending demise, are taken as a "given" and not discussed. Appealing to a captive and known audi-ence, these essays argue the case for radical nationalism, seces-sion and the abandonment of any other course or approach.

O'Meara insists that attempts to save the white race by re-forming or winning control of the United States of America are doomed to failure. The USA is far too far down the path of ra-cial mongrelization, says O'Meara, to be saved by a transfer of power within currently existing political structures. One essay, a friendly but firmly critical essay on the late Sam Francis, un-derlines this argument and insists that the only option open to the white race, at least in the United States (the line between the fate of the white race as a whole and specifically in the USA is not clearly drawn in these essays) is secession. Drawing in-spiration from the nationalist movement of his Irish ancestors, Michael O'Meara looks forward to the creation of an independ-ent White Nationalist state set up upon the soil of the North American continent.

O'Meara despairs of the failure of even racially aware whites to understand this. "Almost as depressing as the thought of our people's extinction is that of the white opposition to it" he begins one essay revealingly entitled, "Against White Reformists," first published on the *Vanguard News Network* in 2007, noting what he calls the "Sisyphean activities" of "racial conservatives" who seek the restoration of a hierarchy within an existing order that is alien and has long been alien to the Aryan spirit of our ancestors. In other words, the system in its entirety is the enemy and not some part of it.

What O'Meara therefore pleads for is not reform but revolution. We are not told whether constitutional rights will be guaranteed in the White Republic, nor what liberal values are to be kept and which to be abandoned, a more than academic point. Many racial activists tend to denounce liberalism in general but become very liberal when their own rights to free speech or a fair trial are at stake.

The despised system has to date been kind enough not to throw Dr. O'Meara into jail for voicing these opinions, because the USA is still blessed with a liberal, yes a liberal Constitution. It is my own view that freedom is indeed under threat in the land of the free but that Dr. O'Meara is not living in the worst of all possible worlds so far as his constitutional rights are concerned.

The danger of rejecting "the system" *in toto* and proclaiming that one is engaged in a battle to the death with it, is that said system might agree and throw off all restraint as per the motto "if they damn me for telling tales they may as well damn me for murder." The fact that Dr. O'Meara can still write and *The Occidental Quarterly* still publish is surely proof that the system remains subject to some restraint. Should all restraint be abandoned and revolutionaries and elite face each other with "no holds barred"? Is this what O'Meara wants? If it is what he wants, why does he continue to write?

The clarity of Dr. O'Meara's intent creates a considerable gulf between the writer of these essays and the major part of those in the USA who think of themselves as right-wingers. The recent Tea Party movement there, apart from being ridden with contradictions, is wedded to the idea of restoring the United States to some former "pre-Lapsarian" state of capitalist innocence.

As many have observed, the Tea Party movement is overwhelmingly white, but unlike Black Panthers or members of La Raza, entirely ignores the racial element of its own instinctive protest. It has become practically a truism to point out that whites are the only racial group lacking in widespread ethnic self-consciousness. Like so many writers before him, O'Meara hopes for the advent of racial self-awareness among white people. He believes that the way to this is not through reform but via separation, a complete break with the government of the United States.

Although hardly mentioned, the spirit of the American Revolution and what Stonewall Jackson called "America's Second Revolution" of 1861, loom large in these pages. Recalling the spirit of the American revolutionaries of the 18th century or explicitly the Irish nationalists of the 20th ("Sinn Fein"—we alone), O'Meara claims that American racial nationalists should seek to "pursue their destiny without interference" while in no way seek to restore the Confederacy or the Third Reich, as Leftists claim.

The underlying notion of "we alone," of a group of comrades/revolutionaries pursuing destiny without interference, characterizes these essays. The explicit rejection of a comparison with the Confederacy or the Third Reich is bewildering, because it is exactly those two historical precedents to which O'Meara seems emotionally attached, and the very notion of secession on American soil calls Fort Sumter to mind.

The call to the tradition of revolution, in this case the Irish and American revolutions, is problematic. Both revolutions had clearly international aspirations and appealed to a brotherhood of man. The Irish tricolor was based on the tricolor of French republicanism, a Masonic and universalist movement. The Masonic roots of the American Revolution are well-known, indeed they are still carried on the back of the one dollar bill.

The claim, made here, that America was defined in racial terms, is not borne out by the facts. The American Republic was indeed created by white men alone, and it can be argued their understanding of the world was that of white men. Their being white men, however, was not the motivation of their rebellion and was not provided as a guiding principle of that revolution, and it was not mentioned at all in any of their revolutionary tracts. Neither the American Constitution nor the Bill of Rights is explicitly (is it even implicitly?) racial, and it is as easily interpreted as a charter of universalism as one of nationalist revolt.

In marked contrast to the Irish Declaration of Independence, which O'Meara likewise admires, the American Declaration of Independence specifically appeals beyond the limit of the land: "We hold these truths to be self-evident, that all men are created equal, that they are endowed by their Creator with certain unalienable Rights, that among these are Life, Liberty and the pursuit of Happiness." These lines have been taken as the beacon and inspiration of universalism and understandably so. White racialists provide every kind of convoluted argument to insist that the words "all men" do not really mean all men at all, but the simplicity of those words and their universal application cannot be shaken.

Michael O'Meara seeks in his essays to draw a permanent distinction between the White Nationalist ethnostate on the one side and all attempts at reform, all conservatism, patriotism, and reformism on the other. Tea Party demonstrators, for all their contradictions, can appeal to a specific national identity. The national identity which O'Meara seeks in the USA is one which will have to be created from scratch.

Hitherto, nationalists the world over have appealed to the call of the blood sometimes, of the land always. O'Meara's nationalism may be a call to the blood, but where is the land? The last Americans to love their land as land went down to defeat in 1865. Since then for Americans "home is where you hang your hat." No attempt is made in any of these essays to state how a love of land will be created out of nothing.

We come back to the ghosts of the Confederacy and National Socialism. Both movements could draw on a love which already existed. White American separatists will have to create theirs.

O'Meara is very familiar with the theses of the French New Right and refers to two writers which the French New Right examined in order to draw lessons for a strategy for our time. One O'Meara accepts and argues should be "taken on board" in the fermenting of a revolutionary consciousness and approach while the other he flatly rejects.

The example he admires is that of Georges Sorel, the French syndicalist. In an essay entitled "The Myth of Our Rebirth" he stresses the importance which Sorel attached to "myth." Sorel understood myth as a force which impelled those who fell under its spell to participate in political action. The action itself then reinforced the symbolic and inspirational force of the original myth. As O'Meara succinctly observes, "Myth . . . is not a description of things or a rational alternative to the present, but an expression of a determination to act" (p. 27).

An example which comes to my mind of this kind of "mythical action" is the sacrifice of Bobby Sands and the other Irish republican hunger strikers, who chose death by slow starvation rather than submit to being treated as common criminals. Sands' sacrifice acquired the status of a myth in the sense which Sorel intended and has been a driving force of Irish republicanism since the day he died.

Unwittingly it seems, O'Meara has put his finger on a fundamental weakness of White Nationalism. This weakness is so fundamental indeed that unless it is mended I believe that white separatism in the United States or anywhere else in the world will continue to be the stuff of fantasy and resentment and not be a serious challenge to prevailing systems.

I share O'Meara's belief in the force of myth, and, although I have not read much of Georges Sorel, I accept the premise in terms of psychology upon which I suppose it to be based, namely that powerful and terrible acts of sacrifice and defiance may create their own momentum and that the demonstration of political power in the form of symbolic gestures creates its own dynamic and draws people to it like a magnet or the center of a whirlpool.

What can we say, then, of a movement which patently

proves itself unable to produce such myth-making figures? Not only does the white racialist movement itself not "create myths" in this way, it pours scorn and bile on those who do. Bobby Sands earned not a crumb of respect from the British nationalist movement (the then leader of the British National Front haughtily dismissed the hunger strikers as "sub-human") and otherwise competed with the popular press in abusive epithets, among which "coward" featured often.

British nationalists have frequently lauded their own bravery, and I do not wish to belittle the courage it takes to sacrifice career and reputation for one's beliefs, but putting one's job on the line, heroic though it is in a way, is not myth-making stuff.

British nationalism did boast one hunger striker as it happens. His name was Robert Relf, a racial nationalist who went on hunger strike in protest against a law which forbad him from publicly putting his house up for sale "to an English family only." He called off his strike for the obvious and very human reason that going on hunger strike is a terrible step that only the bravest of the brave can carry out to the end. In other words he became hungry, and he failed to carry his plan out. It was human of Relf to have balked; I doubt I would ever have the depth of courage to carry out such an awful act myself.

The fact remains that racial nationalists have so far been very poor in the creation of martyrs. The least they could do is show a little awe if not respect in face of the really terrible sacrifices which others make for their beliefs. It is not right to say that white separatists have no martyrs. True, they seem to be flawed or possibly cranks, but does one examine the creators of a myth with a magnifying glass?

There is one obvious myth creator in the Sorelian sense in the history of White Nationalism. His name is Robert J. Mathews. His actions may be regarded from one perspective as those of a felon, from another perspective as those of a hero. I would expect him to feature frequently in these pages, but it is not so. If Michael O'Meara mentions Bob Mathews more than once I missed it. Here is the only reference I noted:

If you want to build a nationalist movement to ensure the

continuity of white America, you appeal to Robert E. Lee and Bob Mathews, to the Battle of the Alamo and Kearney's Workingmen, to the Stars and Bars and the sustaining voices of those quintessential representatives of America's white culture, the Carter family. (p. 44)

The writer cited by the French New Right from whom O'Meara emphatically does not wish lessons to be drawn, is Antonio Gramsci. He talks of Gramscism but is obviously so repelled by the thought of using Gramsci's example that Gramsci is not even cited in the Index at the end of the book.

Antonio Gramsci was a founding member of the Italian Communist Party. In his *Prison Notebooks* he argued that a political revolutionary movement needs to be aware of the institutions that not only wield but also radiate power. A favorite word of Gramsci's was "hegemony." By hegemony Gramsci referred to the opinion formers on the one hand and the wielders of power on the other, whose sympathizers could play a decisive role in the fortune of revolutionaries, revolutionary writers, and thinkers.

O'Meara somewhat narrowly interprets this as just a theory of the "long march through the institutions." "The notion," writes O'Meara (p. 97), "that racialists follow the Left's Gramscian 'march through the institutions' is . . . unserious. Covington's Northwest Volunteer Army is a hundred times more realistic than the thought of re-establishing the integrity of white life through elections or an expanded media." Good pure radical stuff, but I can't help wondering whether some members Robert Mathews' Silent Brotherhood, who received stiff jail sentences for their part in money laundering and bank robbery, might be wondering today in prison (where many of them today still languish) if a little more "Gramscian" infiltration among judges and juries and a prior White Nationalist trudge through an institution or two might not have served their turn very nicely.

Gramsci was not writing about restoring anything (nor was the New Left). Gramsci was writing about revolution. Elsewhere, O'Meara is dismissive about those who have any kind of truck with what he calls "the reformist snare" (p. 97). It is, he writes, "the system itself, communicating vessel of the Jews' lunar spirit, that de-Aryanizes us, contaminates our blood, and seeks our destruction."

O'Meara also argues that reformism has not worked because it has not succeeded in moving back the tide of color or the decline of Western/Aryan man. One point is that it is impossible to say with certainty what the current state of the world would be like if reformists had not acted at all. Secondly, and more importantly, such a radical position does not admit of compromise, but compromise is not what Gramsci was writing about. He was writing about strategy. One may admire Robert Mathews' courage while questioning his strategy.

One whose strategy O'Meara does admire is that of Harold Covington. An entire chapter of a book running to only 153 pages is devoted to Covington's *Northwest Trilogy*, of which O'Meara is clearly an ardent admirer.

Covington waxes eloquent in his writings on the hopelessness of mere theory and the need for action.

O'Meara's chapter on Covington is headed with a quotation from Adolf Hitler: "Those who want to live, let them fight, and those who do not want to fight in this world of eternal struggle do not deserve to live." This is probably taken from *Also sprach Zarathustra* which is itself a twist to the Book of Job: "The life of man upon earth is warfare and his days are like the days of the hireling." *Militia est vita hominis.*

Covington's trilogy is very similar to William Pierce's *Turner Diaries*, which it closely resembles in content, plot, purpose, and ideology. O'Meara describes it as "infinitely more readable and convincing than William Pierce's *Turner Diaries* (now one of our classics) but has probably sold only a fraction as many copies." "Infinitely more readable" strikes me as a trifle exaggerated, but I agree that it makes for more lively reading than Pierce's plodding text. Apparently unlike O'Meara, I was struck by the similarities in the two works more than by the differences. The differences are ones of style. Simply put, Covington is a born storyteller and colorful writer, and Pierce, a physicist by profession, was not.

If Covington did not propagate the radical political views

that he does, he could easily have become a reasonably successful novelist and be living today in some comfort with "wife and two veg" in a leafy New England suburb. He is the typical "malcontent" known to the Elizabethans, who would have been advanced if he were not out of favor with the powers that be. That makes men dangerous. Hitler, the frustrated painter and architect, was another.

Covington has narrative talent and puts it to good use in his lengthy yarn, which at times is a cliffhanger; but in terms of political intent and approach I see no difference between his work and Pierce's. Covington like Pierce describes a situation in the near future where whites are pushed to the point that they can tolerate ZOG no longer and take up arms.

Both books depict two-dimensional characters parachuted out of the crudest possible military propaganda manual. In both books non-white, especially Jewish, opponents of the heroic movement are painted much as earlier Christian preachers depicted the devils out of hell. Covington waxes lyrical (Pierce is never lyrical) in depicting the sheer fiendishness of everyone fighting the White Nationalists, and gloats over their inevitable fate. In short, this is a sort of *Star Wars* for White Nationalists.

The book is about action and is a call to arms. Mr. Covington has nothing but scorn for armchair nationalists, and O'Meara quotes him thus: Those among us who continue to emphasize the need to educate or awaken people, he argues, usually end up doing "nothing more than hide behind an email address while playing with the computer in one's basement rec room, with a bowl of nachos and a cold brewski beside the mouse" (p. 66). Covington's is a highly entertaining and probably accurate depiction of many an American white racial "activist."

Arguably, this collection of essays is remarkable less for what it includes as what it so markedly excludes. There is nothing here on economics (other than a projection of forthcoming financial collapse), nothing at all on the degradation of the environment, no examination of real historical martyrs, only a nodding reference to the one person who really carried the dream of white separatism into hard deeds, and most astonish-

ing of all, no analysis and apparently no interest in contemporary separatist movements of our time.

This is O'Meara on Dmitry Orlov and the likely or inevitable
collapse of the current capitalist financial system: "Society as a
whole will be forced back to a less complex mode of operation:
centralized forms of control will wane; things will suddenly
become 'smaller, simpler, less stratified, and less socially differentiated'; regions and communities will assume a greater
centrality of tasks. Whether there will ensue a Hobbesian 'war
of all against all' is anybody's guess" (p. 134). It could be from
a Millenarian tract of any number of religious sects.

Michael O'Meara is hardly the exception among White Nationalists in treating economics with scant interest, but this lack
of interest, so typical and so prevalent among White Nationalists, is a serious flaw.

The whites in whose name Michael O'Meara wishes to see
his republic, who are they? One other subject not mentioned in
this book, although in this case perhaps understandably, is eugenics. Will the White Republic have any selection process for
whites? From a book entitled "Toward the White Republic" I
would hope for at least a few pointers regarding this difficult
question. There is nothing.

Another gap in these essays is ecology and the deterioration
of the natural environment, on which subject O'Meara, who
can spare several pages for Covington's trilogy, finds here
nothing whatsoever to say. Nationalists generally tend to pay
lip service to this subject but never seem to get very serious
about it. The world is in many ways divided between those
who want continued change and innovation in the capitalist
sense and those who, for whatever reason, want to cry halt. As
the desecration of the planet continues, particularly under the
weight of the so-called "emerging markets" demanding the
living standards of the West, a refusal to draw a clear line on
the issue looks increasingly like another demonstration of provincialism, isolationism, and historical irrelevance.

When White Nationalists are silent on this subject of environmental degradation (and here I mean not lip service but
concrete workable solutions) they make themselves even more

irrelevant on the battlefield of world politics than they already are. "Toward the White Republic" does not pay lip service to ecological protest, for the simple reason that it does not cover the subject at all. In an essay entitled "Why I Write," where the reader might expect a listing of O'Meara's chief concerns, all that is offered is a critique of reformist racial movements and misguided nationalism. It is difficult not to conclude from this that ecology and economics belong to the many issues for and about which Dr. O'Meara would not and does not care to write.

Covington does have something to say about environmentalism. He explicitly dismisses environmentalist concerns in his writing. Saving a small species of bird at the expense of loggers' jobs is, he writes, insane and in his novel, *The Brigade*, zoning orders are condemned as a kind of yuppie plot. (Plenty of Jewish writers could heartily endorse such robust anti-green views and several have indeed expressed themselves in almost identical language to Covington's — Ayn Rand and Charles Krauthammer come to mind.)

To my mind the most remarkable omission of all, and the most inexplicable, is that regarding separatist movements long past, recent, and present throughout the world. In the last thirty years up to the present day, the world has been convulsed by separatist movements. Some have been successful, some have not, some have been armed, some have been peaceful, some have been Marxist, some socialist, some nationalist. One would expect that anyone who is serious in seeking the separation of white ethnics from the main body of the United States to create a new ethnostate, would avidly study the many examples around the world in order to gain inspiration from others' successes and to learn from others' mistakes. The success of Bangladesh and the failure of the Tamil Tigers, the success of Southern Sudan and the failure of Quebec, must all contain their lessons. How can it be that these are not cited and studied? I cannot avoid the suspicion that there is both a complacency and provincialism at work here. This lack of reference to real separatist movements coupled with a discussion of a fantasy separatist movement in a novel, proves, if proof were needed, that white separatists still believe that their aims can be

282   *North American New Right*, vol. 1, 2012

achieved in a vacuum and that the rest of the world can go hang.

There may be the occasional nod in the direction of each ethnic group having the right to pursue its own destiny, but when push comes to shove, there seems to be no concern for any group but whites. This is a fatal error. I am convinced that whites will only achieve the kind of autonomy spoken of in this book when a substantial number of non-whites share their views and their desire to separate. "We alone" in this context is a recipe for continued desolation and disaster.

I reject wholeheartedly the "all or nothing approach" of Harold Covington, the man who despises those who isolate themselves in the computer rec room, the man whom O'Meara obviously admires. This all or nothing approach leads to abject failure and will continue to do so as long as it is proposed and practiced. If people studied separatist movements around the world, they would see that success is usually if not always linked to outside and inside support and sympathy. Insurgents who rely only on themselves have never to my knowledge been successful.

To be honest, however, I am not as dedicated as Dr. O'Meara because I am not inspired by the alternative on offer. I do not like the system under which I labor, and in principle I would not be unhappy to see it disappear, but to be replaced by what? Mr. Covington's racialist Utopia, the healthy dictatorship of square jawed Aryan lookalikes? I wonder if I cannot even find it in my heart to still prefer the devil I do know than Covington's dubious Utopia. Anyway, the radicalization of white working people will not take place as the result of reading novels, however inspirational. It can take place through the failure of the system on the one hand and myth building sacrifice on the other coupled with realistic political acumen.

I am far from hostile to the notion of separatism, but it is time that someone came to grips with the issues at stake, namely overpopulation, the environment, cross-border alliances, social incoherence, modern genetics, and new media technology, and examine white racial survival in terms of these and the other developments, which matter and must matter not only to a future White Republic but also to any fledgling White Nationalist movement.

Mr. Covington and Dr. O'Meara are right that most people are not inspired by the written word, no matter how brilliant. (There are exceptions, Robert Mathews being one of them, inspired by a book *Which Way Western Man?*) It is physical action that inspires and imposes the force of myth upon others, the action of the angel, the warrior, the prophet, and of course the martyr, the action of those sent against time to stop and challenge time.

When that time comes and those persons are there, I shall know it. I shall not, I think, be writing about them as I am now. I shall not have time for writing then. The myth will have drawn me out. In the meantime, in preparation, those who might one day break away should not dismiss options casually. They should seek examples from which they can learn, and they should point to those examples, and they should have better responses than the prevailing elite to the challenges of the day and be seen by growing numbers of people as having those better answers. Then they will not find themselves blindly banging their heads against a prison wall, which has been and continues to be the fate of White Nationalists these many years.

TAKING OUR OWN SIDE*

KEVIN MACDONALD

Michael J. Polignano
Taking Our Own Side
Edited by Greg Johnson
Foreword by Kevin MacDonald
San Francisco: Counter-Currents Publishing, 2010

The triumph of the cultural Left is an ongoing disaster to America and every other Western country. The result is stultifying intellectual conformity in all the elite institutions of society, particularly the educational system. All levels of the educational system are rigorously policed to ensure ideological conformity, with the result that college graduates—especially college graduates—emerge zombie-like, mouthing politically correct platitudes they heard from their brilliant professors, mindlessly looking forward to an impossible future of racial harmony where the white minority adapts seamlessly and joyously to life among their non-white brothers.

Michael Polignano somehow managed to overcome all that. And what's really amazing is that he did it while still a college student. Overcoming the propaganda is a remarkable achievement at any age, but is especially difficult for young people. Not only have they been subjected to this massive propaganda assault since kindergarten, they have to overcome the natural human proclivity to conformity that is especially strong among young people. I am ashamed to say that I was hopelessly conformist in college and grad school. Even after becoming ever more disenchanted with the Left (I was happy Reagan was elected), I couldn't really get out of the narrow confines of the political mainstream.

---

* This is Kevin MacDonald's Foreword to *Taking Our Own Side*.

Mike Polignano gets it. This is about racial survival: "A proposed moral principle cannot conflict with the survival of the race." He is a biologist by training, and it shows. He has a clear understanding of group interests:

> The reality is: The races are at war with one another. The different human races are distinct subspecies, with distinct temperaments and talents, some of which conflict dramatically. It is an iron biological law that when two distinct subspecies try to occupy the same ecological niche in the same geographical region, there will be group conflict. . . . But since we're rational creatures, humans also have [another] option: voluntary separation. This last option preserves racial uniqueness and eliminates interracial competition, allowing each race to shape the course of its own future.

Mike Polignano rejects white guilt. We have to develop a sense of urgency to reverse the tide that is swelling against us: "In this time of racial peril, the highest and noblest thing any of us can do is work together to ensure the survival and flourishing of the white race, so it can give birth to new Leonardos and Newtons and Teslas." I couldn't agree more.

Multiculturalism then becomes not a source of strength, but the ideology of white dispossession—nothing more than "an attempt to replace white cultures with non-white cultures—or, more precisely, with fantasies, lies, and sanitized half-truths about non-white cultures designed to make them seem spiritually and morally superior."

And as he notes, "Social ostracism is a small thing to risk considering what's at stake." Indeed, he correctly sees whites as "too polite, too concerned to accommodate and demonstrate goodwill to non-white invaders." It is a politeness fueled at least partly by the desire not to be ostracized, not to take views that oppose what all the "smart people" in the universities and the elite media believe. Going against it takes a lot of intellectual confidence and a very thick skin.

Mike Polignano is a race realist in every sense of the word.

Although he sees whites as having made unique and irreplaceable contributions to civilization, he also advocates eugenics. The white gene pool could be improved by providing incentives for the best and the brightest to have children.

Eugenics is an idea that that was once championed by progressive thinkers of all political persuasions but has fallen into disfavor because the contemporary Left rejects any acknowledgment that genes influence important behaviors like IQ— despite the overwhelming evidence from research. Nowadays, there is an automatic, knee-jerk accusation of Nazi sympathies whenever eugenics is mentioned. But the research is quite clear that genetic influences explain most of the variation in intelligence. And that implies that eugenic breeding practices would indeed be effective.

Polignano is also a race realist when it comes to race differences in IQ. The Left quickly noticed that civil rights laws and an equal playing field did not result in equal outcomes. The result has been affirmative action designed to magically create a non-white elite with all the same skills as the people they are displacing accompanied by massive propaganda featuring brilliant blacks and stupid whites. The result is:

> a Potemkin village increasingly populated by non-whites who, regardless of their real merits, have been promoted a rung or two above those merits because of their race. Television and the movies portray a fantasy world filled with dumb blondes and black doctors, lawyers, judges, inventors, and computer geniuses. But behind the façade hides a vast, squalid reality of false promises, false hopes, and outright falsehoods about race—all premised on the refusal to accept racial inequality as a natural fact.

Polignano is also a realist when it comes to Jewish influence. He has a hilarious spoof on the "Differently Intelligent" and the "National Association for the Advancement of Retarded People" where all the advocates for these unfortunate souls are highly accomplished people with obvious Jewish names:

The NAARP was founded and staffed by the law firm of Wiesel, Wiener, Liehr, Ratner, and Cohen (Ari Wiesel, JD, Harvard, SAT 1560; Barry Wiener, JD, Yale, SAT 1470; Aaron Liehr, JD, Harvard, SAT 1510; Shulamith Ratner, JD, Harvard, SAT 1520; and Adam Cohen, JD, Yale, SAT 1420). (Mr. Wiener returned to private practice in 1999 after the passage of the Equalization of Opportunity Act and has won multi-billion dollar settlements in class action suits on behalf of DI individuals.)

Although this is satire, it points to a real issue: Very intelligent Jews from the very best schools have used their abilities to engineer the Potemkin village of black and Latino accomplishment — not to mention altering the law on church-state relations and promoting the "rights" of immigrants, legal and illegal: the Jewish elite hostile to the traditional white majority of America.

Polignano also points to two key traits of Jews that make them such formidable enemies to white America and the West: (1) Their powerful sense of collectivism — that Jews have a strong sense of Jewish communal interest and have a remarkable agreement on the basic issues they see as benefiting Jews — particularly issues such as immigration and multiculturalism in the US, and support for Israel as an ethnically exclusive Jewish state. (2) The Jewish hatred of Christianity "which over the centuries has given rise to terrible persecutions whenever Jews have gained political power." This is exactly right.

One very encouraging aspect of Mike Polignano's story is that it shows that a smart and inquisitive college student can bypass political correctness and plug into powerful scientific research that supports a race realist perspective. It goes without saying that such research would not be mentioned in classrooms at the vast majority of American universities, except perhaps to call attention to the "sloppy scholarship" and "moral turpitude" of the scientists who produced it. The good news is that well-informed discussions of this body of research as well as quite a few of the original academic papers are readily available online.

As a result, Polignano has extensive discussions of quite a

few of the leading figures in this academic movement, including Frank Salter and Arthur Jensen. His encounter with Jensen's research seems to have been pivotal. His column on Jensen in the Emory student newspaper not only caused an uproar on campus, it doubtless led to a deep understanding of the current academic environment. He was subjected to a forum pitting six hostile professors (none psychologists) against an undergrad who was expected to defend Jensen's position.

Imagine his disgust when some professors agreed in private that Jensen might be right but were too cowardly to come out and say so in public. Remember, at least some of these people had tenure and couldn't have been fired from their jobs for expressing agreement with Jensen. But they could be sure that they could forget about being invited to academic cocktail parties or getting any grants from the university for their travel or research. What a commentary on the contemporary academic world:

> I came to realize that an extremely nasty and highly motivated minority of faculty and students held the campus in the grip of fear. The purpose of my public humiliation was clear: It was a warning. Anyone who publicly acknowledged scientific facts or personal experiences about the reality of race could expect the same treatment.
>
> Arthur Jensen is the Galileo of our times. And to its eternal shame, Emory University refused to look into the telescope.

This is exactly the sort of experience that would turn a bright student away from even thinking about wanting to get a teaching or research position in the academic world. Seeing what can happen when one takes seriously the views of someone like Jensen with impeccable academic credentials would certainly be daunting. One could only look forward to hostility, ostracism, and academic unemployment if one went that route. Recent research indicates that graduate students self-select on the basis of their political beliefs: Controlled for IQ, conservatives avoid the academic profession, while people on the Left find a welcome home there. Thus the academy becomes ever more one-sidedly Leftist.

If there is one thing I wish Mike Polignano had done, it is to write about his personal subjective experience of being the focal point of all this hostility on the Emory campus. Did students walk up to him and angrily denounce him? Did faculty members give him condescending looks, implying that, "as anyone with any brains knows, Jensen is a crackpot"? Was he forced to be a loner, or did he find a group of students on campus who offered social support?

I have had quite a bit of experience with the personal shunning and hostility that views like race realism elicit on college campuses these days. I never did really adjust to it. And in my case, I couldn't rely on anyone on campus who really agreed with me intellectually, although there were a few gestures of friendliness. The result was that encountering faculty members or even some students would lead to a lot of anxiety.

It must have been much worse for Polignano if only because the urge to fit in is much stronger in young people. And while I have tenure, he must have been looking ahead to a life where his views would forever taint his chances of really getting ahead in multicultural America. When a lot of students look back at college, it's a pleasant blur of parties, socializing, and studying — not memories of hostility and ostracism.

People like Mike Polignano are a rare and courageous breed. We need a lot more like him. And we have to find ways to support them financially as they continue their careers as effective writers and activists on behalf of the white majority of America.

Counter-Currents/*North American New Right*,
September 23, 2010

A SERIOUS CASE

F. ROGER DEVLIN

Guillaume Faye
Archeofuturism:
European Visions of the Post-Catastrophic Age
London: Arktos, 2010

> "The modern world is like a train full
> of ammunition running in the fog."
> — Robert Ardrey

Most thought described as "conservative" is a kind of political *hygienics*: it takes its bearings by what is natural, normal, or best in the social order. One hazard of its focus on right order is to leave us unprepared in extraordinary situations. Thus, we all know otherwise intelligent conservatives who would continue, even as blood was running in the streets, to talk of the need for electing fiscally responsible Republicans to office. The best treatment for this sort of blindness is a crash course in political *pathology* such as the book under review.

Author Guillaume Faye was for many years a luminary of Alain de Benoist's Group for the Research and Study of European Civilization. Beginning from the principle "no Lenin without Marx," Benoist conceived his activities as part of a Gramscian (or Cochinian) strategy to undermine the hegemony of liberalism. In the early 1980s, remembers Faye, each issue of Benoist's journal *Éléments* was "an ideological barrage that sparked outraged reviews from the mainstream press," and people sat up and took notice of the *Colloques parisiens* his organization sponsored. The well-educated men of this "New Right," as it came to be called, looked down on the young *Front National* as a "microscopic group of good-for-nothings," and even barred "that pirate-faced old soldier" Jean-Marie Le Pen from their meetings.

Yet within a few years the tables were turned, as dissatisfied New Rightists flocked to the Front. Any misgivings they had about Le Pen's vulgarity were outweighed by the impression that his organization was where *something was happening*. Faye, too, eventually concluded that the New Right had become a mere literary salon: "from 1986 I began to feel that a clique spirit and literary pagan romanticism were prevailing over historical will. . . . In order to prove effective, ideological and cultural action must be supported by concrete political forces which it integrates and extends."

Archeofuturism marks the author's return to the political arena after an absence of twelve years. Its first chapter is devoted to a friendly critique of his former colleagues. For example, he finds in New Right publications an overemphasis upon folkloric aspects of European heritage: Breton bonnets, Scandinavian woodcarvings, and the like. Such charming but innocuous traditions have their equivalents among all peoples on earth. Faye would rather maintain "the creative primacy of Western civilization" represented by our tradition of scientific research, philosophy and engineering, as well as our unparalleled artistic and literary high culture.

Faye also considers the New Right wedded to a faulty political paradigm in which "America"—conceived narrowly as the Hollywood/Wall Street/Foggy Bottom axis—is the enemy. This way of thinking is well-expressed in the title of Benoist's book *Europe-Third World: The Same Struggle*. Benoist invites the entire non-American world (even Muslims!) to "a fruitful exchange of dialogue among parties clearly situated in relation to one another." In other words: multiculturalism with one place at the table reserved for white Europeans. Faye rightly dismisses this as "a Disneyland dream."

Starting from what Faye considers a correct Nietzschean assessment of primitive Christianity as an egalitarian, leveling and ethnomasochistic movement, the New Right launched an ill-considered attack on the folk Catholicism of ordinary Frenchmen. Meanwhile, they ignored their proper target: a return to the "Bolshevism of antiquity" among the high clergy, marked by immigrationism and self-ethnophobia. This latter tendency is identical with what James C. Russell has identified as the "de-Germanization of Christianity." The New Right would have done better to ally itself with Catholic traditionalists in combating it rather than to alienate these natural allies.

Lastly, while the New Right professed admiration for the German jurist Carl Schmitt, it never made any practical application of his concept of the *Ernstfall*: the "serious case" which cannot be met within the normal framework of constitutional law. When Hannibal is at the gates of Rome, when the Royal Guards mutiny—no appeal can be made to law. Such contingencies can only be met with the virtue of *prudence*, i.e., the ability to make sound judgments about what to do in particular cases.

This blind spot may be fatal, for Faye is convinced that the liberal regime is driving Western civilization towards an *Ernstfall* the likes of which the world has never seen. He describes it as a "convergence of catastrophes." Elements include: the failure of multiracialism, the disintegration of family structures, disruption in the transmission of cultural knowledge and social disciplines, the replacement of folk culture by the passive consumption of industrially produced mass culture, increasing crime and drug use, the decay of community, anti-natalism, nuclear proliferation and the re-emergence of viral and microbial diseases resistant to antibiotics, public debt, and the privileging of speculative profits, i.e., the construction of our economy atop the stilts of investor confidence rather than upon the solid ground of production.

Furthermore, liberal ideology has propounded a utopian ideal of universal "development," whereby every last African hellhole is supposed to become an affluent, tolerant, democratic, and efficient consumerist society. The nations of the South were won over to this project, dazzled by the deceptive prospect of economic growth. They set in motion a process of industrialization that has devastated the natural environment, undermined their traditional cultures, and created social chaos, including urban jungles like Calcutta and Lagos. Resentment at the broken promise of "development" runs deep; the resurgence of religious fanaticism is one of its expressions.

Under the banner of "inclusion," the liberal regime is now importing legions of immigrants who will function as the fifth column of an aggressive South. "The ethnic war in France has already started," writes Faye in 1998, seven years before *les émeutes des banlieues*.

These are the lines of catastrophe which Faye expects to converge in about the second decade of this century. His prophecy is reminiscent of Andrei Amalrik's 1969 essay *Will the Soviet Union Survive Until 1984?* — which, of course, proved uncannily accurate. Still, the wise reader will not want to overstress Faye's time frame; much is clear about the crisis we face, but not even the angels in heaven know the day or the hour.

The author emphasizes that the impending meltdown presents us with opportunities: "When people have their backs against the wall and are suffering piercing pains, they easily change their opinions." The stormy century of iron and fire that awaits us will make people accept what is currently unacceptable. The Right today must position itself to be perceived as the natural alternative when the inevitable crisis hits. This means discrediting Leftist pseudo-dissent, which is merely a demand for the intensification of official ideology and praxis. It also means acquiring a monopoly over alternative thought: not by imposing a party line, but by uniting all healthy forces on a European level and abandoning provincial disputes and narrow doctrines.

Faye's book is intended as "a sort of mental training for the post-catastrophic world." The title *Archeofuturism* refers to the principles appropriate to reconstructing our civilization. "Archaic" must be understood according to the root sense of the Greek noun *archè*: both "foundation" and "beginning." The *archai* are anthropological values which "create and are unchangeable" while referring to the central notion of "order."

Such foundational values include:

the distinction of sex roles; the transmission of ethnic and folk traditions; spirituality and priestly organization; visible and structuring social hierarchies; the worship of ancestors; rites and tests of initiation; the re-establishment of organic communities (from the family to the folk); the de-individualization of marriage [and] an end to the confusion between eroticism and conjugality; the prestige of the warrior caste; inequality of social status—not the unjust and frustrating implicit inequality we find today in egalitarian utopias, but explicit and legitimated inequalities; duties that match rights, hence a rigorous justice that gives people a sense of responsibility; a definition of peoples—and of all established groups or social bodies—as diachronic communities of destiny rather than synchronic masses of individual atoms.

Faye calls these "the values of justice." We need not doubt they will return once the hallucinations of equality and individual emancipation have dissipated, for they follow from human nature itself.

The real danger is that we may end up having them imposed on us by Islam rather than reasserting them ourselves from our own historical memory. For Islam is the symbolic banner of Southern *revanchisme,* and the mindset of the South remains archaic. It takes for granted the primacy of force, the legitimacy of conquest, ethnic exclusivity, aggressive religiosity, machismo, and a worship of leaders and hierarchic order. Muslim employment of liberal cant—complaints of "discrimination" and "intolerance"—are the merest fig leaf for a Machiavellian "strategy of the fox" against Europe. In order to oppose the invaders, we must revert to an archaic mindset ourselves, abandoning the demobilizing handicap of modern humanitarianism.

Faye is perhaps at his best explaining the behavior and motivations of the "petty, inglorious princes who pretend to be governing us." For example, he notes the increasing importance of "consultation" in French political life; authorities "consult" representatives of various approved interest groups, such as labor unions and non-white ethnic blocs, and then formulate policy on the basis of the lowest common denominator of agreement between them. The point of this exercise is to avoid the risks and responsibilities of actual *leadership.* (Try to imagine De Gaulle behaving this way.) But it is presented to the public as a wonderful way of "modernizing democracy."

A related symptom is the rise of negative legitimization, or what the author calls the "big bad wolf tactic":

> Politicians no longer say, "Vote for us, because we've got the right solutions and we'll improve your living conditions." That is positive legitimization. Instead they say (implicitly) "Vote for us, since even though we're a bunch of good-for-nothings, bunglers and bullies, at least we will protect you from fascism."

Four years after these words were written Le Pen made the presidential run-offs and, sure enough, all the *bien-pensants* showed up at the polls with clothespins on their noses to support the crook Chirac!

Egalitarian reform serves as a convenient pretext for the elites to enact measures whose practical effect is to entrench their own position. Thus, they have sabotaged the French educational system by eliminating selectivity and discipline. But it is only these which give the talented outsider an honest chance against the untalented insider. As Pareto put it: the more rigorous the (rationally planned) selection in a social system, the greater the turnover in the elite. Without objective standards, on what grounds can one argue against elite self-perpetuation?

But the regime's most breathtaking hypocrisy is found in its demonization of the National Front. The Front has broken the tacit ground-rules of the managerial regime by "engaging in politics where it has been agreed that one should only engage in business"; it has sought popular trust with a view to implementing a program, where the established parties "communicate" and maneuver with a view to re-election. Timid careerists denounce the Front as a threat to the Republic because they fear it as a threat to themselves.

Faye considers the National Front a genuinely revolutionary party. Yet he apparently has never been a member, and is not really a French nationalist. In his view, Le Pen's romantic and backward-looking devotion to the French state embodies a great deal of latent Jacobinism. It is this state, after all, which has naturalized millions of Afro-Asiatic "youths" who do not see themselves as French at all. Moreover, a nation state, even run on patriotic principles, would be an entity too small to defend the French *ethnos* effectively in the contemporary world. Would a federal European state be any more capable of doing so? "I believe it would," says Faye, "provided it is exactly the opposite of the European state currently being built."

Those who believe that an imperial and federal European state would "kill France" are confusing the political sphere with the ethno-cultural one. The disappearance of the Parisian regime would in no way threaten the vigor and identity of the people of France. Moreover, argues Faye, a European federal state would breathe new life into autonomous regions: Brittany, Normandy, Provence, etc.

The European Union is a ghastly bureaucratic mess, but it is also one of the forces in being. Why turn our backs on it or work to destroy it when we might instead hijack it and turn it to our own purposes? Faye calls for the transformation of the EU into "a genuinely democratic and no longer bureaucratic European government with a real parliament and a strong and decisive central power." He describes this position as *European Nationalism*, and dreams of a Eurosiberian Federation extending from Brest to the Bering Strait.

While Faye disagrees with Benoist's interpretation of America as an enemy (*hostes*), he continues to view her as a rival and opponent (*inimicus*). This American reviewer does not grasp why the case for including a chastened post-imperial United States in a Northern Federation would be any weaker than the case for including Russia.

The Eurosiberian Federation is to be characterized by a two-tier economy. The elite (20% of the population) will continue to live according to the techno-scientific economic model based on ongoing innovation. They would form part of a global exchange network of about one billion people, including the elites of other civilizational blocs. As Faye notes, "the essence of technological science is not connected to egalitarian modernity, but has its roots in the ethno-cultural heritage of Europe, and particularly ancient Greece."

Among the first exploits of this new elite shall be exploring the "explosive possibilities of genetic engineering." These include inter-species hybrids, man-animal chimeras, semi-artificial "biolithic" creatures, and decerebrated human clones. Faye is utterly contemptuous of moral or religious scruples in this domain, which he oddly attributes to the ideology of liberal modernity more than to Christianity.

The remainder of humanity would live in archaic, neo-traditional communities. The techno-scientific portion of humanity would be under no obligation to help (i.e., "develop") everybody else, but neither would they have any right to interfere in their affairs.

In sum, for the elite: Promethean achievement, linear time and futuristic technology; for the rest: neo-feudalism, cyclic time, and timeless, "archaic" values.

But it is not clear how the elite could avoid interfering in the affairs of people they are supposed to *govern*. Moreover, how would the elite perpetuate itself? It seems clear that Faye does not intend a hereditary aristocracy. Perhaps there is some sort of test or initiatory ordeal for prospective members. But then families would be divided between the classes, which would involve many difficulties. In the fictional portrayal of his ideal future society which closes the book, Faye refers in passing to something called "the Party." This reviewer would need to hear *a lot* more about this shadowy organization before signing on to Faye's proposals. The two-tiered economy is altogether the least satisfactorily worked out part of the book.

Yet the author is aware that men never get what they plan for: somewhat grandiloquently, he calls this *heterotelia*. And he distinguishes "worldview" (an idea of civilization as a goal and some values) from "ideology" and "doctrine" (applications to society and what tactics to use). So we can follow him for the first mile.

Archeofuturism should have a bracing effect on anyone more accustomed to reading the despondent Cassandras of paleoconservatism. "Realism," he reminds us, "is often disheartened fatalism":

Those who blame others, enemies and the political climate for their own failures do not deserve to win. For it is in the logic of things for enemies to oppress you and circumstances to prove hostile. The mistake lies in exorcising reality by adopting the morals of intention as opposed to those of consequences.

We must reject the pretext that radical thought would be "persecuted" by the system. The system is foolish. Its censorship is as far from stringent as it is clumsy, striking only at mythic acts of provocation and ideological tactlessness. Talent always prevails over censorship, when it is accompanied by daring and intelligence. A Right wing movement can only prove successful through the virtue of courage.

So there is no excuse for being taken by surprise when the liberal regime disregards its own principles in order to fight us (as the British establishment has done with the British National Party). Of course we should publicize and ridicule their inconsistencies, but it is silly to be indignant over them: repression simply means that the regime recognizes us as an *Ernstfall*, a mortal threat, and that is precisely what a serious Right ought to be. Attempts to shut us down are symptoms of growing success and should strengthen our resolve.

Counter-Currents/*North American New Right*,
December 14, 2010

METAPHYSICS OF WAR

DEREK HAWTHORNE

Julius Evola
Metaphysics of War:
Battle, Victory and Death in the World of Tradition
Aarhus, Denmark: Integral Tradition Publishing, 2007

Metaphysics of War is a collection of sixteen essays by Italian Traditionalist Julius Evola (1898–1974), published in various periodicals in the years 1935–1950.

These essays constitute what is certainly the most radical attempt ever made to justify war. This justification takes place essentially on two levels: one profane, the other sacred. At the profane (meaning simply "non-sacred") level, Evola argues that war is one of the primary means by which heroism expresses itself, and he regards heroism as the noblest expression of the human spirit. Evola reminds us that war is a time in which both combatants and non-combatants realize that they may lose their lives and everything and everyone they value at any moment. This creates a unique moral opportunity for individuals to learn to detach themselves from material possessions, relationships, and concern for their own safety. War puts everything into perspective, and Evola states that it is in such times that "a greater number of persons are led towards an awakening, towards liberation" (p. 135):

> From one day to the next, even from one hour to the next, as a result of a bombing raid one can lose one's home and everything one most loved, everything to which one had become most attached, the objects of one's deepest affections. Human existence becomes relative—it is a tragic and cruel feeling, but it can also be the principle of a catharsis and the means of bringing to light the only thing

which can never be undermined and which can never be destroyed. (p. 136)

So far, these ideals may seem quite similar to those espoused by Ernst Jünger—and indeed Evola alludes to him in one place in the text (p. 153), and is uncharacteristically positive. (Usually when Evola refers to a modern author it is almost always to stick the knife in.) However, Evola goes well beyond Jünger, for he adds to this ideal of heroism and detachment a "spiritual" and even supernatural dimension (this is the "sacred" level I alluded to earlier). In essential terms, Evola argues that the heroism forged in war is a means to transcendence of this world of suffering and to identification with the source of all being. He even argues that the hero may attain a kind of magical quality.

Unsurprisingly, Evola attempts to situate his treatment of heroism in terms of the doctrine of the "four ages," a staple of Traditionalist writings. The version of the four ages most familiar to Western readers is the one found in Ovid, where the ages are gold, silver, bronze, and iron. However, Evola has squarely in mind the Indian version wherein the Iron Age (the most degraded of all) is referred to as the *Kali Yuga*. To these correspond the four castes of traditional society, with a spiritual, priestly element dominating in the first age, the warrior in the second, the merchant (or, bourgeois, the term most frequently used by Evola) in the third, and the slave or servant in the fourth.

When the bourgeoisie dominates in the third age, "the concept of the nation materializes and democratizes itself"; "an anti-aristocratic and naturalistic conception of the homeland is formed" (p. 24). Ironically, when I read this I could not help but think of Fascist Italy and National Socialist Germany. To the liberal mind, fascism and Nazism both are "ultra-conservative" (to put it mildly). From the Traditionalist perspective, however, both are modern, populist movements. And National Socialism especially found itself caught up in reductionist, biological theories of "the nation." Nevertheless, Evola writes that "fascism appears to us as a reconstructive revolution, in that it affirms an aristocratic and spiritual concept of the nation, as against both socialist and internationalist collectivism, and the democratic and demagogic notion of the nation" (p. 27). In other words, whatever its shortcomings may be, fascism is for Evola a means to restore Tradition. Evola also writes approvingly of fascism having elevated the nation to the status of "warrior nation." And he states that the next step "would be the spiritualization of the warrior principle itself" (p. 27). Of course, it seems to have been Heinrich Himmler's ambition to turn his SS into an elite corps of "spiritual warriors." One wonders if this was the reason Evola began courting members of the SS in the late 1930s (a matter briefly discussed in John Morgan's Introduction to this volume).

Evola tells us that the end of the reign of the bourgeoisie opens up two paths for Europe. One is a shift to the subhuman, and Evola makes it clear that this is what Bolshevism represents. The fourth age is the age of the slave and of the triumph of slave morality in the form of communism. The other possibility, however, is a shift to the "superhuman." As Evola has said elsewhere, the Kali Yuga may be an age of decline but it presents unique opportunities for self-transformation and the attainment of personal power. ("A radical destruction of the 'bourgeois' who exists in every man is possible in these disrupted times more than in any other," p. 137.) Those who "ride the tiger" are able not just to withstand the onslaught of negative forces in the fourth age, but actually to use them to rise to higher levels of self-realization. War is one such negative force, and Evola maintains that the idea of war as a path to spiritual transformation is a Traditional view.

According to Evola, the ancient Aryans held that there are two paths to enlightenment: contemplation and action. In traditional Indian terms, the former is the path of the brahmin and the latter of the kshatriya (the warrior caste). Both are forms of yoga, which literally means any practice that has as its aim connecting the individual to his true self, and to the source of all being (which are, in fact, the same thing). The yoga of action is referred to as *karma yoga* (where *karma* simply means "action"), and the primary text which teaches it is the Bhagavad-

Gita. Evola returns again and again to the Bhagavad-Gita throughout *Metaphysics of War*, and it really is the primary text to which Evola's philosophy of "war as spiritual path" is indebted. The work forms part (a very small part, actually) of the epic poem *Mahabharata*, the story of which culminates in an apocalyptic war called Kurukshetra. On the eve of battle, the consummate warrior Arjuna (the Siegfried of the piece) surveys the two camps from afar and realizes that on his enemy's side are many men who are his friends and relations. When Arjuna reflects on the fact that he will have to kill these men the following day, he falters. Fortunately, his charioteer—who is actually the god Krishna—is there to teach him the error of his ways. Krishna tells Arjuna that these men are already dead, for their deaths have been ordained by the gods. In killing them, Arjuna is simply doing his duty and playing his role as a warrior. He must set aside his personal feelings and concentrate on his duty; he must literally become a vehicle for the execution of the divine plan.

One might well ask, what's in it for Arjuna? The answer is that this following of duty becomes a path by which he may triumph over his fears, his passions, his weaknesses—all those things that tie him to what is ephemeral. Following his duty becomes a way for Arjuna to rise above his lesser self and to connect with the divine. This is not mere piety or "love of God." It is a way to tap into a superhuman source of power and wisdom. The result is that Arjuna becomes more than merely human.

In fact, Krishna puts Arjuna in a situation in which he must fight two wars. One, the "lesser" war is external—it is the one fought on the battlefield with swords and spears. The other, "greater" war is internal and is fought against the internal enemy: "passion, the animal thirst for life" (p. 52). Evola places a great deal of emphasis on this distinction. What Krishna really teaches Arjuna is that in order to fight the lesser war, he must fight the greater one. Really, unless one is able to conquer one's weaknesses, nothing else may be accomplished. This opens up the possibility that there may be "warriors" who never fight in any conventional, "external" wars. These would be warriors of the spirit. Evola believes that one can be a true warrior without ever lifting a sword or a gun, by conquering the enemy within oneself. And he mentions initiatic cults, like Mithraism, which conceived of their members on the model of soldiers.

Nevertheless, the focus in *Metaphysics of War* is really on actual, physical combat as a means to spiritual transformation. Evola tells us that the warrior ceases to act as an ordinary person, and that a non-human force transfigures his action. The warrior who does not fear death becomes death itself. This is one of the major lessons imparted by Krishna in the Bhagavad-Gita. It is not just a matter of "waking up" or becoming tougher and harder (as it is in Jünger). Evola clearly suggests that there is a supernatural element involved, though his remarks are far from clear. He writes that "the one who experiences heroism spiritually is pervaded with a metaphysical tension, an impetus, whose object is 'infinite,' and which, therefore, will carry him perpetually forward, beyond the capacity of one who fights from necessity, fights as a trade, or is spurred by natural instincts or external suggestion" (p. 41). Elsewhere Evola states that when the "right intention" is present "then one has given birth to a force which will not be able to miss the supreme goal" (p. 48). Heroic experiences seem "to possess an almost magical effectiveness: they are inner triumphs which can determine even material victory and are a sort of evocation of divine forces intimately tied to 'tradition' and 'the race of the spirit' of a given stock" (p. 81).

The suggestion here is that the experience of combat, fought with the right intention, results in a kind of ecstasy (an "active ecstasy" as Evola says on p. 80). The Greek *ekstasis* literally means "standing outside onself." In combat one is lifted out of one's ordinary self and, more specifically, out of one's concern with the mundane cares of life. One enters into a state where one ceases even to care about personal survival. It is at this point that one has ceased to identify with the "animal" elements in the human personality and has tapped into that part of us that seems to be a divine spark. This is not, however, an intellectual state or "realization." Instead, it is a new state of being, which pervades the entire person. The ancient Germans called it *wut* and *odhr*. And from these two words derive two of the names of the chief Germanic god: Wotan and Odin. Odin is not, however, conceived simply as the god of war; he is also the god of wisdom and spiritual transformation. In this state of ecstasy, one feels oneself lifted above the merely human; one's senses and reflexes become more acute, one's movements more graceful, life suddenly comes into perspective and is seen as the transient affair that it really is, and one feels invincible, capable of accomplishing anything. (A dim simulacrum of this is experienced in athletic competition.) One has, in fact, become a god.

Evola ties this achievement of self-transformation through combat into a "general vision of life," which he expresses in one of the most memorable metaphysical passages in this small volume:

> [L]ike electrical bulbs too brightly lit, like circuits invested with too high a potential, human beings fall and die only because a power burns within them which transcends their finitude, which goes beyond everything they can do and want. This is why they develop, reach a peak, and then, as if overwhelmed by the wave which up to a given point had carried them forward, sink, dissolve, die and return to the unmanifest. But the one who does not fear death, the one who is able, so to speak, to assume the powers of death by becoming everything which it destroys, overwhelms and shatters—this one finally passes beyond limitation, he continues to remain upon the crest of the wave, he does not fall, and what is beyond life manifests itself within him. (p. 54)

Throughout *Metaphysics of War*, Evola describes the various virtues of the warrior. These are the characteristics one must have to be effective in battle, and receptive to the sort of experience Evola describes. Again, however, it is very clear that he believes that all those who follow a path of spiritual transformation are warriors. Evola describes the warrior as without any doubt or hesitation; as having a bearing that suggests he "comes from afar"; as holding a world-affirming outlook. The warrior takes pleasure in danger and in being put to the test. (The lesson here for all of us, Evola says, is to find the meaning in adversity, and to take hardships as calls upon our nobility.) The warrior regards as comrades only those he can respect; he has a passion for distance and order; he has the ability to subordinate his passions to principles. The warrior's relations with others are direct, clear, and loyal. He carries himself with a dignity devoid of vanity, and loathes the trivial.

Above all, however, Evola emphasizes the importance of detachment:

> detachment towards oneself, towards things, and towards persons, which should instill a calm, an incomparable certainty and even, as we have before stated, an indomitability. It is like simplifying oneself, divesting oneself in a state of waiting, with a firm, whole mind, with an awareness of something that exists beyond all existence. From this state the capacity will also be found of always being able to commence, as if *ex nihilo*, with a new and fresh mind, forgetting what has been and what has been lost, focusing only on what positively and creatively can still be done. (p. 137)

Evola offers us a vision of life as a member in a spiritual army. The standard, liberal view of the military is in effect that it is a necessary evil, and that the military and its values are not a suitable model for individual lives or societies. Evola argues instead that true civilization is conceived in heroic and "virile" terms. Readers of Evola's other works will be familiar with his concept of "spiritual virility." Mere physical virility is the element in man that he shares with other male animals. But this is not true or absolute manhood. True manhood is achieved in the spirit, in developing the sort of hardness, detachment, and perspective on life that is characteristic of the warrior. René Guénon (a major influence on Evola) called the modern age "the reign of quantity." It is typical of our time that we have come to see manhood entirely in terms of quantities of various kinds: how many pounds one can bench press or squat; numbers of sexual partners; inches of height; inches of penis; the number of zeros in one's bank balance; the number of cylinders in one's engine, etc. Just as in Huxley's *Brave New World*, our masters have striven to create a society without conflict; a "nice" and "tolerant" society. And women have invaded virtually every arena of competition that used to be exclusively male and ruined them for everyone. Under such circumstances, how is spiritual virility to develop? It is no surprise that our conception of virility is a purely physical and quantitative one. Evola evidently saw in fascism a means to awaken spiritual virility in the Italian male. He says that the starting point for fascist ethics is "scorn for the easy life" (p. 62).

Unlike other thinkers on the Right, Evola never was particularly interested in biological conceptions of race, because he believed that human nature as such was irreducible to biology. He opposed reductionism, in short, and believed in a spiritual (i.e., non-material) component to our identity. Evola articulates his views on race in much greater detail elsewhere. Here he reminds us of his belief in a "super race" of the spirit: a race of men who are like-souled, and not necessarily like-bodied. Nevertheless, Evola realized the connection between the body and the spirit. He did not believe that all the (biological) races are equally fitted for achieving heroism. What Evola was most concerned to combat was a racialism that reduced heroism or mastery to simple membership in a race defined by certain biological characteristics. For Evola, heroism is really achieved in a step beyond the biological, and in mastery over it.

One will also find little in Evola that celebrates "the nation." Evola's ideal of heroism transcends national identity. This comes out most clearly in his discussion of the Crusades: "*In fact, the man of the Crusades was able to rise, to fight, and to die for a purpose which, in its essence, was supra-political and supra-human,* and to serve on a front defined no longer by what is particularistic, but rather by what is universal" (p. 40, italics in original). Having written this, however, Evola immediately realized that the powers that be might see this (correctly) as implying that it is the achievement of heroism *as such* that is important, not merely the achievement of heroism in service to one's people. A further implication of this, of course, is that the hero is raised above his people. And so Evola writes in the next paragraph, "Naturally this must not be misunderstood to mean that the transcendent motive may be used as an excuse for the warrior to become indifferent, to forget the duties inherent in his belonging to a race and to a fatherland" (pp. 40–41). Evola is not really being disingenuous here. Taking a cue again from the Bhagavad-Gita, one can say that it is the performance of one's duty to race and fatherland that is the path to liberation. But as the wise man once said, when the raft takes us to the other shore, we do not put it on our backs and carry on with it. As Rajayoga teaches, there is no god (and certainly no country) above an awakened man. Evola is a fundamentally a philosopher of the left hand path, not a conservative. This individualistic element in him is troublesome for many on the Right, and it is one of the primary reasons why he was unable to wholly reconcile himself to fascism.

Nine of these essays were written during the Second World War, and it is interesting to see how Evola situates his understanding of the conflict within his philosophy. In one essay written on the eve of the war, Evola states that:

> If the next war is a "total war" it will mean also a "total test" of the surviving racial forces of the modern world. Without doubt, some will collapse, whereas others will awaken and arise. Nameless catastrophes could even be the hard but necessary price of heroic peaks and new liberations of primordial forces dulled through grey centuries. But such is the fatal condition for the creation of any new world—and it is a new world that we seek for the future. (p. 68)

It is doubtful that the war's outcome either surprised or demoralized Evola. As noted earlier, he believed strongly in a cyclical view of history, and saw our age as a period of inevitable decline. It could not have surprised him that the combined forces of bourgeois and Bolshevik prevailed. In the final essay of in this volume, published five years after the end of the war, Evola reflects that "what is really required to defend 'the West'" against the forces of barbarism "is the strengthening, to an extent perhaps still unknown to Western man, of a heroic vision of life" (p. 152).

Evola makes it clear that his position is not an unqualifiedly pessimistic one. The Kali Yuga is not the final age; history is cyclical, and a new and better age will follow this one. In each period, the stage is set for the next. The actions of those who resist this age set the stage for what is to come. Hence, though speaking and acting on behalf of truth may seem futile given the degradation that surrounds us, ultimately our resistance is part of the mechanism of the great cosmic wheel which will, in time, swing things back to truth and to Tradition. In the act of resisting, heroism is born in us and instantly we become creatures who no longer belong to this age, who "come from afar." We become beacons pointing the way to the future, and simultaneously back to a glorious past. Evola writes that "a teaching peculiar to the ancient Indo-Germanic traditions was that precisely those who, in the dark age, in spite of all, resist, will be able to obtain fruits which those who lived in more favorable, less hard periods could seldom reach" (p. 61).

Metaphysics of War is required reading for all those interested in the Traditionalist movement. But it will be of special appeal to a certain sort of man, who scorns the easy life and seeks to give birth to something noble and heroic in himself.

Counter-Currents/*North American New Right*,
September 13, 2010

THE EPIC OF ARYA

AMANDA BRADLEY

Abir Taha
The Epic of Arya:
In Search of the Sacred Light
Milton Keynes: AuthorHouse, 2009

In Abir Taha's philosophical novel, Arya is a goddess in human form. Born in the Kali Yuga, the darkest age of the world, she is a symbol of the divine spark (*ātman*) that resides in every human. As she struggles to overcome her humanity, especially her *woman*ness, the reader also is given insight into the inner alchemical process that can make men into gods.

Arya meets several guides throughout her journey, and visits a number of cities that exemplify the greed, superficiality, and degeneracy that define the Kali Yuga. One village contains people who worship the moon—often considered an indication of a non-Traditional society that exalts the feminine principle over the masculine, and of people who follow the path of the ancestors rather than the solar path of the gods. Arya does find a kindred spirit—an old man who is a Sun worshiper. Through their conversation, she starts to feel that there is a secret group of beings who are awake, evoking similarities to the secret chiefs described in Karl von Eckartshausen's *The Cloud Upon the Sanctuary*, legends of the Great White Brotherhood, or Madame Blavatsky's Ascended Masters.

Arya finds no receptive ears to her message of freedom, truth, and responsibility, and the rest of the *Epic* recounts Arya's quest to find Hyperborea, where the Master Race was born.

She receives guidance from a prophet, who tries to convince her that the great Northern race no longer exists. Against his pleadings, she continues her quest, only to find he was correct. She comes across "a gloomy, overcrowded, noisy city teeming with people scurrying here and there in a chaotic manner, countless lonely atoms going their separate ways, impervious to the grey hell in which they were living" (p. 241). The city is called the pride and envy of the world, yet to Arya's refined senses it contains only "the deafening sound of the chaos of the senses and the unbearable noise of greed" (p. 241).

After meeting several more characters, including a *Chandala* (an untouchable in the Hindu caste system) and a knight, she meets the King of the World, the ruler of the sacred land of Shambhala. He gives her the keys to overcome herself and find the long-lost kingdom: "Shambhala is only real to those who live the glorious Unity of Being, and it is only visible to those who see beyond what the blind human eyes see" (p. 342), echoing the words of Pindar in his Tenth Pythian Ode: "neither by ship nor on foot would you find / the marvelous road to the assembly of the Hyperboreans."

The ideas in *Arya* are the same as those found in the writings of Traditionalists, the New Right, and Western esotericism: aristocracy, the coming race, the overman, Hyperborea, Ultima Thule, and philosopher kings. Taha has written two books on similar themes—*Nietzsche's Coming God, or the Redemption of the Divine* (Paris: Éditions Connaissances et Savoirs, 2005) and *Nietzsche, Prophet of Nazism: The Cult of the Superman – Unveiling the Nazi Secret Doctrine* (Bloomington, Indiana: AuthorHouse, 2005).

In fact, the best way to approach Taha's *Epic* is as another *Thus Spoke Zarathustra*, with the plot serving more as a means to express her *Weltanschauung* rather than a literary device. Arya's dialogues echo those of *Zarathustra* (Taha even uses the same "thus spoke" mantra), and of Krishna and Arjuna in the Bhagavad-Gita. This novel of ideas is heartfelt, and it's obvious that Taha is honest in the Preface when she says the story was written with her blood and tears, as the insights this "spiritual bible" contains are profound. Those familiar with Traditionalist doctrines may find that some sections are too repetitive, with concepts repeated several times in different words. Readers new to Traditionalist thought, however, will appreciate the emphasis on uncommon ideas like anti-egalitarianism and anti-modernity.

Because *The Epic of Arya* is about a goddess, women may find the story especially appealing as they will identify more with sections that deal with Arya's struggles to overcome human love for divine. A few sections mention finding the goddess within, but these can apply equally to finding the god within, and true seekers of wisdom will see beyond such nuances to pearls of wisdom.

THE KALI YUGA: THE AGE OF VICE

The Epic of Arya is set in the Kali Yuga, the last age in the Hindu cycle of ages (which roughly correspond to the ages outlined by Hesiod in *Works and Days*). In the Golden Age, men and gods lived on the earth together. In the Kali Yuga (or Dark Age), mankind is the furthest removed from God and the most spiritually decadent. This age is ruled by the demon Kali, a negative manifestation of the god Vishnu. The Kali Yuga is described in the Vishnu Purana as a time when Brahmanical clothing constitutes a Brahman; when agriculture is abandoned for mechanization; the Earth is honored for mineral treasures and is exploited; there is no transcendent connection to sacraments like marriage; men are fixated on money; and women are selfish. As Arya puts it, "in the Golden Age, before the hotchpotch of mob rule melted races and classes into a maelstrom from hell, there was one divine race on earth" (p. 182).

Being born in such a world is distressing to Arya—she is alone with no kindred soul. Even when she reaches a city lauded by the masses, Arya is disgusted:

You call yourselves "civilized," but yours is the civilization of accumulation and mediocrity bearing the banner of justice and equality, a sham civilization which buries all higher aspirations in the stagnant mud of materialism, and drowns all will to elevation in the murky waters of degeneracy. (p. 257)

MERITOCRACY AS THE TRUE ARISTOCRACY

Another main theme of *Arya* is that of hierarchies, as opposed to the egalitarianism prevalent in the world today. *The*

Epic of Arya does not extol an aristocracy based on blood or material possessions, but a meritocracy like that described by Plato in *The Republic*.

Hereditary aristocracy makes even less sense in the Kali Yuga than other times, since it brings a degeneration of form that does not allow Traditions to be passed by blood, as "True superiority is seldom inherited" (p. 209). *Arya* is interesting in part because of the many descriptions given for what is truly noble:

- ❖ Something that cannot be bought or sold
- ❖ Something that cannot be inherited or given, only earned
- ❖ Not related to titles, but to abilities
- ❖ Determined by how much someone gives, not owns
- ❖ Involves merit, talent, honor, duty, and honesty
- ❖ The real aristocrat is: "a complete human being, a synthetic man, an accomplished person. He combines a healthy body with a brilliant mind and a noble soul, a radiant spirit and beauty within and without. But the soul is primary, and a pure soul is more beautiful than the most perfect body" (p. 216).
- ❖ "All greatness is humble and magnanimous, all baseness is wicked and conceited" (p. 229).

RACE OF THE SPIRIT

The Epic of Arya expresses a concept of race similar to that of Julius Evola, Oswald Spengler, and Francis Parker Yockey — the notion of a race of the spirit. Arya does not come by this view naturally, however: For most of the book she is obsessed with finding her true sons, others of her race who are from the North. When she eventually finds the city she longs for, however, the people there are as crude, materialistic, and greedy as those of any other place. Familial and racial connections have lost their transcendent connections, and the men she finds are simply the "unworthy sons that every mother has" (p. 199).

According to the doctrine of the Yugas, in the Golden Age, race was an indication of an inner quality. A person was formed from a substance that represented his true nature.

Thus, the beautiful body revealed a beautiful soul and noble character, and male and female souls formed corresponding bodies. It is the opposite of the current Dark Age, when most men no longer possess true virility and pariahs comprise the ruling class who desecrate the sacred earth.

In addition to not being applicable in the Kali Yuga, the biological doctrine of race also is a hindrance to enlightenment. Arya is told:

> Cling to no nation, no tribe, and no creed, these are but chains of enslavement to the limited and the transient. How could you call a nation your own, you whose soul dwells with the gods? How could you embrace but one creed, when Truth is the source of all creeds. (p. 374)

Not only is the biological determinist view of race invalid in the Kali Yuga, it also is disproved by the very nature used to support it. The *Epic* illustrates this point when Arya is told: "how many beautiful flowers contain the deadliest poison! How many worms dwell in the loveliest apples! Do not cling much to form, Arya, for it deceives ... and though spirit moulds the form, yet the form is *not* the spirit!" (p. 108).

The discourse on race also comments on the notion of a chosen people: "Eternal Religion has no holy land or chosen people" (p. 33), and again, "There are *no* chosen people, save those who have chosen out themselves" (p. 116). Arya also comments on Yahweh, the God of the Hebrew Bible: "let this god from the desert stay away from me, away from us *truly* chosen ones— we who have chosen Pan over Yahweh—for *his* lost tribes are doomed to aimlessly wander the earth in search of a promise that never was" ... "That is the curse of the gods: those who stray from the Inner Path shall nowhere feel at home and never find peace, though they may wander the earth in search of their lost soul; the desert remains their only home" (p. 38).

If race is not determined by blood or soil, a question naturally arises as to how a race of the spirit could be defined. *The Epic of Arya* has an answer for this question as well:

A race is a spiritual brotherhood of blood and honor; it is defined by the dream that it shares, the truth that it reveres and fights for, the god that it venerates . . . and only he or she who shares *my* truth and believes in *my* god do I call a brother or a sister, a son or a daughter, for blood means little if it does not serve the soul. (p. 50)

THE HERD & THE OVERMAN

Another Nietzschean concept in *Arya* is the *Übermensch*. In *Zarathustra*, Nietzsche wrote, "man is something which ought to be overcome." Arya is told that there are no races anymore, only masters and slaves, godmen and undermen. Some need a god "before whom you can all be slaves—but equal slaves" (p. 67). These are the people who fulfill themselves only through their slavery (p. 67).

Nietzsche's notion of being a bridge appears in *Arya* as well: "Hence the Higher Man, that god in the making, remains trapped between heaven and earth—while men are trapped between earth and hell" (p. 115). Arya eventually learns that she should focus not on bridging the gap between herself and the herd, but on bridging the gap between the human and the god.

The plight of godmen, then, is to endure the agony of humanity while remaining divine in spirit: "choosing the cold dangers of the pure and innocent wilderness to the warm comfort of the filthy and decadent human wastelands of civilization; for where herds live, there you find the wastelands and the deserts of the spirit; and where no man has set foot, there the air remains pure and undefiled, and a ray of hope shines on the horizon of a better tomorrow" (p. 139).

The Epic of Arya is such a ray of hope, a connection to the transcendent to help guide mankind through the end of the Kali Yuga to the establishment once again of the Golden Age.

Counter-Currents/*North American New Right*,
July 2, 2010

ANDROPHILIA: A MANIFESTO

DEREK HAWTHORNE

Jack Malebranche (Jack Donovan)
Androphilia: A Manifesto
Baltimore, Md.: Scapegoat Publishing, 2006

Near the end of *Androphilia*, Jack Donovan writes, "It has always seemed like some profoundly ironic cosmic joke to me that the culture of men who love men is a culture that deifies women and celebrates effeminacy. Wouldn't it make more sense if the culture of men who are sexually fascinated by men actually idolized men and celebrated masculinity?" (p. 115).

He has a point there. As Donovan notes, homosexual pornography is almost exclusively focused on hypermasculine archetypes: the lumberjack, the Marine, the jock, the cop, etc. (I am going to employ the term "homosexual," despite its problematic history, as a neutral term to denote same-sex desire among men. I am avoiding the term "gay," for reasons that will soon be apparent.) So why are homosexuals, who worship masculine men, so damn queeny? Most straight men (and women too) would offer what they see as the obvious answer: homosexuals are not real men. They are a sort of strange breed of womanly man, and it is precisely the *otherness* of masculine men that attracts them so. This is, after all, the way things work with straight people: men are attracted to women, and vice versa, because they are other. We want what we are not. Therefore, if a man desires another man then he must not be a real man.

What makes this theory so plausible is that so many self-identified homosexuals do behave in the most excruciatingly effeminate manner. They certainly seem to be not-quite-men. Donovan thinks (and I believe he is correct) that it is this womanish behavior in homosexuals that bothers straight men so much—more so, actually, than the fact that homosexuals have sex with other men in the privacy of their bedrooms.

Donovan objects to effeminacy in homosexuals as well, but he sees this effeminacy as a socially-constructed behavior pattern, as a consequence of the flawed logic that claims "since we're attracted to what's other, if you're a man attracted to a man you must not be a real man." Having bought into this way of seeing things, the "gay community" actually encourages its members to "camp it up" and get in touch with their feminine side. They think they are liberating themselves, but what they don't see is that they have bought into a specific set of cultural assumptions which effectively rob them of their manhood, in their own eyes and in the eyes of society.

Donovan argues, plausibly, that homosexual attraction should be seen as a "variation in desire" among men (p. 21). Homosexuals are men—men who happen to be attracted to other men. Their sexual desire does not make them into a separate species of quasi-men. This is a point that will be resisted by many, but it is easily defended. One can see this simply by reflecting on how difficult it is to comprehend the homosexuals of yore in the terms we use today to deal with these matters. There was, after all, unlikely to have been anything "queeny" (and certainly not cowardly) about the "Sacred Band" of Thebes—a contingent of warriors consisting of same-sex couples. And the samurai in feudal Japan were doing it too—just to mention two examples. These are not the sort of people one thinks of as "sensitive" and who one would expect to show up at a Lady Gaga concert, were they around today. It is unlikely that Achilles and his "favorite" Patroclus would have cruised around with a rainbow flag flying from their chariot. These were manly men, who happened to sexually desire other men. If there can be such men, then there is no necessary disjunction between homosexuality and masculinity. QED.

In essential terms, what Donovan argues in *Androphilia* is that homosexuals should reject the "gay culture" of effeminacy and reclaim masculinity for themselves. Ironically, gay culture is really the product of an internalization of the Judeo-Christian demonization of same-sex desire, and its insistence that homosexuality and masculinity are incompatible. Donovan wants gays to become "androphiles": men who love men, but who are not defined by that love. "Gay men" are men who allow themselves to be defined entirely by their desire, defined into a separate segment of humanity that talks alike, walks alike, dresses alike, thinks alike, votes alike, and has set itself apart from "breeders" in fashionable urban ghettos. "Gay" really denotes a whole way of life "that promotes anti-male feminism, victim mentality, and leftist politics" (p. 18). (This is the reason Donovan often uses "homo" instead of "gay": gay is a package deal denoting much more than same-sex desire.) He argues that in an effort to promote acceptance of men with same-sex desire, homosexuals encouraged others to regard them as, in effect, a separate sex—really, almost a separate race. "Gay," Donovan remarks, is really "sexuality as ethnicity" (p. 18). As a result, gay men have cut themselves off from the fraternity of men and, arguably, trapped themselves in a lifestyle that stunts them into perpetual adolescence. Donovan asks, reasonably, "Why should I identify more closely with a lesbian folk singer than with [straight] men my age who share my interests?"

Many of those who have made it this far into my review might conclude now that *Androphilia* is really a book for homosexuals, and doesn't have much to say to the rest of the world. But this is not the case. Donovan's book contains profound reflections on sexuality and its historical construction (yes, there really are some things that are historically constructed), the nature of masculinity, the role of male bonding in the formation of culture, and the connection between masculinity and politics. This book has implications for how men—all men—understand themselves.

Donovan attacks head-on the attempt by gays to set themselves up as an "oppressed group" on the model of blacks and women, and to compel all of us to refrain from uttering a critical word about them. He attacks feminism as the anti-male ideology it is. And he zeroes in on the connection, taken for granted by nearly everyone, between gay culture and advocacy of Left-wing causes. *Androphilia*, in short, is a book that belongs squarely on the political Right. It should be no surprise to anyone to discover that Donovan has been busy since the publication of *Androphilia* writing for sites like *Alternative Right* and *The Spearhead*.

Donovan himself was a part of the gay community when he was younger, but never really felt like he belonged. He so much as tells us that his desire for men is his religion; that he worships masculinity in men. But it seemed natural to Donovan that since he was a man, he should cultivate in himself the very qualities he admired in others. His desire was decidedly not for an "other" but for the qualities that he saw, proudly, in himself. (He says at one point, "I experience androphilia not as an attraction to some alien opposite, but as an attraction to variations in sameness," p. 49.)

Donovan is certainly not alone. It's natural when we think of homosexuals to visualize effeminate men, because those are the ones that stand out. If I asked you to visualize a Swede you'd probably conjure up a blonde-haired, blue-eyed Nordic exemplar. But, of course, a great many Swedes are brunettes (famous ones, too; e.g., Ingmar Bergman). The effeminate types are merely the most conspicuous homosexuals. But there also exists a silent multitude of masculine men who love men, men whom no one typically pegs as "gay." These men are often referred to as "straight-acting"—as if masculinity in a homosexual is necessarily some kind of act. These men are really Donovan's target audience, and they live a tragic predicament. They are masculine men who see their own masculinity as a virtue, thus they cannot identify with what Donovan calls the Gay Party (i.e., "gay community") and its celebration of effeminacy. They identify far more closely with straight men, who, of course, will not fully accept them. This is partly due to fear ("is he going to make a pass at me?"), and partly, again, due to the prevailing view which equates same-sex desire with lack of manliness. The Jack Donovans out there are lost between two worlds, at home in neither. Loneliness and sexual desire compels such men to live on the periphery of the gay community, hoping always to find someone like themselves. If they have at all internalized the message that their desires make them less-than-men (and most have), then their relationship to masculinity will always be a problematic one. They will always have "something to prove," and always fear, deep down, that perhaps they are inadequate in some fundamental way.

Androphilia is therapy for such men, and a call for them to form a new identity and group solidarity quite independent of the "gay community." On the one hand, Donovan asserts that, again, homosexuality should be seen as a "variation in desire" among men; that homosexuals should see themselves as men first, and not be defined entirely by their same-sex desire. On the other hand, it is very clear that Donovan also has high hopes that self-identified androphiles will become a force to be reckoned with. He writes at one point, "While other men struggle to keep food on the table or get new sneakers for Junior, androphiles can use their extra income to fund their endeavors. This is a significant advantage. Androphiles could become *leaders* of men in virtually any field with comparative ease. By holding personal achievement in high esteem, androphiles could become more than men; they could become *great* men" (p. 88).

Is Jack Donovan—the androphile Tyler Durden—building an army? Actually, it looks more like he's building a religion, and this brings us to one of the most interesting aspects of *Androphilia*. Repeatedly, Donovan tells us that "masculinity is a religion," or words to that effect (see especially pp. 65, 72, 76, 80, 116).

A first step to understanding what he is talking about is to recognize that masculinity is an ideal, and a virtue. Men strive to cultivate masculinity in themselves, and they admire it in other men. Further, masculinity is something that has to be achieved. Better yet, it has to be *won*. Femininity, on the other hand, is quite different. Femininity is essentially a state of being that simply comes with being female; it is not an accomplishment. Women *are*, but men must *become*. If femininity has anything to do with achievement, the achievement usually consists in artifice: dressing in a certain manner, putting on makeup, learning how to be coy, etc. Femininity is almost exclusively bound up with being attractive to men. If a man's "masculinity" consisted in dressing butch and not shaving, he would be laughed at; his "masculinity" would be essentially effeminate. (Such is the masculinity, for example, of gay "bears" and "leatherman.") Similarly, if a man's "masculinity" consists entirely in pursuing women and making himself attractive to them, he is scorned by other men. (Ironically, such "gigolos" are often far more effeminate mama's boys than many homosexuals.) No, true masculinity is achieved by accomplishing something difficult in the world: by fighting, building something, discovering something, winning a contest, setting a record, etc. In order for it to count, a man has to overcome things like fear and opposition. He has to exhibit such virtues as bravery, perseverance, commitment, consistency, integrity, and, often, loyalty. Masculinity is inextricably tied to virtue (which is no surprise—given that the root *vir-*, from which we also get "virile," means "man"). A woman can be petty, fickle, dishonest, fearful, inconstant, weak, and unserious—and still be thought of as 100% feminine.

A woman can also be the butchest nun, women's lacrosse coach, or dominatrix on the planet and never be in any danger of someone thinking she's "not a real woman." With men, it's completely different. As the example of homosexuals illustrates, it is quite possible to have a Y chromosome and be branded "not a real man." Masculinity, again, is an ideal that men are constantly striving to realize. The flip side of this is that they live in constant fear of some kind of failure that might rob them of masculinity in their eyes or the eyes of others. They must "live up" to the title of "man." Contrary to the views of modern psychologists and feminists, this does not indicate a "problem" with men that they must somehow try to overcome. If men did not feel driven to make their mark on the world and prove themselves worthy of being called men, there would be no science, no philosophy, no art, no music, no technology, no exploration.

"But there would also be no war, no conflict, no competition!" feminists and male geldings will shriek in response. They're right: there would be none of these things. And the world would be colorless and unutterably boring.

As Camille Paglia famously said, "If civilization had been

left in female hands, we would still be living in grass huts." She also said, "There is no female Mozart because there is no female Jack the Ripper." What this really means is that given the nature of men, we can't have Mozart without Jack the Ripper. So be it.

It should now be a bit clearer why Donovan says that "masculinity is a religion." To quote him more fully, "masculinity is not just a quality shared by many men, but also an ideal to which men collectively aspire. Masculinity is a religion, one that naturally resonates with the condition of maleness. Worship takes place at sports arenas, during action films, in adventure novels and history books, in frat houses, in hunting lodges" (p. 65).

Earlier in the book he writes:

> All men appreciate masculinity in other men. They appreciate men who are manly, who embody what it means to be a man. They admire and look up to men who are powerful, accomplished or assertive. . . . Men respectfully acknowledge another man's impressive size or build, note a fierce handshake, or take a friendly interest in his facial hair. . . . Sportscasters and fans speak lovingly of the bodies and miraculous abilities of their shared heroes. . . . While straight men would rather not discuss it because they don't want to be perceived as latent homosexuals, they do regularly admire one another's bodies at the gym or at sporting events. (p. 22)

None of this is "gay," "latently gay," or "homoerotic." This is just men admiring manliness. One of the sad consequences of "gay liberation" (and Freudian psychology) is that straight men must now police their behavior for any signs that might be read as "latency." And gay liberation has destroyed male bonding. Just recently I re-watched Robert Rossen's classic 1961 film *The Hustler*. In the opening scene, an old man watches a drunken Paul Newman playing pool and remarks to a friend, "Nice looking boy. Clean-cut. Too bad he can't hold his liquor." No straight man today would dream of openly admiring another man's appearance and describing him as "nice looking," even though there need be nothing sexual in this at all.

Of course, there *is* something decidedly sexual in androphilia. The androphile admires masculinity in other men also, but he has a sexual response to it. An androphile may admire all the same qualities in a man that a straight man would, but the androphile gets turned on by them. Here we must note, however, that although the straight man admires masculinity in men he generally spends a lot less time reflecting on it than an androphile does. And there are innumerable qualities in men (especially physical qualities) which androphiles notice, but which many straight men are completely oblivious to. In fact, one of the characteristics of manly men is a kind of obliviousness to their own masculine attractiveness. Yes, straight men admire masculinity in other men and in themselves — but this is often not something that is brought fully to consciousness. No matter how attractive he may be, if a man is vain, his attractiveness is undercut — and so is his masculinity. Men are attractive — to women and to androphiles — to the extent that their masculinity is something natural, unselfconscious, unaffected, and seemingly effortless. Oddly, *lack of self-consciousness* does seem to be a masculine trait. Think of the single-minded warrior, uncorrupted by doubt and introspection, forging ahead without any thought for how he seems to others, unaware of how brightly his virtue and heroism shine.

What all this means is that androphilia is *masculinity brought to self-consciousness*. To put it another way, the androphile is masculinity brought to awareness of itself. It is in the androphile that all that is good and noble and beautiful in the male comes to be consciously reflected upon and affirmed. It is in androphiles like Jack Donovan that the god of masculinity is consciously thematized as a god, and worshipped. Masculinity is a religion, he tells us again and again.

Now, I said a few lines earlier that *lack* of self-consciousness seems to be a masculine trait. If in androphiles a greater self-consciousness of masculinity is achieved, doesn't this mean that androphiles are somehow unmasculine? Actually what it means is that they are potentially *hyper*-masculine. It is true that we admire unselfconscious figures like Siegfried or Arjuna, because they seem to possess a certain purity. But such men are always ultimately revealed to be merely the plaything of forces over which they have no control. Greater still than a naïve, unselfconscious purity is the power of an awakened man, who consciously recognizes and cultivates his virtues, striving to take control of his destiny and to perfect himself. This is part and parcel of the ideal of *spiritual virility* Julius Evola spoke of so often.

The difference between Siegfried and Arjuna is that the latter had the god Krishna around to awaken him. Krishna taught him that he is indeed a plaything of forces over which he has no control. But Arjuna then *affirmed* this, affirmed his role in the cosmic scheme as the executioner of men, and became the fiercest warrior that had ever lived.

Most men unconsciously follow the script of masculinity, pushed along by hormones to realize the masculine ideal—usually only to find the same hormones putting them in thrall to women and, later, children. Androphiles consciously recognize and affirm masculinity, and because their erotic desires are directed towards other men, they have the potential to achieve far more in the realm of masculine accomplishment than those who, again, have to "struggle to keep food on the table or get new sneakers for Junior." Thus, far from being "unmasculine," androphiles have it within their power to become, well, *Overmen*. Androphiles have awakened to the god in themselves and other men. There is an old saying on the Left Hand Path: "There is no god above an awakened man." There is also no man above an awakened man. So much for the idea that a man's love for other men is a badge of inferiority.

Implicit in the above is something I have not remarked on thus far, and that Donovan does not discuss: the duality in the masculine character. It is a rather remarkable thing, as I alluded to earlier, that testosterone both makes a man want to fight, to strive, and to explore—and also to inseminate a woman and tie himself down to home and family. Of course, without that latter effect the race would die out. But it is nevertheless the case that men are pulled in two directions, just by being men: towards heaven and towards earth. To borrow some terms from Evola again, they have within themselves both *uranic* and *chthonic* tendencies. Modern biologists have a way of dealing with this: they insist that all of life is nothing but competition for resources and reproduction. Thus, all of men's uranic striving, all of their quest for the ideal, all of their adventures and accomplishments, are nothing more than ways in which they make themselves more attractive to females. This is sheer nonsense: nothing but the mindset of modern, middle-class, henpecked professors projected onto all of nature.

The truth is that men strive to realize the ideal of masculinity in ways that not only have nothing to do with the furtherance of the species, but are often positively inimical to it. Perhaps the best and most extreme example of masculine toughness one could give is the willingness of the samurai to disembowel themselves over questions of honor. Men strive for ideals, often at the expense of life. Masculinity has a dimension that can best be described as supernatural—as above nature. Women are far more tied to nature than men are, and this (and not sexist oppression) is the real reason why it is almost exclusively men who have been philosophers, priests, mystics, scientists, and artists. It is woman's job to pull man back to earth and perpetuate life.

One way to look at androphilia is that it is not just the masculine come to consciousness of itself, but the masculine ridding itself of the "natural." This "natural" side of the man is not without value (again, without it we would go extinct), but it has almost nothing to do with what makes men great. The androphile is free to cultivate the *truly* masculine aspects of the male soul, because he is free of the pull of the feminine and of the natural. This has to have something to do with why it is that so many great philosophers, artists, writers, mystics, and others, have tended to be androphiles. In 1913, D. H. Lawrence wrote the following to a correspondent:

> I should like to know why nearly every man that approaches greatness tends to homosexuality, whether he admits it or not: so that he loves the *body* of a man better

than the body of a woman—as I believe the Greeks did, sculptors and all, by far. . . . He can always get satisfaction from a man, but it is the hardest thing in life to get one's soul and body satisfied from a woman, so that one is free for oneself. And one is kept by all tradition and instinct from loving a man.

The androphile, again, is masculinity brought to consciousness of itself—and in him, it would seem, much else is brought to consciousness as well. For what else are science, philosophy, religion, art, and poetry but the world brought to consciousness of itself? These things—which are almost exclusively the products of men—are what set us apart and make us unique as a species. Human beings (again, almost exclusively men), unlike all other species, are capable of reflecting upon and understanding the world. We do this in scientific and philosophical theories, but also in fiction, poetry, and painting. Some of us, of course, are more capable of this than others—capable of achieving this reflective stance towards existence itself. And it would seem that of those men that are, some carry things even further and become fully aware of the masculine ideal that they themselves represent. And they fall in love with this. Sadly, androphile writers, artists, poets, etc., have often bought into the notion that their desire for other men makes them unmasculine and, like Oscar Wilde, have shoe-horned themselves into the role of the decadent, effeminate aesthete.

I think that when Donovan describes masculinity as a religion this is not just a desire to be provocative. I think he does experience his admiration for men as sacred. If this is the case, then it is natural for men who feel as he does to insist that such a feeling *cannot* be indecent or perverse. Further, it is natural for them to wonder why there are men such as themselves. What I have tried to do in the above reflections (which go beyond what Donovan says in his book) is to develop a theory of the "cosmic role," if you will, of the masculine itself, and of the androphile. I believe Donovan is thinking along the same lines I am, though he might not express things the same way. He writes at one point:

Masculinity is a religion, and I see potential for androphiles to become its priests—to devote themselves to it
and to the gods of men as clergymen devote their lives to
the supernatural. What other man can both embody the
spirit of manhood and revere it with such perfect devotion? This may sound far-fetched, but is it? If so, then
why? Forget about gay culture and everything you asso-
ciate with male homosexuality. Strip it down to its raw
essence—a man's sexual desire for men—and reimagine
the destiny of that man. Reimagine what this desire focused on masculinity could mean, what it could inspire,
and who the men who experience it *could* become. (p.
116)

There is much else in *Androphilia* that is well-worth discussing, though a review cannot cover everything. Particularly
worthy of attention is Donovan's discussion of masculinity in
terms of what he calls physical masculinity, essential masculinity, and cultural masculinity. Then there is Donovan's discussion of masculine "values." These really should be called "virtues" (especially given the etymology of this word—mentioned
earlier—Donovan has missed a bit of an opportunity here!).
The language of "values" is very modern. What he really has in
mind is virtues in the Aristotelian sense of *excellences* of the
man. Donovan lists such qualities as self-reliance, independence, personal responsibility, achievement, integrity, etc. He
starts to sound a bit like Ayn Rand in this part of the book, but
it's hard to quarrel with his message. The book ends with a
perceptive discussion of "gay marriage," which Donovan opposes, seeing it as yet another way in which gays are aping
straight relationships, yearning narcissistically for society's
"approval."

This is really a superb book, which all men can profit from,
not just androphiles. If one happens to be an androphile, however, one will find this is a liberating and revolutionary work.

Counter-Currents/*North American New Right*,
October 4, 2010

SIR NOËL COWARD, 1899–1973

JAMES J. O'MEARA

Noël Coward
The Noël Coward Reader
Ed. Barry Day
New York: Knopf, 2010

> "The only thing that really saddens me over my demise is that I shall not be here to read the nonsense that will be written about me and my works and my motives. . . . There will be lists of apocryphal jokes I never made and gleeful misquotations of words I never said. What a pity I shan't be here to enjoy them."
>
> —*The Noël Coward Diaries*, March 19, 1955[1]

> "White"—from a list of things with "style," solicited from Sir Noël for an ad by Gillette razor blades.

One is so used to today's notion of the artist as an outsider, tortured or haughty as the case may be, or perhaps proudly degenerate, that it can come as a shock to find, or recall, that the artist has usually been, and more importantly seen himself as, a productive and grateful member of society, whatever its flaws; even a patriot.

Ah, but what of the homosexual artist? Surely here we can find a true outsider. According to the victimology of the Left, life "before Stonewall" was one long uncut period of gay bashing and oppression, subtle or overt.

The point of such a mythology is to convince the homosexual that by accepting the manufactured "gay" identity, and thus

---

[1] Noël Coward, *The Noël Coward Diaries*, ed. Graham Payn and Sheridan Morley (New York: Da Capo, 2000).

contributing to the Left's project of destroying and reconstructing Western civilization, he will be rewarded with both vengeance now and a bright future in an entirely new gay-friendly
world.

Well, it wasn't that way, and it needn't be that way. As the
late English New Right theorist Alisdair Clarke put it:

> After the 1967 de-criminalization in the UK, homosexuals
> faced a choice between re-integrating with European civi-
> lization in a way not possible for 1,500 years (i.e., since
> the Jewish heresy of Christianity infiltrated the Roman
> Empire), or siding with the Marxist, Maoist, New Left
> enemies of European civilization, the ones who brought
> "Gay Liberation" from Manhattan to London. Instead of
> taking up our traditional responsibility of defending and
> glorifying our civilization, as did so many homosexuals
> in the past like Frederick II and von Humboldt, we sup-
> ported of those who would destroy that very same civili-
> zation.[2]

In this context, it may be instructive to examine the case of
Sir Noël Coward, "The Master," who practically invented the
idea of "The Englishman" in the 20th century, as an example of
such full-hearted, un-ironic "defending and glorifying our civilization."

Was Coward a "conservative"? It seems odd to those who
remember him, if at all, as the campy cabaret entertainer of the
'50s and '60s. When Coward's *Diaries* were published in 1982,
Variety was puzzled: "It's a bit startling to discover that Coward was a 'political reactionary,'" quoting his views on Suez:
"The good old imperialism was a bloody sight wiser than all
this woolly-headed, muddled 'all men are equal' humanitarianism which has lost us so much pride and dignity and prestige
in the modern world."[3]

---

[2] Alisdair Clarke, "Paris Shockwaves" at his blog *Aryan Futurism*
http://aryanfuturism.blogspot.com/2006/08/paris-shockwaves.html
[3] Philip Hoare, *Noël Coward: A Biography* (Chicago: University of

Rather than accepting such loaded terms as "reactionary," we can certainly designate Coward as a "conservative" or "man of the Right" as Paul Gottfried has recently defined the term:

> The Right by its nature is anti-egalitarian and favors hierarchy over the idea (or chimera) of universal individual equality. It is also committed to preserving organic institutions in which families and communities can survive. It is profoundly skeptical of any scheme that seeks to advance some notion of human perfection, and especially in the modern world, the Right should be fighting doggedly against social engineering and leveling.[4]

Jere Real reviewed the work of Coward back in 1976 and came to the same diagnosis, but with this useful caveat:

> [A] conservative may desire simultaneously order in society and the toleration of personal non-conformity, he can doubt the existence of equality in the abstract but hope for the greatest variety in human experience. This combination—the orderly society combined with considerable expression of individual eccentricity—exists in our time, almost as nowhere else, in the England of a writer such as Noël Coward.[5]

With the publication of *The Noël Coward Reader*, which chronologically mixes excerpts from his public work and private diaries and letters, we can now take a synoptic look at six decades of artistic public work and private rumination and not

---

Chicago Press, 1998), p. 521.

[4] Paul Gottfried, "Cannon Fodder" at http://www.alternativeright.com/main/blogs/untimely-observations/canon-fodder/

[5] Jere Real, "The Playwright as Bohemian Tory," *Intercollegiate Review* vol. 11, no. 2 (Winter–Spring 1976). Available online at http://www.firstprinciplesjournal.com/print.aspx?article=487&loc=b&type=cbtp)

only see that Coward deserves, as Real suggested, Russell Kirk's sobriquet, Bohemian Tory, but also some idea of how he came to be that way.

The *Reader* is a big, well-organized, finely produced volume, but it suffers from a couple of odd flaws. First, it claims that "to date, there has never been a Noël Coward reader; this is the first"; in fact, *The Cream of Noël Coward* was published in 1996 by the Folio Society.[6] One might claim this was a "limited edition," but it is still easily available online for half the price of the *Reader*. More importantly, although the *Reader* is three times larger, it ignores *Not Yet the Dodo*, which as we will see is Coward's most explicit discussion of homosexuality, the artist, and society; it even claims that "A Song at Twilight" from the previous year is "the only time he touched upon the subject of homosexuality in his work" (*Reader*, p. 546). What could explain this curious omission?

Despite Coward's reputation, and carefully constructed pose, as the quintessence of high-class sophistication and airy panache, his biographers have shown how the man was shaped by his distinctly unglamorous childhood, what the *Reader* calls the "refined suburban poverty" and proud of it to the end of his life:

> How fortunate I was to have been born poor. If Mother had been able to send me to private school, Eton and Oxford or Cambridge, it would probably have set me back years. I have always distrusted too much education and intellectualism. . . . My good fortune was to have a bright, acquisitive but not, *not* an intellectual mind, and to have been impelled by circumstances to get out and earn my living.[7]

He earned that living as a hard-working child actor, which he considered to have taught him quite a lot about the "basic

---

[6] Noël Coward, *The Cream of Noël Coward*, ed. Michael Cox (London: The Folio Society, 1996)

[7] *Diaries*, December 21, 1967.

facts of life by the age of fourteen."

What were those facts of life? Here is John Simon's sum-mary of them:

> Yet no one loved England (climate apart) and its common people more than Coward, as his friend the queen was first to acknowledge. "England may be a very small is-land, vastly overcrowded, frequently badly managed," he wrote, "but very much the best and bravest in the world." Repeatedly he flaunts his pride in the Scottish and English blood to which he owes his success.[8]

That success, early on, came from work that, though super-ficially as "decadent" and "modern" as the Bright Young Products of Oxbridge, was actually bringing the critical eye of a practical, working-class mind to their intellectual pretensions.

Like his contemporary Evelyn Waugh, Coward created a character, what Kenneth Tynan later called his "protective pose" (*Reader*, p. 522), which made him seem to be of that very milieu, while employing a subtle wit to create aesthetically pleasing and enjoyable works that also mockingly expose the flaws in "the modern age."

As Guillaume Faye advises, "It is mocking and 'eccentric' brainwaves that should lay the foundations" for any critique, a principle also well known to the Surrealists ("Gravity lies in what does not appear serious" — André Breton) and the Situa-tionists ("subversive ideas can only come from the pleasure principle" — Raoul Vaneigem).[9]

Coward was far from a flapper or a toff, but rather an hon-est and sympathetic participant-observer and conservative crit-ic, in the same way Burroughs played with crime and drugs

---

[8] John Simon, "Sir Noël's Epistles," *New York Times*, November 25, 1967, a review of Noël Coward, *The Letters of Noël Coward*, ed. Barry Day (New York: Knopf, 1997), available online at http://www.nytimes.com/2007/11/25/books/review/Simon-t.html

[9] Quotes in Guillaume Faye, *Archeofuturism: European Visions of the Post-Catastrophic Age*, trans. Sergio Knipe (London: Arktos Media, 2010), p. 57.

and Kerouac with irresponsibility, but were not themselves "Beat" as that "lifestyle" was distilled from their works by the mass media. In the same way Coward writes of hopelessly romantic couples while privately, in his letters and diaries disdaining the very idea of "love."

The pose was solidified for all time after his first major success, his play *The Vortex* (which was almost banned until a surprisingly perceptive civil servant noted that this mélange of drugs and incest served a serious aim, and observed that "if we ban this we shall have to ban *Hamlet*") when he allowed himself to be photographed in Chinese garb, in bed, with a look of "advanced degeneracy" caused (he later said) by the flashbulb. But his teasing interviews were designed to leave the same impression: his mind is "frightfully depraved" and "a mass of corruption" due to incessant visits to "opium dens, cocaine dens" (*Reader*, p. 103).

There is certainly no attempt to advance any kind of "gay agenda." The "camp" of *Demi-Monde* was a serious attempt to explore morality that had been shattered but not destroyed by the First World War (as he says quite openly in his Preface) and *Bitter Sweet* is intended as parody of Wilde, not hagiography.

Eventually real or affected decadence led to a nervous breakdown, where his treatment involved composing a list of good and bad qualities—among the former: "common sense."

Gradually, his "exploration" of modernity modulated to an open disillusionment with this life of bobbed hair and cigarettes; were people *really* happy?

> By dancing
> Much faster
> You're chancing
> Disaster
> Time alone will show
> ("Poor Little Rich Girl")

"These words from me may surprise you" indeed; and three years later, in 1928, Coward is even more emphatic, and specific:

But I know it's vain
To try to explain
When there's this insane
Music in your brain . . .
Nigger melodies
Syncopate your nerves . . .
And when the lights are starting to gutter
Dawn through the shutters
Shows you're living in a world of lies.
("Dance Little Lady")

Indeed, as Spengler observed five years later (in a book published by same house as *The Noël Coward Reader* today), "jazz music and Negro dancing [are performing] the Dead March for a great Culture."[10]

All this subtly subversive work culminated in 1931, when encapsulating the "essential psychology" of his time in the classic song "Twentieth Century Blues."

One might think, if one were under the "general perception" of him, that the ensuing Depression and war would leave a campy social critic like Coward without a subject. But what was called for was patriotism and belief in the British spirit, and these were hardly alien.

And while it would be inaccurate and even absurd to think Coward welcomed the war, it did give him the opportunity to exercise his profoundly conservative instincts in a more open, as it were out of the closet, fashion.

Coward's patriotic work was on two fronts; one was more public than ever, to buck up British spirits with a play, *Blythe Spirits*, a song, "London Pride," and a movie, *In Which We Serve*. "To make that film he had to overcome extraordinary opposition from high up, only to have it turn into a major artistic and morale-building hit."[11]

---

[10] Oswald Spengler, *The Hour of Decision, Part One: Germany and World-Historical Revolution*, trans. Charles Francis Atkinson (New York: Alfred A. Knopf, 1934), pp. 227–28.

[11] John Simon, "Sir Noël's Epistles."

The other was more secretive: undercover work promoting, among other things, US involvement in the war. Though some conservatives might prefer the "isolationist" side from today's perspective, Coward, like Lindbergh after Pearl Harbor, was simply defending his homeland from attack by outsiders.

This is again consistent with Gottfried's notion of "conservative":

> [F]riend/enemy distinctions are natural to how people live. The way out of this situation, even when it becomes heated, should not be through international administrative regulation of individual human lives for the sake of perpetual peace and brother- or sisterhood. Such utopian efforts can only lead to tyranny and the utter destruction of traditional ways of life. The best we can do in dealing with conflict is to control and channel violence through timely diplomacy and only if absolutely necessary, military interventions.

Rooted in real connection to his country, Coward's patriotism did not entail any ideological demonizing of the German enemy, or a demand for "unconditional surrender" (the typical motive of the modern war of "humanism" versus "enemies of humanity"), and certainly no dream of a post-war "world administration," whose actual manifestations, displacing the beloved Empire, he despised. As Guillaume Faye has said:

> It is possible to be a "patriot," someone tied to his subcontinental motherland, without forgetting that this is an organic and vital part of the common folk whose natural and historical territory . . . extends from Brest to the Bering Strait.[12]

No modern neocon or liberal ideologue could have the sense of his enemy's humanity that would allow him to see the ironic humor in a song like:

---

[12] *Archeofuturism*, p. 20.

Don't let's be beastly to the Germans
When our victory is ultimately won,
It was just those nasty Nazis who persuaded them to
    fight
And their Beethoven and Bach are really far worse than
    their bite
Let's be meek to them —
And turn the other cheek to them
And try to bring out their latent sense of fun.
Let's give them full air parity
And treat the rats with charity,
But don't let's be beastly to the Hun.

Certainly the BBC didn't appreciate it.

Oddly enough, Churchill loved the song; but maybe he just loved forcing Coward over and over to jump up and sing it on command. In any event, Coward's authentic patriotism was miles from the war-mongering ideologue Churchill, and the two hardly saw eye to eye on anything involving the war. Churchill rebuffed his offer to work for the war effort, disparaging his talk of "intelligence" (though Coward pointed out that he was talking of his own talent, not "Intelligence" in quotes, *à la* James Bond) and suggested he "sing to the troops while the shooting goes on" ("not practicable," Coward later sniffed).

Churchill was no doubt part of the "higher authorities" who didn't want him involved with the film *In Which We Serve*, and Coward, rightly as later documents showed, suspected Churchill had personally torpedoed his knighthood for the ensuing film.

For his part Coward hardly granted Churchill the reverence today's neocons demand; he considered him "a spoiled petulant gaga old sod."[13]

Coward was hardly committed to idolizing the Yanks (who still seem to think that "the war" began in January 1942, by which time Britain had been in action for three years).

---

[13] Graham Payn, *My Life with Noël Coward* (New York: Applause Books, 2000), p. 135.

In Coward's *Middle East Diary*, he made several statements that offended many Americans. In particular, he commented that he was "less impressed by some of the mournful little Brooklyn boys lying there in tears amid the alien corn with nothing worse than a bullet wound in the leg or a fractured arm."[14]

Tame, it would seem, but one can sense the sneer underlying "mournful little Brooklyn" and "the alien corn" and the corresponding -witz's and -steins it implies. After protests from both the *New York Times* and the *Washington Post*, the Foreign Office urged Coward not to visit the United States.

One is also reminded of a similar incident, around the same time, involving General Patton and an apparently malingering soldier. Coward and Patton (who once proposed a tank uniform of green leather jumpsuit and gold helmet) belonged to an earlier generation that expect soldiers to get out there and get results, whatever their taste in haberdashery; today's macho commanders worry about "gays" but haven't won a war since, well, Patton.

And speaking of "macho," the incident also gave him an opportunity to demonstrate the usefulness of his "campy" persona, when backed by genuine physical courage. As fellow spy David Niven tells the story:

> Now [on the day that *Stars and Stripes* headlined "Kick this bum out of the country"], Noël opened in Paris with Maurice Chevalier, whom the American soldiers were sure was a collaborator, and with Marlene Dietrich, whom they were sure was a German spy. . . . I went to see Noël before the performance and I said . . . what are you going to do about it? Sir Noël said, "First I shall calm them, and then I shall sing some of my very excellent songs." So I went out and stood at the back by the exit, and Noël came on to a deathly hush, which he's not used

---

[14] Robert Calder, *Beware the British Serpent: The Role of Writers in British Propaganda in the United States, 1939–1945* (Montreal: McGill-Queen's University Press, 2004), pp.102–04.

to. A deathly hush. And then he looked at them and said, "Ladies and Gentlemen, and all you dear, dear, sniveling little boys from Brooklyn . . ." And they fell down and absolutely loved it.

But the Navy was his true love:

I love the Navy, I inherited my affection for it, all my mother's family were Navy. Admirals and Captains. I love everything to do with the Navy. To start with they've got the best manners in the world and I love the sea and Navy discipline, which is very hard. It wouldn't have frightened me because I'm quite disciplined anyway, and I'm used to accepting discipline. I would have loved to have been in the Navy.[15]

The combination of pride in family heritage and personal predilection for self-discipline are expressed honestly, while in these days of "gay sensibility" as well as official "don't ask, don't tell" policies they seem almost "camp."

Even Churchill's opposition couldn't stop his writing and acting in the classic film, *In Which We Serve*, a tribute to his friend, Lord Mountbatten, as well as to the regular sailors, whom he demanded be detailed to the production instead of actors. That confidence in the "ordinary man" was rewarded by performances that led the Admiralty Head of Personnel to exclaim: "By Jove, Coward, that convinces me you were right to ask for a proper ship's company, *real* sailors. No actors could have possibly done that" (*Reader*, p. 432).

Although it must be said that when he gave his patriotism too free a hand (in the war time isolationist bashing *Time Remembered*, the pre-War *Post-Mortem* or the post-War *Peace in our Time*) it tended to become strident and a bit hysterical, forgetting his first rule of the dandy's pose: "The greatest thing in the world is not to be obvious — over ANYTHING."

---

[15] Charles Castle, *Noël: Biography of Noël Coward* (New York: Doubleday, 1973), p. 173.

If the early Coward developed an aristocratic veneer for sol-
idly working class values, and the wartime Coward was a simple spokesman for a patriotism considered old-fashioned if not
criminal, the post-War Coward now became the "surprisingly"
reactionary. Coward hadn't changed; what had changed was
England. Having won the war, would it now win the peace?

Coward had his doubts; the post-War "Festival of Britain"
was like Britain itself: "the last word in squalor and completely
ungay" causing him to riposte with the lugubriously conservative, almost Guénonian "Bad Times are Just Around the Cor-
ner":

> There are bad times just around the corner.
> There are dark clouds travelling through the sky.
> And it's no good whining
> About a silver lining.
> For we know from experience they won't roll by.

The '50s were indeed a bad time for Coward, who was put
on the shelf by critics who found him, and his work, terribly
old-fashioned, though the public never deserted him.

His send-up of "modern" art, *Nude with Violin*, based, of
course, not on rival "theories" but his own experience as an
amateur painter, ran for over a year but was ignored by the
critics. "**Sebastien**: I don't think anyone knows about painting
anymore. Art, like human nature, has got out of hand."

Since he wasn't taken seriously in the theatre anymore,
Coward even tossed aside the pose and began to speak over
the heads of the critics, directly to the public, in a serious of articles for the *Sunday Times*, "Consider the Public." Here he diagnosed and rebuked the bad new playwrights, who were:

> [B]igoted and stupid to believe that tramps and prostitutes
> . . . are automatically the salt of the earth [or] that reasona-
> bly educated people who behave with restraint in emo-
> tional crises are necessarily "clipped," "arid," "bloodless,"
> and "unreal."

Coward also lambasted the bad new actors who use a pretentious and unreliable "Method" to justify an inflated sense of their own "intellects" as well as a contempt for audiences, actors of the older generation, and the theatre itself, expressed mainly through coprophiliac stage business, slovenly dress, and dirty fingernails; and above all, the bad new critics, whose "old-fashioned class consciousness and inverted snobbism" (the Leftist as the true reactionary!) leads them to assume that any successful West End play is "automatically inferior" to a shoestring production in the East End, and who mislead the actors and writers by over-praising anything that "happens to coincide with the racial, political and social prejudices of a handful of journalists."[16]

Against all this Coward praised simple, unpretentious craft—"You must have the emotion to know it, then you must learn how to use the emotion without suffering it"—which he had honed the hard way entertaining troops; "Noël distrusted every emotion on stage and dealt solely in the illusion."[17] And above all, respect for theatrical tradition, and the audience itself, without which there would be no theatre at all.

The critics sneered, but as usual the public applauded Coward's common sense, and the *Times'* letters column had to be cut short.

Sadly, not much would have to be rewritten for publication in, say, *The New Criterion*; today actors like De Niro and Theron undergo grotesque physical metamorphoses for roles (satirized in the recent *Tropic Thunder* by Robert Downey's character who preps for a role "by working in a Beijing textile factory for eight months"), writers seek only to shock and disgust their passive audiences, and critics impose a rigid, class-conscious code of political correctness and crap-Freudianism.

And there was bad politics as well; here comes that "reactionary" stuff, though confined to his *Diaries*:

The British Empire was a great and wonderful social,

---

[16] Payn, pp. 322–37.
[17] Payn, p. 42.

economic, and even spiritual experience and all the parlour pinks and eager, ill-informed intellectuals cannot
convince me to the contrary.[18]

Bad actors and bad critics were one thing he could "rise
above," to use his characteristic expression, but not the parlor
pinks. The tax-happy welfare state drove him out of his native
land; at a professional ebb and subjected to scorn for leaving,
Coward typically replied: "An Englishman is the highest example of a human being who is a free man. As an Englishman I
have a right to live where I like." That turned out to be Jamaica,
where he was indeed able to "conserve," as the *Reader* puts it, a
little bit of the old England. By 1963 he had concluded that "the
England we knew and loved was betrayed at Munich, revived
for one short year in 1940 and was supreme in adversity, and
now no longer exists."[19]

The next year, with the Beatles, the '60s began in earnest. As
Philip Larkin put it in *"Annus Mirabilis"*: "Sexual intercourse
began/In nineteen sixty-three/(which was rather late for me)—
/Between the end of the *Chatterley* ban/And the Beatles' first
LP."

In "Swinging London," along with a new freedom of expression in the theatre, there was a perhaps surprising Coward
renaissance. Coward now began to openly discuss homosexuality; first, in a one act play, *A Song at Twilight*, where letters
revealing a homosexual affair threaten an elderly, knighted
writer living in Switzerland (where Coward now lived, but still
without the knighthood). Here the homosexual angle anchors a
fairly conventional melodrama, based on Max Beerbohm but
with a bit of Maugham tossed in. Certainly "today's youth" is
not courted:

Sir Hugo: I detest the young of today. They are grubby,
undisciplined and ill-mannered. They also make too
much noise.

---
[18] *Diaries*, February 3, 1957.
[19] *Diaries*, 1963.

But there were also hints of a libertarianism that Coward would soon present explicitly:

> **Carlotta**: To outside observers my way may seem stupid and garish and, later on perhaps, even grotesque. But the opinion of outside observers has never troubled me unduly. I am really only accountable to myself.

Or simply: "**Sir Hugo**: My inner feelings are my own affair."

But he chose verse, always the home of "his secret heart," to once and for all address the question of the homosexual and society; or rather, typically, the homosexual and his everyday family.

While the Britain's Wolfenden Report, a decade before Stonewall, may have brought the issue to society's attention and thus on Coward's agenda, for Coward the '60s promised not the chance to overthrow or otherwise remake society in some utopian formula for absolute "freedom" (the "freedom" of those grubby, undisciplined, ill-mannered and noisy youths, actors, and critics) but rather a chance for good old English common sense (always to be distinguished from media-programmed proles) to be heard from on such issues as homosexuality.

In the title piece of *Not Yet the Dodo*, common sense is expressed by the family maid to her employer, a mother of conventional middle-class morals who has finally realized her son is a theatrical homosexual:

> "If you want my opinion," she said, "I think
> We're both of us wasting our breath,
> You can't judge people by rule of thumb
> And if we sit gabbing till Kingdom Come
> We'll neither one of us sleep a wink
> And worry ourselves to death.
>
> People are made the way they're made
> And it isn't anybody's fault.
> Nobody's tastes can quite agree

Some like coffee and some like tea
And Guinness rather than lemonade
And pepper rather than salt."

Here Coward had the opportunity, towards the end of a long, professionally successful but, the Left ideologues would imagine, privately thwarted and persecuted life (nursing perhaps a grudge at the knighthood that would be denied him until the last moment in 1970), to pen an explosion of rage and expose society's rottenness, like the "kitchen sink" dramatists he had deplored (but, typically, personally befriended) in the '50s. Instead, Coward delivered a paean to the common sense, live-and-let-live conservatism of his working class roots.[20] As he wrote in his diary at the time: "I have always distrusted too much education and intellectualism. Always dead wrong about things that really matter."[21]

This is one of the passages where Real locates his fundamental conservatism:

[It] lies, I think, in the manner in which these acts are presented. In every instance, such nonconforming behavior is shown to be individualized; true, it is the individual's right, but it is also his or her responsibility. In other words, the problem — if there is one — is the individual's, not society's. Coward may seem to endorse a "new morality," but he also implies that personal morality is ultimately just that, personal. . . .

In summary, therefore, it might be said that Coward's attitude was one of maximum toleration of independence and non-conformity for the responsible individual. However, on larger societal issues of order, patriotism in times

---

[20] Faye describes his view, opposing not only "repression (or) banning" of homosexuality, but also homosexual "marriage," as "*common sense*, a notion with which the French Left — the most stupid Left in the world — has been in conflict with since 1789 thanks to its ideological hallucinations" (*Archeofuturism*, p. 107).

[21] *Diaries*, December 21, 1967.

of crisis, tradition, national loyalty, skepticism about man's perfectibility, and the inherent flaws of human nature, he was consistently conservative. Because of these views and his accompanying total trust in the intelligence of many average men, he qualifies, perhaps as much as any literary figure of our time, for that appellation Russell Kirk so frequently invokes, the Bohemian Tory.

One might find this redolent of the kind of vulgar libertarianism that is anathema to many conservatives, including Kirk. Rather, I suggest it has its analogues in an almost Nietzschean recognition of different moralities for different people (without his anti-social bias), or rather, for those who can make themselves different people, and thus be worthy of their own morality.

It may also suggest the Absolute Individual of Baron Evola (and who was more of a "Bohemian Tory" than the Baron, at least in his younger, Dadaist days, or when he toured Soviet Russia in white tie and tails to annoy the commissars?) or the four castes and differentiated ethics of Traditional India (and it is interesting that other than Guénon, the only Traditionalist who actually lived in a traditional society was Alain Daniélou, who roamed pre-war India with his lover in a silver motor home and reports that it was being a European that made him outcaste, and as a result his sexuality was of no interest to anyone).

The editors of the earlier anthology, *The Cream of Noël Coward*, were correct to include it as "a fitting capstone" to the book and his life's work, "because it celebrates the people and the country which Coward knew so well and the values which he always stood for: loyalty, courage, and good manners."

Counter-Currents/*North American New Right*,
December 7–8, 2010

ARKHAM ASYLUM:
AN ANALYSIS

JONATHAN BOWDEN

Arkham Asylum: A Serious House on Serious Earth
Story by Grant Morrison, art by Dave McKean
New York: DC Comics, 1989

Arkham Asylum claims to be among the most "adult" comics ever produced, and, although there are a few other candidates, it does merit this accolade up to a point. It has also inspired numerous spinoffs, including video games. Elsewhere I have written about a Batman and the Joker team-up comic from the mid-seventies, but this was deliberately circumscribed by the Comics Code Authority and lacked a mature sensibility.[1]

Note: By "adult," I am not referring to a predilection for transgression, low-grade, or "edgy" material here. Most of these attempts in popular culture are faintly ludicrous, it has to be said. No. What I am referring to is transgression of the philosophical limitations placed on such narratives by an insistent Dualism. This leads to a totally uncomplicated schema where the forces of light and darkness ply their trade in a Manichean way.

The first point of departure is in the treatment of mental illness. Nearly all of the villains in this institution for the criminally insane are regarded (by the story-line) as mad, bad, and dangerous to know. They are all considered to be responsible for their actions irrespective of their madness. In this respect, Ark-

---

[1] *The Brave and the Bold*, A Team-up comic featuring Batman and the Joker, DC Comics, no. 111, March 1974, reviewed as "Batman and the Joker," Counter-Currents/*North American New Right*, November 14, 2010, http://www.counter-currents.com/2010/11/batman-the-joker/

ham—in a fictionalized New York City called Gotham—resembles a British mental hospital such as Broadmoor. This establishment was erected in Berkshire in the 1850s as the prototypical institution for the criminally insane—even though such descriptions are studiously avoided.

All of the super-villains contained herein—the Joker, Two-Face, Crock, Black-mask, Doctor Destiny, the Mad Hatter, the Scarecrow, Clay Face, Maxie Zeus, Tweedle-Dum and Tweedle-Dee, Professor Milo, etc.—are all held to be accountable for their crimes, but treatable. This accords with the liberal-humanist notion (based on Pelagianism) that Man is naturally good, rational, kind, humane, and non-criminal. The facts of Man's post-animalian state completely militate against this, of course, but don't forget that we're dealing with an ideology here.

Several psychotherapists are employed in the institution in order to treat the maniacs contained therein. When the lunatics take over the asylum (quite literally), some of them even volunteer to remain with their charges. They have a responsibility, you see.

Just like in a real hospital, a range of treatments (whether medical or ideological) is tried: paint-spot/Rorschach tests, word association mind-games, as well as classic Freudianism—whereas some of the other "therapies" are obviously from the Behavioral school. The director of the institution even uses severe ECT (Electro-Convulsive Therapy) on the "patients." This is interesting for two reasons: one, the anti-psychiatric movement campaigned against this from the 1960s onwards; and, two, it indicates the biological basis of mental illness. It can only be physically assailed if it is somatic to begin with.

In fact, those who are criminally insane fall into two large categories. The offences that they commit—murder, rape, cannibalism, etc.—tend to be rather similar, but the originating conditions are very distinct. The two categories are psychopathia and schizophrenia. Interestingly, the word psychopath (reduced to "psycho" in popular language) is now deeply "offensive" or politically incorrect. It has got to the point that certain staff in these hospitals can be disciplined if they make use of it.

Psychopathia is a birth condition—that is, persons suffering from an advanced personality disorder are born and not made. Psychopaths begin torturing animals about age of 4 to 6 and then proceed onto young children later. They regard killing their own species as the equivalent of swatting a fly. Likewise, for them rapacity is normal sex. It appears that psychopaths are hard-wired to believe that life happens to be a constant war-zone of each against all . . . and that love is hatred, quite literally.

They are relatively incapable of lying, unlike normal humans who are mendacious all the time. (Note: this is usually to survive social situations without conflict.) Psychopaths live for conflict, believe life to be worthless, and have utter contempt for social workers, parole board types, concerned professors, and do-gooders who attempt to help them. They often advocate the harshest punishments for criminals of their sort (excluding possibly themselves); they would love to apply such indignities with the maximum amount of torture or humiliation. Psychopaths lack certain female chromosomes (if male) which soften the ferocity of the male nature and prepare it for camaraderie, fatherhood, paternalism, and the softer virtues.

One of the most famous psychopaths in criminology was Peter Kurten (the basis for Fritz Lang's film *M*) who was executed in Germany in the early 1930s. This occurred during that authoritarian half-way house period (typified by a whiff of Conservative Revolutionism) between the end of Weimar and Hitler's rise.

The Joker is certainly a psychopath, but in Arkham Asylum he is presented as suffering from Tourette's Syndrome. This is a clever notion, because Tourette's is a complicated diagnosis with both positive and negative characteristics. (Mozart is believed to have suffered from it, for instance.) The simplistic thing to say is that Tourette's is a tic-based condition which is both genetic and inherited (i.e., strictly biological). The Joker's mindless and repetitive desire to be rude, upset social order, utter blasphemies, and be mentally sadistic (whilst grinning inanely) are all part-and-parcel of it.

Yet, if we probe deeper, the Joker can also be diagnosed as suffering from Super Sanity: his ego is completely suppressed and experience washes over him continuously. He has no filter in relation to hyper-reality (in other words) and is therefore incapable of a conservative gesture; whether linguistically, morally, violently, sexually, etc. Everything is in the moment—he is a pure Existentialist without remit or prior expectancy. With him, Being is becoming—to use philosophical language. He bears a strong resemblance—as a result of this—to the personality of Caligula, the mad Roman emperor, as designated in Robert Graves' *I, Claudius* and *Claudius the God*, as well as Albert Camus' absurdist play. To bring it to a point: the Joker, like the Mad God Caligula, can embrace you, flirt with you, assassinate you, and dance with the corpse—while laughing continuously . . . as well as having tears of mock-genuine sadness flowing down his cheeks. "I've done away with my best friend, but he deserved it" would be a typical remark.

Batman, by point of contrast, is everything which is ordered, finite, prior, Right-wing, apriori, anti-atheistic (in a metaphysical sense), and Objective . . . philosophically. Bruce Wayne (Batman) is a metaphysical Objectivist, a Fascist; the Joker (by dint of contrast) is an anarchist. Yet anarchism and fascism are tied together by virtue of their dialectical inversions of one another. Scratch Nietzsche and you move to Stirner (in the center of this spectrum); scratch Stirner and you end up with the individualistic element in Bakunin, for example. You can also go back along the spectrum as well.

Another consideration arises: the notion of the anarcho-fascist or Right-wing anarchist (a combination of Batman and the Joker). This would include a great number of artists, such as Céline, D. H. Lawrence, Wyndham Lewis, Gottfried Benn, Ernst Jünger, Yukio Mishima, Drieu La Rochelle, T. E. Lawrence, Ezra Pound, and so forth. A new conundrum also arises here: most far Right leaders (unlike the majority of their followers) exhibit Anarch traits, the most notorious political artist of the 20th century being Adolf Hitler, of course. (Note: the supporters of such movements tend to be much more conservative than their leaders, *per se*; they look to such individuals to provide the rebellious conformism, aggressive normalcy, and transgressive stoicism that the Right needs.)

But if we might return to Arkham Asylum proper: one of

the other major tropes is the treatment of homosexuality. Interestingly, the writer, a Scottish creator called Grant Morrison, wished to visualize the Joker as an effeminate (if threatening) transvestite replete with French bodice and underwear. This is to accentuate the grinning red-lips, green hair, palsied or blanched skin, string tie, purple jacket and slacks, and green dress-shirt of the original. To link inversion with a psychopathic clown (i.e., a negative image) is relatively reckless on Morrison's part . . . given that any such treatment would be considered "politically incorrect."

In Italian neo-Realist cinema after the Second World War (for instance) two lesbians were used as a dark or sinister portrayal of fascism, but negative depictions of inversion are rare in contemporary media. (This is contrary to the Liberal-Left view that "homophobia" lurks as an omnipresent catch-all.) The last sinister depiction which I can recall is the triumvirate of villains in the Humphrey Bogart version of *The Maltese Falcon*. This starred, quite memorably, Sidney Greenstreet as the eponymous Fat Man. I remember a bourgeois Marxist catalog from the 1980s at the National Film Theatre (in Britain) describing the villainous troupe's portrayal as an example of "bigotry."

Nonetheless, Morrison's schemata for the Joker continues—with him embodying an inverted sadism in contrast to Batman's gruff, no-nonsense, Josef Thorak-laced, and straight as an arrow sensibility. There are also some terrific scenes in this *folie à deux* (so to say); one of which occurs at the end of the piece. In this particular, Batman starts wrecking the asylum with an axe, and, as he does so, one of the maniacs runs down various corridors (in this Bedlamite labyrinth, you understand) screaming "the Bat—the Bat; he's destroying EVERYTHING!" To which Blackmask responds, "You see, Joker; he's too powerful, you should never have let him in here." In a great panel, drawn and painted by Dave McKean, the Joker screams as a false martyr: "That's it! Go on, blame me, go on . . . do!" All of this is accompanied by the quiff of emerald hair and the manic smile—amid tons of greasepaint—which just grins on and on without mirth. Just how far the author, Morrison, is aware of any symmetry with Otto Weininger's *Sex and Character* is a moot point, however. In his own mind, he is probably trying to create the "wildest" version of Batman on record, nothing more.

In finality, *Arkham Asylum* goes quite a long way towards considering Batman as a putative Superman (in a Nietzschean sense). First of all, he has to overcome distaste at going in the place to begin with; then he must confront his own "demons" — by virtue of the mentally questionable state of someone who dresses up as a bat in order to beat up criminals for a living. Also, Batman seems hesitant in the face of the Joker's triumphant lunacy inside the Asylum where he can posture as the Lord of Misrule. In one revealing moment he refers to an Arkham run by lunatics as the "real world." Presumably, in this context, the world outside the gates superintended by Commissioner Gordon is unreal.

Nevertheless, Batman goes through a series of tests — even a crucifixion *manqué* — as he gradually conquers the place and subdues it to his will. Over time he sidesteps Harvey Dent's (Two-Face's) deconstruction from dualism, beats down upon Clayface's disease, refuses the nightmares of Doctor Destiny, or the serendipity of Professor Milo. Likewise, he emerges from the Scarecrow's cell unscathed and confronts the man-Alligator, Croc, in a clash of the Titans. Yet, throughout the whole process, he is getting stronger and stronger . . . as he engages in personal transcendence or self-over-becoming. Until, by the end of this film on paper, he can absorb the insanity of the place, sublimate it, purge it, throw it forward, and then clamber out on top of it.

By the time the drama ends, Batman makes a move to rejoin the waiting police (headed by Gordon) and the media outside. The criminal lunatics remain inside where they belong, but in a strangely subdued way. The fascistic hero may have lanced the boil (granted), but he has only been able to do so by re-integration, fanaticism for a cause outside oneself, and the adoption of a strength greater than reason. At the end (although sane) he has incorporated part of the Joker's Tarot (The Fool or the Hanged Man) into his own purview. To use an Odinic or pagan device, he is walking with Weird or embracing his own Destiny (fate) — i.e., the will which lies at the end of the road where you will the end's refusal. In this state — perhaps — a fictionalized variant on the end of the Charlemagne Division exists. Remember: they fought on to the end in a fire-torn Berlin because they had no country of their own to return to.

It is intriguing to point out the states which a form of entertainment for children can begin to approach. But it's only a funny book, isn't it?

Counter-Currents/*North American New Right*,
December 31, 2010

CHRISTOPHER NOLAN'S BATMAN MOVIES: WEAPONIZING TRADITIONALISM, TRANSVALUING VALUES

TREVOR LYNCH

Batman Begins

In *Batman Begins* (2005) and its sequel *The Dark Knight* (2008), director Christopher Nolan breaks with the campy style of earlier Batman films, focusing instead on character development and motivations. This makes both films psychologically dark and intellectually and emotionally compelling.

Nolan's casts are superb. Although I was disappointed to learn that David Boreanaz—the perfect look, in my opinion—had been cast as Batman right up until the part was given to Christian Bale, it is hard to fault Bale's Batman. He may be too pretty. But he has the intelligence, emotional complexity, and heroic physique needed to bring Batman to life. (Past Batmans Adam West, Michael Keaton, and George Clooney were jokes, but Val Kilmer was an intriguing choice.)

Batman Begins also stars Michael Caine, Gary Oldman, Liam Neeson, Cillian Murphy, Ken Watanabe, Rutger Hauer, and Morgan Freeman as one of those brilliant black inventors and mentors for confused whites so common in science fiction. In *The Dark Knight*, Bale, Caine, Oldman, Murphy, and Freeman return, and the immortal Heath Ledger *is* the Joker.

Batman Begins falls into three parts. In the first part we cut between Bruce Wayne in China and flashbacks of the course that brought him there. I despise the cliché that passes for psychology in popular culture today, namely that a warped psyche can be traced back to a primal trauma. So I was annoyed to learn that young Bruce Wayne became obsessed with bats when he fell down a well and was swarmed by them, and that he became a crime-fighter because his wealthy parents were gunned down in front of him by a mugger. Haunted by these traumas, billionaire Bruce Wayne ended up dropping out of Princeton to immerse himself in the criminal underworld, eventually ending up in a brutal Chinese prison.

Wayne is released by the mysterious Mr. Ducat—played by the imposing and charismatic Liam Neeson—who oversees his training in a mysterious Himalayan fortress run by "The League of Shadows," an ancient order of warrior-ascetics led by Ra's al Ghul (Ken Watanabe). The League follows the Traditional teaching that history moves in circles, beginning with a Golden Age and declining into a Dark Age, which then collapses and gives place to a new Golden Age. The mission of the League of Shadows is to appear when a civilization has reached the nadir of decadence and is about to fall—and then give it a push. (Needless to say, they do not have a website or a Facebook page. Nor can one join them by sending in a check.)

The League's training is both physical and spiritual. The core of the spiritual path is to confront and overcome one's deepest fears using a hallucinogen derived from a Himalayan flower. In a powerful and poetic scene of triumph, Bruce Wayne stands unafraid in the midst of a vast swarm of bats. The first time I watched this, I missed the significance of this transformation, which is an implicit critique of "trauma" psychology, for traumas are shown to be ultimately superficial compared with the heroic strength to stand in the face of the storm. It is, moreover, perfectly consistent with the conviction that nature is ultimately more powerful than nurture.

Bruce Wayne accepts the League's training but in the end rejects its mission. He thinks that decadence can be reversed. He believes in progress. He and Ducat fight. Ra's al Ghul is killed. The fortress explodes. Wayne escapes, saving Ducat's life. Then he calls for his private jet and returns to Gotham City.

In act two, Bruce Wayne becomes Batman. Interestingly enough, Batman is much closer to Nietzsche's idea of the "Superman" than the Superman character is. Superman isn't really a man to begin with. He just looks like us. His powers are just "given." But a Nietzschean superman is a man who makes himself more than a mere man. Bruce Wayne conquers nature, both his own nature and the world around him. As a man, he makes himself more than a man.

But morally speaking, Batman is no *Übermensch*, for he remains enslaved by the sentimental notion that every human life has some sort of innate value. He does not see that this morality negates the worth of his own achievement. A Batman can only be suffered if he serves his inferiors. Universal human rights—equality—innate dignity—the sanctity of every sperm: these ideas license the subordination and ultimately the destruction of everything below—or above—humanity. They are more than just a death sentence for nature, as Pentti Linkola claims. They are a death sentence for human excellence, high culture, anything in man that points above man.

Of course Batman's humanistic ethic has limits, particularly when he makes a getaway in the Batmobile, crushing and crashing police cars, blasting through walls, tearing over rooftops. Does Bruce Wayne plan to reimburse the good citizens of Gotham, or is there a higher morality at work here after all?

In act two, Batman begins to clean up Gotham City and uncovers and unravels a complex plot. In act three, we learn who is behind it: The League of Shadows. We learn that Neeson's character Ducat is the real Ra's al Ghul, and he and the League have come to a Gotham City tottering on the brink of chaos—to send it over the edge. Of course Batman saves the day, and Gotham is allowed to limp on, sliding deeper into decadence as its people lift their eyes towards the shining mirages of hope and eternal progress that seduce and enthrall their champion as well.

Batman Begins is a dark and serious movie, livened with light humor. It is dazzling to the eye. The script was co-authored by Christopher Nolan and Jewish writer-director David Goyer. There are a few politically correct touches, such as Morgan Freeman (although I find it impossible to dislike Morgan Freeman) and the little fact that one of Wayne's ancestors was an abolitionist, but nothing that really stinks.

Batman Begins touches on many of the themes that I discerned in my reviews of Guillermo del Toro's *Hellboy* and *Hellboy II*.[1] Again, the villains seem to subscribe to the Traditionalist, cyclical view of history; they hold that the trajectory of history is decline; they believe that we inhabit a Dark Age and that a Golden Age will dawn only when the Dark Age is destroyed; and they wish to lend their shoulders to the wheel of time. That which is falling, should be pushed. The heroes, by contrast, believe in progress. Thus they hold that a better world can be attained by building on the present one.

This is a rather elegant and absolutely radical opposition, which can be exploited to create high stakes dramatic conflict. What fight can be more compelling than the people who want to destroy the world versus the people who want to save it?

This raises the obvious question: Who in Hollywood has been reading René Guénon and Julius Evola — or, in the case of *Hellboy*, Savitri Devi and Miguel Serrano? For somebody inside the beast clearly understands that a weaponized Traditionalism is the ultimate revolt against the modern world.

Counter-Currents/ *North American New Right*,
September 23, 2010

The Dark Knight

In my review of Christoper Nolan's *Batman Begins*, I argued that the movie generates a dramatic conflict around the highest of stakes: the destruction of the modern world (epitomized by Gotham City) by the Traditionalist "League of Shadows" versus its preservation and "progressive" improvement by Batman.

I also argued that Batman's transformation into a Nietzschean *Übermensch* was incomplete, for he still accepted the reigning egalitarian-humanistic ethics that devalued his superhu-

---

[1] http://www.counter-currents.com/2010/08/hellboy/ and http://www.counter-currents.com/2010/08/hellboy-ii-the-golden-army/

man striving and achievements even as he placed them in the service of the little people of Gotham.

This latent conflict between an aristocratic and an egalitarian ethic becomes explicit in Nolan's breathtaking sequel *The Dark Knight*, which is surely the greatest supervillain movie ever. (The greatest superhero movie has to be Zack Snyder's *Watchmen* [2009].)

PHILOSOPHIZING WITH DYNAMITE

The true star of *The Dark Knight* is Heath Ledger as the Joker. The Joker is a Nietzschean philosopher. In the opening scene, he borrows Nietzsche's aphorism, "Whatever doesn't kill me, makes me stronger," giving it a twist: "I believe whatever doesn't kill you, simply makes you . . . *stranger*." Following Nietzsche, who philosophized with a hammer, the Joker philosophizes with knives as well as "dynamite, gunpowder, and . . . gasoline."

Yes, he is a criminal. A ruthless and casual mass murderer, in fact. But he believes that "Gotham deserves a better class of criminal, and I'm going to give it to them. . . . It's not about money. It's about sending a message. Everything burns." In this, the Joker is not unlike another Nietzschean philosopher, the Unabomber, who philosophized with explosives because he too wanted to send a message.

The Joker's message is the emptiness of the reigning values. His goal is the transvaluation of values. Although he initially wants to kill Batman, he comes to see him as a kindred spirit, an alter ego: a fellow superhuman, a fellow freak, who is still tragically tied to a humanistic morality. Consider this dialogue:

> **Batman**: Then why do you want to kill me?
> **The Joker**: I don't want to kill you! What would I do without you? Go back to ripping off mob dealers? No, no, NO! No. *You . . . you . . . complete me.*
> **Batman**: You're garbage who kills for money.
> **The Joker**: Don't talk like one of them. You're not! Even if you'd like to be. To them, you're just a freak, like me! They need you right now, but when they don't,

they'll cast you out, like a leper! You see, their morals, their code, it's a bad joke. Dropped at the first sign of trouble. They're only as good as the world allows them to be. I'll show you. When the chips are down, these . . . these civilized people, they'll eat each other. See, I'm not a monster. I'm just ahead of the curve.

The Joker may want to free Batman, but he is a practitioner of tough love. His therapy involves killing random innocents, then targeting somebody Batman loves.

DEATH, AUTHENTICITY, & FREEDOM

The basis of the kinship the Joker perceives between himself and Batman is not merely a matter of eccentric garb. It is their relationship to death. The Joker is a bit of an existentialist when it comes to death: "in their last moments, people show you who they really are." Most people fear death more than anything. Thus they flee from it by picturing their death as somewhere "out there," in the future, waiting for them. But if you only have one death, and it is somewhere in the future, then right now, one is immortal. And immortal beings can afford to live foolishly and inauthentically. People only become real when they face death, and they usually put that off to the very last minute.

The Joker realizes that there is something scarier than death, and that is a life without freedom or authenticity.

The Joker realizes that mortality is not something waiting for him *out there* in the future. It is something that he carries around *inside him* at all times. He does not need a *memento mori*. He feels his own heart beating.

Because he knows he can die at any moment, he *lives* every moment.

He is *ready* to die at any moment. He accepts Harvey Dent's proposal to kill him based on a coin toss. He indicates he is willing to blow himself up to deter the black gangster Gambol—and everybody believes him. He challenges Batman to run him down just to teach him a lesson.

In his mind, the Joker's readiness to die at any moment may

be his license to kill at any moment.

The Joker can face his mortality, because he has learned not to fear it. Indeed, he has come to love it, for it is the basis of his inner freedom. When Batman tries to beat information out of the Joker, he simply laughs: "You have nothing, nothing to threaten me with. Nothing to do with all your strength." Batman is powerless against him, because the Joker is prepared to die.

The Joker senses, perhaps mistakenly, that Batman could attain a similar freedom.

What might be holding Batman back? Could it be his conviction of the sanctity of life? In *Batman Begins*, Bruce Wayne breaks with the League of Shadows because he refuses the final initiation: taking another man's life. Later in the movie, he refuses to kill Ra's al Ghul (although he hypocritically lets him die). In *The Dark Knight*, Batman refuses to kill the Joker. If that is Batman's hangup, the Joker will teach him that one can only live a more-than-human life if one replaces the love of mere life with the love of liberating death.

LESSONS IN TRANSVALUATION

Many of the Joker's crimes can be understood as moral experiments and lessons.

1. When the Joker breaks a pool cue and tosses it to Gambol's three surviving henchmen, telling them that he is having "tryouts" and that only one of them (meaning the survivor) can "join our team," he is opposing their moral scruples to their survival instincts. The one with the fewest scruples or the strongest will to survive has the advantage.

2. The Joker rigs two boats to explode, one filled with criminals and the other with the good little people of Gotham. He gives each boat the detonator switch to the other one, and tells them that unless one group chooses to blow up the other by midnight, he will blow up both boats. Again, he is opposing moral scruples to survival instincts.

The results are disappointing. The good people cannot act without a vote, and when they vote to blow up the other ship, not one of them has the guts to follow through. They would rather die than take the lives of others, and it is clearly not because they have conquered their fear of death, but simply from a lack of sheer animal vitality, of will to power. Their morality has made them sick. They don't think they have the right to live at the expense of others. Or, worse still, they all live at the expense of others. This whole System is about eating one another. But none of them will own up to that fact in front of others.

Batman interprets this as a sign that people "are ready to believe in goodness," i.e., that the Joker was wrong to claim that, "When the chips are down, these . . . these civilized people, they'll eat each other." The Joker hoped to put oversocialized people back in touch with animal vitality, and he failed. From a biological point of view, eating one another is surely healthier than going passively to one's death *en masse*.

3. The Joker goes on a killing spree to force Batman to take off his mask and turn himself in. Thus Batman must choose between giving up his mission or carrying on at the cost of individual lives. If he chooses to continue, he has to regard the Joker's victims as necessary sacrifices to serve the greater good, which means that humans don't have absolute rights that trump their sacrifice for society.

4. The Joker forces Batman to choose between saving the life of Rachel Dawes, the woman he loves, or Harvey Dent, an idealistic public servant. If Batman's true aim is to serve the common good, then he should choose Dent. But he chooses Dawes because he loves her. But the joke is on him. The Joker told him that Dawes was at Dent's location, so Batman ends up saving Dent anyway. When Batman tells the Joker he has "one rule" (presumably not to kill) the Joker responds that he is going to have to break that one rule if he is going to save one of them, because he can save one only by letting the other die.

5. As Batman races towards the Joker on the Batcycle, the Joker taunts him: "Hit me, hit me, come on, I want you to hit me." The Joker is free and ready to die at that very moment. Batman, however, cannot bring himself to kill him. He veers off and crashes. The Joker is willing to die to teach Batman simply to kill out of healthy animal anger, without any cant about rights or due process and other moralistic claptrap.

6. Later in the film, Batman saves the Joker from falling to

his death. He could have just let him die, as he did Ra's al Ghul. The Joker says:

> Oh, you. You just couldn't let me go, could you? This is what happens when an unstoppable force meets an immovable object. You are truly incorruptible, aren't you? . . . You won't kill me out of some misplaced sense of self-righteousness. And I won't kill you because you're just too much fun. I think you and I are destined to do this forever.

Again, one has the sense that the Joker would have been glad to die simply to shake Batman out of his "misplaced sense of self-righteousness."

At the risk of sounding like the Riddler:

Q: What do you call a man who is willing to die to make a philosophical point?
A: A philosopher.

MATERIALISTIC VERSUS ARISTOCRATIC MORALS

Modern materialistic society is based on two basic principles: that nothing is worse than death and nothing is better than wealth. Aristocratic society is based on the principles that there are things worse than death and better than wealth. Dishonor and slavery are worse than death. And honor and freedom are better than wealth.

We have already seen that the Joker fears death less than an inauthentic and unfree life. In one of the movie's most memorable scenes, he shows his view of wealth. The setting is the hold of a ship. A veritable mountain of money is piled up. The Joker has just recovered a trove of the mob's money—for which he will receive half. Tied up on top of the pile is Mr. Lau, the money launderer who tried to abscond with it.

One of the gangsters asks the Joker what he will do with all his money. He replies: "I'm a man of simple tastes. I like dynamite, and gunpowder, and . . . gasoline." At which point his henchmen douse the money with gasoline. The Joker continues: "And you know what they all have in common? They're cheap." He then lights the pyre and addresses the gangster: "All you care about is money. Gotham deserves a better class of criminal, and I'm going to give it to them."

Aristocratic morality makes a virtue of transforming wealth into something spiritual: into honor, prestige, or beautiful and useless things. Trading wealth for spiritual goods demonstrates one's freedom from material necessity. But the ultimate demonstration of one's freedom from material goods is the simple destruction of them.

The Indians of the Pacific Northwest practice a ceremony called the "Potlatch." In a Potlatch, tribal leaders gain prestige by giving away material wealth. However, when there was intense rivalry between individuals, they would vie for honor not by giving away wealth but by destroying it.

The Joker is practicing Potlatch. Perhaps the ultimate put-down, though, is when he mentions that he is only burning *his share* of the money.

THE MAN WITH THE PLAN

Gotham's District Attorney Harvey Dent (played by Nordic archetype Aaron Eckhart) is a genuinely noble man. He is also a man with a plan. He leaves nothing up to chance, although he pretends to. He makes decisions by flipping a coin, but the coin is rigged. It has two heads—two faces.

The Joker kidnaps Harvey Dent and Rachel Dawes and rigs them to blow up. He gives Batman the choice of saving one. Batman races off to save Dawes but finds Dent instead. Dawes is killed, and Dent is horribly burned. Half his face is disfigured, and one side of his coin (which was in Rachel's possession) is blackened as well. Harvey Dent has become "Two-Face."

The Joker, of course, is a man with a plan too. Truth be told, he is a criminal mastermind, the ultimate schemer. (Indeed, one of the few faults of this movie is that his elaborate schemes seem to spring up without any time for preparation.) When the Joker visits Dent in the hospital, however, he makes the following speech in answer to Dent's accusation that Rachel's death was part of the Joker's plan.

Do I really look like a guy with a plan? You know what I am? I'm a dog chasing cars. I wouldn't know what to do with one if I caught it. You know, I just . . . *do* things.

The mob has plans, the cops have plans. . . . You know, they're schemers. Schemers trying to control their little worlds. I'm not a schemer. I try to show the schemers how pathetic their attempts to control things really are. . . . It's the schemers that put you where you are. You were a schemer, you had plans, and look where that got you. I just did what I do best. I took your little plan and I turned it on itself. Look what I did to this city with a few drums of gas and a couple of bullets. Hmmm?

You know . . . You know what I've noticed? Nobody panics when things go "according to plan." Even if the plan is horrifying! If, tomorrow, I tell the press that, like, a gang banger will get shot, or a truckload of soldiers will be blown up, nobody panics, because it's all "part of the plan." But when I say that one little old mayor will die, *well then everyone loses their minds!*

Introduce a little anarchy. Upset the established order, and everything becomes chaos. I'm an agent of chaos. Oh, and you know the thing about chaos? It's fair!

The Joker's immediate agenda is to gaslight Harvey Dent, to turn Gotham's White Knight into a crazed killer. "Madness," he says, "is like gravity. All you need is a little push." This speech is his push, and what he says has to be interpreted with this specific aim in mind. For instance, the claim that chaos is "fair" is clearly *a propos* of Dent's use of a two-headed coin because he refuses to leave anything up to chance. (Chaos here is equivalent to chance.) Dent's reply is to propose to decide whether the Joker lives or dies based on a coin toss. The Joker agrees, and the coin comes up in the Joker's favor. We do not see what happens, but the Joker emerges unscathed and Harvey Dent is transformed into Two-Face.

THE CONTINGENCY PLAN

But the Joker's speech is not merely a lie to send Dent over the edge. In the end, the Joker really isn't a man with a plan, and the clearest proof of that is that *he stakes his life on a coin toss.* Yes, the Joker plans for all sorts of contingencies, but he knows that the best laid plans cannot eliminate contingency as such. But that's all right, for the Joker embraces contingency as he embraces death: it is a principle of freedom.

The Joker is in revolt not only against the morals of modernity, but also its metaphysics, the reigning interpretation of Being, namely that the world is ultimately transparent to reason and susceptible to planning and control. Heidegger called this interpretation of Being the *"Gestell,"* a term which connotes classification and arrangement to maximize availability, like a book in a well-ordered library, numbered and shelved so it can be located and retrieved at will. For modern man, "to be" is to be susceptible to being classified, labeled, shelved, and available in this fashion.

Heidegger regarded such a world as an inhuman hell, and the Joker agrees. When the Joker is arrested, we find that he has no DNA or fingerprints or dental records on file. He has no name, no address, no identification of any kind. His clothes are custom made, with no labels. As Commissioner Gordon says, there's "nothing in his pockets but knives and lint." Yes, the system has him, but has nothing on him. It knows nothing about him. When he escapes, they have no idea where to look. He is a book without a barcode: unclassified, unshelved, unavailable . . . free.

For Heidegger, the way to freedom is to meditate on the origins of the *Gestell,* which he claims are ultimately mysterious. Why did people start thinking that everything can be understood and controlled? Was the idea cooked up by a few individuals and then propagated according to a plan? Heidegger thinks not. The *Gestell* is a transformation of the *Zeitgeist* that cannot be traced back to individual thoughts and actions, but instead conditions and leads them. Its origins and power thus remain inscrutable. The *Gestell* is an *"Ereignis,"* an event, a contingency.

Heidegger suggests that etymologically *"Ereignis"* also has the sense of "taking hold" and "captivating." Some translators render it "appropriation" or "enowning." I like to render it "enthrallment": The modern interpretation of Being happened, we know not why. It is a dumb contingency. It just emerged. Now it enthralls us. We can't understand it. We can't control it. It controls us by shaping our understanding of everything else. How do we break free?

The spell is broken as soon as we realize that the idea of the *Gestell*—the idea that we can understand and control everything—cannot itself be understood or controlled. The origin of idea that all things can be understood cannot be understood. The sway of the idea that all things can be planned and controlled cannot be planned or controlled. The reign of the idea that everything is necessary, that everything has a reason, came about as sheer, irrational contingency.

The Joker seeks to break the power of the *Gestell* not merely by *meditating* on contingency, but by *acting from it*, i.e., by *being* an irrational contingency, by being an agent of chaos.

He introduces chaos into his own life by acting on whim, by just "doing things" that don't make sense, like "a dog chasing cars": staking his life on a coin toss, playing chicken with Batman, etc. When Batman tries to beat information out of the Joker, he tells him that "The only sensible way to live in this world is without rules."

Alfred the butler understands the Joker's freedom: "Some men aren't looking for anything logical, like money. They can't be bought, bullied, reasoned, or negotiated with. Some men just want to watch the world burn."

The Joker introduces chaos into society by breaking the grip of the System and its plans.

He is capable of being an agent of chaos because of his relationship to death. He does not fear it. He embraces it as a permanent possibility. He is, therefore, free. His freedom raises him above the *Gestell*, allowing him to look down on it . . . and laugh. That's why they call him the Joker.

IN ALL SERIOUSNESS

I like the Joker's philosophy. I think he is right. "But wait," some of you might say, "the Joker is a monster! Heath Ledger claimed that the Joker was 'a psychopathic, mass murdering, schizophrenic clown with zero empathy.' Surely you don't like someone like that!"

But remember, we are dealing with Hollywood here. In a "free" society we can't suppress dangerous truths altogether. So we have to be immunized against them. That's why Hollywood lets dangerous truths appear on screen, *but only in the mouths of monsters:* Derek Vinyard in *American History X*, Travis Bickle in *Taxi Driver*, Bill the Butcher in *Gangs of New York*, Ra's al Ghul in *Batman Begins*, the Joker in *The Dark Knight*, etc.

We need to learn to separate the message from the messenger, and we need to teach the millions of people who have seen this movie (at this writing, the seventh biggest film of all time) to do so as well. Once we do that, the film ceases to reinforce the system's message and reinforces ours instead. That's what I do best. I take their propaganda and turn it on itself.

What lessons can we learn from *The Dark Knight*?

Batman Begins reveals a deep understanding of the fundamental opposition between the Traditional cyclical view of history and modern progressivism, envisioning a weaponized Traditionalism (The League of Shadows) as the ultimate enemy of Batman and the forces of progress.

The Dark Knight reveals a deep understanding of the moral and metaphysical antipodes of the modern world: the Nietzschean concept of master morality and critique of egalitarian slave morality, allied with the Heideggerian concept of the *Gestell* and the power of sheer irrational contingency to break it.

The Joker weaponizes these ideas, and he exploits Batman's latent moral conflict between Nietzschean self-overcoming and his devotion to human rights and equality.

In short, somebody in Hollywood understands who the System's most radical and fundamental enemy is. They know what ideas can destroy their world. It is time we learn them too.

Let's show these schemers how pathetic their attempts to control us really are.

Counter-Currents/ *North American New Right*,
September 27, 2010

ABOUT THE AUTHORS

ALAIN DE BENOIST is the leading theorist of the European New Right. He is the editor of *Nouvelle École* and *Krisis*. His most recent title in English is *Beyond Human Rights: Defending Freedom* (London: Arktos, 2011).

KERRY BOLTON, Ph.D., Th.D., is the author of *Artists of the Right: Resisting Decadence* (San Francisco: Counter-Currents, 2012), *Revolution from Above* (London: Arktos, 2011), and many other books and essays.

JONATHAN BOWDEN, 1962–2012, was an English writer, artist, and orator. His many books include *Our Name is Legion* (London: The Spinning Top Club, 2011).

AMANDA BRADLEY is an American writer who focuses on religion, Western esotericism, and women's issues.

JEF COSTELLO is a writer living in New York City.

HAROLD COVINGTON is the Chairman of the Northwest Front and the author of the Northwest Quintet.

F. ROGER DEVLIN, Ph.D., is the author of *Alexander Kojève and the Outcome of Modern Thought* (Lanham, Md.: University Press of America, 2004) and many essays and reviews.

JULIUS EVOLA, 1898–1974, was one of the leading Traditionalist thinkers of the 20th century and the author of *Revolt Against the Modern World* (1934) and many other books and essays.

GUILLAUME FAYE is a leading thinker of the European New Right. His most recent book in English is *Why We Fight: Manifesto of the European Resistance* (London: Arktos, 2011).

DEREK HAWTHORNE is a writer living in New York City.

JULEIGH HOWARD-HOBSON is a poet and essayist living in Portland, Oregon.

North American New Right, vol. 1, 2012

GREG JOHNSON, Ph.D., is the author of *Confessions of a Reluctant Hater* (San Francisco: Counter-Currents, 2010).

ALEX KURTAGIĆ is the author of the dystopian novel *Mister* (Guildford, U.K.: Iron Sky Publishing, 2009) and many essays.

TREVOR LYNCH is an American movie critic and the author of *Trevor Lynch's White Nationalist Guide to the Movies* (San Francisco: Counter-Currents, 2012).

KEVIN MACDONALD, Ph.D., is Professor of Psychology at California State University, Long Beach, and author of *The Culture of Critique* (Westport, Conn.: Praeger, 1998) and many other books and articles.

JAMES J. O'MEARA is a writer living in New York City. His blog is http://jamesjomeara.blogspot.com/

MICHAEL O'MEARA, Ph.D., is the author of *New Culture, New Right: Anti-Liberalism in Postmodern Europe* (Bloomington, Ind.: 1stBooks, 2004) and *Toward the White Republic* (San Francisco: Counter-Currents, 2010).

EDOUARD RIX is a French writer on the European Right.

TED SALLIS is an American writer on race, politics, and culture.

JOHN SCHNEIDER is an American writer on politics.

ROBERT STEUCKERS is a prominent member of the European New Right. The author of countless essays, articles, and reviews, he is Editor of Euro-Synergies, the leading New Right webzine, http://euro-synergies.hautetfort.com/

BRYAN SYLVAIN is a writer living in Southern California.

DOMINIQUE VENNER is a French historian. He is the editor of *Nouvelle revue d'histoire* and the author of many books and articles. His most recent book is *Le choc de l'Histoire: Religion, mémoire, identité* (Versailles: Via Romana, 2011).

MICHAEL WALKER is a writer living in London.

www.ingramcontent.com/pod-product-compliance
Lightning Source LLC
Chambersburg PA
CBHW020333270326
41926CB00007B/166